CRITIQUE AND CONSTRUCTION
A Symposium on Roberto Unger's *Politics*

CRITIQUE AND CONSTRUCTION

A Symposium on
Roberto Unger's *Politics*

Edited by
ROBIN W. LOVIN
Divinity School of the University of Chicago
and
MICHAEL J. PERRY
Northwestern University School of Law

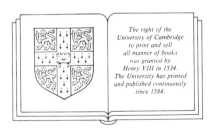

CAMBRIDGE UNIVERSITY PRESS

Cambridge

New York   Port Chester   Melbourne   Sydney

Published by the Press Syndicate of the University of Cambridge
The Pitt Building, Trumpington Street, Cambridge CB2 1RP
40 West 20th Street, New York, NY 10011, USA
10 Stamford Road, Oakleigh, Melbourne 3166, Australia

© Cambridge University Press 1990

First published 1990

Printed in the United States of America

Library of Congress Cataloging-in-Publication Data
Critique and construction: a symposium on Roberto Unger's Politics /
edited by Robin W. Lovin and Michael J. Perry.

p.   cm.

ISBN 0-521-35208-8

1. Unger, Roberto Mangabeira. Politics, a work in constructive
social theory. 2. Sociology. 3. Political sociology. I. Lovin,
Robin W.   II. Perry, Michael J.
HM24.C767   1990
306.2′092 – dc20

89-23850
CIP

British Library Cataloguing in Publication Data
Critique and construction: a symposium on Roberto Unger's
Politics.

1. Politics. Theories of Unger, Roberto Mangabeira
I. Lovin, Robin W. II. Perry, Michael J.
320.5′092′4

ISBN 0-521-35208-8 hard covers

CONTENTS

A NOTE ON THE AUTHORS

ROBERT P. BURNS is Professor of Law at the Northwestern University School of Law, where he practices criminal and civil rights law in its legal clinic. He earned his law degree and his doctorate, with honors, from the University of Chicago, where he was a National Science Foundation Fellow in the History and Philosophy of Science and a Danforth Foundation Kent Fellow in the Philosophy of Law. His publications include *Hannah Arendt's Constitutional Thought* in AMOR MUNDI: PERSPECTIVES ON THE THOUGHT OF HANNAH ARENDT (1987); *The Enforceability of Mediated Agreements: An Essay on Legitimation and Process Integrity*, 2 OHIO ST. J. DIS. RES. 93 (1986); *Blackstone's Theory of the 'Absolute' Rights of Property*, 54 CIN. L. REV. 67 (1985); *The Federalist Rhetoric of Rights and the Instrumental Conception of Law*, NORTHWESTERN U. L. REV. 949 (1985); and *A Lawyer's Truth: Notes for a Moral Philosophy of Litigation Practice*, 3 J. L. & REL. 229 (1985). Professor Burns' contribution to this Symposium is entitled *When the Owl of Minerva Takes Flight at Dawn: Radical Constructivism in Social Theory*.

J.C. CLEARY is Professor of Religion at Wesleyan University, Middletown, Connecticut. His work includes A BUDDHA FROM KOREA (forthcoming); and ZEN DAWN: EARLY ZEN TEXTS FROM TUN HUANG (1986). He has translated, with Thomas Cleary, HSUEH-TOU, THE BLUE CLIFF RECORD (1977). Professor Cleary is co-author, with Patrice Higonnet, of an article in this symposium entitled *Plasticity into Power: Two Crises in the History of France and China*.

CHARLES DAVIS, Professor of Religion at Concordia University in Montreal, is known for his work on the relation between religion and politics. His recent publications include WHAT IS LIVING, WHAT IS DEAD IN CHRISTIANITY TODAY: BREAKING THE LIBERAL-CONSERVATIVE DEADLOCK (1986); and THEOLOGY AND POLITICAL SOCIETY (1980), a work that originally was given as the Hulsean Lectures at the University of Cambridge in 1978. Professor Davis' contribution to the symposium is entitled *Religion and the Making of Society*.

JOHN DUNN is a Fellow of Kings College and Reader in Politics at the University of Cambridge. His pathbreaking work in the area of political theory includes RETHINKING MODERN POLITICAL THEORY: ESSAYS 1979–83 (1985); LOCKE (1984); and THE POLITICS OF SOCIALISM: AN ESSAY IN POLITICAL

THEORY (1984). His article in this Symposium is entitled *Unger's Politics and the Appraisal of Political Possibility.*

WILLIAM A. GALSTON, Professor of Public Affairs at the University of Maryland and Senior Research Scholar at the Institute for Philosophy and Public Policy, University of Maryland, is a respected political theorist who has also served as an adviser to politicians such as Walter Mondale. His recent publications include JUSTICE AND THE HUMAN GOOD (1980); and KANT AND THE PROBLEM OF HISTORY (1975). His contribution to this Symposium is entitled *False Universality: Infinite Personality and Finite Existence in Unger's* Politics.

GEOFFREY HAWTHORN is a Reader in Sociology and Politics at the University of Cambridge. He is known for his work in social and political theory, including POPULATION AND DEVELOPMENT (1978); and ENLIGHTENMENT AND DESPAIR: A HISTORY OF SOCIOLOGY (1976). His article in this Symposium is entitled *Practical Reason and Social Democracy: Reflections on Unger's* Passion *and* Politics.

PATRICE HIGONNET, Professor of History at Harvard University, is a renowned historian of the French Revolution. His publications include SISTER REPUBLICS: THE ORIGINS OF FRENCH AND AMERICAN REPUBLICANISM (forthcoming); CLASS, IDEOLOGY, AND THE RIGHTS OF NOBLES DURING THE FRENCH REVOLUTION (1981); and *Le sens de la Terreure,* 35 COMMENTAIRE 436 (1986). His contribution, co-authored with J.C. Cleary, is entitled *Plasticity into Power: Two Crises in the History of France and China.*

J. ALLAN HOBSON, M.D., is the Director of the Laboratory of Neurophysiology, Department of Psychiatry, Harvard Medical School. A pioneer in the "new psychiatry," Dr. Hobson has published THE RETICULAR FORMATION REVISITED (1980); *Psychoanalysis on the Couch,* 1986 ENCYCLOPEDIA BRITANNICA MED. & HEALTH ANN. 74–91; and *Sleep Mechanisms and Pathophysiology: Some Clinical Implications of the Reciprocal Interaction Hypothesis of Sleep Cycle Control,* 45 PSYCHOSOMATIC MED. 2 (1983). His contribution to this Symposium is entitled *Psychiatry as Scientific Humanism: A Program Inspired by Roberto Unger's* Passion.

TONY JUDT is a Professor of History and Professor in the Institute of French Studies at New York University. His widely respected work in politics and modern history includes MARXISM AND THE FRENCH LEFT: STUDIES ON LABOUR AND POLITICS IN FRANCE, 1830–1981 (1986); and SOCIALISM IN PROVENCE, 1871–1914: A STUDY IN THE ORIGINS OF THE MODERN FRENCH LEFT (1977). Professor Judt's article in this Symposium is entitled *Radical Politics in a New Key?*

ROBIN W. LOVIN is Associate Professor of Ethics and Society at the Divinity School of the University of Chicago. His publications include CHRISTIAN

FAITH AND PUBLIC CHOICES: THE SOCIAL ETHICS OF BARTH, BRUNNER, AND BONHOEFFER (1984); *Rethinking Values Formation: The Education and Political Contexts,* 68 SOUNDINGS 5 (1985); and *The School and the Articulation of Values,* 96 AM. J. ED. 143 (1988). He is the editor of RELIGION AND AMERICAN PUBLIC LIFE (1986). Professor Lovin is co-editor of this Symposium and author of the Introduction.

MICHAEL J. PERRY is Professor of Law at the Northwestern University School of Law, where he teaches constitutional law, constitutional theory, and moral and political philosophy. His publications include MORALITY, POLITICS, AND LAW (1988); THE CONSTITUTION, THE COURTS, AND HUMAN RIGHTS (1982); *Freedom of Expression: An Essay on Theory and Doctrine,* 78 NORTHWESTERN U. L. REV. 1137 (1983); *Why the Supreme Court was Plainly Wrong in the Hyde Amendment Case,* 32 STANFORD L. REV. 1113 (1980); and *Modern Equal Protection: A Conceptualization and Appraisal,* 79 COLUM. L. REV. 1023 (1979). Professor Perry is co-editor of this Symposium.

RICHARD RORTY is Kenan Professor of the Humanities at the University of Virginia. He is the author of PHILOSOPHY AND THE MIRROR OF NATURE (1979), CONSEQUENCES OF PRAGMATISM (1982), and CONTINGENCY, IRONY, AND SOLIDARITY (1988). He also edited THE LINGUISTIC TURN (1967) and co-edited PHILOSOPHY IN HISTORY (1984). He is currently writing a book on Martin Heidegger. Professor Rorty's contribution to this Symposium is entitled *Unger, Castoriadis, and the Romance of a National Future.*

WILLIAM H. SIMON, Professor of Law at Stanford University and Visiting Professor of Law at Harvard Law School, is known for his work in legal theory. His publications include *The Invention and Reinvention of Welfare Rights,* 44 MD. L. REV. 1 (1985); and *Visions of Practice in Legal Thought,* 36 STAN. L. REV. 469 (1984). His contribution to the Symposium is entitled *Social Theory and Political Practice: Unger's Brazilian Journalism.*

CASS R. SUNSTEIN is Professor of Law and Professor of Political Science at the University of Chicago. A renowned legal scholar in the areas of administrative and constitutional law, Professor Sunstein's publications include *Constitutionalism After the New Deal,* 101 HARV. L. REV. (1987) (forthcoming); *Lochner's Legacy,* 87 COLUM. L. REV. 873 (1987); *Interest Groups in American Public Law,* 38 STAN. L. REV. 29 (1986); and *Legal Interference with Private Preferences,* 53 U. CHI. L. REV. 1129 (1986). Professor Sunstein is also a co-author of CONSTITUTIONAL LAW (1986) (with G. Stone, L. Seidman & M. Tushnet). His contribution to this Symposium is entitled *Routine and Revolution.*

DAVID M. TRUBEK is Voss-Bascom Professor of Law and Director of the Institute for Legal Studies at the University of Wisconsin-Madison. He has written on social and legal theory, the sociology of law, legal practice and politics, civil procedure and litigation. His publications include *Max Weber's Tragic Modernism and the Study of Law in Society,* 20 L. & Soc. Rev. 573 (1986); *Where the Action Is: Critical Legal Studies and Empiricism* (co-authored with W. Felstiner, H. Kritzer, A. Sarat, and J. Grossman), 36 Stan. L. Rev. 623 (1984); and *The Costs of Ordinary Litigation,* 31 UCLA L. Rev. 72 (1983). Professor Trubek's contribution to this Symposium is entitled *Programmatic Thought and the Critique of the Social Disciplines.*

David E. Van Zandt, Associate Professor of Law at the Northwestern University School of Law, holds in addition to a law degree a doctorate in sociology from the London School of Economics. His publications include *Neutralizing the Regulatory Burden: The Use of Equity Securities by Foreign Corporate Acquirers,* 13 Sec. L. Rev. 583 (1981). Professor Van Zandt's article in this Symposium is entitled *Commonsense Reasoning, Social Change, and the Law.*

Cornel West is Professor of Religion and Director of the Afro-American Studies Program at Princeton University. A leading philosopher of religion, Professor West has published Prophesy Deliverance!: An Afro-American Revolutionary Christianity (1982); and *Race and Social Theory: Towards a Genealogical Materialist Analysis,* in The Year Left 74–90 (Sprinkler et al. eds. 1987). He is also the co-editor, with John Rajchman, of Post-Analytic Philosophy (1985). His contribution to this Symposium is entitled *Between Dewey and Gramsci: Unger's Emancipatory Experimentalism.*

A NOTE ON CITATIONS

In order to provide uniformity to the citations used in this Symposium, references to Roberto Unger's works will be standard throughout. The citation will be in the following form: FALSE NECESSITY at 630. The complete bibliographical information and the short forms are given below.

—The three volumes of R. UNGER, POLITICS: A WORK IN CONSTRUCTIVE SOCIAL THEORY (1987) will be cited separately.
> —R. UNGER, SOCIAL THEORY: ITS SITUATION AND ITS TASK (1987) will be cited as SOCIAL THEORY.
> —R. UNGER, FALSE NECESSITY: ANTI-NECESSITARIAN SOCIAL THEORY IN THE SERVICE OF RADICAL DEMOCRACY (1987) will be cited as FALSE NECESSITY.
> —R. UNGER, PLASTICITY INTO POWER: COMPARATIVE-HISTORICAL STUDIES ON THE HISTORICAL CONDITIONS OF ECONOMIC AND MILITARY SUCCESS (1987) will be cited as PLASTICITY INTO POWER.

—R. UNGER, PASSION: AN ESSAY ON PERSONALITY (1984) will be cited as PASSION.

—Unger, *The Critical Legal Studies Movement,* 96 HARV. L. REV. 561 (1983), *reprinted in slightly revised form as* R. UNGER, THE CRITICAL LEGAL STUDIES MOVEMENT (1986): references to the *Harvard Law Review* version will be cited as *The Critical Legal Studies Movement;* references to the book will be cited as THE CRITICAL LEGAL STUDIES MOVEMENT.

—Unger, *A Program for Late Twentieth-Century Psychiatry,* 139 AM. J. PSYCHIATRY 155 (1982) will be cited as *Late Twentieth-Century Psychiatry.*

—R. UNGER, LAW IN MODERN SOCIETY: TOWARD A CRITICISM OF SOCIAL THEORY (1976) will be cited as LAW IN MODERN SOCIETY.

—R. UNGER, KNOWLEDGE AND POLITICS (1975) will be cited as KNOWLEDGE AND POLITICS.

Professor Unger has indicated he will write a Part II of *Politics.* In this upcoming work, he plans to develop his ideas about "the transformation of personal relations that extends the institutional program of empowered democracy."[1]

---

[1] FALSE NECESSITY at 630.

INTRODUCTION: ROBERTO UNGER'S *POLITICS*

Robin W. Lovin

Politics has often been considered the most inclusive search for the human good. The most important human aims come to fruition in political communities, and the more specialized forms of knowledge are ancillary to this effort to understand those goals we have in common. To know human beings is in the end to know what enables and constrains their life together in political communities, and it is in those broad communities, rather than in the narrower confines of personal relationships and economic efforts, that persons most fully express themselves.

Aristotle launched these expansive claims for politics in Western thought, against the winds of Plato's complaint that politics would never amount to anything until philosophers were kings, and against his own assertion that contemplation, *theoria,* is the highest human good. Medieval theologians complicated the picture with a supernatural good which could only be achieved by God's grace, but even for Thomas Aquinas, the good of the community was the highest goal that persons could seek by their own natural powers. It was only in modern times that political thinkers began to define their aims in less ambitious terms—not, to be sure, because they assigned knowledge of the human good to some other line of inquiry, but because they believed it was not to be had.

Roberto Mangabeira Unger has sought to return politics to that expansive inquiry, but in a way that challenges the idealized, static pictures of human good in classical politics no less than it criticizes the narrow, positivistic understandings of law and society that characterize the modern period. In his early writing, and in his courses at Harvard Law School, Unger treated law as a product of its social context, rather than a discourse that moves according to its own independent logic.[1] As an active participant in the politics of Brazil and in his new theoretical formulations in *Politics,* Unger thinks about social contexts in ways

---

[1] KNOWLEDGE AND POLITICS, LAW IN MODERN SOCIETY, and THE CRITICAL LEGAL STUDIES MOVEMENT. Unger's association with the Critical Legal Studies movement reflects a way of reading the social context of law that marks a break with some of his earlier writing, but it also continues the basic theme that law must be understood in terms of social context and function. *See also* M. KELMAN, A GUIDE TO CRITICAL LEGAL STUDIES (1987).

that transcend the North Atlantic starting point of previous social theory. The result is a "program of empowered democracy" that aims at a comprehensive transformation of modern social relationships.

Unger's political program requires a rethinking of the human sciences through which modern society understands persons and their relationships. Some of the provocative new directions in Unger's thought appeared in his proposal for a new psychology, *Passion: An Essay on Personality,* which appeared in 1984. Unger has tried to show that politics is intimately connected to these developments in social theory. What we think we can know about human needs, about history, about the working of institutions, and about transcendent human aspirations shapes our politics. But more important, politics is the medium in which we bring this knowledge into being. Unger hints, in a cryptic remark at the end of *Knowledge and Politics,* that this may even include that knowledge of theological ends that the medieval writers placed beyond the reach of politics.[2]

This radical version of the relationship between knowledge and politics, which makes politics the source of knowledge as well as the place where it is put to use, dominates *Politics: A Work in Constructive Social Theory.* As Unger notes on the very first page of the three volumes, "No one has ever taken the idea of society as artifact to the hilt."[3] That is precisely what he proceeds to do, through more than a thousand pages that range across the intellectual problems of modern social theory (*Social Theory*), an alternative social theory for a radical democratic politics (*False Necessity*), and comparative studies that illustrate the main themes of the new theory (*Plasticity into Power*).

The originality and scope of Unger's work provokes an equally broad response. Not only legal theorists and social scientists, but philosophers, theologians, and historians will find ideas in *Politics* that challenge the conventional wisdom of their disciplines. These possibilities for discussion were already apparent in a lecture that Unger delivered at the University of Chicago Divinity School in May, 1985. After several days of stimulating conversations, during which the editors learned of Unger's plans for *Politics,* we decided that it would be important to offer an early response to the volumes that would draw contributors from the full range of relevant disciplines. Accordingly, we drew up a list of potential authors and invited them to contribute to a symposium on Unger's new work. The assignment, as will be apparent in these essays, was not to produce a book review of *Politics,* but to use Unger's essay as a starting point for reflection on their own disciplines and to evaluate his points in light of their own constructive work. Thanks to the kind cooperation of Professor Unger and Cam-

---

[2] KNOWLEDGE AND POLITICS at 294-95.
[3] SOCIAL THEORY at 1.

bridge University Press, the symposium authors received advance copies of the manuscript of *Politics,* and were able to complete their essays for a special issue of the *Northwestern University Law Review,*[4] published just a few months after the publication of *Politics* itself. Those essays, together with new contributions by Robert Burns, Richard Rorty, and David Trubek, make up this volume.[5]

THE CRITIQUE OF LIBERALISM

Unger's *Politics* is sharply critical of the political systems that have emerged along with the industrialization of the developed, capitalist economies. His call for a politics that is more attentive to human aims and goods links him to the critical reassessment of political liberalism that has received much attention in North American political thought in recent years. A quick survey of the contributors to this volume who have been part of that discussion shows, however, that their alternatives to liberalism develop in ways quite different from Unger's proposal. William Galston offers the most concise formulation of Unger's relationship to the contemporary critics of political liberalism: Unger's *Politics* has a "classical form" with an "anti-classical content" (16). Like the classical political theorists, Unger calls for a turn to a politics that includes knowledge, goals, and human goods, but he sees those elements in quite different terms.

The "anti-classical content" of Unger's essay will, for many readers, obscure the "classical form." Unger does not aim at the creation of an ideal political community that is legitimated by its correspondence to human nature. *Politics* is a demand for radical freedom that consistently upsets all settled ways of doing things. Joy and human fulfillment lie in the recognition of this radical freedom and an escape from the anxieties and oppressions that inevitably arise when it is denied. This revolutionary world view is embedded more in the human soul than in the determinism of Marxist materialism. Its antecedents, as Cass Sunstein notes, are in Nietzsche and Sartre (46, 48). Its method, Robert Burns argues, begins with the necessity of radically free choice (134).

The notion that human beings can live, and live well, in the absence of settled expectations, runs counter to the political wisdom that sees the ordering of life in ways that permit stable expectations as the great achievement of Western law. Unger demands the overthrow of institutions and customs, not only because they oppress or because they permit the accumulation of power and resources in a few hands,

---

[4] 81 NORTHWESTERN UNIVERSITY LAW REVIEW (Summer 1987).

[5] A version of Trubek's essay has also appeared in the AMERICAN JOURNAL OF SOCIOLOGY. The NORTHWESTERN UNIVERSITY LAW REVIEW symposium also included articles by Milner Ball and Drucilla Cornell.

but simply because they are static, because they obscure the radical freedom that marks every social arrangement as a human artifact. In Unger's view, persons have rights—"destabilization rights"—to a political order that acknowledges their existential freedom.[6] This disvaluation of continuity and stability in political life leaps forth from almost every page of *Politics,* and if it is all the reader sees, Unger's theory soon appears neither as classical politics with an anti-classical content (Galston), nor as a new articulation of radical politics (Judt, 115), but as a sort of Western version of "Crazy Zen" which, as Cleary and Higonnet remind us, serves in some forms of Eastern thought to disorder thinking about politics altogether (276).

Beyond the startlingly new political proposals, however, there remains much in Unger's *Politics* that connects with more moderate revisions of liberalism. Perhaps the most important of these connections is a skepticism about the emphasis on results that characterized earlier, utilitarian versions of liberalism. What seemed to Bentham to be a liberation of human ingenuity from superstitious tables of duties appears two hundred years later to be a license to sacrifice the human individual to the requirements of social progress. It seems axiomatic, but also important, to say that there are some things that we may not do to persons, not only in pursuit of our private goals, but in pursuit of the social good, or even out of regard for their own good. Hence the concept of rights takes an important place in political philosophy, in Unger's radical vision no less than in the modified liberalism of John Rawls or Ronald Dworkin.[7]

Persons must be protected, but Unger stresses the difference between protecting persons and stabilizing systems of property and political power that only make it easier to oppress them. The continual unmaking and remaking of social arrangements that Unger calls for in his political program must not be read in isolation from the concern for persons and their relationships which limits and guides the political experiments. "The commitment of empowered democracy to expand the scope of context-revising conflict makes it all the more important to assure the individual that his basic security, and the security of those closest to him, will be protected. If he lacks this assurance, the institutionalized controversies and reinventions of social life will quickly become intolerable to him, and he will see each as a threat to himself."[8]

The system of rights that characterizes empowered democracy is, in fact, very extensive. "Market rights" establish and limit the claims that persons and groups may make against the supply of capital avail-

---

[6] FALSE NECESSITY at 530-35.
[7] FALSE NECESSITY at 508-39. For a more detailed treatment of Unger's differences with Rawls and Dworkin, see Burns (135-39) and Hawthorn (92-93).
[8] FALSE NECESSITY at 514.

able in the society, and regulate their relationships with one another as temporary holders of a share of that supply. "Immunity rights" cover the basic concerns for personal security, encompassing not only the freedoms we ordinarily associate with the term, but the protections from extreme material want that political theorists usually call "welfare rights." The new category of "destabilization rights" indicates the seriousness with which Unger takes the political process of conflict, challenge, and reorganization. Persons in an empowered democracy have rights to insure that institutions do not accumulate wealth and power in ways that insulate them from such challenges. A "destabilization right" demands a certain vulnerability in powerful institutions and groups. Finally, as a counterpoint to the apparent instabilities of empowered democracy, there are "solidarity rights," the right of persons to establish relations of trust and reliance between themselves.

It is clear that Unger intends these rights, with the expectations they generate and the forms of security they provide, to be as prominent a part of the experience of empowered democracy as the conflicts and changes that continually remake the social institutions. It is less clear how their constraints will be effected:

> The remaking of the system of rights is not a separate task of institutional reconstruction, as if we could change the constitutional form of government, the style of conflict over the control and uses of governmental power, the regime of capital, the organization of work, and *then* the content and form of legal entitlements. It is rather the indispensable expression of all those other changes. But this expression is not transparent or automatic. It poses specific problems and clarifies hidden connections.[9]

The revised system of rights must be incorporated into the workings of empowered democracy itself, not applied as an external constraint on them, though doubtless there must be something like a system of courts to make these demands explicit and prevent them from being neglected or subverted. Unger suggests that destabilization rights might best be enforced by a separate branch of government, distinct from anything we would now recognize as the legislature or judiciary. It is in the nature of some of these rights, especially some solidarity rights, however, that they cannot be enforced by anything more rigorous than the social reliance placed on trust and the social opprobrium that attaches to those who prove untrustworthy. The rights that appear in *Politics,* then, are far more diverse in kind than the rights we are used to thinking about in liberal political theory, and their claims cover far more than the enforceable minimums we often associate with legal rights. Nevertheless, they are there, and they allow individuals the

---

[9] FALSE NECESSITY at 509.

measure of security they need to participate in the risks and joys of political creativity.

In the end, then, Unger's revolutions are Jeffersonian (Sunstein, 48; West, 261). He sees the chief threat to human aspirations not in social disorder, but in the deadening stability of regimes that limit innovation and concentrate resources in the hands of those who already have them. To be sure, some people will be hurt by the rapidity of change. Those whose identity and satisfactions are tied to a certain niche in the economic and social hierarchy must know that empowered democracy will not protect *their* expectations. But every system of rights is also a statement of what other claims and hopes must be denied when they come into conflict with the claims protected by rights. The pace of life in an empowered democracy might prove more rapid than most North Atlantic liberals have thought safe, but persons would not wander unprotected in this shifting landscape, nor would these revolutions be allowed to devour their children. To that extent, Unger's system of rights serves the purpose that rights have always served in modern polities that have replaced the security of ascribed status with the unpredictable possibilities of achievement.

SOCIAL THEORY AND POLITICAL POSSIBILITY

Unger's concerns with human goods and human rights show a connection between his *Politics* and contemporary critiques and reformulations of liberalism that one might miss by concentrating only on the innovative elements of his political program. The program itself could only be envisioned by someone whose political experience has taught him that, in Auden's words, "nothing can save us that is possible."[10] The close fit between the program of *Politics* and Unger's concrete advice to a restored Brazilian democracy (Simon, 330-32) shows where his hopes really lie. "For him, none of the rich North Atlantic democracies are home" (Rorty, 30). Empowered democracy is envisioned by its author not against the backdrop of rust-belt cities, two-party politics, and pension-fund socialism, but in a setting of vast, untapped resources, where such stability as has been achieved has rested on a base of authoritarianism, inequality, and economic dependency.[11] Before one dismisses the vision, it is well to remember that more of the world is like that than is like Pittsburgh and Detroit. The bounds of possibility, as Rorty suggests (31), may have appeared wider when those places were new.

---

[10] W. H. Auden, *For the Time Being: A Christmas Oratorio,* in COLLECTED POEMS (1976) at 274.

[11] See Unger's characterization of Brazilian culture as reported in Simon (308-11). See also Hawthorn (112) on the fit between Unger's line of argument and the historical development of Latin American politics.

Unger, however, aims to do far more than oppose a weary liberalism with a romantic vision. He is convinced that the failure to appreciate the program of empowered democracy, when it is not motivated by a self-interested commitment to the present order, is largely the result of an inability to see the constant remaking of the social context as a real possibility. That curious failure of imagination in modern intellectuals can be traced, in turn, to a social determinism that is a pervasive feature of social theory. Whether we look at society through the lenses provided by Marx, or Durkheim, or any of a number of lesser figures, we see a range of possibilities for the future that is largely determined by causal forces already at work in the present and limited by a virus-like tendency of present social structures to replicate themselves in the future with a bare minimum of adaptive modifications. We do not remark on this determinism as a feature of our social theory because it seems equally present in any of the alternative theories to which we may turn. Consequently, we begin to see the determinism as a feature of reality, rather than a limitation in our way of understanding it. So long as we think that the outcomes of social conflict are predetermined and could be known in advance by a sufficiently penetrating social science, we cannot take the conflicts with the seriousness that the program of empowered democracy requires:

> The fighting is not in earnest in the sense that the conflicts over the formative contexts of social life or over the procedures for social problem solving and interest accommodation take place under the controlling influence of forces the contenders cannot master and do not even fully understand. The fighting may also not be in earnest in the sense that whatever the intentions of the disputants, only a narrow range of possible outcomes can stand the test of practical reality. Inflexible economic, technological, or psychological imperatives determine which forms of governmental or economic organization can and cannot work.[12]

Intellectual clarity about the program of empowered democracy thus requires us to discard the idea that history has a script. This implies nothing less than a complete rethinking of the ideas of social theory on which modern conceptions of politics and its possibilities rest. An adequate social theory must be consistently anti-naturalistic. That is, it must carry through the critical analyses by which psychology, economics, and sociology have shown that property rights, hierarchies of authority, market systems of distribution, and other features of social life that seem to have the permanence and inevitability of nature are in fact historically contingent social creations. But a consistent anti-naturalism must also understand that the "deep structures" of historical development and social evolution that provided the explanatory frameworks for these earlier critical analyses were themselves creations of human intellect

---

[12] FALSE NECESSITY at 135.

and not the discovery of inexorable forces that operate in nature. For Unger, Marx's analysis of the forces at work in the internal contradictions of capitalism provides at once the most developed example of this "deep structure" theory and the key elements for a social theory that would move beyond its misleading determinism.[13]

Unger thus introduces a far-reaching skepticism into his treatment of social science, a skepticism that cuts in precisely the opposite direction of the skepticism that prepared the way for social science at the beginning of the modern period. In the seventeenth and eighteenth centuries, doubt about our knowledge of the human good led Hobbes and others to speculate on the possibility of a knowledge of human beings—their ideas and ultimately their social institutions—that would rest strictly on causal explanations that would integrate them into the larger world of natural forces.[14] This has not led, as those innovators expected, to the enhancement of human control of events, but to the enervating sense that we are the powerless creatures of forces we are unable to master. Only a new skepticism, directed this time at deterministic causal explanations in the human sciences, can achieve the liberation that the original revolt against a static, divinely ordained pattern of human life once promised.

It is in this penetrating criticism of "false necessity" that many readers find Unger's most important contribution. In setting the stage for his own political alternatives, Unger formulates the intellectual problems of social science in a way that also challenges those whose interest in these issues is chiefly theoretical. The program for a new politics is also a program for a new form of social science, without which the politics has no way of explaining its hopes for social transformation or for understanding the human relationships that might emerge in a new political order. At the same time, Unger sees with a clarity perhaps unmatched since Max Weber how one's understanding of social theory directs and limits one's political role. In the process he challenges those of Weber's heirs who would invoke the "value neutrality" of their scientific inquiry as a refuge from political commitment.[15]

Many readers agree, then, that Unger's call for a "radically antinaturalistic social theory"—which extends to the study of personality as well as institutions—is a benchmark in critical studies of the presuppositions and goals of modern social science. There is less agreement with the substance of the alternative view of theory, persons, and politics that Unger proposes.

John Dunn perhaps best summarizes the tenor of these criticisms

---

[13] FALSE NECESSITY at 96-100.

[14] *See* J. YOLTON, THINKING MATTER: MATERIALISM IN EIGHTEENTH CENTURY BRITAIN (1983).

[15] On Weber's views, see the essay *Science as a Vocation*, in FROM MAX WEBER (H. H. Gerth and C. W. Mills eds. 1946) at 129.

when he notes that Unger's view rests on "a taut but oddly stable balance between an intense scepticism and an at least equally intense faith" (71). It is Dunn's judgment that "Over time . . . Unger's scepticism and preoccupation with institutional form are likely to prove more instructive than the ardor of his faith" (89).

Criticisms of the program of empowered democracy tend to center around two general themes: First, there are questions whether Unger's anti-naturalistic approach has escaped constraints on human projects so completely as he had hoped. Second, there are questions whether Unger's system of rights is so closely tied to his anti-naturalism that it becomes implausible once the anti-naturalism is called into question.

Unger's anti-naturalism substitutes for the idea of a fixed human nature the concept of "formative contexts."[16] A formative context is the set of assumptions and patterns of social organization that provide the framework for the routines and practices of a given society. A formative context is what reduces the infinite possibilities of human life to the realities of a particular social order. While a formative context sets a perhaps rather narrow, and apparently rather permanent range of possibilities for any individual, the idea is to stress that contexts themselves are social artifacts, susceptible to remaking in ways that remake the persons who live in them.

Critics who imagine empowered democracy as a scene of constant social flux often mistake the point of Unger's anti-naturalism. His discussion of formative contexts is not intended to make more rapid change plausible, but to alert us to illusions that arise because important social changes are necessarily so slow:

> Rather than attempt neatly to separate an unchanging core and a variable periphery of human nature, we can simply impose an ad hoc, loosely defined constraint. The successful realization of the program must not require any abrupt or drastic change in the predispositions we now experience . . . We *can* choose who or what to become, but only so long as we go step by step, never expect to move very far at any one time, and resist the temptation to mistake our strongest current desires for a permanent kernel of human nature.[17]

We must avoid the caricatures of Unger's work that suggest he sees persons as protean creatures with no important sources of satisfaction except to revel in constant change. Still, whether the pace of change be fast or slow, it is important to ask whether it is true that there are no constraints on change beyond the formative contexts that are susceptible to our remaking. David Van Zandt offers a detailed criticism of this idea. He formulates an alternative microsocial theory which suggests that ideas of human nature are not simply explanations

---

[16] *See* SOCIAL THEORY at 3-4, 130-33.
[17] FALSE NECESSITY at 559.

introduced after the fact to justify a fixed social structure, but are part of the commonsense understanding that allows persons to make plans and engage in cooperative activities in the first place (Van Zandt, 176-94). Hobson (210) devotes less attention to his own alternative, but clearly thinks that Unger gives too little attention to the persistent features of human life that do not yield to incremental change. The suspicion lingers among these readers that there are requirements of human flourishing that are not accounted for by the plasticity Unger finds in formative contexts, and that may not be fully satisfied by the invigorating exercise of context smashing, even when the pace of change is tolerable and people are confident of their immunity rights. As Geoffrey Hawthorn points out, "These considerations suggest that the 'qualified introspection' that Unger urges us to exercise on his conception of passion is as likely to lead us to dissent as to convince us that his particular conception of human nature and its possibilities match our existing dispositions" (101).

Unger might well reply that those who doubt that persons can flourish in a situation where contexts are regularly remade are probably rather comfortable with the context in which they now find themselves. Their conception of what persons want and require may, in short, rest on an ideological commitment to existing social systems, and not on any real insight into human nature. That rebuttal would have to be taken seriously. Rorty, with his appreciation of the vitality and openness of the developing countries in which Unger is at home, might join in the argument on Unger's side (34). But it is hard to know how an argument that Van Zandt or Hobson is the victim of his own ideology could be supported without appeal to just the sort of "deep structure" theory that Unger wants to avoid. To say that people's view of human nature is ideologically blinkered is to claim that their experience can only be understood by appeal to a theory that not only is not part of their experience, but actually runs counter to it. Marx and Freud have provided us with highly successful examples of such theories, but Unger says that his theory is of another sort. Indeed, it has to be of another sort if he is not to constrain our political imagination with his *Politics* in the same way that he contends other social theorists have done with their deep structures. The only way to adjudicate the case between Unger and Rorty, on the one side, and Van Zandt or Hobson, on the other, is to submit their accounts of what life is like to the ordinary experience of thoughtful people and ask which view, in that discussion, seems more true or correct.[18]

---

[18] Hawthorn argues the stronger point that such a discussion cannot, in the nature of the case, lead to even provisional *truths* about how we ought to lead our lives. "Someone may think me foolish, even mad, to live as I do, but he cannot show me that I am actually wrong" (Hawthorn, 100).

The question of what persons really need to live well is more than an incidental accompaniment to the larger issues of social organization raised in *Politics*. The system of rights which keeps political risks to individuals within limits is closely connected to the anti-naturalism of Unger's social theory. Unlike liberal rights doctrines, which attempt to define a realm of discretionary action in which individuals may pursue their own goods, Unger intends his system of rights to "soften the opposition between devotion to the common good and the pursuit of private interests."[19] The system of rights defines the kind of good life that will be possible in an empowered democracy. It does not simply clear a space which individuals may fill with whatever good they can make to fit.

By most criteria of theoretical elegance, this close fit between the understanding of persons and the political account of their rights is a great achievement. It does reduce the opposition between private interests and the common good, and it makes the lines of argument by which the system of rights might be justified more clear. But it also makes the plausibility of the political program rather closely dependent on the plausibility of the anthropology (Trubek, 240).

Where the fit between personality and rights is looser, we might endorse the system of rights even if we disagreed about the needs, goals, and motivations of persons. In Unger's work, doubts about the description of personality lead at once to questions about the adequacy of the system of rights. Thus, Milner Ball has written:

> To take but one example, bringing so-called relative equality to Native Americans and eliminating the so-called enduring subjugation practiced by tribes continue to be favored inspirations for destroying them. What looks like archaic, pre-modern submission from the outside may from the inside prove to be a fulfilling, experimental venture in trust. The rights granting immunity from Unger's empowered democracy leave no room for such non-Spartan or truly different people. In addition, I can see no room in empowered democracy for the Thomas Mertons of the world, and none for the untimely born and the untimely dead whose claims to humanity, so far as I can tell, would be trampled upon as much as they are now. Only the agile of mind, foot, and political instinct would survive.[20]

Unger's critics, then, raise persistent questions about the adequacy of his understanding of persons and about the impact of this narrowly modern anthropology on his system of politics. Some who strongly endorse his criticism of previous social theory suggest that he has replicated some of the mistakes in his own constructive work. The problem may lie neither in the determinism of "deep structure" theories, nor in the reductionism of positivism, but in the limits of the

---

[19] FALSE NECESSITY at 509.
[20] Ball, *The City of Unger,* 81 NORTHWESTERN UNIVERSITY LAW REVIEW (Summer 1987) at 641.

theoretical enterprise itself, in its tendency to provide system at the expense of diversity and to overwhelm the prudent wisdom of practice with a relentless demand for consistency. Dunn's suggestion that Unger's skepticism will prove a more useful guide to political practice than Unger's faith is one expression of this judgment (Dunn, 89). Cleary and Higonnet call for a more "Taoist" politics that reflects a similar tempering of theory by experience (Cleary and Higonnet, 281-83). So, perhaps, does Charles Davis' contrast between "making" and "doing" in the creation of social systems (Davis, 244).

There can be little doubt that Unger would reject any suggestion that his critique of previous social theory points us away from theory altogether. Given the choice Dunn formulates between Unger's skepticism and Unger's faith, Unger himself would doubtless choose faith. He belongs to what Cornel West calls "Third-Wave left romanticism" (West, 256), to those who, though they are critical of Marxism, are not yet ready to reject Marx's project. At a time when the intellectual fashion is to be post-Marxist, postmodern, and postpolitical, Unger's assessment of modernity is something like Chesterton's comment about Christianity, that the thing has not so much been tried and found wanting as it has been unwanted, and therefore not tried.

To give modernity its chance, however, it may be necessary to go all the way back to the beginning. Overcoming "false necessity" is not just a matter of avoiding the deep structure social theories that shatter politics by depicting persons as mere effects of forces that they cannot understand or control. It requires rethinking the first moves by which modern thinkers sought to replace human purposes with natural causes in their accounts of political community. Unger's anti-naturalism, rejecting the determinist naturalism implicit in the theoretical enterprise that runs from Hobbes, through Marx, to the present, must eventually find itself face to face with an older, even Aristotelian, naturalism. That version of naturalism says that how persons live together politically must be a function of what we know to be their good. The "classical form" which Galston (16) notes in Unger's work is no accident. It results from his questioning of the self-imposed limitations of modern political thought.

Most of the participants in this symposium share Unger's dissatisfaction with liberal and/or deep structure theories, and so they appreciate the "classical form." The repeated question of the critics, however, is whether the "anti-classical content" is adequate to the task of defining a political context that would protect a reasonably full range of human goods, including those that happen to be inherently less politically aggressive or temporarily less popular.

The discussion on that issue is likely to continue for some time, if the vigor of these contributions to it or the longevity of its classical antecedents is any indication. Unger promises a further treatment of the transformation of personal relations in an empowered democracy as part II of *Politics*. It is our hope that the essays in this volume will help to insure that neither the present three volumes, nor any future parts of *Politics*, will be read exclusively as exercises in social theory. They belong in a much larger discussion of human aims and possibilities that social theory, though it has often foreclosed it, was intended to open.

FALSE UNIVERSALITY: INFINITE PERSONALITY AND FINITE EXISTENCE IN UNGER'S *POLITICS*

William A. Galston

I. INTRODUCTION

A decade ago, Daniel Bell argued against what he termed the "monolithic" view of society.[1] Whatever may have been true of classical and medieval communities, Bell contended, Western industrial societies are characterized not by integration, but by disjunction. There is no single spirit that animates these societies. Rather, they are divided into different realms, each guided by its own principle: the techno-economy, the operating principle of which is efficiency; the polity, the legitimacy of which is based on the concept of free and equal citizens; and culture, increasingly dominated by the modernist ideal of unlimited self-expression. Within this framework, Bell suggested, one can discern the following structural sources of tension in modern societies:

> [B]etween a social structure (primarily techno-economic) which is bureaucratic and hierarchical, and a polity which believes, formally, in equality and participation; between a social structure that is organized fundamentally in terms of roles and specialization, and a culture which is concerned with the enhancement and fulfillment of the self and the "whole" person. In these contradictions, one perceives many of the latent social conflicts that have been expressed ideologically as alienation, depersonalization, [and] the attack on authority . . . .[2]

Roberto Unger's project in *Politics* is to argue that these contradictions can be overcome. Specifically, Unger contends that the principle of what Bell calls "culture"—the enhancement and fulfillment of the self—is the axis around which all of society must be reconstructed. Economic roles and hierarchies that constrain self-expression must be dismantled. Legal-constitutional forms that restrict the free play of the human imagination must be reconstituted. Fortunately, Unger argues, to accord normative primacy to self-assertion is not to surrender other desirable features of modern life. Plastic, nonhierarchical economic institutions are not merely compatible with but actually necessary for the attainment

---

[1] D. BELL, THE CULTURAL CONTRADICTIONS OF CAPITALISM (1976).

[2] *Id.* at 14.

of material prosperity. Rights-based political institutions can be redesigned to accommodate the democratic clash of imaginative projects while preserving individual security against tyranny. We need neither embrace the rigors of civic-republican virtue to achieve democracy nor accept the repressiveness of the Protestant ethic to ensure prosperity; the modernist ideal of personal liberation will be functional in every sphere of life. We can, in short, realize the old Enlightenment dream of a rational society in which our most treasured goals are no longer in ultimate conflict.

From this normative vantage point, Unger launches a vigorous attack on contemporary liberal polities. (He acknowledges—but does not dwell on—parallel failings of Marxist-Leninist societies.) Unger contends that Western societies are frozen into rigid roles and hierarchies. Political systems of checks and balances impede both democratic self-expression and egalitarian social reconstruction. A combination of social rigidity, political gridlock, and imaginative stultification locks liberal politics into futile cycles of reform and retrenchment. Even European social democracy—the fullest realization of liberal aspirations—fails to liberate the individual's practical, emotional, and cognitive capacities. For these reasons, we cannot be satisfied with a program of incremental changes pursued through current institutions. Rather, we must seek to destabilize these institutions in order to move toward their radical transformation.

It is not my purpose in this Essay to subject Unger's concrete political analyses and proposals to detailed scrutiny. For the record, I should say that his account of roles and hierarchies is unpersuasive in its denial of the considerable fluidity characteristic of modern socioeconomies; that his critique of political checks and balances is blind both to their capacity for strong democratic action and to their ability to protect individuals against collective tyranny; and that his account of reform cycles ignores the ways in which liberal societies have been noncyclically transformed over the past century. Moreover, the practical lesson of recent generations is that aggressive contempt for social democracy does not promote the fulfillment of radical aspirations. The effort to "leap over" social democracy is more likely to produce traditionalist counterreaction than cultural revolution. In short, Unger's prescriptions rest on a dramatically flawed diagnosis of contemporary society; they minister to ills the very existence of which most individuals would deny. As I shall argue, this gulf between Unger's vision and ordinary consciousness forces his argument in elitist and coercive directions radically at odds with his professed intentions.

Unger's *Politics* is an ambitious attempt to combine the synoptic explanatory claims of modern social theory with the normative aspirations of traditional political philosophy. While each of these elements deserves full exploration, it is the complex relation of Unger's thought to the normative philosophical tradition that serves as the focus of my remarks.

The normative strand of Unger's work may be described as an effort to restore the form of classical political philosophy, but with an anticlassical content. Unger endorses the classical strategy: a description of individual human flourishing or happiness as the basis for a normative account of society. But he rejects the classical depiction of structured, delimited human nature in favor of a post-Christian, modernist account of free, unbounded human personality.

Three key features of Unger's thought express his fidelity to the classical project. Against the strictures of Machiavelli and Marx—but in line with the thinkers of antiquity—he insists that normative social theory culminates in a concrete vision of a good society (in classical terms, a "utopia"). Like Aristotle, he argues that the good society is justified through its propensity to permit and promote individual *eudaemonia*. Finally, like Plato, he believes that the structure of society mirrors the structure of the self, that the political community is the human soul writ large.

At the same time, Unger contemptuously rejects the classical account of human nature, and with it, the classical depiction of the good society. "[T]he classical moralizing doctrines of the virtues and the vices," he declares, are a species of "superficial sentimentality."[3] The decisive break with these doctrines—the revolutionary view of human existence developed by the great modernist artists and authors—is "[o]ne of the most important events in the history of modern culture. . . . Compared with this modernist view of the self, earlier images of man look shoddy and unconvincing."[4] As a result, the classical conception of society, which culminated in an account of natural order and hierarchy, must be supplanted by forms of social organization compatible with the modernist revolution.

The isomorphism between self and society rests on the troubled relation between formative structures and formed activities. Unger rejects the primacy of character or of fixed, habitual patterns of behavior in favor of a fluid capacity to act on imagination and desire. Similarly, he rejects a sharp distinction between stable constitutional institutions and the vagaries of ordinary politics in favor of a continuum characterized throughout by openness and revisability. To be sure, he tempers modernist iconoclasm with the antiskeptical claim that some individual virtues and collective institutions can be rationally defended. But the defense rests on the modernist premise that infinite personality can never adequately be contained in any set of rules, roles, or structures.

There are, then, two distinct standpoints from which Unger's nor-

---

[3] PASSION at 297.

[4] *Id.* at 296.

mative theory may be questioned. First, one may reject the very project of constructing and justifying a utopia as ungrounded and useless. Alternatively, one may accept the general utopian strategy, but criticize the specific content of Unger's vision.

This Essay adopts the latter approach. I shall criticize Unger's modernist conception of the self as being unduly dismissive of individual character and contemptuous of everyday life. I shall criticize his conception of society for its failure to grasp the justification of hierarchy and the requirements of order. At the same time, my objections to the content of his argument arise in the context of a considerable sympathy for its intention and form.

II. The Visionary/Utopian Form of Unger's Work

To avoid misunderstanding, let me enumerate the premises of Unger's argument that I shall not question. I shall grant (as others may not) that it is possible to give an account of human nature or personality that is not simply relative to a particular time, place, and circumstance; that one can move from this account to moral conclusions about individuals, a movement mediated by the moral weight accorded to human striving; and that one can further move from this normative account of the individual to the justification of a specific vision of the good society. In short, I would agree with Unger that visionary (or, in my terms, "utopian") thought is both theoretically possible and practically necessary.[5]

Most human action is both conscious and purposive. However, these two elements do not coexist harmoniously; consciousness dissolves our immediate, unreflective purposive certainty, leaving doubt and irresolution. Moral philosophy is the vector sum of the destruction of our immediate purposes and our enduring need for grounds of action. Its object is to provide reflective grounds capable of withstanding skeptical corrosion. Utopian thought is the political branch of moral philosophy.

Utopias are images of ideal communities; utopian thought makes explicit and justifies the bases upon which such communities are held to be ideal. For example, Plato's *Republic* contains both the image of a class-divided community and a defense of the principles of specialization and meritocracy that underlie that division.

Utopian thought performs three related political functions. First, it guides our deliberation, whether in devising courses of action or in choosing among exogenously defined alternatives. Second, it justifies our actions; the grounds of action are reasons that others ought to accept and—given openness and the freedom to reflect—can be led to accept. Third, it serves as the basis for evaluating existing institutions and prac-

---

[5] The following remarks are based on my previous work, W. GALSTON, JUSTICE AND THE HUMAN GOOD 14-16, 31-32 (1980).

tices. The *locus classicus* is the *Republic*, in which the completed ideal is deployed in Plato's memorable critique of imperfect regimes.

Utopian thought attempts to specify and justify the principles of a comprehensively good political order. Whatever their bases, these principles share certain general features.

First, utopian principles are universally valid in their intention, both temporally and geographically.

Second, the idea of the good order arises out of our experience, but does not mirror it in any simple way and is not circumscribed by it. Imagination may combine elements of experience into a new totality that has never existed; reason, seeking to reconcile the contradictions of experience, may transmute its elements.

Third, utopias exist in speech; they are "cities of words."[6] This does not mean that they cannot exist, only that they need not exist. This "counterfactuality" of utopia in no way impedes its evaluative function.

Fourth, utopian principles may come to be realized in history, and it may be possible to point to real forces pushing in that direction. But our approval of a utopia is not logically linked to the claim that history is bringing us closer to it or to an identification of an existing basis for the transformative actions that would bring it into being. Conversely, history cannot validate principles by itself. The movement of history (if it is a meaningful totality in any sense) may be from the more to the less desirable; the proverbial dustbin may contain much of enduring worth.

Fifth, although not confined to actual existence, the practical intention of utopia requires that it be constrained by possibility. Utopia is realistic in that it assumes human and material preconditions that are neither logically nor empirically impossible, even though their simultaneous presence may be both unlikely and largely beyond human control to effect.

Possibility is a limiting condition of utopian thought for two reasons. First, if an imagined state of affairs is not possible, it cannot serve as a ground of criticism. It would be absurd to dream of a world in which we no longer needed to eat, and then to criticize human beings on that basis for manifesting dependence and destructiveness in their relation to food. This criterion of possibility emerges in moral theory in the principle that "ought implies can." Obligation ceases in the face of impossibility, and praise and blame are not applicable to acts or events over which the agent can have no control. Second, an impossible state of affairs is not an appropriate object of endeavor, and therefore is not a suitable guide for practice. As Aristotle pointed out, we may long for the impossible, but we choose and act in the belief that our goal is possible. Action guided by longing for the impossible leads either to despair or to a frenzy of destructive rage at the world's permanent resistance. Utopian

---

6 *See* PLATO, REPUBLIC § 592b, at 238 (G.M.A. Grube trans. 1974).

seriousness is the mean between abstract negation and the cynical or un-thinking acceptance of facticity.

The difficulty is determining the limits of possibility, a concept that has many different meanings. Something is *logically* possible when it can be conceived without contradiction. But, as Kant observed, a logically possible concept

> may none the less be an empty concept, unless the objective reality of the synthesis through which the concept is generated has been specifically proved; and such proof . . . rests on principles of possible experience, and not on the principle of analysis (the law of contradiction). This is a warning against arguing directly from the logical possibility of concepts to the real possibility of things.[7]

We may call an object of possible experience *categorically* possible. Not everything categorically possible, however, is *nomologically* possible. It is categorically possible, for example, that the constants in well-en-trenched laws of nature could be other than they are; but from a scientific standpoint these constants are brute facts, limiting the range of causal events and human interventions. Finally, not everything nomologically possible is *practically* possible. Relative to a given set of facts, a state of affairs may be impossible to attain, even though a nomologically possible alteration of those facts would render it possible. The concept of practi-cal possibility has both technological and political application. Given present knowledge and techniques, it is impossible to fly to Sirius; given present challenges, real or perceived, it is impossible to persuade Con-gress to make a ninety percent cut in the defense budget.

We may now say that a political state of affairs is a fantasy when it is logically or categorically, but not nomologically, possible. It is a utopia when it is nomologically possible, whether or not it is practically possi-ble. The gap between nomological and practical possibility is the sphere of serious political action.

Unger wavers in his account of possibility as a limiting condition on utopia. On the one hand, he insists that there is no context-independent conception of possibility. This proposition, combined with his under-standing of contexts as radically incomplete, would seem to undercut any determinate account of possibility as a constraint on utopian thought.[8] On the other hand, Unger deploys a conception of possibility as a stan-dard for preferring some utopias to others. "Stability," he insists, is a key criterion: "A social scheme is unstable if it fails to reckon with be-havioral predispositions or material constraints that work to disrupt it."[9] In short, the abstract correspondence of a utopian vision with one's pre-ferred ideals is not enough to validate that vision. It also must meet

---

7 I. KANT, CRITIQUE OF PURE REASON A597-B625, at 503 n. (N.K. Smith trans. 1965) (2d ed. 1787).

8 SOCIAL THEORY at 173, 184.

9 PASSION at 48.

certain empirical conditions. In practice, then, Unger proceeds in a manner that is consistent with the tradition of utopian thought. But his apparent embrace of a specific understanding of possibility stands in tension—if not outright contradiction—with his blanket rejection of context-independent conceptions of possibility.

III. THE MODERNIST ACCOUNT OF PERSONALITY

I turn now from the visionary/utopian form of Unger's argument to its modernist content. This section deals with the modernist account of personality. The following section turns to the modernist account of society. The Essay concludes with some general reflections on modernist theory.

For Unger, the essence of human personality is that it is "infinite." It has the capacity to transcend all contexts: traits of character, moral rules, political institutions, cognitive structures, etc. No one context is hospitable to the full range of practical, passionate, political, or philosophic projects that personality can imagine. This infinity is not just an abstract capability, but—in the old language of teleology—an immanent impulse as well. The health of each individual personality is incompatible with its acceptance of the constraints inherent in specific contexts. Indeed, vice, psychological illness, and simple unhappiness are all consequences of the failure to relieve the tension between personal desire and contextual constraint. Modernist visionaries identified and struggled with this tension. Their struggle may have taken the form of an artistic fringe in conflict with bourgeois society. But its inner meaning is a universal truth about the human condition. The vague but spreading apprehension of this truth is now evoking disquiet and longing among men and women everywhere.

Unger's modernist account of personality rests on a sharp distinction between "character" and "self." Character is the set of routinized habits and dispositions that channel individual behavior into fixed patterns. Self, on the other hand, is the dual capacity to reject routine patterns of conduct and to imagine and act on alternatives to them.[10]

This distinction provides the point of departure for my critique of modernism. That individuals have a capacity to question and revise settled features of their existence cannot be denied. But Unger's separation of self and character is far too sharp. His thesis is reminiscent of Kant's bifurcation between phenomenal and transcendental consciousness, and it encounters the same difficulties. Our traits of character are not related to our existence in the mode of external possessions or physiological stimuli. These traits are not what we *have* and *feel*, but rather what we *are*. Our identities as persons are constituted largely by learned or inherited patterns of behavior. The consciousness that struggles against these

---

[10] *Id.* at 109, 111, 114.

patterns nevertheless is implicated in them. Personal change results not from a struggle of self against character, but rather from a mobilization of some traits of character against others. Ambition can be made to counteract sloth; courage can overcome shame.

Even if we grant Unger's distinction between routinized character and fluid self, it does not follow that the latter is to be given normative preference. The mere fact that we are able to upset settled patterns in favor of new experiences does not mean that we should do so. The fact that the imagination can counterpose itself to moral rules does not mean that these rules should be transgressed. At one point, Unger characterizes the view of individual behavior underlying his proposed political institutions as "the ability to entertain fantasies about possible forms of self-expression or association and to live them out."[11] This ability, he continues, is the "diurnal repetition for social life of what the Marquis de Sade recommended for sex: the strenuous enlargement of enacted possibility."[12] To this I would reply: there is no more solace to be found in the total liberation of fantasy than in its total repression—a maxim I would have thought emerges clearly enough in de Sade's own texts.

This point may be broadened. Unger projects a boundless hostility to the "vast spiritual sloth" and "overwhelming apathy" that allegedly characterize ordinary human experience.[13] Rejecting the solace most of us find in ordered existence, he insists that to understand deeply "is always to see the settled from the angle of the unsettled."[14] He even finds in the forcible destruction of everyday patterns the fount of moral insight:

[T]he growth of the transforming and ennobling passions . . . and the ability of these passions to penetrate the crust of everyday perception and habit seem to depend upon loss and sacrifice . . . . [T]he primary form of loss and sacrifice is the sacrifice and the loss of your settled place in a settled world. This is the event that allows you to distinguish the gold from the tinsel: the opportunities of human connection from the forms of established society, and the disclosures of incongruous insight or disobedient desire from the distraction and the narcosis of habit.[15]

So steelworkers are ennobled by unemployment? Husbands and wives are ennobled by shattering divorces? Parents are ennobled by the death of children? Lebanon's citizens are ennobled by civil war? The most charitable response to Unger's proposition is that disaster strengthens some of these unfortunate human beings but destroys the others. A franker response is that his proposition is a classic example of theoretical deduction swamping experiential truth. As for the alleged pharmacolog-

---

11 FALSE NECESSITY at 579.

12 Unger included this passage in a widely-circulated manuscript of FALSE NECESSITY, deleting it only in the final published version. Had it been retained, it would have appeared at 579.

13 PASSION at 165.

14 SOCIAL THEORY at 65.

15 PASSION at 73.

ical properties of habit, the relentless modernist quest for peak experiences is more of a narcotic than the stable patterns of daily life could ever be.

The preference for the unsettled over the settled, the impulse to imagine and to act out context-smashing transgressions, is indeed characteristic of modernist artists, authors, and revolutionaries. But Unger mistakes the part for the whole. His criticial error is to assume that the motives and satisfactions of a tiny elite somehow constitute the (hidden) essence and desire of all human beings. A world restructured to accommodate the iconoclastic cravings of modernist visionaries is a world from which everyone else would recoil in dread. Most human beings find satisfaction within settled contexts and experience the disruption of those contexts not as empowerment, but rather as deprivation. The everyday life that Unger holds in such contempt is not the imposition of the few on the many. It retains its customary form precisely because it is the mode of existence best suited to the overwhelming majority of the human race.

Modernists typically represent themselves as the vanguard of broad popular movements. In reality, however, modernism is an elite doctrine and practice masquerading as populism. Modernist novels and music have failed to attain any measurable mass influence, spawning instead a split between the iconoclastic tastes of a narrow elite and the enduring popular demand for naturalism and tonality. Modern art, sculpture, and architecture have achieved a greater measure of acceptance, but only by shedding their adversarial stance toward bourgeois culture and becoming either economically functional or visually decorative. In no instance has modernism transformed the broad public outlook, which remains esthetically and morally conservative.

Therefore, to the extent that modernism craves transformative efficacy, it is driven toward "revolution from above"—that is, toward coercion. It is no accident that in its rage against the stolid persistence of bourgeois society, modernism has repeatedly flirted with fascism. Nor is it an accident that Unger's political modernism, ostensibly justified in the name of the greatest possible openness to individual expression, culminates in the forcible destruction of traditional ways of life. Unger is admirably—if chillingly—candid on this point:

> [P]eople have . . . always put their sense of basic security in the maintenance of particular social roles, jobs, and ways of life. Any attempt to indulge this conception of security would prove incompatible with the institutions of the empowered democracy and with the personal and social ideals that inspire them . . . . [P]eople can and should wean themselves away from a restrictive, rigidifying view of where they should place their sense of protection.[16]
> They and, if not they, their children will discover that the security that matters does not require the maintenance of a narrowly defined mode of

---

[16] FALSE NECESSITY at 524.

life. They reach this conclusion in part . . . by awakening to a conception of the personality as both dependent upon context and strengthened through context smashing.[17]

To summarize this strand of Unger's argument, modernist social theory rests on a normative conception of personality that is valid for, and binding upon, everyone. Today, some of us accept this conception while others stubbornly resist it. Within suitably constructed institutions, we all will (eventually) come to experience the correctness of the modernist vision. And in the interim, while our generation has not yet been re-educated (or replaced by suitably socialized children), we will certainly not be "indulged." Instead, we will be shaken out of our narcoleptic trance and purged of stubborn habits. We will be forced to be free.

Unger anticipates a certain resistance to this proposal on the part of the "classical liberal," who recognizes that modernist social theory culminates in totalitarian interventions in areas that even traditional despots are content to leave alone. Unger concedes the factual accuracy of this accusation, but seeks to transmute its moral meaning:

> [T]he classical liberal is wrong to think . . . that an institutional order can . . . draw a watertight distinction between the public institutions of a people and the forms of close association or intimate experience to which the people are drawn. . . . The authority of the radical project lies in its vision of the individual and collective empowerment we may achieve by cumulatively loosening the grip of rigid roles, hierarchies, and conventions . . . . But it does not claim to be indifferent to the choice among alternative styles of association.[18]

Would it not be more honest to say that we have a *choice* between constructing society in accord with the traditionalism of the many or with the iconoclasm of the few? The former alternative propels the modernist elite to the fringes of society, where it assumes an adversarial stance toward established institutions. But the latter alternative evokes a traditionalist counterreaction to the practices of advanced culture, a response that (depending on circumstances) can take the form of either a relatively benign conservatism or a far more virulent fascism.

Unger is systematically—almost wilfully—blind to the origins and dangers of contemporary "populist" movements. The false universality of his conception of personality obscures the dominant cultural clash of our time. Ironically, a social philosophy that takes as its point of departure the unmasking of suppressed strife ends by smothering genuine strife in a theoretical structure that suppresses some of the most fundamental human differences.

IV. THE MODERNIST ACCOUNT OF SOCIETY

The chief virtue of political institutions, Unger believes, is to be

---

17 *Id.* at 514-15.
18 *Id.* at 558.

maximally open to the infinite variety of practical and emotional arrangements that human beings may devise. All social contexts are restrictive to some extent. But unalloyed modernist iconoclasm, Unger argues, overlooks differences among contexts in the degree of constraint they impose. Institutions go astray when they needlessly constrict human possibilities by freezing society into rigid roles and hierarchies. Restrictive polities thus are characterized by a sharp distinction between basic structures, which are highly resistant to revision, and the routine activities that occur within these structures. The good society, on the other hand, builds opportunities for challenge and change into its basic institutions. In so doing, it narrows the breach between contexts and routines, and it enables each individual to participate as a self-determining personality in the reconstructions of fundamental social arrangements. Unger's proposed constitution is thus a "structure-destroying" superstructure[19] that "preserves in its determinate existence the marks of an original indefinition"[20] and is "designed to prevent any definite institutional order from taking hold in social life."[21]

No brief discussion can adequately confront Unger's lengthy, complex institutional argument. Out of necessity, I shall focus on what I take to be his basic premises, offering in each instance a counterproposal.

Unger Thesis No. 1: Far from resting on—or reflecting—a natural order, society is a pure artifact originating in, but freezing, struggle among human beings.[22]

Counterthesis: Society is neither purely natural nor purely artificial. Human beings are naturally drawn together into political communities whose goals, moreover, include such natural ends as survival, security, and material adequacy. These facts impose certain constraints on the possible range of institutional arrangements and political programs. At the same time, the specific forms such communities assume will be determined largely by differences in human belief and will. Social theory goes astray if it understands society either through the analogy of determinate natural growth or in the image of unconstrained artistic creation. Unger commits the latter error.

Unger Thesis No. 2: All hierarchies are unnatural, rigid structures that thwart human flourishing and lack rational justification. For that reason, to open hierarchies up to the possibility of scrutiny and revision is to initiate the process of their dissolution.[23]

Counterthesis: Some hierarchies are both rationally justifiable and conducive to individual self-assertion: the authority of parents over children, teachers over students, skilled artisans over apprentices and, more

---

[19] *Id.* at 572.

[20] *Id.* at 573.

[21] *Id.* at 572.

[22] SOCIAL THEORY at 10, 145-46.

[23] FALSE NECESSITY at 8-9.

generally, the authority of those who have special knowledge or competence that promotes the attainment of shared ends over those who do not. If members of a society agree on certain ends, and if the achievement of those ends is in part a function of knowledge or competence, in principle there can be rational social and political authority.

Unger Thesis No. 3: All contexts that resist revision thwart human flourishing. The more revisable the context, the better: "[O]ver the long run, the practical, moral, and cognitive advantages to be won by disentrenching formative contexts outweigh in the strength and universality of their appeal the benefits to be gained by entrenching these contexts further."[24]

Counterthesis: Rather than constraining us, some revision-resisting contexts actually liberate us. In the arts, such conventions as baroque harmony, the sonnet, and the blues have provided enabling structures within which explosions of creativity have occurred. In social relations, such institutions as indissoluble marriage may promote intimacy and personal growth—a point that even Unger ultimately concedes.[25] Similarly, in politics relatively stable contexts may provide arenas within which conflicting proposals and ways of life may be tested against one another without risking the escalation of conflict into community-threatening bitterness and violence.

Because circumstances change unpredictably and dramatically, the structural context of political life—the "constitution"—must be open to revision. But the art of constitution-making is not, as Unger would have it, to maximize revisability. It is rather to locate the appropriate mean between rigidity and anarchy. So, for example, the United States Constitution does not require unanimous consent of the states to pass constitutional amendments, but does require more than a bare majority. One may argue (as some did after the defeat of the Equal Rights Amendment) that this requirement gives excessive veto power to relatively small minorities. But few believe that constitutional amendments should be as easy to pass as ordinary legislation.

The critique of Unger's norm of maximum revisability rests on logical as well as prudential grounds. If political dialogue cannot produce unanimity, then some structure of decision-rules is needed to determine when the views of a portion of the community are deemed to have become binding on the whole community. Within this structure, institutions, laws, and social arrangements may be exposed to revision. But the structure itself cannot be challenged—at least not in the same way. The constitutional provision that proposed constitutional amendments require a three-quarters majority for passage can be changed only through an amendment that itself receives a three-quarters majority. There are

---

[24] THE CRITICAL LEGAL STUDIES MOVEMENT at 94.

[25] PASSION at 267.

only two alternatives to respect for basic structures: The appeal to principles of legitimacy underlying these structures (as in the Framers' resort to state ratification conventions against the letter of the Articles of Confederation), and the resort to revolutionary force. Each of these strategies may indeed be justified in many instances. But the point is that no structure can be made so comprehensively revisable as to rule out the need for its disruption in certain extreme circumstances. One cannot wholly efface the distinction between context and routine.

Unger Thesis No. 4: Political change is properly conceived as isomorphic with scientific change. The ideal of maximum institutional revisability

> is the political counterpart to an ideal of objectivity in science that relies not on the incorrigibility of self-evident propositions but on the universal and accelerated corrigibility of every feature of an explanatory practice, including the very conception of what it means to explain something. This comparison represents more than a vague parallel; it is . . . a precise and revealing convergence.[26]

Counterthesis: This comparison represents a failure to understand the fundamental difference between scientific and political change. At their best, scientists form a rational community; that is, the authority of particular scientific propositions rests solely on their ability to withstand skeptical scrutiny. To be sure, habitual beliefs and practices can impede the operation of scientific inquiry and retard the acceptance of new propositions. But the sway of tradition, strictly speaking, is a perversion of science. In a political community, on the other hand, the authority of particular propositions rests in part on familiarity and habit. Of course, mere existence should not sustain the status quo. But reason is not enough either. Without the practical familiarity born of habit, political propositions cannot be rendered effectively binding on a community. Excessive openness to revision undermines the very foundation of law, and with it, the very possibility of a community not ruled by force. The realistic political alternative to habitual practices is not pure reason, but a destructive oscillation between anarchy and tyranny.

V. GENERAL REFLECTIONS ON MODERNIST THEORY

At the heart of Unger's project is a vision of the human situation as infinite personality trapped in the coils of a finite world. This depiction, a secularized transcription of what Unger calls the "Christian-romantic tradition,"[27] leads to a "social iconoclasm expressive of man's ineradicable homelessness in the world."[28] Yet there is a crucial difference between the original tradition and Unger's appropriation of it. In Christianity, the infinite human subject can find satisfaction only in an

---

[26] SOCIAL THEORY at 46.

[27] PASSION at vii.

[28] *Id*. at 24.

infinite object that also is a subject. The human longing for infinity leads toward an encounter with God. For Unger, on the other hand, the concept of an infinite object entirely disappears. The infinite impulse instead must express itself in ceaseless efforts to reconstitute personal encounters between, or social relations among, human beings.

I cannot help wondering whether, in thus replacing God with man, Unger is not placing more weight on the individual/social world than it can rightly bear. Is the realm of personal love and social attachments an appropriate venue for the enactment of transcendent desire? Can we love our neighbors as ourselves without an overarching canopy of Divine love? And can we hope to transform politics into an arena for the practice of faith, hope, and charity? Or is the advice of the original Christian not infinitely wiser: Render unto Caesar what is Caesar's, and unto God what is God's?[29] Unger urges us to seek the infinite in the endless reconstitution of the finite. But this is a formula for the endless disruption of human life in pursuit of a goal that no permutation of that life can provide. It is sounder, I believe, to eschew the idolatry of this world, to insist that infinite longing can find its satisfaction only in an infinite object, and to acknowledge that in the absence of such an object, man truly is a useless passion.

Unger will have none of this. Within the modernist frame—the spirit of social iconoclasm—he describes human existence as a quest for the "basic freedom that includes an assurance of being at home in the world."[30] To be sure, this longing is "impractical." But it has an "attainable element"—a "vision of empowerment that touches every aspect of our experience."[31] Society realizes that vision "by laying its practical and imaginative order ever more open to correction."[32] And so do individuals. By opening our characters and settled ways of life to challenge and change, "we keep ourselves in the state of permanent searching . . . that nearly amounts to a secular salvation."[33]

But how can we search without hope of finding? If we know in advance that every context is ultimately incommensurable with our longing for the infinite, why take seriously the endless ardor of secular striving? Modernism and hope are incompatible, unless through the mediation of illusion. But illusion is precisely what no modernist—Unger included—can accept.

Yet the driving impulse of Unger's enterprise is hope: on the political level, hope that a form of association can be established which reconciles and achieves such diverse values as liberty, equality, democracy, security, prosperity, and self-expression; and on the theoretical plane,

---

[29] *Matthew* 22:21; *Mark* 12:27; *Luke* 20:25.
[30] PASSION at 107.
[31] *Id.* at 263.
[32] *Id.* at 264.
[33] *Id.* at 266.

hope that in the teeth of corrosive modernist skepticism, a form of affirmative discourse nonetheless can be defensibly practiced. I have already noted the ways in which Unger's political hopes seem incompatible with his modernist point of departure. It remains only to show that his theoretical hopes are similarly vitiated.

Unger asserts that thought, like social life, can have no absolute context. At the same time, he insists that modernist thought can consist in more than "ultra-theory"—that is, in more than a series of negative gestures dramatizing the facticity of existence. "Super-theory"—affirmative discourse built on modernist foundations—is a real possibility.

Perhaps so. But it is instructive to see what happens when it is attempted. Unger's work is reminiscent of nineteenth-century social theory—a synoptic series of broad claims to general validity. Indeed, I have never before encountered prose crafted so relentlessly in the prophetic mode, so incessantly proferring universal truths. The secularized Christian-romantic understanding of personality is not merely true now, for us; it is true vis-á-vis heroism, Aristotelianism, Confucianism; it is true *simpliciter*. The revisionary understanding of society is not merely true in the late twentieth century for advanced industrial societies; it is true (perhaps especially true), for example, for Third World nations as well.

I do not mean to criticize these universal claims of truth. Indeed, I believe that every moral or social theory must make them eventually. My point is rather that in putting forward these claims, not just as internal criticism, but as visionary insight, Unger violates his own modernist canons. Like Hegel—like so many theorists since Hobbes—his own affirmations cannot be contained in his general account of human thought. Unger implicitly claims for himself an exemption from contextuality: whatever may be true for others, his own prophetic powers have achieved the status of absolute understanding.

In the last analysis, then, Unger's theory is not a generic break with the Aristotelian naturalism he decries. It is rather a substantive alternative to that naturalism *within the same sphere of theoretical discourse and aspiration*. As such, it must be evaluated not as super-theory—there is no such thing—but rather as theory in the classic sense. Unger's theory must stand not on the radical novelty of its approach—for it has none—but rather on the rigor of its arguments and on the persuasiveness of its account of the human condition. It has been the burden of this Essay to suggest that, judged by these canons, Unger's achievement falls far short of his aspirations.

UNGER, CASTORIADIS, AND THE ROMANCE OF A NATIONAL FUTURE

Richard Rorty

Roberto Mangabeira Unger is a Brazilian philosopher. "Brazilian philosophy" has as little resonance as "American philosophy" did a hundred years ago. But in 1882 Walt Whitman, comparing Carlyle's "dark fortune-telling of humanity and politics" with "a far more profound horoscope-casting of those themes—G. F. Hegel's," wrote as follows:

> Not the least mentionable part of the case, (a streak, it may be, of that human with which history and fate love to contrast their gravity) is that although neither of my great authorities [Carlyle and Hegel] during their lives consider'd the United States worthy of serious mention, all the principal works of both might not inappropriately be this day collected and bound up under the conspicuous title: *Speculations for the use of North America, and Democracy there, with the relations of the same to Metaphysics, including Lessons and Warnings (encouragements too, and of the vastest,) from the Old World to the New.*[1]

Try pasting that title on your copy of Unger's *Politics*, having first altered "North America" to "South America," "Old World" to "Northern Hemisphere," and "New" to "Southern." It is not inappropriate. Though few of our great authorities presently consider Brazil worthy of serious mention, spaces left blank in the minds of one century's authorities often get filled in, quite quickly and surprisingly, during the next. Try beginning your reading of Unger's book with pages 64–79 of the first volume ("The Exemplary Instability of the Third World" and "A Brazilian Example").[2] Remember that Unger—though he has put

---

[1] W. WHITMAN, *Carlyle from American Points of View* in PROSE WORKS 171 (1900) (emphasis in original).

[2] The three volumes of Unger's three-volume POLITICS: A WORK IN CONSTRUCTIVE SOCIAL THEORY (1987) are titled SOCIAL THEORY: ITS SITUATION AND ITS TASK [hereinafter SOCIAL THEORY], FALSE NECESSITY: ANTI-NECESSITARIAN SOCIAL THEORY IN THE SERVICE OF RADICAL DEMOCRACY [hereinafter FALSE NECESSITY], and PLASTICITY INTO POWER: COMPARATIVE-HISTORICAL STUDIES ON THE INSTITUTIONAL CONDITIONS OF ECONOMIC AND MILITARY SUCCESS [hereinafter PLASTICITY INTO POWER]. All three volumes were published simultaneously by Cambridge University Press. Unger's previous books are: KNOWLEDGE AND POLITICS (1975), LAW IN MODERN SOCIETY (1976), PASSION: AN ESSAY ON PERSONALITY (1984), and THE CRITICAL LEGAL STUDIES MOVEMENT (1986). Unger was born in Brazil in 1947, was educated there and in Europe, and has been Professor of Law at Harvard since 1972. Citation to Unger's work in this article will conform to the style established in the Unger Symposium issue of the Northwestern University Law Review, 81 Nw. U.L. REV. (1987).

in many years of hard work here in North America, changing the curricula of many of our law schools and the self-image of many of our lawyers—is a man whose mind is elsewhere. For him, none of the rich North Atlantic democracies are home. Rather, they are places where he has gathered some lessons, warnings, and encouragements.

Whitman prefaced *Leaves of Grass* with a comparison between the closed-down character of Europe and the openness of the American future:

> Let the age and wars of other nations be chanted, and their eras and characters be illustrated, and that finish the verse. Not so the great psalm of the republic. Here the theme is creative, and has vista.[3]

In *Democratic Vistas* he urges that psalm has barely begun:

> Far, far, indeed, stretch, in distance, our Vistas! How much is still to be disentangled, freed! How long it takes to make this American world see that it is, in itself, the final authority and reliance![4]

As his book goes along, Whitman continually looks from the gloriously possible to the sickeningly actual—from the American future to the facts of the Gilded Age—and back again. His naive hope invariably prevails over his sophisticated disgust. Compare Unger on Brazil in 1985:

> Indefinition was the common denominator of all these features of the life of the state. . . . All this indefinition could be taken as both the voice of transformative opportunity and the sign of a paralyzing confusion. At one moment it seemed that new experiments in human association might be staged here; at the next, that nothing could come out of this disheartening and preposterous blend of structure, shiftlessness, and stagnation.[5]

Again,

> At this time in world history, an attitude once confined to great visionaries had become common among decent men and women. They could no longer participate in political struggle out of a simple mixture of personal ambition and devotion to the power and glory of the state. They also had to feel that they were sharing in an exemplary experiment in the remaking of society. A person who entered Brazilian politics in this spirit wanted his country to do more than rise to wealth and power as a variant of the societies and polities of the developed west. He wished it to become a testing ground for . . . the options available to mankind.[6]

To get in the right mood to read passages like these, we rich, fat, tired North Americans must hark back to the time when our own democracy was newer and leaner—when Pittsburgh was as new, prom-

---

[3] W. WHITMAN, *Preface, 1855, to first issue of Leaves of Grass,* in PROSE WORKS, *supra* note 1, at 264.

[4] W. WHITMAN, *Democratic Vistas,* in PROSE WORKS, *supra* note 1, at 226.

[5] SOCIAL THEORY at 69–70.

[6] *Id.* at 75–76.

ising, and problematic as São Paulo is now. Irving Howe describes "the American newness" of one hundred and fifty years ago as a time when "people start to feel socially invigorated and come to think they can act to determine their fate."[7] He continues bleakly: "What is it like to live at such a time? The opposite of what it is like to live today."[8]

Howe's bleakness, which I and many of my contemporaries share, comes from the fear that what Unger calls "the cycles of reform and reaction" that make up politics in the United States are simply not up to the demands of the times. This bleakness is increased by our inability to imagine any better goal than the next cycle of reform. On the one hand, we recognize that, for example, "Automation is progressing much more rapidly than the decretinization of American senators."[9] On the other hand, we see these cycles of reform and reaction as the operation of free institutions—institutions it took two hundred years of hard work, and lots of good luck, to construct. These institutions, increasingly rackety and ineffectual as they are, seem to be all we have got, and all we can really imagine having. So we content ourselves with saying that, as institutions go, ours are a lot better than the actually existing competition. Unger has us dead to rights when he speaks of "the rich, polished, critical and self-critical but also downbeat and Alexandrian culture of social and historical thought that now flourishes in the North American democracies."[10] Our high culture, at the end of the twentieth century, resembles the culture that Whitman saw at the end of the nineteenth when he looked toward Europe.[11]

In *Politics,* Unger is reacting against this bleak defensiveness and resignation. He sometimes thinks of the tragic liberalism of us Alexandrians as an inexplicable failure of imagination, and sometimes as an exasperating weakness of will. What makes him different from most theorists who are critical of American liberalism is his orientation toward the future rather than the past—his hopefulness. Most radical critics of American institutions (for example, the admirers of Althusserian, Heideggerian, or Foucauldian social thought—the people for whom Harold Bloom has invented the sobriquet "The School of Re-

[7] I. Howe, The American Newness: Culture and Politics in the Age of Emerson 17 (1986).

[8] *Id.* at 17. At the end of this book, Howe bravely says that " 'The newness' will come again. It is intrinsic to our life." *Id.* at 89. Maybe it will, but I would not know how to write a scenario for its return.

[9] C. Castoriadis, The Imaginary Institution of Society 83 (K. Blamey trans. 1987).

[10] Social Theory at 223. The term "Alexandrian" carries connotations of decadent scholasticism and of political impotence.

[11] There was, in fact, more in Europe to see than Whitman, who was not very well-informed, saw. See, for example, James Kloppenberg's account of the social democratic intellectuals in France, Germany, and Britain in the 1880s. J. Kloppenberg, Uncertain Victory: Social Democracy and Progressivism in European and American Thought, 1870–1920 (1986). I am not sure there is more in contemporary North Atlantic culture than Unger sees.

sentment"[12]) would not be caught dead with an expression of hopefulness on their faces. Their reaction to American inertia and impotence is rage, contempt, and the use of what they call "subversive, oppositional discourse," rather than suggestions about how we might do things differently. Whereas people like Howe and myself would love to get some good ideas about what the country might do (and dream of the election of, if not another Lincoln, at least another FDR), the School of Resentment washes its hands of the American experiment. Since these people have also been disappointed, successively, in Russia, Cuba, and China, they now tend to wash their hands of *all* "structures and discourses of power" (the Foucauldian term for what we used to call "institutions").

By contrast, when Unger is not berating us for our lack of hope and failure of nerve, he is sketching alternative institutions—a rotating capital fund, a government department of destabilization, and so on. He predicts, accurately, that the people who still take Marxism as a model of what a social theory should look like will reject his suggestions as reformist tinkering, as inadequately oppositional. With equal accuracy, he predicts that we downbeat, Alexandrian, social democratic liberals will view them as utopian. Still, the distance between the Unger of *Politics* (as opposed to the Unger of a dozen years back, the author of *Knowledge and Politics*[13]) and us Alexandrians is a lot less than that between Unger and the School of Resentment. For our reaction is, more accurately: "Utopian, but, God knows, worth trying; still, you'll never get it into a Democratic, much less a Republican, platform."

This is where Brazil comes in. If Unger were your ordinary universalizing social theorist—as he sometimes, alas, makes himself out to be—names of particular countries would not be relevant. But he is rather (as the caption of an early, nasty review of *Politics* put it) "a preposterous political romantic"[14]—as preposterous as Whitman, albeit better read. Being a political romantic is not easy these days. Presumably it helps a lot to come from a big, backward country with lots of raw materials and a good deal of capital accumulation—a country that has

---

[12] Conversation with Harold Bloom, Professor of Humanities, Yale University.

[13] For the difference between the two books, see Unger's postscript (written in 1983) to the second edition of KNOWLEDGE AND POLITICS. As Unger says there, he had become "much less anxious to emphasize the dependence of liberal ideas upon certain basic conceptions of modern speculative philosophy that first took recognizable form in the seventeenth century," and much more ready to grant that "the classic nineteenth-century forms of liberalism" represent "one of the great modern secular doctrines of emancipation." *Id.* at 339. This decreased emphasis on "philosophical presuppositions" seems to me an important step forward. For an example of the over-philosophized description of "liberalism" which, alas, many readers took away from KNOWLEDGE AND POLITICS, see Ryan, *Deconstruction and Social Theory: The Case of Liberalism* in DISPLACEMENT: DERRIDA AND AFTER 154 (M. Krupnick ed. 1983).

[14] Holmes, *The Professor of Smashing: The Preposterous Political Romanticism of Roberto Unger,* The New Republic, Oct. 19, 1987, at 30.

started to lurch forward, even though frequently falling over its own feet. It must also help, ironically enough, to come from a country that cannot hope to achieve what the North Atlantic has achieved in the way of equality and decency by the same means: reliance on a free market in capital and on compromises between pressure groups. As Unger says, "For many third world countries the route of empowered democracy [that is, something like Unger's own alternative institutions] may represent less the bolder alternative to social democracy than the sole practical means by which even social-democratic goals can be achieved."[15]

Unger writes that

> Much in this work can be understood as the consequence of an attempt to enlist the intellectual resources of the North Atlantic world in the service of concerns and commitments more keenly felt elsewhere. In this way I hope to contribute toward the development of an alternative to the vague, unconvinced, and unconvincing Marxism that now serves the advocates of the radical project as their lingua franca. If, however, the arguments of this book stand up, the transformative focus of this theoretical effort has intellectual uses that transcend its immediate origins and motives.[16]

I am interpreting *Politics* in the light of the first two sentences of this passage. I have doubts, however, about the third sentence. As a pragmatist, I think philosophy is at its best when it is content to be "its own time apprehended in thought" and lets transcendence go.[17] As a Kuhnian,[18] I have doubts about whether argument plays much of a role in scientific or political Gestalt-switches. Arguments (whose premises must necessarily be phrased in familiar vocabularies) often just get in the way of attempts to create an unfamiliar political vocabulary, a new *lingua franca* for those trying to transform what they see around them. If Unger is able to supply future leaders of Third World social movements with a non-Marxist and non- "behavioral science" *lingua franca*—one that will help them brush aside the conventional wisdoms offered by the KGB and the CIA—he will have done something so important as to dwarf argumentation. He will have done for Third World leaders of the next century what Dewey tried to do for the North American intelligentsia of the first, more optimistic, half of the twentieth. Among other things, he will have helped make them aware that, as Dewey put it, "philosophy can proffer

---

[15] FALSE NECESSITY at 395.

[16] SOCIAL THEORY at 223–24.

[17] The phrase comes from the Preface to G. F. Hegel's PHILOSOPHY OF RIGHT 11 (Knox trans. 1942). Hegel continues: "It is just as absurd to imagine that a philosophy can transcend its contemporary world as it is to fancy that an individual can overleap his own age, jump over Rhodes." *Id.*

[18] T. S. Kuhn, in THE STRUCTURE OF SCIENTIFIC REVOLUTIONS (1962), emphasizes the importance of the adoption of new vocabularies, as opposed to the use of arguments phrased in old vocabularies, for scientific progress.

nothing but hypotheses, and that these hypotheses are of value only as they render men's minds more sensitive to the life about them."[19]

Realizing that Unger is a *Brazilian* philosopher lets us Alexandrians convert our initial reaction to his book to something more like, "We hope to Heaven these imaginary institutions do sell in Brazil; if they should actually *work* there, maybe then we could sell them here. The Southern Hemisphere might conceivably, a generation hence, come to the rescue of the Northern." This amounts to saying that if there is hope, it lies in the Third World. But this is not to say, with Winston Smith, "If there is hope, it lies in the proles."[20] For the Third World is not an undifferentiated mass of immiserated men and women. It is a set of diverse nations, and if it is ever to have hope it will be for a diverse set of national futures.

The School of Resentment sometimes suggests, following Lukács and Foucault, that the immiserated share a common "consciousness"— which can be set over against all "discourses of power" or "ideologies."[21] This suggestion that there is something "deep down"—something ahistorical and international under what we powerful, discursive types have been inscribing on the bodies of the weak—makes this school feel justified in toying with anarchism, with the idea that everything would be all right if we could just get "power" off everybody's backs.[22] Members of this School will be shocked and indignant to find that Unger does not assume that the initial agents of transformation in the Third World will be workers and peasants. He thinks they will be petty-bourgeois functionaries:

> In countries with a strong statist tradition the lower rungs of the governmental bureaucracy constitute the most likely agents for the development of such floating resources. For example, in many Latin American nations whole sectors of the economy (e.g., agriculture) are closely supervised and coordinated by economic bureaucrats: public-credit officers and agronomists. . . . But the bureaucracies are typically mined by a multitude of more or less well-intentioned, confused, unheroic cryptoleftists—middle-class, university-trained youth, filled with the vague leftist ideas afloat in the world. The ambiguities of established rules and policies and the failures of bureaucratic control can supply these people with excuses to deny a fragment of governmental protection to its usual beneficiaries and make it available to other people, in new proportions

---

[19] J. DEWEY, RECONSTRUCTION IN PHILOSOPHY 22 (1948).

[20] *See* G. ORWELL, 1984, in THE PENGUIN COMPLETE NOVELS OF GEORGE ORWELL 783 (1951).

[21] *See* Habermas' discussion of this link between Lukács and Foucault. J. HABERMAS, THE PHILOSOPHICAL DISCOURSE OF MODERNITY 280 (F. Lawrence trans. 1987).

[22] For an acute analysis of the sources of such fantasies, see B. YACK, THE LONGING FOR TOTAL REVOLUTION: PHILOSOPHICAL SOURCES OF SOCIAL DISCONTENT FROM ROUSSEAU TO MARX AND NIETZSCHE (1986) (discussing Rousseau, Kant, Schiller, Hegel, Marx, and Nietzsche).

or in new ways. . . . The result is to create a floating resource—one the transformers can appropriate or fight about.[23]

"Well-intentioned, confused, university-trained young crypto-leftists" is a reasonable description of the thousands of recently graduated lawyers who, influenced by Unger and other members of the Critical Legal Studies Movement, are now helping make institutions in the United States slightly more flexible and decent. It is also a good description of the only allies Gorbachev is likely to have in his effort to restructure Russian institutions—namely, the more Winston-like members of the Outer Party.[24] If Unger's description of his hoped-for allies seems wry and self-mocking, it is. He would *like* to identify himself with the victimized masses. Who, two thousand years after Christ and a hundred years after Zola, would not? But in *Politics,* the romanticism of *Knowledge and Politics* is balanced by a calculation of current possibilities.

Toward the end of *The Critical Legal Studies Movement,* Unger admitted that

> there is a disparity between our intentions and the archaic social form that they assume: a joint endeavor undertaken by discontented, factious intellectuals in the high style of nineteenth-century bourgeois radicalism. For all who participate in such an undertaking, the disharmony between intent and presence must be a cause of rage. We neither suppress this rage nor allow it the last word, because we do not give the last word to the historical world we inhabit. We build with what we have and willingly pay the price for the inconformity of vision to circumstance.[25]

This paragraph is typical of Unger at his best, and illustrates what separates him from the School of Resentment. He does not give the last word to the time he lives in. He also lives in an imaginary, lightly sketched, future. That is the sort of world romantics *should* live in; their living there is the reason why they and their confused, utopian, unscientific, petty bourgeois followers can, occasionally, make the actual future better for the rest of us.[26]

The School of Resentment, made up of people who can single-handedly deconstruct a large social theory faster than a Third World

---

[23] FALSE NECESSITY at 410. *Compare* SOCIAL THEORY at 76:

It was also vital [in the Brazilian context] to avoid the path toward isolation that had helped defeat or tame the European leftist parties and to renounce the preconceptions about feasible class alliances underlying that path. You could not, for example, assume that the only alternative to a politics of unremitting hostility to the petty bourgeoisie or the salaried middle classes was an alliance with the national entrepreneurs and landowners against the foreigner.

[24] For Orwell's distinction between the Inner Party and the Outer Party, see his 1984, *supra* note 20, at 863.

[25] THE CRITICAL LEGAL STUDIES MOVEMENT at 118–19.

[26] See N. ROSENBLUM, ANOTHER LIBERALISM: ROMANTICISM AND THE RECONSTRUCTION OF LIBERAL THOUGHT (1987) for a good account of the relation between liberalism and romanticism.

village can construct a small elementary school, does not take kindly to romance. These people are modernists, maybe even *post*modernists. They have celebrated all the eras and characters, and they *like to* finish their verses with a dying fall, for example:

> While this America settles in the mold of its vulgarity,
>   heavily thickening to empire
> And protest only a bubble in the molten mass, pops and
>   sighs out, and the mass hardens,
> I sadly remember that the flower fades to make fruit,
>   the fruit rots to make earth.[27]

When these people do social theory, they push aside the tradition of Locke, Jefferson, Mill, Dewey, and Habermas and turn to a tradition that began with Hegel and is continued in Heidegger's downbeat story of the destiny of the West. Hegel made bud-flower-and-fruit his archetypal dialectical triad. His idea of a social theory was a retrospective narrative, written by someone whose "shape of life had grown old."[28] Such a scenario either ends with the present (as Hegel and Heidegger prudently ended theirs) or else forecasts (as Marx and Mao did) a new kind of human being—someone on whose body "power" has inscribed nothing, someone who will burst the bounds of all the vocabularies used to describe the old, tattered palimpsests. Since the School of Resentment is, nowadays, mostly "post-Marxist," it tends to favor the former sort of scenario. So it relishes phrases like "late capitalism," "the end of the metaphysics of presence," "after Auschwitz," and "post-X (for any previous value of X)." Its members outdo each other in belatedness. They tend to accept some version of the story of the West as a long slide downhill from better days (the time of "organic community" or "the *polis*" or some such—a time before "structures of power" started scrawling all over us). They see no redeeming features in the present, except perhaps for their own helpless rage. When Heidegger describes the West as successively discrediting the notions of "the supersensory world, the Ideas, God, the moral law, the authority of reason, progress, the happiness of the greatest number, culture, civilization,"[29] they nod in recognition. Ah yes, "the greatest happiness of the greatest number"—at least we now see through *that* pathetic apology for the Panoptic State.

If my criticism of this School seems harsh, it is because one is always harshest on what one most dreads resembling. We tragic liberals are ourselves easily seduced by the lines I quoted from Jeffers' "Shine,

---

[27] R. Jeffers, *Shine, Perishing Republic,* in READING POEMS 582 (W. Thomas & S. Gerry ed. 1941).

[28] *See* G. HEGEL, *supra* note 17, at 13.

[29] Heidegger, *The Word of Nietzsche: God is Dead,* in THE QUESTION CONCERNING TECHNOLOGY AND OTHER ESSAYS 65 (W. Lovitt trans. 1977).

Perishing Republic."[30] We are continually tempted by the urge to sit back and grasp our time in thought rather than continuing to try to change it. Even though we can still manage two cheers for America— even America under Reagan—a romantic like Unger sees little difference between us and the School of Resentment. For the only difference between us and the Resenters is that we regret our lack of imagination, whereas they make a virtue of what they think a philosophico-historical necessity.

Our only excuse is, once again, to appeal to national differences— to say, in effect, "Maybe it's easier in Brazil, but it's pretty hard here." Political imagination is, almost always, national imagination. To imagine great things is to imagine a great future *for a particular community,* a community one knows well, identifies with, can make plausible predictions about.[31] In the modern world, this usually means one's nation. Political romance is, therefore, for the foreseeable future, going to consist of psalms of *national* future rather than the future of "mankind." Officially, to be sure, we are all supposed to be "past" nationalism, to be citizens of the human race. We are all supposed to believe, with the Marxists, that nationalism is just "mystification." But Castoriadis gives this pretense the treatment it deserves:

> To say: 'The proof that nationalism was a simple mystification, *and hence something unreal,* lies in the fact that it will be dissolved on the day of world revolution,' is not only to sell the bearskin before we catch the bear, it is to say: 'You who have lived from 1900 to 1965 and to who knows when, and you, the millions who died in the two wars . . . all of you, you are *in*-existent, you have always been in-existent with respect to true history. . . . True history was the invisible Potentiality that *will be,* and that, behind your back, was preparing the end of your illusions.'[32]

Castoriadis and Unger are willing to work with, rather than deconstruct, the notions that already mean something to people presently alive—while nonetheless not "giving the last word to the historical world they inhabit."[33] That is another way in which both differ from the School of Resentment. The latter School is interested not in building with what we have, but in penetrating to the "repressed" reality behind the "ideological" appearances. Resenters admire in Marxism precisely what Unger and Castoriadis distrust: the insistence on getting the "underlying realities" right, on doing theory first and getting to

---

[30] *See supra* text accompanying note 27. Consider, for example, Gore Vidal's account of America's transition from Republic to Empire in his historical novels and polemical essays. Vidal is a paradigmatically Alexandrian figure, still trying to be a liberal, but unable to repress his excitement over the rumors about the barbarians.

[31] Consider the nationalism that runs through E. P. Thompson's discussion of Perry Anderson in his THE POVERTY OF THEORY (1978), as well as through Orwell's THE ROAD TO WIGAN PIER (1937).

[32] C. CASTORIADIS, *supra* note 9, at 149 (emphasis in original).

[33] *See* THE CRITICAL LEGAL STUDIES MOVEMENT at 119.

political utopias later. Though members of this School accept in meta-theory the Heidegger-Derrida view—that the reality-appearance distinction is the archetypal "binary opposition" from whose clutches we must escape—in their theoretical practice they wallow in it.[34]

Castoriadis and Unger escape this temptation because they adopt the attitude toward philosophy which I earlier quoted from Dewey. The "anti-naturalism" of Unger's book comes down to the least common denominator of Hegel, Marx, and Dewey: the claim that "the formative contexts of social life . . . or the procedural frameworks of problem solving and interest accommodation . . . [are] nothing but frozen politics: conflicts interrupted or contained" plus the desire "to deprive these frameworks or contexts of their aura of higher necessity or authority."[35] This anti-naturalism fits together nicely with Castoriadis' claim that "the imaginary—as the social imaginary and as the imagination of the psyche—is the logical and ontological condition of 'the real.' "[36] Just as in the individual psyche, moral character is "conflict interrupted or contained," so is the moral character of a society—that is, its institutions.

Unger urges the "thesis that everything in our ideas about the world, including our conceptions of contingency, necessity, and possibility, is sensitive to changes in our empirical beliefs."[37] This holistic, Quinean thesis provides what he calls "the philosophical setting of an antinaturalistic social theory."[38] "Setting" is the right word. It is not so much a "foundation" for such a theory as an excuse not to take philosophy as seriously as the Marxists or the Resenters take it. That thesis helps one accept Unger's claim that "everything is politics"—that if politics can create a new form of social life, there will be time enough later for theorists to explain how this creation was possible and why it was a good thing. Quinean holism helps assure romantics that we humans are lords of possibility as well as actuality—for possibility is a function of a descriptive vocabulary, and that vocabulary is as much up for political grabs as anything else.[39]

---

[34] See the (by now vast) literature on how to combine the "totalizing" aims of Marxism with the anti-totalizing aims of "post-modernism." *See, e.g.,* Jay, *Epilogue: The Challenge of Poststructuralism,* in MARXISM AND TOTALITY 510–37 (1984).

[35] SOCIAL THEORY at 145.

[36] C. CASTORIADIS, *supra* note 9, at 336.

[37] SOCIAL THEORY at 180.

[38] SOCIAL THEORY AT 170, AND *compare id.* at 223.

[39] I have developed this point about Romanticism in *The Contingency of Language,* LONDON REV. OF BOOKS, May 8, 1986, at 11, by reference to Donald Davidson's radicalization of Quine's holistic philosophy of language, especially his treatment of metaphor. Castoriadis makes the same point when he describes *legein,* the use of one vocabulary rather than another, as a "primordial institution," and says that "at this level identitary logic *cannot* seize hold of the institution, since the institution is neither necessary nor contingent, since its emergence is not determined but is that on the basis of which and by means of which alone something determined exists." C. CASTORIADIS, *supra* note 9, at 258 (emphasis in original).

This latter point—the least common denominator of Quine, Wittgenstein, and Dewey—provides the backup for Castoriadis' claim that what matters in a social thinker is the bits to which argumentation is irrelevant:

> What the greatest thinkers may have said that was truthful and fecund was always said *despite* what they thought of as being and as thinkable, not because of what they thought or in agreement with it. And, to be sure, it is in this *despite* that their greatness is expressed, now as ever.[40]

In other words, if there is social hope it lies in the imagination—in people describing a future in terms which the past did not use. "The *only* thing that is not defined by the imaginary in human needs," Castoriadis says, "is an approximate number of calories per day."[41] Every other "constraint" is the fossilized product of some past act of imagination—what Nietzsche called "truth," namely, "[a] mobile army of metaphors, metonyms and anthropomorphisms . . . a sum of human relations which have been enhanced, transposed, and embellished poetically and rhetorically, and which after long use seem firm, canonical, and obligatory to a people."[42]

Certain constraints may come to seem so firm, canonical, and obligatory to a people that their sense of themselves as a community will not outlast the elimination of those constraints. This is what we tragic liberals fear may be the case in the contemporary United States—and, more generally, in the rich North Atlantic democracies. The institutions that empowered our past (for example, inheritable private property) may strangle our future—with the poor and weak getting strangled first, as usual. The institutions that are our only protection against quasi-fascist demagogues may also be the constraints which prevent us from renouncing our insolent greed. The only way to fight off the Pat Robertsons or the Militant Tendency may be to cooperate with the George Bushes and the Kenneth Bakers. The only way to elect a Democratic President or a Labor Prime Minister may be to promise spoils to corrupt trade unions. Maybe North Atlantic politics have frozen over to such a degree that the result of breaking the ice would be something even worse than what we have now. That, at least, is the specter that haunts contemporary North Atlantic liberals.

We tragic liberals realize wistfully that back in the 1880s we too might have seen illimitable vistas. We might have been the young John Dewey rather than the aging Henry Adams. We might have read Carlyle without discouragement, Whitman without giggles, and Edward Bellamy with a wild surmise. Nowadays, despite our fears, we still insist that it was lucky for the United States—not just for its poets and professors

---

[40] *Id.* at 200 (emphasis in original).
[41] *Id.* at 265.
[42] F. NIETZSCHE, *On Truth and Lie in an Extra-Moral Sense,* in THE VIKING PORTABLE NIETZSCHE (W. Kaufmann trans. 1954).

but also for its miners and sharecroppers—that our predecessors *did* read them that way. For in the intervening hundred years things actually got a *lot* fairer, more decent, more equal. People who had read those books had a lot to do with *making* them so. A century after Whitman's death it may seem that, as Orwell said, "the 'democratic vistas' have ended in barbed wire."[43] But we covered a lot of ground before our century, and our hope, began to run out. Maybe the Brazilians (or the Tanzanians, or *somebody*) will be able to dodge around that barbed wire—despite all that the superpowers can do to prevent them.

Unger's book offers a wild surmise, a set of concrete suggestions for risky social experiments, and a polemic against those who think the world has grown too old to be saved by such risk-taking. It does not offer a theory about Society, or Modernity, or Late Capitalism, or the Underlying Dynamics of anything. So, if Unger is going to have an audience, it may not be in the rich North Atlantic democracies. The intellectuals here may continue to find him "preposterous," because he does not satisfy what we have come to regard as legitimate expectations. He does not make moves in any game we know how to play. His natural audience may lie in the Third World—where his book may someday make possible a new national romance. Maybe someday it will help the literate (that is, the petty-bourgeois) citizens of some country to see vistas where before they saw only dangers—see a hitherto undreamt-of national future instead of seeing their country as condemned to play out the role that some foreign theorist has written for it.

One of the most helpful ways to think about such a possibility is given by Castoriadis' analogy between the individual psyche and the social whole:

> There comes a time when the subject, not because he has discovered the primal scene or detected penis envy in his grandmother, but through his struggle in his actual life and as a result of repetition, unearths the central signifier of his neurosis and finally looks at it in its contingency, its poverty and its *insignificance*. In the same way, for people living today, the question is not to understand how the transition from the neolithic clans to the markedly divided cities of Akkad was made. It is to understand—and this obviously means, here more than anywhere else, to act—the contingency, the poverty and the insignificance of this 'signifier' of historical societies, the division into masters and slaves, into dominators and dominated.[44]

From Castoriadis' angle, the efforts of nineteenth-century German philosophers (and of their ungrateful heirs, the contemporary School of Resentment) look like attempts to discover the primal scene, or to unmask grandmother's penis envy (and, more recently, grandfather's

---

[43] G. ORWELL, *Inside the Whale,* in COLLECTED ESSAYS 127 (1966).

[44] C. CASTORIADIS, *supra* note 9, at 155.

womb envy). The same doubts arise even about relatively unphilo-
sophical social theory—social theory that ignores local (and, in particular, national) differences in favor of "underlying dynamics." Given
Castoriadis' analogy, it is hard to believe that patient study of Man, or
of Society, or of Capitalism, will tell us whether the division into domi-
nators and dominated is "natural" or "artificial," or which, if any,
contemporary societies are "ripe" for the elimination of this division,
or what "factors" will determine whether or not this possibility will be
realized. Such discussion seems as remote from the project of imagining a new national future as are hydraulic models of libidinal flow from
what actually happens on the couch. Such models may help the analyst
to make an incisive diagnostic remark, but they are of no help in
predicting the wildly idiosyncratic and unpredictable incident in the
"struggle of actual life" that suddenly permits that endlessly repeated
remark to mean something to the patient. Nor do they help in predicting the course of the analysis from that point onward.

Both Unger's slogan "everything is politics" and Castoriadis' analogy help us see why, insofar as social theory declines to be romantic, it
is inevitably retrospective, and thus biased toward conservatism. As
Hegel said, it typically tells us about the rise of a form of life that has
now grown old—about possibilities which are, by now, largely exhausted. It tells us about the structure of what, with luck, our descendants will regard as our neurosis, without telling us much about what
they will regard as "normal." It abstracts from national histories, which
is like abstracting from the particular family in which a particular patient grew up. It tends to dismiss as "irrational" whatever purely local
factors falsify its generalizations and predictions. This is just as unhelpful as telling the patient that his resistance to the analyst is "irrational."

Liberal social theorists resist Unger's and Castoriadis' suggestion
that release from domination, if and when it comes, will come not in the
form of "rational development" but through something unforeseeable
and passionate. Most of the twentieth century's political surprises, liberals rightly point out, have been unpleasant ones. Romanticism, after all,
was common to Mussolini, Hitler, Lenin, and Mao—to all the leaders
who summoned a nation to slough off its past in an act of passionate self-
renewal, and whose therapy proved far worse than the disease—as well
as to Schiller, Shelley, Fichte, and Whitman. So it is tempting for us
liberals to say that the slogan "everything is politics" is too dangerous to
work with, to insist on a role for "reason" as opposed to "passion."

The problem we face in carrying through on this insistence is that
"reason" usually means "working according to the rules of some familiar language-game, some familiar way of describing the current situation." We liberals have to admit the force of Dewey's, Unger's, and
Castoriadis' point that such familiar language-games are themselves
nothing more than "frozen politics," that they serve to legitimate, and

make seem inevitable, precisely the forms of social life (for example, the cycles of reform and reaction) from which we desperately hope to break free. So we have to find something else for "reason" to mean. This effort to reinterpret rationality is central to Habermas' work, and culminates in his distinction between "subject-centered reason" and "communicative reason"—roughly, the distinction between rationality as appeal to the conventions of a presently-played language-game and appeal to democratic consensus, to "argumentative procedures" rather than to "first principles."[45]

But the idea of "argumentative procedures" for changing our description of what we are doing—for example, changing our political vocabularies from Mill's to Marx's, or from Althusser's to Unger's— seems inapplicable to the way in which patients grasp the contingency, poverty and insignificance of the central signifiers of their neuroses. To say that the aim of social change should be a society in which such procedures are all that we need—in which passionate, romantic, only retrospectively arguable breaks with the past are no longer necessary— is like saying that the aim of psychoanalysis should be "normal functioning." Of course it should, but that does not make psychoanalysis a less hit-or-miss, a more rational, procedure. Of course we should aim at such a society, but that does not mean that the only sort of social change we should work for is the kind for which we can offer good arguments. Unger has no more idea than do his readers whether his rotating capital fund will work—any more than Madison had of whether the separation of powers would work, or than an analyst has of whether a given remark will get through to a given patient. The only "argument" such people can give for such experiments is "Let's give it a try; nothing *else* seems to work."

This was, to be sure, also Hitler's and Mao's "argument." But we should not use this resemblance between Unger and Mao to make Unger look bad or Mao good. Rather, we should realize that the notion of "argumentative procedures" is not relevant to the situation in which nothing familiar works and in which people are desperately (on the couch, on the barricades) looking for something, no matter how

---

[45] As Habermans explains:

Subject-centered reason finds its criteria in standards of truth and success that govern the relationships of knowing and purposively acting subjects to the world of possible objects or states of affairs. By contrast, as soon as we conceive of knowledge as communicatively mediated, rationality is assessed in terms of the capacity of responsible participants in interactions to orient themselves in relation to validity claims geared to intersubjective recognition. Communicative reason finds its criteria in the argumentative procedures for directly or indirectly redeeming claims to propositional truth, normative rightness, subjective truthfulness, and aesthetic harmony.

J. HABERMAS, *An Alternative Way Out of the Philosophy of the Subject: Communicative versus Subject-Centered Reason,* in THE PHILOSOPHICAL DISCOURSE OF MODERNITY, *supra* note 21, at 294, 314.

unfamiliar, which might work. What remains relevant is, roughly, freedom of speech. Whether a given romantic, once in power, allows such freedom (of newspapers, universities, public assemblies, electoral choices, and so on) is, though not an infallible index, the best index we have of whether he or she is likely to do his or her nation some good. To my mind, the cash-value of Habermas' philosophical notions of "communicative reason" and "intersubjectivity" consists in the familiar political freedoms fashioned by the rich North Atlantic democracies during the last two centuries. Such notions are not "foundations" or "defenses" of the free institutions of those countries; they *are* those institutions, painted in the philosopher's traditional "gray on gray."[46] We did not learn about the importance of these institutions as a counterweight to the romantic imagination by thinking through the nature of Reason or Man or Society; we learned about this the hard way, by watching what happened when those institutions were set aside.

More generally, I doubt that any philosophical reworking of the notion of "rationality," or of any similar notion, is going to help us sort out the de Sades from the Whitmans, the Heideggers from the Castoriadises,[47] or the Hitlers from the Rosa Luxemburgs. "Everything is politics," in this context, means that what political history cannot teach, philosophy cannot teach either. The idea that theorizing, or philosophical reflection, will help us sort out good from bad romantics is part of the larger idea that philosophy can anticipate history by spotting "objectively progressive" or "objectively reactionary" intellectual movements. This is as bad as Plato's idea (recently resurrected by Allan Bloom[48]) that philosophers can distinguish "morally healthy" from "morally debilitating" kinds of music. We cannot hope to avoid

---

[46] *See* G. HEGEL, *supra* note 17, at 13.

[47] Habermas describes Castoriadis as combining the "the late Heidegger [and] the early Fichte in a Marxist fashion." J. HABERMAS, *supra* note 21, at 329–30. The description is accurate enough as far as it goes. It will also do for Unger, for like Castoriadis, he can make good use of the late Heideggerian idea of "world-disclosure." Were Habermas to criticize Unger, he would, I should imagine, do so along the same lines at he criticizes Castoriadis in his *Excursus on Cornelius Castoriadis: The Imaginary Institution,* in THE PHILOSOPHICAL DISCOURSE OF MODERNITY, *supra* note 21, at 327–35. He would say that, like Castoriadis, Unger "assimilat[es] intramundane praxis to a linguistic world-disclosure hypostatized into a history of Being." *Id.* at 332.

A full reply to these pages of Habermas would require a separate paper. Here I can only remark that Castoriadis no more *assimilates* these two than the pscyhoanalyst assimilates the patient's day-to-day "struggle in his actual life" to the unconscious fantasies that dictate the terms in which the patient describes that struggle. It is one thing to say that the language we currently use for describing our individual or social situation is an imaginative product—one that may, with luck, be replaced by another such product—and another to say that recognizing this fact is incompatible with taking this language seriously. It is just not the case that such recognition "prejudices the validity of linguistic utterances generally," *id.* at 331, nor that on Castoriadis' view "social praxis disappears in the anonymous hurly-burly of the institutionalization of ever new worlds from the imaginary dimension." *Id.* at 330.

[48] *See* A. BLOOM, THE CLOSING OF THE AMERICAN MIND 68 (1987).

risky social experiments by discerning the presence or absence of dubious overtones (for example, "bourgeois ideology," "authoritarianism," "irrationalism," "the philosophy of subjectivity") in the discourse of those who advocate such experiments.

In order to conclude on a concrete note, I shall discuss one such experiment. Suppose that somewhere, someday, the newly-elected government of a large industrialized country decreed that everybody would get the same income, regardless of occupation or disability. Simultaneously, it instituted vastly increased inheritance taxes and froze large bank transfers. Suppose that, after the initial turmoil, it worked: that is, suppose that the economy did not collapse, that people still took pride in their work (as streetcleaners, pilots, doctors, canecutters, Cabinet ministers, or whatever), and so on. Suppose that the next generation in that country was brought up to realize that, whatever else they might work for, it made no sense to work for wealth. But they worked anyway (for, among other things, national glory). That country would become an irresistible example for a lot of other countries, "capitalist," "Marxist," and in-between. The electorates of these countries would not take time to ask what "factors" had made the success of this experiment possible. Social theorists would not be allowed time to explain how something had happened that they had pooh-poohed as utopian, nor to bring this new sort of society under familiar categories. All the attention would be focused on the actual details of how things were working in the pioneering nation. Sooner or later, the world would be changed.

Castoriadis, like Edward Bellamy a hundred years ago, advocates such an experiment, but he sensibly declines to offer an argument for it:

> If . . . I have maintained for twenty-five years that an autonomous society ought immediately to adopt, in the area of "requittal", an absolute equality of all wages, salaries, incomes, etc., this springs neither from some idea about any natural or other "identity/equality" of men, nor from theoretical reasoning . . . this is a matter of the imaginary significations which hold society together and of the *paideia* of individuals.[49]

The success of such an experiment would be the analogue of a patient getting better as a result of coming to see, "in his actual life and as a result of repetition," the "contingency, poverty and insignificance" of "the central signifier of his neurosis." The French had heard incisive diagnoses many times, but one summer morning in 1789 they woke up conscious of the contingency, poverty, and insignificance of the three Estates, the lilies of Bourbon, and the Catholic Church—of the imagi-

---

[49] C. Castoriadis, Crossroads in the Labyrinth 329 (K. Soper & M. Ryle trans. 1984). The equalization of incomes was central to the imagination of the so-called Old Left here in the North Atlantic. No passage in *Animal Farm* did more to create ex-Communists than the one about how the Pigs managed to monopolize the milk and the apples. But it is the sort of option that the more up-to-date, theoretical, and resentful Left rarely discusses.

nary significations that had been holding their social life together, had been essential to the meaning of "France." Things in France did not work out very well at first, but the world was, eventually, changed for the better. European national neuroses began to have different sorts of central signifiers.

A large part of the irrelevance to the Third World of the Cold War, and of talk about "capitalism" and "socialism," is that the obstacles to equalization of income, and to a *paideia* that is *not* centered around the attainment of wealth, are pretty well the same in the United States and in Russia.[50] More broadly, the imaginary significations that hold society together are pretty much the same in both places. No single change could do more to expose the contingency, poverty, and insignificance of some of the central signifiers of the national neuroses of both superpowers than some third country's success at equalizing incomes. To say, as I have been saying here, that if there is hope it lies in the imagination of the Third World, is to say that the best any of us here in Alexandria can hope for is that somebody out there will do something to tear up the present system of imaginary significations within which politics in (and between) the First and Second Worlds is conducted. It need not be equalization of incomes, but it has to be something *like* that—something so preposterously romantic as to be no longer discussed by us Alexandrians. Only some actual event, the actual success of some political move made in some actual country, is likely to help. No hopeful book by Unger or Habermas,[51] any more than one more hopeless, "oppositional," unmasking book by the latest Resenter, is going to do the trick. Unger, however, has an advantage over the rest of us. His advantage is not that he has a "more powerful theory," but simply that he is aware of "the exemplary instability of the Third World"[52] in a way that most of us are not. His theoretical writing is shot through with a romanticism for which we Alexandrians no longer have the strength. His book has a better chance than most to be linked, in the history books, with some such world-transforming event.

---

[50] This is the kernel of truth in all the loose, resentful, Heideggerian talk about Russia and America being "metaphysically speaking the same" and in all the loose, resentful analogies between the Gulag and the "carceral archipelagoes" of the democracies. See Foucault's discussion of the latter analogies in POWER/KNOWLEDGE: SELECTED INTERVIEWS AND OTHER WRITINGS 134 (C. Goordeon ed. 1980).

[51] Habermas ends *The Philosophical Discourse of Modernity* with an expression of "the dream of a completely different European identity . . . taking shape at a time when the United States is getting ready to fall back into the illusions of the early modern period under the banner of a 'second American revolution.' " *The Normative Content of Modernity,* in THE PHILOSOPHICAL DISCOURSE OF MODERNITY, *supra* note 21, at 366. I think Habermas is too pessimistic about the United States and probably too optimistic about Europe, but I suspect such differences of opinion merely reflect the local patriotisms of different suburbs of Alexandria. Presumably the boundaries between these suburbs are invisible from Brazil.

[52] *See* SOCIAL THEORY at 64.

ROUTINE AND REVOLUTION

Cass R. Sunstein

The most prominent theories of public life in American law tend to be rooted in conceptions of virtue, welfare, or autonomy. For example, modern interest-group pluralism is defended on the ground that it respects private preferences, thus enhancing autonomy, and accurately aggregates private interests, thus promoting welfare.[1] The principal competitors to pluralism stem from republican theories of politics, which are designed to profit from and to cultivate virtue in political actors, whether citizens or representatives. Republican theories[2] also draw on a conception of politics that sees freedom in the selection rather than the implementation of ends. The dispute between pluralist and republican theories turns out to be a disagreement about the meaning and place of freedom, welfare, and virtue in public life.

Roberto Unger's *Politics* rejects these positions and places in their stead a distinctive theory of human nature and a distinctive approach to politics.[3] The institutional proposals in *Politics*—embodying what Unger calls "empowered democracy"—are designed to break down the distinctions between routine and revolution and to facilitate individual and collective self-transformation. It should not be hard to see that this system departs dramatically from those based on the conceptions of virtue, autonomy, and welfare that have influenced modern democratic theory.

This Essay is organized in three parts. The first explores the relationship between Unger's approach and eighteenth-century constitutionalism, the principal target of Unger's institutional proposals. The second compares Unger's system of "empowered democracy" with the various understandings of public life that have dominated American constitutional theory since its inception. I explore the relationships among Unger's approach and the more conventional alternatives. The final part of the Essay examines Unger's conception of the relationship between democracy and constitutionalism. The task for the future, I suggest, is to minimize the pathologies of traditional constitutionalism in systems that

---

[1] *See infra* Sections II and IIA.

[2] *See infra* Section IIB.

[3] Sartre and Nietzsche have obviously influenced the view presented in *Politics*; see other pieces in this Symposium for discussion.

have at least partly abandoned the goal of limited government. Unger's institutional proposals would not be likely to accomplish that task. For this reason, the program of *Politics*—a romantic, impressively learned, sometimes vague and repetitive, excessively rhetorical, seemingly self-contradictory work—ultimately points in the wrong direction.

I. THE TARGET: EIGHTEENTH-CENTURY CONSTITUTIONALISM

The major target of Unger's institutional proposals is eighteenth-century constitutionalism, which was designed to promote a wide variety of goals. Prominent among them was a desire to insulate basic institutional arrangements from fundamental change and to guard against dramatic intrusions on private property. In this way, the system was intended to limit the redistribution of wealth,[4] a purpose that grew out of Lockean understandings of the institution of private property.

Eighteenth-century constitutionalism also attempted to control the dangers posed by the existence of well-organized private groups, or "factions." National representation and the system of checks and balances were designed to minimize the possibility that any particular group would be able to exercise control over governmental power in order to redistribute wealth or opportunities in its favor.[5] A related but distinct goal was to diminish the likelihood of self-interested representation: the possibility that representatives would obtain and act upon interests diverging from those of the people at large. The fear that the rulers might oppose the ruled played an important part in efforts to promote political accountability, and the framework of the American Constitution was designed to limit the risk that representatives might act on interests independent of those of the governed.[6]

Finally, eighteenth-century constitutionalism reflected an effort to distinguish between different kinds of politics. Constitutional politics are revolutionary in character; they involve the citizenry at large and call forth a measure of far-sightedness and civic virtue. As a general rule, conventional politics contains less of both, and necessarily involves narrower issues and at least a measure of factional manipulation.[7] In all of these respects, traditional constitutionalism distinguished between the routine operation of politics and the occasional revolutionary moments that serve as the backdrop for the system.

The institutional proposals in *Politics* amount to a wholesale attack on eighteenth-century constitutionalism. *Politics* diagnoses the problem

---

[4] See the close of *The Federalist No. 10*, citing as reasons for the proposed constitutional framework its ability to offset "a rage for paper money, for an abolition of debts, for an equal division of property, or for any other improper or wicked project."

[5] *See* THE FEDERALIST NOS. 10 & 51 (J. Madison).

[6] This is the meaning of the notion that "ambition" should be made to "oppose ambition" in THE FEDERALIST NO. 51 (J. Madison).

[7] *See* Ackerman, *Discovering the Constitution*, 93 YALE L.J. 1013 (1984).

of modern liberal democracies as "routine without reason": a system of politics in which people debate the distribution of marginal shares. The result, Unger claims, is a series of reform cycles, in which large issues are not addressed because the power of an unquestioned and even unidentified "formative context" severely limits political possibilities and hopes. For Unger, the overriding purpose of a revised system of institutional arrangements is to ensure that fundamental issues[8] should be continually "up for grabs." The system should be structured to facilitate its frequent and fundamental revision. The distinction between routine and revolution should be eliminated;[9] checks and balances should disappear. Massive transformations should be easy to accomplish. The distinction between constitutional and ordinary politics is made much less sharp.

For example, Unger proposes a separate "destabilization" branch, authorized to break down entrenched arrangements.[10] The system of checks and balances is to be abandoned in favor of one that facilitates large-scale transformation.[11] The legislative and executive branches are not to be mutually constraining. If the legislative branch fails to implement the president's program in its entirety, the latter can call for new elections.[12] Among Unger's category of rights is the "destabilization right," affording an opportunity to disturb settled systems. A distinct branch of government is to be charged with disseminating and providing access to information; the goal is to ensure against the rigidities that might be produced by citizen ignorance of public affairs. The basic purpose of the system as a whole is to ensure that the system is capable of constant and fundamental self-revision.

In many respects, Unger's conception of politics is neo-Jeffersonian. Jefferson also argued in favor of frequent constitutional amendment and was hospitable to "turbulence."[13] Both, he thought, would engage the public as a whole in matters of general importance. Such notions fit well

---

[8] Unger does, however, immunize from revision both the basic system of rights and the institutional structures designed to ensure that fundamental issues remain up for grabs. Political actors may not attempt to bring about stability or durability in institutional arrangements or political roles. In this sense, they are prohibited from "smashing" the basic "context" set up by Unger. These forms of fixity create considerable awkwardness for the system.

[9] In this respect the approach falls within the general tradition set out in B. YACK, THE LONGING FOR TOTAL REVOLUTION: PHILOSOPHIC SOURCES OF SOCIAL DISCONTENT FROM ROUSSEAU TO MARX TO NIETZSCHE (1986).

[10] [T]he power responsible for systematic interventions should be a branch apart . . . . They should have at their disposal the technical, financial, and human resources required by any effort to reorganize major institutions and to pursue the reconstructive effort over time.

Such a branch of government must have a wide latitude for intervention. Its activities embrace, potentially, every aspect of social life and every function of all the other powers in the state.

FALSE NECESSITY at 453.

[11] See Unger's critique of checks and balances. *Id.* at 72, 207, 266.

[12] *See id.* at 457-61.

[13] Jefferson suggested that turbulence is "productive of good. It prevents the degeneracy of government, and nourishes a general attention to . . . public affairs. I hold . . . that a little rebellion

with Unger's approach, though Unger of course takes the notion of turbulence much further than did Jefferson. One can, moreover, find good reasons to support this approach, at least in some settings. The atrophied character of modern public life, in which citizens participate little in public affairs, might be altered if dramatic political shifts became likely—if, as Unger puts it, the issues of politics had to do with more than marginal distributive shares. The goods that accompany participation—education, feelings of community, personal growth of various sorts[14]—might be well served by such a system. *Politics* might be understood as a general effort to respond to Weberian concerns about the effects of rationalization on the possibilities of social life; some of the proposals could be salutary here.

Another point in favor of Unger's system derives from the fact that factional power can manifest itself in resistance to change as well as in change itself—a point missed by traditional constitutionalism, largely because of its emphasis on private property and its choice of a status quo baseline from which to measure factionalism.[15] Unger's treatment of the problem is persuasive here.[16] The ability of well-organized groups to block measures that might be approved democratically, or to set the agenda,[17] poses a large problem for modern liberal democracies. Traditional constitutionalists saw factional power in what they regarded as government action—alteration of the existing distribution of wealth and entitlements—rather than inaction,[18] and Unger's proposals are intended to remedy this defect. Liberal democracy poses an occasional risk of calcification, in which established practices become unrevisable, and oppressive rules are entrenched; the institutional proposals in *Politics* are designed to redress this problem. A recent example of a movement capturing some of Unger's goals is the student effort of the 1960s, when some basic issues were put "up for grabs" in a period of collective mobilization.

In all of these respects, the institutional proposals of *Politics* are designed to invigorate public life, to reduce the risks of rationalization and entrenched authority, and to promote participation in the workings of government—goals that point to genuine defects in modern democra-

---

now and then is a good thing." Letter from Jefferson to Madison (Jan. 30, 1787), *reprinted in* THE PORTABLE THOMAS JEFFERSON 416-17 (M. Peterson ed. 1975).

[14] *See* C. PATEMAN, PARTICIPATION AND DEMOCRATIC THEORY (1970); *cf.* J. ELSTER, SOUR GRAPES: STUDIES IN THE SUBVERSION OF RATIONALITY (1983) (showing that some or all of these goods are "essentially byproducts").

[15] *See* Sunstein, *Constitutionalism After the New Deal*, 101 HARV. L. REV. (1987) (forthcoming); Sunstein, *Lochner's Legacy*, 87 COLUM. L. REV. 873 (1987).

[16] *See* FALSE NECESSITY at 370.

[17] *See* S. LUKES, POWER: A RADICAL VIEW (1974); Bachrach & Baratz, *The Two Faces of Power*, 56 AM. POL. SCI. REV. 947 (1962).

[18] *See* Hale, *Coercion and Distribution in a Supposedly Non-coercive State*, 38 POL. SCI. Q. 470 (1923).

cies. The institutional proposals of *Politics* are intended to counter the stagnation built into political systems in which private groups have disproportionate, but sometimes invisible, power. *Politics* thus carries forward some conventional liberal themes, as Unger suggests in his description of his own project as "superliberalism."[19] But the institutional proposals point in unpromising directions.

II. THREE CONCEPTIONS OF PUBLIC LIFE

Unger's system can usefully be approached by comparing it with the three conceptions of public life that have undergirded traditional public law. The first conception, which we might call pluralist, treats politics as a struggle among self-interested private groups for limited social resources; the goal is to ensure that politics accurately aggregates private interests. The second conception, associated with traditional republican thought, regards politics as a forum in which citizens participate in choosing shared values. The third conception, which we might call Madisonian, treats politics as a system in which representatives, rather than citizens, engage in the processes of politics. In the Madisonian system, those processes are an effort to decide on values rather than to implement preferences; politics has a deliberative component.

Each of these conceptions is grounded in principles of autonomy, welfare, or virtue. The pluralist understanding, for example, is defended on grounds of both autonomy and welfare. Pluralism is primarily concerned to respect private preferences and in that sense might be thought to promote autonomy. At the same time, a system of preference aggregation might be justified on welfare grounds, rooted as it is in utilitarian concerns. Republicanism, by contrast, tends to be defended on grounds of virtue and autonomy. Political participation is supposed to profit from and produce virtue in the citizenry. Republicanism also proceeds from an antipluralist conception of autonomy, one that sees personal freedom in selection of values and that defines political freedom as collective self-determination.[20] Madisonian republicanism is designed to profit from and to promote virtue in political representatives,[21] but it is intended as well to serve the goals of autonomy and welfare. The allocation of political power to representatives is supposed to promote a healthy division of labor and to leave the people as a whole free to pursue their disparate conceptions of the good life.

---

19 FALSE NECESSITY at 588.

20 *See* Michelman, *The Supreme Court, 1985 Term—Foreword: Traces of Self-Government*, 100 HARV. L. REV. 4 (1986).

21 *See, e.g.*, THE FEDERALIST No. 57 (A. Hamilton) (suggesting that the first "aim of every political constitution is . . . to obtain for rulers men who possess most wisdom to discern, and most virtue to pursue, the common good of society").

A. Pluralism

Under the pluralist conception, politics is a kind of market. Citizens have preferences, which are treated as prepolitical and which should be aggregated in political outcomes. This aggregation is the "public interest" produced by the political system. In a well-functioning political process, as in any other well-functioning market, the purpose is to ensure that both numbers and intensities of preferences are reflected in the outcome. Politics thus amounts to a struggle among self-interested groups for scarce social resources.

Implicit in the pluralist conception is a theory of representation that counsels representatives accurately to reflect constituent desires, in terms of number and intensity of preferences. It follows from this understanding that a lack of widespread political participation is hardly a problem, but instead reflects general satisfaction with the system. Participation is a form of "demand" generated by the failure of the system to satisfy citizen preferences. The absence of widespread participation demonstrates that the process is close to the equilibrium point. Citizens may be ignorant or apathetic about politics; neither is a source of serious concern. Political participation is not valued above other activities in which citizens may involve themselves. It is not a distinct means of promoting human development, feelings of community, or self-realization.

Pluralism has a long pedigree in American constitutional thought. Elements of pluralist thought can be found in the writings of Gouverneur Morris and Alexander Hamilton. More recently, political scientists and economists have explored pluralism as a predictive tool and as a normative good.[22] But several risks threaten to undermine a pluralist system.

1. *Market Failure.*—Under a pluralist approach, the central defect in a political system is a failure in the political market. It is not altogether clear what such a failure might look like, but a familiar example is a diffuse, weakly organized group that suffers significantly from public or private conduct[23] because it is unable to participate effectively in the political marketplace. A somewhat more controversial example, of special importance in American law, is the discrete and insular minority subject to pervasive prejudice or hostility on the part of the majority.[24] It is unclear whether such groups can be brought into the usual category of "market failure." The special solicitude for them is probably attributable to a normative judgment about the nature of the "preferences" that typi-

---

[22] *See, e.g.*, R. DAHL, A PREFACE TO DEMOCRATIC THEORY (1956); D. MAYHEW, CONGRESS: THE ELECTORAL CONNECTION (1974); Becker, *A Theory of Competition Among Pressure Groups for Political Influence*, 98 Q.J. ECON. 371 (1983); Peltzman, *Constituent Interest and Congressional Voting*, 27 J.L. & ECON. 181 (1984); Stigler, *The Theory of Economic Regulation*, 2 BELL J. ECON. 3 (1971).

[23] *See* Ackerman, *Beyond* Carolene Products, 98 HARV. L. REV. 713 (1985).

[24] *See* J. ELY, DEMOCRACY AND DISTRUST: A THEORY OF JUDICIAL REVIEW (1980).

cally produce discriminatory legislation.[25] But at least on occasion, market failures of various sorts will be a source of concern in a pluralist system.

2. *Aggregation and Related Problems.*—Pluralist approaches seek to aggregate private preferences in political outcomes. But there are severe difficulties in the aggregation process. Cycling problems, strategic behavior, and other difficulties make it unlikely that majoritarianism will accurately implement private preferences.[26] A large problem for pluralist theory is to devise mechanisms to eliminate or reduce these risks. Because it depends on voting, majority rule is also indifferent to variations in intensity of preferences. And in light of free-rider problems and transaction costs, the outcomes of representative government are unlikely to reflect accurately private preferences.[27]

3. *Rights.*—Pluralist theory places no limits on the pursuit of self-interest by political actors. "Rights" may appear as illegitimate side-constraints on the operation of the political market.[28] To some, however, the potential intrusion on rights is the most dangerous feature of pluralist bargaining. Under this view, it is necessary to constrain pluralist systems by declaring certain areas to be off-limits to government. Such areas may consist of rights of privacy, property, or nondiscrimination.

4. *Social Disintegration.*—As Tocqueville emphasized, a pluralist conception of politics can undermine social integration.[29] Politics becomes, in this scenario, a war of all against all or at best a matter of bargaining; the ultimate risk is a citizenry that is alternately passive and factious. For those who believe that political decisions should encourage and reflect the public interest rather than promote self-interest, the pluralist approach carries significant risks of destroying social cohesion.

5. *Bad Preferences.*—The pluralist understanding treats private preferences as exogenous variables; indeed, in some settings pluralism can be seen as the obliteration of reason by will. For this reason pluralism will be unattractive to those who believe that private preferences should not always be respected. And even if elements of pluralism are accepted, some private preferences should be subject to critical scrutiny

---

25 *See* Ackerman, *supra* note 23.

26 *See* K. Arrow, Social Choice and Individual Values (1963); B. Barry & R. Hardin, Rational Man and Irrational Society?: An Introduction and Sourcebook (1982); A. Feldman, Welfare Economics and Social Choice Theory (1980); D. Mueller, Public Choice (1979).

27 *See* R. Hardin, Collective Action (1982).

28 *See* R. Posner, Economic Analysis of Law (3d ed. 1986) (discussing the first amendment).

29 A. de Tocqueville, Democracy in America (J.P. Mayer & M. Lerner eds., G. Lawrence trans. 1966).

and review. Laws prohibiting discrimination on the basis of race and gender have their origin, at least in part, in a belief that the preferences giving rise to such discrimination are distorted or objectionable. In particular, recent advances in psychology, political theory, and economics have suggested that some kinds of preferences suffer from cognitive or motivational defects. Some preferences, for example, result from the attempt to adapt to the absence of available opportunities; they are not autonomous. Other preferences depend on misperceptions of the facts. In these circumstances, a system based on private preferences may substantially sacrifice autonomy, welfare, or both.[30] A system that subjects preferences to scrutiny, and considers their origins and effects, might be preferred to approaches that merely aggregate preexisting preferences.

6. *Bad Laws.*—Pluralism might also increase the likelihood of undesirable lawmaking. Under competing theories, laws must be supported by argument and dialogue; they cannot simply be fought for or be the product of self-interested "deals." Such competing conceptions make private preferences an insufficient basis for legislation. Political actors— either citizens or legislators—must appeal to a broader public good. This requirement imposes a disciplining effect on the sorts of measures that can be proposed and enacted.[31]

These considerations apply even if one might imagine a pluralist system free from the distorting effects of "market failure." Even a well-functioning pluralist system, in which private preferences are accurately reflected and aggregated, will suffer from the various distortions produced by any scheme in which self-interest, represented in private preferences taken as exogenous variables, is the driving force behind political outcomes.

B. *Republicanism*

Under traditional republican thought, politics is a process of public discourse and debate by which values are chosen and implemented. In this view, preferences do not filter into the political process as exogenous variables. The purpose of politics is to deliberate about values, not simply to implement them. Discussion and dialogue are critical features of the political process. Moreover, political behavior is not in any simple sense self-interested. The processes of politics cannot be assimilated to ordinary markets precisely because of the operation of "practical reason" in settling disputes.[32]

---

[30] *See* Goodin, *Laundering Preferences*, in FOUNDATIONS OF SOCIAL CHOICE THEORY (J. Elster & A. Hylland eds. 1986); Sunstein, *Legal Interference with Private Preferences*, 53 U. CHI. L. REV. 721 (1986).

[31] A point emphasized by Tocqueville. *See* A. DE TOCQUEVILLE, *supra* note 29.

[32] Michelman, *supra* note 20; *see also* M. NUSSBAUM, THE FRAGILITY OF GOODNESS: LUCK AND ETHICS IN GREEK TRAGEDY AND PHILOSOPHY 290-317 (1986).

Under this view, politics is valued above other activities. Significantly, it helps the citizen develop his faculties, increases the likelihood of desirable laws, and promotes a sense of community among the public. But republicanism is subject to significant risks of its own.

1. *Corruption.*—The problem of corruption arises from the danger that participants in politics will attempt to promote their self-interest and use the notion of the common good as a disguise.[33] If corruption occurs, the republican conception of politics is at risk. Civic virtue is necessary for the system to function. Considerations of this sort formed the starting point for Madison's rejection of traditional republicanism. He believed that traditional republics produced factional strife, endangering both private rights and the public good.[34]

2. *Rights.*—The threat to "rights" arises under the republican approach as well as under other conceptions of politics. Two aspects of the problem are distinctive here. First, for republicans, rights tend not to be regarded as prepolitical; they are typically regarded as a product of politics; they can be overridden if the deliberative process so concludes. Second, the risk to rights arises largely because of the dangers posed by corruption. In a well-functioning republic, constraints on the operation of the political process—in the form of fundamental rights—would not be necessary. But in any event, the republican understanding furnishes no guarantee against violation of rights.

3. *Turbulence.*—In some versions, a republican process may both lead to and suffer from turbulence and instability. In the framing of the Constitution, this point emerged most clearly in the debate between Jefferson and Madison on the frequency of constitutional amendment. Jefferson argued that the Constitution should be amended every generation. Frequent amendments would promote popular participation in the workings of government, ensure civic virtue, and prevent social disintegration. For Madison, however, such an approach threatened property rights and social stability. Frequent amendment, he wrote, would produce "the most violent struggle between the parties interested in reviving and those interested in reforming the antecedent state of property."[35] It was necessary to create checks preventing self-interested private groups from usurping governmental power in order to distribute wealth or opportunities in their favor. The discussion in *The Federalist No. 10* of the disastrous consequences of direct democracy is probably the most familiar treatment of the subject.

---

[33] *See* J. DIGGINS, THE LOST SOUL OF AMERICAN POLITICS: VIRTUE, SELF-INTEREST, AND THE FOUNDATIONS OF LIBERALISM (1984).

[34] This is a principal theme of *The Federalist No. 10.*

[35] Letter from Madison to Jefferson (Feb. 14, 1790), *reprinted in* THE MIND OF THE FOUNDER: SOURCES OF THE POLITICAL THOUGHT OF JAMES MADISON 232 (M. Meyers rev. ed. 1981).

For some, however, the potential for turbulence is a virtue rather than a vice. It prevents the system from becoming intolerably self-insulating. To Jefferson, for example, even turbulence "is productive of good. It prevents the degeneracy of government, and nourishes a general attention to the public affairs. . . . [A] little rebellion now and then is a good thing."[36]

4. *Totalitarianism.*—The problem of totalitarianism may arise in any system that sets out a conception of the public good that is distinct from the aggregation of private interests. Under an approach that forbids citizens from appealing to satisfaction of private preferences, the notion of a unitary public good may be used as a means of imposing a particular and partisan conception of the public interest on the citizenry. Moreover, republican thought is sometimes associated with approaches that take the good as prior to the right and that reject "neutrality" as an undesirable constraint on government.[37] Current and recent experiences with totalitarian governments suggest that such fears are not fanciful.

5. *Power.*—A system in which citizens are allowed to participate and to deliberate on political outcomes will be unsatisfactory if power is distributed in such a way as to distort deliberative processes.[38] Discussion and deliberation may be ineffectual where there are widespread disparities in power and influence. Politics must, in this view, be accompanied by exercises of power on the part of the disadvantaged. Deliberation on the part of the citizenry will accomplish little if the deliberations are constrained by ideas that ensure that certain aspects of the existing order are taken for granted.

Classical republicanism exemplified this danger, for republican thought flourished at a time in which social roles and traditional hierarchies were regarded as natural, fixed, and largely inviolable. It is unclear whether and how the republican conception of politics might fit with a system in which social roles are fluid. Moreover, the notions of "public interest" and "common good" threaten to ignore differences between the perspectives of divergent social groups.

C. Madisonian Republicanism

A third conception of public life, prominent at the time of the framing of the American Constitution, borrows elements from the pluralist and republican approaches. Under this view, politics is properly under-

---

[36] Letter from Jefferson to Madison, *supra* note 13.

[37] *See generally* LIBERALISM AND ITS CRITICS (M. Sandel ed. 1984). Recent efforts to generate a kind of liberal republicanism are responsive to this problem. *See* B. ACKERMAN, RECONSTRUCTING AMERICAN LAW (1984); Michelman, *supra* note 20; Sunstein, *Interest Groups in American Public Law*, 38 STAN. L. REV. 29 (1986).

[38] *See* J. ELSTER, *supra* note 14, at 33-42.

stood as a means of selecting values rather than simply aggregating and implementing preferences; it is above all deliberative. But the deliberative tasks are entrusted to representatives rather than to the citizenry. Citizens at large are for a variety of reasons unable or unwilling to participate in the tasks of politics. But it would be intolerable, under this view, to allow politics to consist merely of bargaining among self-interested private groups. There is a common good distinct from the aggregation of private interests; such interests should not be taken as exogenous. The solution is to allow representatives, chosen by the people, to engage in deliberative tasks.

In extreme form, this view is associated with Burke's understanding of representation, in which legislators assumed a role akin to that of Platonic guardians deliberating far above their constituents. A less extreme version can be found in Madison, whose understanding of representation consisted of a mixture of Burkean and pluralist elements.[39] For Madison, the role of the representative was to deliberate, not to respond mechanically to existing constituent pressures. Madisonian representatives were not, however, to undertake their deliberations in a vacuum. Political accountability was designed to ensure that their decisions would not stray far from the desires of their constituents. But whether Burkean or Madisonian, this view produces serious difficulties as well.

1. *Factionalism.*—The problem of factionalism—according to Madison, the central problem of politics—arises from the danger that self-interested private groups will obtain undue power over governmental processes, using public force to distribute wealth or opportunities in their favor. This concern has been associated, as an historical matter, with solicitude for private property, and the desire to insulate representatives from constituent pressures has sometimes been seen as an effort to protect private property from democratic intrusions.

There is not, however, a necessary connection between a concern with faction and a desire to protect the existing distribution of wealth. Redistribution of property may be justified, or even necessary, in order to fulfill some normative conception of proper income distribution. Under such a conception, a reallocation of property rights might not be understood as "redistribution" at all. Indeed, particular distributions of private property could themselves be seen as triumphs for self-interested factions. Concerns about factional power can therefore accommodate a wide range of views about the proper role of government.

2. *Self-interested Representation: Rulers v. Ruled.*—The problem of self-interested representation arises from the risk that representatives will attempt to implement their own private interests rather than the interests of the community as a whole. This problem is especially acute in

---

[39] *See generally* Sunstein, *supra* note 37.

a Burkean or Madisonian system, in which representatives are not tightly controlled by their constituents; pluralist conceptions of government are often the response. The system of checks and balances is designed to control self-interested representation at the same time that it tends, by making government action harder, to insulate the existing distribution of wealth from public intrusion.

3. *Rights.*—As in the republican and pluralist conceptions, there is in Madisonian republicanism a risk of disrespect for private rights. A traditional solution is a "bill of rights" that declares certain spheres to be off-limits to legislators.

4. *Power.*—As under the classical republican understanding, and for the same reasons, maldistributions of power may infect the operation of the Madisonian system. Deliberative processes may be distorted by such maldistributions.

5. *Self-insulation and Stability.*—Under the Madisonian framework, representatives are insulated in order to ensure that a more moderate view prevails; checks and balances operate as a check on significant change. In these respects the Madisonian system tends to preserve the status quo. Stability is highly valued. For those who perceive stability as a protection of the existing (and unjustified) distribution of property and as a devaluation of public life, this effect is far from an unambiguous good.

6. *Citizen Withdrawal: The Absence of Participation.*—Hamilton stressed that the American Constitution, unlike all republican approaches that had preceded it, was characterized by a "total exclusion of the people in their collective capacity" from governmental processes.[40] This exclusion of the citizenry at large has been deplored by many as the most objectionable feature of the Constitution; it was also, as we have seen, a major concern for Jefferson. The risk posed by Madisonian republicanism is that the role of the citizen in government is so small and peripheral that citizens will eventually withdraw from politics altogether. The result is similar to the problem of social disintegration that threatens pluralist approaches to government. Implicit and necessary to Madisonian republicanism was the use of federalism or other forms of decentralization that ensured other institutions in which citizens could participate. Tocqueville's intermediate organizations fulfilled part of this role. The traditionally important role of the states in American government has been justified on these grounds.

---

[40] THE FEDERALIST No. 63 (A. Hamilton).

III. UNGER'S "EMPOWERED DEMOCRACY"

The institutional proposals described in *Politics* are designed to implement "empowered democracy." Among the characteristics of Unger's discussion is a high level of ambiguity and abstraction, combined with considerable rhetorical flourish. Analytical precision is sometimes absent here. To some degree Unger's institutional framework might be understood as proposing marginal changes in existing systems; indeed, parts of the framework can be seen as conservative. Moreover, some elements of the discussion contradict each other; there are many themes in *Politics*, and the most individualistic parts of the book coexist uneasily with the treatment of solidarity. The discussion that follows reads *Politics* as setting out the radical framework that Unger purports to seek. This reading of the book makes it distinctive, though, as we shall see, it makes it more vulnerable as well.

A. *Underlying Premises of the System*

The "empowered democracy" described in *Politics* is a departure from all of the traditional understandings. The system is designed to invigorate public life, to break down the distinction between routine and revolution, and thereby to satisfy at least some classical republican goals; but it is to do this without relying on republican appeals to civic virtue. In these respects, the approach is designed to reject the traditional opposition between self-interest and civic virtue as the alternative driving forces of political life. Unger believes that the opposition is a false one, depending on particular institutional arrangements, and that by subjecting formative contexts themselves to politics, it is possible to generate a system in which the opposition is dissolved.[41] In this respect *Politics* reflects a significant departure from Unger's *Knowledge and Politics*, which attempted to transcend liberal "antinomies" through a neo-republican theory of organic groups.[42]

The foundation for Unger's system is neither virtue nor welfare in the traditional sense; nor is it autonomy, at least not in any familiar incarnation. Unger argues for his system in two ways. First is the strategy of "internal justification":[43] argument that starts from the premise of a

---

[41] The constitution of empowered democracy does not oppose private desires and collective devotions. Instead, it robs this polemical contrast of its force. It does so by enabling people more easily to extend the humdrum practice of pursuing interests within a framework of unquestioned institutional and imaginative assumptions into the extraordinary activity of questioning this framework. Thus, the practice of fantasy and enactment that the institutional program encourages is less a public militancy than an extension of the ordinary activity of defining goals and pursuing them. Its chosen expression is not civic pomp and heroic striving but the activity of a working life. And its favorite devices are conversations rather than meetings, conversations that continue when the meetings end.
FALSE NECESSITY at 591.

[42] *See* KNOWLEDGE AND POLITICS.

[43] FALSE NECESSITY at 368-95.

particular, received view of democracy, operates within that received tradition, suggests how the current system fails to satisfy its own goals, and leads in the direction of alternative arrangements. The second strategy is the "visionary" portrayal of approaches to social life that depart radically from current systems.

To the extent that there is a foundational value in *Politics*, it is captured in the related notions of "empowerment," "self-assertion," and "context smashing." Unger's emphasis on self-assertion reveals the radically individualistic character of much of *Politics*. For Unger, self-assertion should be seen

> less as the depiction of a limited, contentious value, to be weighed against competing values, than as a summation of our strivings for happiness. If the effort to formulate such views of self-assertion has a central theme, it may be the struggle to resolve the conflict between the imperative of engagement in shared forms of life and the dangers of dependence and depersonalization such engagement brings.[44]

The basic point emerges even more clearly in a later discussion:

> Both altruism and harmony are deemphasized in [the] reconstructed image of community. Insofar as they continue to play a role, they do so for the sake of their contribution to the view of community as a zone of heightened mutual vulnerability. *In this zone people may experiment more freely with ways to achieve self-assertion through passionate attachments.*[45]

Unger says similarly that a "driving force of the constitutional program is the desire to do justice to the human heart, to free it from indignity and satisfy its hidden and insulated longing for greatness in a fashion it need not be fearful or ashamed of."[46]

The institutional mechanisms described in *Politics* are structured so as to increase the opportunities for individual and collective self-revision. From the standpoint of traditional approaches, Unger's system is paradoxical in its willingness to embrace vigorous public life without community. Indeed, some pluralist premises are largely accepted, even extended. One of Unger's central metaphors, frequently repeated, suggests that matters should be "up for grabs"; the metaphor is revealing here, especially when one considers its literal meaning. The objection to current democratic practice is not that it is based on raw exercises of power or self-interest. Unger argues instead that the fundamental problems stem from the routinized character of political life and the fact that some issues are immunized from the process of "fighting" and "conflict." Consider in this regard the character of Unger's rhetoric: "smashing" of contexts, "fighting," "grabs," "struggle over the mastery and uses of governmental power," and "conflict" are key terms here.

Unger is critical of classical republicanism because, in his view, it

---

44 *Id.* at 351-52.
45 *Id.* at 536 (emphasis added).
46 *Id.* at 584.

represents an optimistic inversion of the current system that is unaccompanied by proposals and strategies that would help bring it about. His system is designed to alter institutional arrangements rather than to offer what he considers an unrealistic, unproductive, and potentially tyrannical appeal to selflessness. Unger claims that his approach is "less a sequel to the classical republican vision than a superliberalism. It pushes the liberal war against privilege and superstition to a point that requires the abandonment of the forms of governmental, economic, and legal organization with which liberalism has traditionally been associated."[47]

The institutional proposals in *Politics* thus have the iconoclastic characteristics described above. For Unger, "the classical liberal technique of dividing central government into a small number of well-defined branches . . . generates a stifling and perverse institutional logic."[48] Instead of checks and balances, Unger constructs a system of multiplied branches with overlapping functions. One branch, for example, is "charged with enlarging access to the means of communication, information, and expertise, all the way from the heights of governmental power to the internal arrangements of the workplace."[49] The same branch would both "make know-how available to those who . . . set up new productive enterprises" and "intervene in all other social institutions and change their operations, by veto or affirmative initiative," when that intervention is "related to the task of securing the conditions that would maximize information about affairs of state and achieve the maximum subordination of expert cadres to collective conflicts and deliberations."[50] Another branch of government would be entrusted with destabilization.[51] Conflicts among branches would be resolved by rules of priority and by devolution of constitutional impasses to the general electorate.[52] The principal representative body would ensure that the party in office actually implemented its program.[53] The goal, building on some forms of European constitutionalism, is to provide frequent opportunities for fundamental transformations of the system.

Unger distinguishes this system from what he calls "the program of social democracy,"[54] which emphasizes participation and redistribution. That program does not involve "radical institutional innovations" of the sort proposed in *Politics*, though it is informed by similar goals. Unger contends that the intentions of social democrats will not be achieved un-

---

47 *Id.* at 588.
48 *Id.* at 449.
49 *Id.* at 450.
50 *Id.* at 451.
51 *Id.* at 453.
52 *Id.* at 456.
53 *Id.* at 460.
54 *Id.* at 389-91.

less there is major institutional change; if current institutions are accepted, neither redistribution nor participation will be brought about.

Significantly, however, Unger urges a system of rights to check the risks posed by the basic institutional structure. Most important, Unger argues for a set of "immunity rights," consisting of power to fend off poverty, violence, violations of civil rights and liberties, and other fundamental intrusions.[55]

B. The Question of Foundations

The first question raised by the institutional proposals of *Politics* goes to the problem of foundations. Imagine a system in which social roles were largely or entirely fluid, fundamental issues were up for grabs, and the distinction between routine and revolution was eliminated. We have seen that the most prominent theories of public life in American law are founded in conceptions of autonomy, welfare, and virtue. Unger rejects all three, and places in their stead a conception of "self-assertion" or "empowerment."[56] At times *Politics* appears to treat self-revision and constant transformation as intrinsic goods; hence the emphasis on placing the fundamental issues "up for grabs." But the question whether self-revision is desirable turns largely on the directions in which the revision leads.

For example, the liberation of women from traditional gender roles does serve the end of autonomy, but not because it is "context smashing" or "self-assertion" for its own sake. The traditional gender roles have been the only realistic option, and their selection is hardly autonomous when it is based on limitations in the feasible set of opportunities.[57] Self-transformation is desirable when it is in the service of freedom or autonomy[58]—when people select their preferences or identity through some exercise of free choice.[59] But constant transformation of self and society—even if the artifactual quality of both is accepted—is hardly an unambiguous good, especially if it is to occur through "fighting" and "conflict"; and if its foundations in autonomy are absent, it might not be desirable at all.

Indeed, the "smashing" of contexts might be destructive of both freedom and welfare; some old contexts should be preserved and some new ones should be avoided. Consider the rejection of contexts in direc-

---

[55] Other rights include market rights, solidarity rights, and destabilization rights.

[56] *Cf.* N. HARTSOCK, MONEY, SEX, AND POWER: TOWARD A FEMINIST HISTORICAL MATERIALISM (1983) (criticizing approaches to politics having such foundations).

[57] *See* J. ELSTER, *supra* note 14, at 109-40.

[58] See B. YACK, *supra* note 9, for a discussion of how the notion of autonomy, as set out by Kant, has been transformed into one of self-transcendence.

[59] There are some large conundrums here; self-determination is always done against a backdrop that is unchosen. For discussion, see T. NAGEL, THE VIEW FROM NOWHERE (1986); M. NUSSBAUM, *supra* note 32.

tions that may be autonomy-reducing: women who are pressured to return to traditional gender roles; doctors who are forced to become manual laborers; farmers who are forced to make their way in urban life; social systems that borrow from fascist premises. Autonomy and personal identity themselves depend on a certain level of acceptance of context, artifactual or not.[60] The displacement of contexts may produce exhilaration, but its frequent occurrence will result in severe forms of stress, alienation, feelings of impotence, and even terror.[61] The "smashing" of context will, in such circumstances, be destructive of autonomy and welfare and hinder the formation of character itself.

Unger's system appears to be an attempt to wed Christian notions of transcendence with conceptions of freedom influenced by existential thought. In parts of *Politics*, freedom itself appears to consist of breaking through fixed roles, whatever their content may be. This accounts for the strikingly procedural, even lawyerly, character of parts of *Politics*, in which such substantive problems as racism, poverty, and sexism are barely mentioned. But some contexts are far worse than others, and the reasons to oppose the most harmful of contexts should go to their content, not to their identity as "contexts." Such substantive arguments are largely absent from *Politics*. The lack of clear foundations for the institutional proposals in *Politics* thus makes it difficult to approve the system as responsive to an appealing conception of freedom.[62]

The roots of the system in "context smashing" also suggest that Unger has exaggerated some peculiar and unappealing tendencies in Enlightenment thought. The central metaphor of context smashing is best understood in terms of separation and self-assertion rather than community and compassion. Unger's driving metaphor, almost Faustian in character, is one of self-transcendence and self-creation. The notion is, literally, one of giving birth to oneself and thus erasure of the mother. Approaches of this sort have been subject to powerful criticism in feminist theory.[63] The governing aspiration is hopelessly unrealistic, and it is likely to lead in destructive directions.

Unger is also unclear in explaining why his system would not incorporate civic virtue, in the classical republican vision, at least in some form. A large literature exists on the possibility of developing systems that generate and profit from citizen involvement in public affairs. Concrete proposals have been offered and sometimes implemented in the ser-

---

[60] *See* A. MacIntyre, After Virtue: A Study in Moral Theory (1981).

[61] Unger is aware of this problem; the immunity right recognized in *Politics* extends partial protection.

[62] *See also* Cornell, *Beyond Tragedy and Complacency*, 81 Nw. U.L. Rev. 693 (1987); J. Elster, Making Sense of Marx 90-91 (1983).

[63] *See* L. Irigaray, Speculum of the Other Woman (G. Gill trans. 1985); *cf.* D. Dinnerstein, The Mermaid and the Minotaur: Sexual Arrangements and Human Malaise (1976); J. Kristeva, Desire in Language: A Semiotic Approach to Literature and Art (1980); M. Nussbaum, *supra* note 32.

vice of the republican conception.[64] Unger's wholesale abandonment of the republican conception of politics is an assertion, undefended empirically or theoretically. The effort to explain how the system of empowered democracy removes the "force" of the contrast between civic virtue and self-interest is quite mysterious. It is hardly clear that the extension of politics into a "questioning" of the basic framework dissolves the distinction between virtue and self-interest. Indeed, the distinction may be especially important when fundamental issues are at stake. Consider controversies over the appropriate distribution of wealth, the proper treatment of racial minorities, and the relationship between the sexes.

The system of *Politics* gives little or no place to practical reason as an element in the process of individual or collective self-transformation.[65] Thus, little premium is placed on discussion and dialogue or deliberative approaches to politics as elements of the system. Instead, "conflict," "struggle over the mastery of power," and "fighting" are the principal determinants of social outcomes. It is unclear whether such terms as "smashing" and "fighting" are meant literally or as metaphors; in any case they are hardly independent goods. In Unger's empowered democracy, political outcomes represent an equilibrium point among hostile forces—everything is "up for grabs." But the foundations of this approach have been effectively criticized by approaches to politics that stress the possibilities of dialogue and empathy in social life.[66] Deliberation is an important filter on enactments, reducing the likelihood that laws will amount to naked transfers of wealth or exercises of power.[67] Deliberation also protects against the degeneration of politics into civil war, profiting from and generating some form of citizenship.[68] Unger's system, moreover, does nothing to filter out distorted or objectionable preferences, which appear to be a permissible element in his system.

C. The System of "Empowered Democracy" in Practice

All this suggests that although Unger's institutional framework might in its ideal form contain some advantages over the current liberal democracies, it would have significant dangers. In actual operation, however, the system would be unlikely to achieve its intended purposes. The notion that individual or collective self-transformation might be constant or continuous is contradicted by historical experience.[69] In practice, systems that attempt to break down the distinction between routine

---

[64] See citations in B. BARBER, STRONG DEMOCRACY: PARTICIPATORY POLITICS FOR A NEW AGE (1984); E. GREENBERG, WORKPLACE DEMOCRACY: THE POLITICAL EFFECTS OF PARTICIPATION (1986); J. MANSBRIDGE, BEYOND ADVERSARY DEMOCRACY (1980).

[65] See M. NUSSBAUM, supra note 32; Michelman, supra note 20.

[66] See N. HARTSOCK, supra note 56; Michelman, supra note 20.

[67] Goodin, supra note 30.

[68] See Pitkin, Justice: On Relating Public to Private, 9 POL. THEORY 327 (1981).

[69] See infra text accompanying note 81.

and revolution tend to be undermined, in the short or long run, by the power of self-interested private actors. There is good reason to be skeptical of approaches that remove institutional checks on fundamental change, especially when they accept, as does Unger, some of the premises of pluralist conceptions of politics.

Pluralism is most palatable if it is accompanied by side constraints on political outcomes. Without such constraints, an approach like that in *Politics* threatens to reintroduce, in especially severe forms, many of the pathologies associated with other conceptions of public life. When power is maldistributed, revolutionary or radical change might increase the authority of well-organized private groups over government. Checks on institutional change often operate largely in the interest of the minority rather than the majority. The poor and the poorly organized may well be the victims of fundamental change.[70] The problem is especially severe if self-interest is the motivation for political action.

Unger anticipates such criticisms and offers two responses. First, Unger claims that if the distinction between routine and revolution is eliminated and institutional changes weaken social roles, so that power is more evenly distributed and self-interest does not point in any particular direction, the problem of faction will be reduced significantly. Some support for this proposition comes from recent work on preference formation. Preferences are not exogenous; they adapt to the available opportunities.[71] In a world in which legal arrangements and individual endowments are different, different preferences can be expected as well. In this respect, Unger's approach might be understood as a variation on Madison's defense of a large republic. The idea is that in a system without fixed positions, "interests" will be so fluid and attenuated that factions will not emerge.

But it is difficult to imagine what a world of genuine fluidity would look like. Indeed, part of individual autonomy might be thought to consist of the ability to have a measure of narrative continuity over time, and Unger's system is designed to prevent that sort of continuity.[72] But Unger does not contend that his system will ensure that people have common (or no) interests. He acknowledges that there will be a plurality of interests, and says that conflicting interests should be the basis for political "fighting." The problem of factionalism thus remains unsolved.

Unger's second response has to do with the various rights created by the system and the existence of a "rotating capital fund" to redistribute income. The system of rights is designed to ensure a form of immunity and protection from the constant fundamental struggles of politics. But it remains to decide how capacious these rights are to be. If they are

---

[70] This will not always be the case. Sometimes institutional checks prevent issues unfavorable to the majority from surfacing at all.

[71] *See* J. ELSTER, *supra* note 14.

[72] *See* E. TUGENDHAT, SELF-CONSCIOUSNESS AND SELF-DETERMINATION (1986).

narrow, the problem of factionalism remains, and the immunities will be insufficient to prevent self-interested struggle over the terms of social life in a way that is destructive of individual identity.[73] But if the rights are broad, the institutional program is seriously threatened. A secure system of rights coexists uneasily within a system in which the fundamental questions are "up for grabs." Thus the interaction between the system of rights and the institutions of "empowered democracy" is ambiguous.[74] Similar considerations apply to the rotating capital fund. That mechanism is not designed to equalize the distribution of wealth and to freeze an equal distribution for all time; such an approach would be fundamentally at odds with Unger's system. The rotating capital fund thus does not eliminate the competition for power or solve the problem of factionalism.

Moreover, it is unrealistic to believe that a system could be created that would remove the fixed interests of powerful private actors or rulers—a point that Unger seems to accept. In any particular regime at any particular moment, both the private and public beneficiaries are likely to be resistant to change and well-situated to prevent it. Unger apparently intends to make such possibilities less likely, but it is hard to see how his system would do so. *Politics* is vague on this critical point.

What this suggests is that Unger's "empowered democracy" is likely to be subject to many of the same pathologies associated with conventional conceptions of politics. In particular, the system is subject to risks generated by the absence of deliberative government—that is, the problems of self-interested representation and factional power associated with Madisonian republicanism, and the dangers of turbulence and authoritarianism associated with classical republicanism.

A significant task for modern constitutional theory is to promote the original safeguards against factional tyranny and self-interested representation in an era in which government inaction is far from an inevitable good, and is even ambiguous as a conceptual category. Indeed, the failure to protect citizens from environmental harm, unsafe conditions in the workplace, poverty, or discrimination on the basis of race and gender might itself be seen as action or as the product of factional power. The ultimate goal is to develop institutional arrangements that will accomplish at least some of the purposes associated with eighteenth- and nineteenth-century constitutionalism in a time in which the substantive agenda of "limited government" has been, at least in part, repudiated, and collective selection of preferences or values frequently seems desirable.

---

[73] *Cf.* Radin, *Property and Personhood*, 34 STAN. L. REV. 957 (1982).

[74] *See* FALSE NECESSITY at 579: "The constitutional basis for this willingness to accept the risks of expanded conflict lies in the guarantee of immunity afforded by a system that precludes entrenched dependence . . . and keeps every issue open for another day. Its higher spiritual significance consists in the assertion of transcendence as diurnal context smashing."

But a system that sees politics as a self-interested struggle opens up fundamental issues to frequent contest and "fighting," and removes institutional checks on change, thus creating serious risks in its effort to achieve the ends of democracy. Madison's sensitivity to the dangers posed by factionalism stemmed in part from his desire to protect the existing distribution of wealth from majoritarian pressures, but one need not share that concern in order to recognize that a system of fixed rights and checks and balances, working to diminish factional power, serves the interests of the politically powerless as much as or more than those of the politically powerful.

IV. CONSTITUTIONALISM AND DEMOCRACY

Unger's institutional proposals are based on his view that eighteenth-century constitutionalism is a threat to democracy. For Unger, fixed institutional arrangements are desirable only as a means of ensuring that fundamental matters are continually "up for grabs." His basic institutional framework is principally designed to ensure against efforts to reinvigorate the distinction between routine and revolution. Both the system of rights and the basic institutional arrangement are intended to promote opportunities for constant revision.

This understanding, however, oversimplifies the relationship between constitutionalism and democracy and disregards the functions of precommitment on the part of political actors. Precommitment occurs when people oblige themselves in advance, in the fashion of Ulysses and the Sirens,[75] to follow or not to follow a particular course of conduct. The phenomenon is closely related to that of "second-order preferences," or preferences about preferences: both individuals and collectivities often have second-order preferences and rely on them in public and private life.[76] Those involved in politics thus may decide to enact second-order preferences through constitutional provisions. Unger's discussion might be seen as an attack on precommitment of that sort. But the discussion raises several questions.

A. Precommitment as Facilitative

For Unger, insulation of the status quo from collective conflict and deliberation is an unambiguous evil. In Unger's view, such insulation was the vice of eighteenth- and nineteenth-century constitutionalism, which failed to take liberalism to its logical conclusion. For a number of reasons, however, a polity may decide to insulate certain arrangements from collective control—not in the interest of calcification, but in the

---

[75] *See* J. ELSTER, ULYSSES AND THE SIRENS: STUDIES IN RATIONALITY AND IRRATIONALITY (1979).

[76] *See* T. SCHELLING, CHOICE AND CONSEQUENCE (1984); THE MULTIPLE SELF (J. Elster ed. 1986).

interest of democracy itself.[77]

If the basic institutional arrangements are settled, the public is liberated to resolve other problems without having to reevaluate these institutional questions. In this respect, stability can be liberating and facilitative rather than confining. A public that continually alters the institutional arrangements governing decision-making might find itself unable to make substantive decisions at all. For example, agreement that laws will be made in a constitutionally specified way makes it easier to enact laws. The issue of how laws must be made can be taken for granted. The ability to take some matters as fixed is emancipating in the same sense as the rules of grammar. If the rules of lawmaking are continually up for grabs, democracy is much harder to achieve.[78] An established institutional framework can promote, rather than impair, democracy.

B. Rights as Democracy-Promoting

The rationale for precommitment parallels the concerns that prompted constitutional guarantees of separation of church and state. When religious issues are subject to political control, factionalism may occur, enduring enmities may form, and other issues may become impossible to resolve. The argument for privatization of religion need not be made solely in terms of "rights." The argument may depend instead on the notion that if certain issues are placed off limits to democracy, democracy will itself be strengthened. In private relationships, people often voluntarily forgo discussion of subjects that will cause stress; so too with politics. The insulation of public issues from public processes may in this sense, quite paradoxically, promote democracy.

This phenomenon suggests that Unger's view that fundamental issues should be constantly "up for grabs" in the interest of democracy oversimplifies the problem. If the fundamental structure is subject to revision, the system may dissolve into one of factionalism and impasse with no questions, fundamental or not, capable of resolution. Unger is persuasive in objecting to the calcified character of aspects of modern politics and to the fact that fundamental issues are sometimes closed off from collective resolution. The strategies of precommitment and privatization pose significant dangers as well. But the institutional structure of *Politics* understates the risks of a system in which everything is always "up for grabs."

---

[77] The most useful recent discussions here are Holmes, *Gag Rules and Democracy*, and Holmes, *Precommitment and Self Rule*, in CONSTITUTIONALISM AND DEMOCRACY (J. Elster & R. Slagstaad eds. forthcoming), on which I draw heavily here.

[78] *See* Holmes, *Precommitment and Self Rule*, *supra* note 77.

C. *Planning, the Rule of Law, and Stability*

The distinction between routine and revolution can be defended on various grounds.[79] For one thing, it promotes planning; people can conduct their affairs without fear of dramatic and sudden change. It also promotes individual security by minimizing drastic alterations of the status quo. In these respects, the distinction promotes the virtues classically associated with the rule of law: stability, checks on discretion and caprice, and predictability over time. All of these virtues serve both economic welfare and (under a certain understanding) freedom.[80] Unger's system is largely indifferent to them.

Moreover, if fundamental issues are "up for grabs," individuals in power may want to use their positions for private gain, and those out of power, fearful of change, may hesitate to perform projects that will take time. Jon Elster's recent discussion of constitutionalism and democracy in Florence in the thirteenth and fourteenth centuries reflects these concerns.[81] The Florentine experience is instructive for Unger's system because its political system was based on similar premises. The frequent shifts in political power, in which routine and revolution were collapsed, led to severe factionalism.

D. *The "Destabilization" Branch*

Unger argues for a branch entrusted with destabilization. Despite the efforts of his system to break down fixed interests, he recognizes that electoral majorities or other powerful actors may succeed in entrenching themselves. The notion behind the "destabilization" branch is that the accountable branches are unlikely to undermine the existing regime, because they are subject to electoral control. Moreover, the courts lack the institutional assets that might enable them to undertake significant social change successfully. Unger thus borrows from the ombudsman model and from the aggressive American courts of the 1960s and 1970s, which reformed mental asylums, prisons, schools, and other institutions.[82] For Unger, the virtue of the destabilization branch is that it will accomplish some of the goals associated with the Warren Court—breaking up entrenched institutional arrangements—but, unlike the judiciary, it will have the tools to carry out its tasks.

Serious problems, however, remain. If the destabilization branch is accountable to and its members are appointed by the other branches, it is unlikely to accomplish its intended functions. It will be subject to polit-

---

[79] *Cf.* A. HIRSCHMAN, SHIFTING INVOLVEMENTS: PRIVATE INTEREST AND PUBLIC ACTION (1982); Ackerman, *supra* note 7.

[80] There are of course serious dangers here as well.

[81] *See* Elster, *Introduction*, in CONSTITUTIONALISM AND DEMOCRACY, *supra* note 77. Elster draws on J. NAJEMY, CORPORATISM AND CONSENSUS IN FLORENTINE ELECTORAL POLITICS 1280-1400 (1982).

[82] *See generally* O. FISS, THE CIVIL RIGHTS INJUNCTION (1978).

ical control, much like modern administrative agencies operating under presidential guidance. A branch subject to other institutions is unlikely to "destabilize" in ways that Unger would approve. But equally severe problems may arise if the destabilization branch has a measure of autonomy. Its particular conception of destabilization may be undesirable. It may seek, for example, to create dramatic disparities in wealth. Granting authority to an entity entrusted with breaking up institutional structures in accordance with its own independent agenda is fraught with risks. However the system is structured, the destabilization branch would generate many of the problems associated with an aggressive judiciary attempting to bring about large-scale social transformation.

Some justifications, treated in the vast literature on judicial review, are available to defend such a system. In particular, many have stressed the failures of pluralist systems that stem from the absence of deliberation or from disparities in political power. But such justifications are uncongenial to Unger's system, which is to some degree grounded on pluralist premises rejected by these alternative systems.

V. CONCLUSION

The institutional proposals in *Politics* are based on a rejection of eighteenth-century constitutionalism, which prized stability, distinguished sharply between routine and revolution, and saw in public life a threat of factionalism. For Unger, institutions should be structured so as to ensure that fundamental issues are constantly up for revision. The distinction between routine and revolution should be broken down; the principal issues should be "cracked open to politics"—left for collective conflict and deliberation. The system appears to be based on a conception of human nature that links Christian notions of self-transcendence with existential approaches to freedom, and sees "self-assertion" and "context smashing" as foundational goods.

The proposals in *Politics* are designed to generate a more vigorous public life and overcome the entrenched quality of the existing distribution of power and the existing set of preferences. The basic approach, however, lacks clear foundations. "Context smashing" and "self-assertion" are not intrinsic goods; their desirability depends on a substantive conception distinguishing between contexts that promote autonomy, welfare, or virtue and those that do not. Moreover, Unger's system underestimates the dangers of putting everything "up for grabs," the risks of factionalism, the possibilities of deliberative democracy, and the facilitative functions of constitutionalism. A system in which fundamental issues are constantly open to "fighting" and "conflict" is likely to be undermined by powerful, well-organized private groups and by self-interested representatives.

Institutional arrangements that can be taken for granted help to facilitate democracy; they need not undermine it. The task for the future is not to ensure that everything is constantly up for grabs, but to design mechanisms to limit factional power and self-interested representation, to facilitate deliberative approaches to democracy, and to promote participation in government in an era in which the traditional constitutional goal of "limited government" has lost some of its appeal.

UNGER'S *POLITICS* AND THE APPRAISAL OF POLITICAL POSSIBILITY

John Dunn

What really is politically possible? How different, over any given period of time, could our collective social and political life be caused to become? Just how is it epistemically appropriate and humanly decent to conceive political possibility?

Few, if any, questions about the meaning of human existence so directly and intimately link personal temperament and cognitive style as the question of what really is politically and socially possible. To equate our more edifying desires with the possible consequences of our political actions is merely an agreeable exercise in self-deception. On the other hand, to identify the contours of our existing social arrangements as the current embodiments of "the ancient laws of society"[1] or as structural preconditions for social and political existence here and now is the most ignominious superstition. But the happy Aristotelian mean between these two types of cognitive indignity is as hard to characterize as it is to locate.

The most striking feature of Roberto Unger's new trilogy[2] is the confidence with which it presses an answer to all of these questions. The answer is arrestingly novel in many respects, though it draws with great cunning and analytical energy upon many strands of modern thinking and historical scholarship. The core of Unger's answer is impressively integral and unmistakably *l'homme même*—a direct expression of Unger's highly idiosyncratic fusion of individual disposition and cognitive style. The answer rests on a taut but oddly stable balance between an intense scepticism and an at least equally intense faith. The scepticism dictates the judgment that we can never under any circumstances know what is politically possible or how different our collective social and political life could be caused to become. But the faith—what Unger calls "the radical project"—insists that this limit on our cognitive powers is an occasion for exultation rather than a ground for mourning and never, under any conceivable conditions, an excuse for lassitude, torpor, or res-

---

[1] A. DE TOCQUEVILLE, THE RECOLLECTIONS OF ALEXIS DE TOCQUEVILLE 116 (A. Teixeira de Mattos trans. 1959).

[2] SOCIAL THEORY; FALSE NECESSITY; PLASTICITY INTO POWER; *see also* THE CRITICAL LEGAL STUDIES MOVEMENT; PASSION.

ignation. For Unger, the message of modern world history is that we should revel in the indeterminacy of the future. Despite all of its horrors, modern history is a story of human empowerment, invention, and self-re-creation, both individual and collective, a history of what Unger calls "negative capability."[3]

Taken on its own, the natural impetus of either element in this combination is deeply distasteful to Unger. At the level of practical reason, the sophisticated scepticism of modern understandings of the character and development of human cognition yields a nasty choice. The choice is between a radical depoliticization of the imagination[4] and a sinister obsession with the manipulative opportunities potentially afforded by fusing esoteric knowledge with condensed social and political power. This second option leaves the task of emancipation of men and women to the social and political cognoscenti.[5] They, in consequence, find themselves claiming a kind of social knowledge which is necessarily unavailable. And along with this, and presumptively licensed by it, they also claim a degree of manipulative control that sets fierce and degrading limits on the freedom of action of their fellow human beings. A wide variety of modern thinkers have explored these dangers, and Unger does not make any especially decisive suggestions on how they can be avoided.[6]

What Unger does offer, however, is a compelling picture of the impossibility, short of thermonuclear war, of sundering the potential for drastic social and political reconstruction from the exercise of modern state power. This theory is of great importance and interest because it conflicts so sharply with the educated political sensibility in most contemporary states—as much in the Russia of Mr. Gorbachev, the India of Mr. Gandhi, and the Japan of Mr. Takeshita, as in the United States of Mr. Reagan or the Italy of Mr. Goria. Unger does not deny the massively routine character of most modern politics. But unlike the effectively habituated observers of modern politics—journalists, politicians, economists, political scientists, and citizens—the strategy of understanding which he deploys resists with the greatest obduracy any equation of intelligibility with fatality.

The theoretical basis for Unger's strategy of understanding is set out

---

[3] "Negative capability" is the modernist index of human progress, a startling existential totalization of Karl Popper's falsifiability criterion for scientific inquiry. *See, e.g.,* K. POPPER, OBJECTIVE KNOWLEDGE: AN EVOLUTIONARY APPROACH (1972).

[4] J. DUNN, *Political Obligations and Political Possibilities,* in POLITICAL OBLIGATION IN ITS HISTORICAL CONTEXT 243-99 (1980) [hereinafter J. DUNN (1980)].

[5] K. MARX, *Theses on Feuerbach,* in 5 K. MARX & F. ENGELS, COLLECTED WORKS 4, 7 (1976).

[6] He does offer an elaborate inventory of recommended practices, *see* FALSE NECESSITY; THE CRITICAL LEGAL STUDIES MOVEMENT, which, if they were implemented, would presumably have the effect of avoiding these dangers. But his own analytical views effectively preclude him from presenting a practical diagnosis of how these arrangements can actually be implemented anywhere in particular.

in his preliminary volume, *Social Theory: Its Situation and its Task*. The strategy itself is deployed to advance Unger's preferred political, social, and economic articulation of the radical project in *False Necessity*, the centerpiece of his present trio of works. But it is in the third volume, *Plasticity into Power*, in which one can most easily see both the source of Unger's own political confidence and the fragility of some aspects of his proposals. In this volume, Unger applies his strategy of understanding to the quest for wealth and power in a wide variety of pre-modern societies. Plasticity, that is, the capacity to alter social forms fluidly and inventively to face fresh challenges and surmount ancient barriers, is itself simply an especially important element of power in modern world history (as it has been more or less urgently throughout the recorded history of our species). To tie the development of plasticity to the steady elimination of personal dependence from large-scale human interrelations (let alone to the elimination of the depersonalization which Unger himself sees as accompanying this) is a formidable challenge and an endless political task. It is the essence of the conservative political wisdom of the Western world that we already know this task to have failed, and that it was always in principle impossible.

Unger virulently rejects this jaded but contemptuous conviction, both for the spiritual vices it discloses and for the intellectual superstitions it inadvertently exemplifies. He cannot, however, offer to replace it with a more invigorating and ingenuous conviction if that conviction claims the same conclusive epistemic authority. The very scepticism necessary to discredit the epistemic pretensions of contemporary conservatism precludes Unger from volunteering counter-convictions that claim a comparable authority. To see so unblinkingly the imperative of plasticity as a fact of power certainly calls into question the political realism of governmental and administrative circles in the modern West with their increasingly enfeebled and Lilliputian sense of alternative possibility.[7]

While the precariousness of existing routines may be bad news for their more persistent beneficiaries, it is not necessarily good news for most other human beings. This is especially apparent in a period such as the present in which weapons of terminal destruction are not merely within the scope of human imagination but permanently poised to carry out their tasks.[8] Unger insists evocatively, throughout *Plasticity into Power* and more intermittently throughout *False Necessity*, that the relentless pressures of military competition—the quest to augment man's

---

[7] This is perhaps even more apparent today in the international monetary, trade, and strategic relations between nations and power blocs, *see* R. KEOHANE, AFTER HEGEMONY: COOPERATION AND DISCORD IN THE WORLD POLITICAL ECONOMY (1984); M. OLSON, JR., THE LOGIC OF COLLECTIVE ACTION (1965); ORDER AND CONFLICT IN CONTEMPORARY CAPITALISM (J. Goldthorpe ed. 1984), which Unger on the whole ignores, than it is in the domestic reform cycles of the capitalist democracies and communist regimes which he considers with some care in FALSE NECESSITY.

[8] P. BRACKEN, THE COMMAND AND CONTROL OF NUCLEAR FORCES (1983).

powers of destruction and coercion—have done as much to impose the imperative of plasticity as have man's efforts to create and produce less equivocal goods.

But the hope of giving plasticity "the focus and authority it lacks"[9] by democratizing the quest for wealth and power and by breaking down the hierarchical division of labor with its sharp distinctions between task-setting and task-implementing, looks especially forlorn in the face of thermonuclear war. It is far from apparent that what we really need today is supplementation of our destructive capabilities; nor is it very plausible that the notably hierarchical and overbearing bureaucratic apparatuses of the two greatest powers in the world will not serve all too adequately to increase these capabilities at a dramatic pace. Given the extreme difficulty of controlling the deployment of nuclear weapons and the stunningly evident need to do so, the existence of these weapons and the possibility of ultimate destruction appear to form at least one context in which the imperative of plasticity has at last met its match. Indeed, since the prospect of uncontrollable individual improvisation in crisis conditions is the most likely cause of irreversible engagement,[10] there is now a strong case for seeing reconstruction of a more dependably hierarchical set of rigidities as the central imperative of human life.[11]

Plasticity into Power thus indicates some of the darker shadows cast by Unger's vision and brings out, in the perfunctoriness of its ending,[12] the contingencies of personal temperament that hold this vision together. His presentation, with its elaborate *ricorsi* of leading themes and its mildly elusive structure, leaves the reader with a choice between a variety of modern superstitions of the left or right and one of two theoretical options—super-theory and ultra-theory—each unmistakably of the left, and each commended by Unger himself. But the construction of this matrix of choice relies heavily on fusing negative epistemological doctrines, pragmatist emphasis on the imperative of social plasticity and the self-estimate of the radical project according to Unger's construction of the latter. This fusion, if it is necessary rather than factitious, may give the imperative of plasticity "the focus and authority that it lacks."[13] But to anyone who disputes Unger's reading of the radical project or finds any version of it fundamentally uncompelling, Unger's fusion of doctrines naturally encourages the opposing judgment that plasticity, fact of power though it may be, in fact possesses no such focus or authority.

The most decisive and bracing feature of Unger's work is its frontal assault on the imaginative torpor of modern social and political under-

---

[9] PLASTICITY INTO POWER at 212.

[10] P. BRACKEN, *supra* note 8.

[11] J. DUNN, RETHINKING MODERN POLITICAL THEORY: ESSAYS 1979-83, at 171-89 (1985) [hereinafter J. DUNN (1985)].

[12] PLASTICITY INTO POWER at 211-12.

[13] *Id.* at 212.

standing. With great acuity he sees something about human existence at an individual, a collective, and even a global level, which only the most brazenly flippant of modern thinkers have seen—and which the latters' lack of analytical curiosity or energy has largely prevented them from comprehending. This vision certainly consorts more comfortably with radical and modernist apprehensions of the human predicament than it does with the sedate enjoyment of assured advantage.[14] But the most conservative thinker or political leader has every reason to face it, simply because it is analytically compelling. *Plasticity into Power* vividly demonstrates the force of this lesson. Unger's own evident fascination throughout his writings with the perspective of power gives even greater emphasis to his understanding of human existence. There could be no more appropriate audience for its stringent implications than the exponents of that broadly conceived politics of social democracy, which Unger very justly characterizes as the current embodiment of conservative political decency in the modern West.

Unger takes the alienated catenal imagery of the setting of modern human existence—the iron cage, the carceral imagination—and gleefully supplants it with the picture of a human habitat seething with possibility. The site of this susurration of possibility, which guarantees its omnipresence from the most intimate of individual circumstances to the most global, is simply the human imagination. This is not a metaphysical thesis. Placing a vision of possibility in the human imagination is perfectly compatible with a monistic determinism, so long as the detailing of the latter remains cognitively inaccessible to real human beings. It certainly conflicts, however, with the most widely esteemed modern techniques of social, political, or economic understanding and with the dominant models of human rationality.[15] Unger's view does not, of course, disturb the internal workings of human rationality nor deprive political understanding of all analytical force. But it cuts each of them decisively away from any determinate foundation in human experience and makes their application to this experience a matter of improvisatory deftness and good fortune.

A world seething with possibility to a degree that humans can never accurately assess, and in relation to which the very idea of such an assessment is profoundly unclear, plainly offers no conclusive warrant for any particular set of actions.[16] But to see the world in this way stimulates a style of social vision very different from that prevailing in the positivist social sciences that Unger excoriates.

---

[14] *Cf.* Raynor, *Philosophy into Dogma: The Revival of Cultural Conservatism*, 16 BRIT. J. POL. SCI. 455-73 (1986).

[15] J. DUNN (1980), *supra* note 4, at 243; *cf.* B. WILLIAMS, MORAL LUCK: PHILOSOPHICAL PAPERS 1973-1980 (1981).

[16] It is one of Unger's principal theses that there never have been, are not, and never will be any such warrants.

One of the best ways to see the force of this conception of social causality or causal theory of history is to focus on Unger's understanding of the character and role of institutions. His greatest political merit is his insistence on the importance to any honorable and effective radical politics of institutional understanding. Unger's theory echoes a very old theme in Western political theory,[17] but one which radical political and social thought in the present century has treated in an overwhelmingly frivolous or disingenuous manner, when it has not elected simply to evade the theme completely.[18]

Unger takes institutions (economic, governmental, legal, military) very seriously. In a sense, he takes them even more seriously than most positivist social scientists. Unger sees institutions as not merely subject at any given time to an operating logic and a range of internal constraints, but also as molders of the personnel of whom they are composed, as well as of the clients or victims upon whom they act. Although he recognizes that institutional niches, or on a larger scale what he calls "formative contexts," do much to constitute human agents and determine the consequences of their actions, as well as to constrain in principle the scope of the outcomes that they can bring about, he is most concerned with the ineliminable capacity to reverse or transcend these limits.[19] Once again, the site of this capacity to negate is the human imagination: there a person may stand back from the importunities of a set of routines or practices, recast these practices, and try again.

For Unger, a context is not formative because of its unique and historically predestined eligibility but because of its relative inelasticity at any particular time and, above all, its deep impact upon the social imaginations of its denizens. We are never merely our habitats, but we are always in large measure their creatures. Formative contexts arise from the restless struggle for power and wealth; and they are shaped by invention, mimesis, and the arbitrary contingencies of historical sequence.[20]

But the same forces that shape formative contexts can also serve to break them and shape their sometimes very different successors. Unger's vision of the history of institutions, like the vision of the history of science developed by Thomas Kuhn's followers, stresses both the capacity

---

[17] *See* Q. SKINNER, THE FOUNDATIONS OF MODERN POLITICAL THOUGHT (1978) (esp. vol. 1: THE RENAISSANCE 44-45).

[18] *Cf.* N. BOBBIO, QUALE SOCIALISMO?: DISCUSSIONE DI UN' ALTERNATIVA (1976). One possible construction of his programmatic volume *False Necessity* is to see it as a revitalization of Utopian socialism, inserted firmly into what Unger himself hopes and believes to be a realistic understanding of world history. Unger thereby hopes to rescue the suppressed promise of petty commodity production: *Proudhon Redivivus. Cf.* C. SABEL & J. ZEITLIN, HISTORICAL ALTERNATIVES TO MASS PRODUCTION, PAST AND PRESENT 108, 133-76 (1985).

[19] Compare the more despondent tone of Barrington Moore's musings on the human capacity to become adjusted to the abominable. B. MOORE, INJUSTICE: THE SOCIAL BASES OF OBEDIENCE AND REVOLT (1978).

[20] J. DUNN (1985), *supra* note 11, at 68-102.

of human practices to reproduce themselves and protect themselves against external challenge, and the sharp discontinuities, inseparable from this capacity, between a self-reproducing practice and its successors. Unger's own political program in *False Necessity* attempts to weaken the self-reproducing capabilities of institutional contexts, and eventually to diminish the discontinuities between their prior and subsequent forms.

To make this conception compelling, Unger complements his account of the nature of human institutions with a denial of the possibility of determinate causal knowledge of their properties. Unger sets out this attack best in *Social Theory*. It combines a relatively determinate negative induction from the history of human cognition, much stressed by recent epistemologists and philosophers of science,[21] with the elusively radical scepticism some draw from the later writings of Wittgenstein, from Quine, or from Heidegger.[22] If all human knowledge simply expresses a form of life, epistemologically grounded pretensions to conclusive social insight are as intellectually threadbare as they are politically impertinent and offensive.[23] But this negative doctrine secretes no definite implications for political judgment,[24] however decisive may be its criticisms of others' claims that their political judgments are grounded in epistemic authority. By itself this negative doctrine provides only the flimsiest of support even for Unger's vision.

The account of the character of human institutions, by contrast, provides more robust aid. Unger's account starts from the "obvious truism" well expressed by Alasdair MacIntyre as long ago as 1971, "that no institution or practice is what it is, or does what it does, independently of what anyone whatsoever thinks or feels about it. For institutions and practices are always partially, even if to differing degrees, constituted by what certain people think and feel about them."[25] Unger's account presses this truism to its limits. His account does not—given Unger's sceptical premises—tell us where exactly these limits lie. Indeed, it insists that we cannot *know* where they do lie. What Unger's account does do, still at a truistic level, is insist that the precise causal character of any institution at any time rests upon what every individual causally associated with it thinks and feels about it.[26] Here, epistemic analysis directly

---

21 H. PUTNAM, REASON, TRUTH AND HISTORY (1981); Jardine, *"Realistic" Realism and the Progress of Science*, in ACTION AND INTERPRETATION: STUDIES IN THE PHILOSOPHY OF THE SOCIAL SCIENCES 127 (C. Hookway & P. Peltit eds. 1978). For those who are not professional philosophers the most influential exponents of this viewpoint in the last two decades have probably been the historian T. S. Kuhn, the philosophers Paul Feyerabend and Ian Hacking, and the more turbulent influences of Heidegger, Foucault, and Derrida.

22 *See* R. RORTY, PHILOSOPHY AND THE MIRROR OF NATURE (1980).

23 J. DUNN (1985), *supra* note 11, at 119-38.

24 R. RORTY, CONSEQUENCES OF PRAGMATISM: ESSAYS 1972-1980 ch. 11 (1982).

25 A. MACINTYRE, AGAINST THE SELF-IMAGES OF THE AGE 263 (1971).

26 This implicitly rejects part of MacIntyre's judgment. *Compare id.*

prompts a sense of social vertigo. The practical dependability and facticity of the social world lurches startlingly and the role of surprise is reincorporated into human history.[27] How human beings see their social setting is never conclusively determined at any level cognitively open to the species. The immediate and volatile relation between belief and desire furnishes an endless resource for astonishing recombinations. Any human institution at any time can tip and buckle under the influence of these forces.[28]

Human beings, therefore, really do make their own history. Most crucially, they make it by precariously constructing and refurbishing their own personalities[29] and by assessing the options presented by the settings in which they live. Unger's repeated and exhilarated insistence that history is always "up for grabs" and that social life is necessarily politics is one temperament's response to this understanding. Barrington Moore's resigned pessimism is another.[30] Compared to Moore's view, Unger's response luxuriates in men's and women's magnificent capacity to find themselves suddenly unable to bear a moment longer the odious conditions of their lives. Little analytical conflict exists, however, between the two perceptions. Both see the human imagination as the site where human history is finally determined, and both arrive at this view while attending to the heavy weight of power and the raw urgency of material need.

Clearly, Unger believes that the sense of closure and finitude in a given historical setting affronts human potentiality. The temperamental basis of this distaste, however, arises less from his restless sense of the absurdity of reifying the hopelessly provisional than it does from his classically radical revulsion at the subjugation of huge numbers of human beings by far fewer of their fellows. The prominence of such subordination and exploitation, sunk deep into the property order and institutionalized division of labor of today's social democratic communities, persistently goads him into programmatic expression of his counter-imagination. The telos of a social habitat at last made fit for human inventiveness and antinomianism—the radical project—lends focus and authority to the blank apprehension of social plasticity through the immense gap it exposes between the desirable and the actual. At times Unger writes as though he were confident that this gap will narrow ineluctably as time goes by. But at other times he frankly recognizes that

---

[27] *Cf.* MacIntyre, *Ideology, Social Science and Revolution*, in 5 COMPARATIVE POLITICS 3, 321-42 (1973).

[28] It is not wholly clear whether Unger believes that this is literally true or whether he merely believes that, for all we can ever know, it always may be; a less exciting possibility and one which would lend less sustenance to the radical project in conditions of adversity.

[29] Frankfurt, *Identification and Externality*, in THE IDENTITIES OF PERSONS 239 (A. Rorty ed. 1976).

[30] *See* B. MOORE, *supra* note 19.

the weight of historical experience gives no firmer warrant for an optimistic eschatology for modern social life than it does for a pessimistic one.

Many of Unger's critics will probably concentrate their fire upon the character of this telos—Unger's idiosyncratic reading of the form of the human good. Even those who see a human society as fundamentally a relation between the imaginations of its members[31] will probably find the ferocity of Unger's insistence on individual imaginative autonomy too extreme to be sane. Those with less euphoric temperaments may well find that Unger's sheer zest for novelty and experiment renders deeply unconvincing his account of most human beings' strongest and most persistent motives.[32] Still others are likely to see his human society of endless participatory deliberation and choice as more of a forum for endlessly futile bickering and the squandering of time and energy than than they are to see it as a promise of linking individuals to their social milieu in a vital flow of interest and enjoyment.[33]

Certainly Thomas Hobbes' estimate of the human rewards of political engagement still presents a formidable challenge to Unger's assessment of the pleasures of a society and polity made safe for the more loquacious amongst the petty bourgeoisie:

[S]ome will say, That a *Popular State* is much to be preferr'd before a *Monarchicall*; because that, where all men have a hand in publique businesses, there all have an opportunity to shew their wisedome, knowledge, and eloquence, in deliberating matters of the greatest difficulty and moment; which by reason of that desire of praise which is bred in humane nature, is to them who excel in such like faculties, and seeme to themselves to exceed others, the most delightfull of all things. But in a Monarchy, this same way to obtain praise, and honour, is shut up to the greatest part of Subjects; and what is a grievance, if this be none? Ile tell you: To see his opinion whom we scorne, preferr'd before ours; to have our wisedome undervalued before our own faces; by an uncertain tryall of a little vaine glory, to undergoe most certain enmities (for this cannot be avoided, whether we have the better, or the worse); to hate, and to be hated, by reason of the disagreement of opinions; to lay open our secret Counsells, and advises to all, to no purpose, and without any benefit; to neglect the affaires of our own Family: These, I say, are grievances. But to be absent from a triall of wits, although those trialls are pleasant to the Eloquent, is not therefore a grievance to them, unless we will say, that it is a grievance to valiant men to be restrained from fighting, because they delight in it.[34]

The public pieties of political life over the two and one-half centuries

---

[31] One example is the modern communitarian Charles Taylor. *See* C. TAYLOR, PHILOSOPHY AND THE HUMAN SCIENCES, 2 PHILOSOPHICAL PAPERS (1985).

[32] Compare the more systematic presentation of his conception of individual psychology in PASSION.

[33] Compare Unger's own misgivings over "the fatal mania of meetings," FALSE NECESSITY at 588.

[34] T. HOBBES, DE CIVE: THE ENGLISH VERSION 136 (H. Warrender ed. 1983). Unger's evoca-

since 1642 have gone Unger's way rather than Hobbes'. It is eminently questionable, however, whether most people's sentiments have accompanied these political pieties. The psychological realism or implausibility of Unger's favored telos and of the conception of human nature it rests upon are obviously in themselves important. They also are important, as Unger frequently reiterates, in appraising political and social possibility not merely in principle, but also in practice. In a rhetorically compelling sneer, Unger insists that those who lack a programmatic vision comparable in scope and grandeur to his own must assess the realism or absurdity of political proposals solely by the degree to which a proposal deviates from existing arrangements, and therefore presume the impossibility of significant change. The resulting torpor in social and political imagination is not, in Unger's eyes, merely spiritually unbecoming. By induction from the history of large-scale social transformation, especially over the last two centuries, it is also quite evidently intellectually ludicrous.

Those who cannot fully share his vision of the form of the human good may ask how much Unger's enriched sense of social and political possibility depends upon this vision: how readily can one recombine the components of his analysis to serve other perceptions of what human beings really do want? To judge this, it may help to go back to Unger's radicalization of MacIntyre's truism about social institutions: that all human institutions are as they are and act as they act in part because some of their participants think and feel as they do. Both analytically and practically, even MacIntyre's truism establishes some minimal level of potential instability in all human institutions. This minimum serves as a limit point to the capacity of the institutions to reproduce themselves compulsively. At its narrowest, false necessity is Unger's name for this window of vulnerability in the stolidest and best protected of human arrangements. The necessity is "false" because it is illusory, often secured in many by false beliefs which the institution fosters amongst its denizens, and bovinely reaffirmed by its less sensitive external observers in their own erroneous estimates of how the institution has to operate. If one sees social reality as the codification of the expectations of a social territory's occupants, or as the range of equally habitual expectations nurtured by social reality's more dedicated external observers, then one sees at least one way the possible may shrink to the narrow confines of the actual. In doing so, however, one also sees this constriction as a product of imaginative indolence or capitulation.

What happens to the conceptualization of social possibility if we remove these imaginative shackles? More crucially, what, if anything, happens to the conceptualization of social probability? As we have already seen, we can more easily identify Unger's answer to the first of these

---

tive preoccupation, especially in *Plasticity into Power*, with the emancipation of men's powers to destroy and with the central historical role of the quest for military efficacy, make Hobbes's challenge all the sharper.

questions than to the second. It is important that, despite the rich array of causal reflection on actual and possible legal, economic, and political institutions set out in *False Necessity*, Unger never really considers quite what it means for a human state of affairs to be probable or improbable. Unger believes that the escape from false necessity would open the way once more to the realization of the radical project—not by historical predestination but through the absence of any knowable and conclusive impediment. The defeat of false necessity would open a vast horizon, far far beyond the thwarted and humiliating intimacies of present day politics. But how should we decide upon the best route towards this horizon? What, outside the comparatively domesticated terrain of North American legal education,[35] might human beings have good reason to do if they found Unger's vision of the causal character of existing social life compelling, that they do not have good reason to do already?

At least three ways exist to envision political agency as essentially futile on a given type of occasion, and Unger plainly is anxious to shake the imaginative hold of each of them. The first, expounded with baroque exuberance by proponents of game theory and the economic analysis of public goods, focuses on the improbability of particular individuals' actions decisively securing a given political outcome, or on the antinomies between individual rationality and collective advantage. In its classic form as embodied in the free rider problem and the prisoners' dilemma, this line of thought has exerted a deeply traumatic effect upon the exercise of civic imagination, eroding the plausibility of civic engagement and subverting its putative human point.[36] Unger is pretty brutal in his handling of modern devotees of civic republicanism,[37] an historical tradition he correctly identifies with a commitment to a savage degree of social discipline and a quite unacceptable degree of flippancy towards the claims of modern liberty, that is, the liberty to act as one pleases.[38]

While he is surprisingly (or perhaps unsurprisingly?) cavalier about the potential impact of the dilemmas of collective choice on the radical project, he brings to bear virtually the whole weight of his conception of human nature upon the dispiriting cultural detritus of the free rider problem and the depleted image of human reward this problem fosters. De-

---

35 *See* THE CRITICAL LEGAL STUDIES MOVEMENT.

36 M. OLSON, JR., *supra* note 7. *But cf.* R. HARDIN, COLLECTIVE ACTION (1982).

37 *See* FALSE NECESSITY at 586-87.

38 B. CONSTANT, DE LA LIBERTÉ DES ANCIENS COMPARÉE À CELLE DES MODERNES, 4 COURS DE POLITIQUE CONSTITUTIONELLE 238-74 (1820). Compare Unger's uncharacteristically insensitive account of Constant's views in THE CRITICAL LEGAL STUDIES MOVEMENT at 41. Unger's reading of the implications of the civic republican tradition echoes the contrast between David Hume's and Adam Smith's "Disdain for all Dependency," J. DUNN (1985), *supra* note 11, at 13, 32, and the social order commended, for example, by Andrew Fletcher of Saltoun, Hont & Ignatieff, *Needs and Justice in the Wealth of Nations: An Introductory Essay*, in WEALTH AND VIRTUE 1 (I. Hont & M. Ignatieff eds. 1983). The best overall presentation of civic republicanism as a tradition of thought and sentiment remains J. POCOCK, THE MACHIAVELLIAN MOMENT (1975).

spite the powerful tendency in modern political thinking to see the implications of free riding as essentially a sequence of problems in institutional design, and despite his own keen and imaginative interest in precisely such problems, Unger himself, much like the civic republicans whose social goals he repudiates, is apt to regard free riding as above all an index of spiritual failure.

He may indeed be exceedingly well advised to see them as such, since none of the more analytic procedures that he develops can shake his initial image of political futility. It is precisely this image of futility that has always pressed most heavily on the great majority of human beings. In addition, this purely individual sense of political futility and impotence is for the most part not an illusion at all. It is not a credulous misidentification of necessity where no such necessity exists, but an eminently reasonable assessment of the limits of individual causal powers.[39] To shake the sense of individual political futility, it must be vision or nothing. In the face of this challenge Unger calls once more upon his own sense of the solidarizing potential of the radical project; its capacity to "lend focus and authority" to the analytically achieved appreciation of social plasticity.[40] If individuals can see their own agency, not as a costly and hazardous contribution unlikely to secure a directly and uniquely imputable gain for anyone, but rather as an element in an intrinsically rewarding collective performance, they will repudiate the free rider problem on their own behalf.

This line of attack differs greatly from Unger's assault on deep-structure social theory and the unstable oscillations between fatalist passivity and feckless opportunism which he sees deep-structure theory as prompting. His diagnosis of the corrupting and bemusing political consequences of deep-structure social theory—and most particularly of its Marxist version[41]—is protracted, searching, and lethally effective.[42] Whereas his exploration of the political weaknesses of deep-structure social theory, however, immediately aids the formation of political judgment, it is quite difficult to distinguish the agitational from the analytical elements in his interpretation of the nature of deep-structure social the-

---

[39] *Cf.* J. DUNN (1980), *supra* note 4, at 243-99.

[40] Of course, like Hobbes, he also fully recognizes social plasticity's potential, along with the potential of any other scheme of orienting beliefs that extends beyond the rational imperatives of self-preservation, for spawning an endless sequence of bitter quarrels. But, unlike Hobbes, Unger revels in this prospect. Also unlike Hobbes, Unger cannot afford to dispense with the potential of the radical project for fusing and inspiring a collective agency that is often self-endangering or even self-sacrificial for each particular individual. Compare, however, D. BAUMGOLD, HOBBES'S POLITICAL THEORY (forthcoming), on Hobbes's difficulties in dispensing with analogous degrees of commitment.

[41] *See* SOCIAL THEORY; FALSE NECESSITY.

[42] Unger has a wonderful ear for leftist cant. But it is in fact hard to imagine an exponent of any strand of modern political faith who could read his work through without occasional twinges of acute discomfort.

ory. Hence even the best intentioned are likely to find it difficult to employ Unger's critique of deep-structure social theory directly in the refinement and disciplining of their own political judgment. This is not simply a matter of Unger's inadvertence. It follows from his intense and arrestingly personal ambivalence about the very idea of political judgment itself. Unger sees political realism, in its characteristic modern forms, either as an epistemically pretentious claim to know what necessarily no one can know, or as a limp capitulation to the actual. Either way, Unger is intensely suspicious of the very attempt to subject political judgment to systematic analysis.

The qualities that he approves in political judgment are, naturally, on display throughout his book. These qualities are most accessible, however, in his more condensed sketch of the virtues appropriate to a cadre in one of the political movements that in his view carry the banner of the emancipatory struggle,[43] even though this struggle aims eventually at "effacing the starkness of the contrast between who is and who is not a cadre."[44] The "realistic, second-best solution to the problem of the cadres,"[45] the non-Platonic solution, is the addition of a relatively small number of people who eschew the polar vices of pious conservatism and sectarian bigotry in favor of the benign mean embodied in Unger's own opinions.[46] The addition of these individuals leavens the substantial lump constituted by their less discerning fellows. Unger plainly sees this as a true realism, by no means conflated with the "realism" of the paralytic conservatives whom he scorns. Just as plainly, Unger regards the elaborate institutional forms which he proposes for the transformative movement, within their own hypothetical terms, as eminently realistic; and by "realistic" he means just what the conservatives whom he views with such contempt would mean by the word. What they disagree about is not what realism is but which social expectations are in fact realistic. It is in their causal beliefs, not in their analytical concepts, that they are genuinely at odds.

Since the late seventeenth century, most Western social and political thinkers of any great force have rested their causal beliefs about societies, economies, and polities, either openly or tacitly upon some conception of probability.[47] Unger's emphasis on the desirability of the "persistent exercise of an almost frenzied inventiveness,"[48] and on the prospective triumph of the "principle of pitiless recombination," while presumably in

---

[43] FALSE NECESSITY at 415-19.

[44] *Id.* at 419.

[45] *Id.* at 418.

[46] This is not an especially novel line of thought, let alone sentiment.

[47] *See* F. FAGIANI, NEL CREPUSCOLO DELLA PROBABILITÀ: RAGIONE ED ESPERIENZA NELLA FILOSOFIA SOCIALE DI JOHN LOCKE (1983); I. HACKING, THE EMERGENCE OF PROBABILITY (1975); B. SHAPIRO, PROBABILITY AND CERTAINTY IN SEVENTEENTH-CENTURY ENGLAND (1983).

[48] FALSE NECESSITY at 503.

some sense inductively grounded, sets him very much at odds with the by now hallowed imaginative framework based on probability. But these views of his do not really furnish him with an alternative analytic matrix which could possibly serve to supplant the old framework. A diffuse expectation of forthcoming surprises, however urgent and eager, is scarcely a framework for analyzing anything. There is, therefore, only a quite arbitrary link between his vividly imagined and carefully considered program of emancipation and his more analytic perspective on the human past. The link is an exercise of will and a reflection of temperament, not a dictate of understanding.

Consider the relation between individual human agents as choosers of their own actions and the same persons as judges of the potential consequences of their possible actions. As choosers of their own actions, human beings perceive, reflect, and judge as best they can. From the perspective of practical reason, and from their own point of view, people are best off if they do not deprecate their capacity for invention and self-discipline before attempting to exert either. None are so inefficacious as those who do not try. From the viewpoint of theoretical reason, however, dismayingly robust epistemic grounds for pessimism may exist even in relation to oneself. These same grounds may carry through, with all too crushing cogency, to any consideration within the bounds of practical reason, of the prospective conduct of one's fellows. For what reasonable alternative is there for any human agent, to conceiving the space on which she or he can and must seek to act, if they are to act at all, as a set of varyingly possible consequences, surrounded by a blank cliff of sheer impossibility? Over time, few things matter more to any human being than the structure of risks and opportunities presented by the prospective conduct of others. Except with the extremes of downside risk, what is likely to happen is almost always more important to a human agent than what just conceivably might happen. If humans are to dissipate the sense of futility that hovers over the vast bulk of individual political agency, from the most routine and conformist to the most intractably subversive, what they must above all alter is their sentiments and not their causal beliefs.

Here Unger confronts two other further sources of the feeling that for most humans most of the time, political agency is irretrievably futile. A fatalist and monistic vision of the historical process deconstructs the very idea of rational agency, offering to individuals, as well as to classes, states, or national communities, a perspective on their own strivings which renders the latter comically self-deceptive. Even a less extreme and analytically determinate structural explanation of large-scale historical change requires the adoption of a sociology of fate in lieu of one of choice, and prescinds firmly from the standpoint of human historical agency.[49] Unger's rejection of this perspective, both in its metaphysically full-blown version and in its analytically more modest and controlled version, follows from his emphasis on imagination's inherent unpredictability, and on the severely provisional character of all human cognitive achievement. Even if the most metaphysically extreme version of determinism were in fact valid, human beings could never ascertain that this was the case and could never construe any definite implications for their own agency that followed from its validity. Whatever they chose to do would, ex hypothesi, follow from its being so.

In a sense Unger adopts the ultra-idealist reading of the fundamental determinants of historical change suggested by John Warr, Unger's mid-seventeenth century English predecessor in radical legal criticism: "But yet the minds of men are the great wheels of things; thence come changes and alterations in the world; teeming freedom exerts and puts forth itself."[50] Unger, however, gives this judgment depth and sociological credibility by offsetting it with his conception of human agency's formative contexts and the heavy imaginative weight of habit and cumulative dismay that crushes the powers of negative capability that he sees as the birthright of every full human being.

In a similar manner Unger's conception of world-historical struggle in the twentieth century supplements a recognition of the causal weight of mimesis, invention, and sheer nerve in determining the course of twentieth century revolutions,[51] with a particularly illuminating insistence on both the necessarily improvisatory character of most revolutionary political struggle and on the endless range of institutional possibilities available to those attempting to reconstruct a social world. Unger is a powerful political critic of the twentieth century revolutionary tradition, who nevertheless understands why this tradition has developed as it has. But he displays not the slightest patience with this tradition's tendency to cling desperately to its most adventitious and blatantly discreditable improvisations. He denies, perhaps a trifle hazardously, that any set of human circumstances is knowably impossible, and refuses to dignify any given set of shabby accommodations to the temporarily convenient with a title to historical necessity. He is an equally sharp critic of twentieth century reformist traditions, though it is striking how little his reading of their largely involuntary self-limitation really differs from the reading of their more pedestrian interpreters.[52]

---

49 J. DUNN (1985), *supra* note 11, at 75, 77-78; T. SKOCPOL, STATES AND SOCIAL REVOLUTIONS (1979).

50 Warr, *The Corruption and Deficiency of the Laws of England*, in 3 THE HARLEIAN MISCELLANY 241 (1744-46), *quoted in* C. HILL, THE WORLD TURNED UPSIDE DOWN 219 (1972).

51 *Cf.* J. DUNN (1985), *supra* note 11, at 68-102; J. DUNN (1980), *supra* note 4, at 217-20; J. DUNN, MODERN REVOLUTIONS (1972).

52 *Cf.* J. DUNN, THE POLITICS OF SOCIALISM: AN ESSAY IN POLITICAL THEORY (1984); A. PRZEWORSKI, CAPITALISM AND SOCIAL DEMOCRACY (1985).

The rejection of a closed set of possible worlds,[53] however much it might or should open up a person's sense of historical possibility, probably will not, for fairly obvious reasons, directly sharpen anyone's political judgment. Addressed to human beings individually, nothing in Unger's *Politics* shakes the rationality for most people in the contemporary world of presuming that political engagement for all but the most obsessive and narrowly motivated will prove in practice hazardous or massively unrewarding, and very probably both. Unger grounds his confidence in human self-emancipation, in effect, on a Platonic philosophical psychology in association with a deeply un-Platonic conception of value for human beings.[54]

The judgment that vision shapes desire, and shifts in vision effectively reshape it, still powerfully challenges the debilitating impact of Hume's naturalist insistence that human beings' inclinations fundamentally determine the reasonableness of their actions.[55] But the judgment that vision shapes desire remains not merely the oldest but also the most robust foundation for genuinely Utopian social thinking, a genre which Unger's present work dramatically revives. The direct address to vision, however, alters what human agents have good reason to do to the extent, and only to the extent, that it changes how they happen to see. The only audience likely to be able to take Unger's work as it was intended is, therefore, the array of ideal cadres—a category predefined to a perilous degree in terms of the theory in the first place. Because they share his sense of what really matters for human beings and what truly is desirable, this array of cadres can develop the passionate pragmatism of Unger's exploration of the vulnerability of existing social and political forms in harmony with the goals that he holds dear, and not in the service of more disparate and distressingly contingent purposes of their own. For most others, however, exposure to Unger's vision, while intellectually striking and agreeably enlivening in itself, is likely to leave the world of politics in very much the same condition as they previously supposed it to be. For even the more sympathetic of such readers, the most lasting aspect of *Politics* is likely to be particular felicities of Unger's institutional explorations and not the diffuse euphoria induced by the first encounter with his text as a whole.

Unger makes the role of modernist legislator, for which he discreetly offers himself, inherently more self-effacing than its ancient predecessor. It is scarcely surprising that he should feel the need to repudiate the mantle of "an omniscient and benevolent Lycurgus" towering over the

---

[53] *Cf.* D. LEWIS, COUNTERFACTUALS (1973).

[54] However "negative capability" is to be understood, it scarcely possesses the stabilizing and orienting potential of Plato's Form of the Good. *See* THE REPUBLIC OF PLATO (F.M. Cornford trans. 1941).

[55] *Contrast* B. WILLIAMS, *supra* note 15.

world of ordinary agents created by his historical action.[56] By virtue of its very commitment to institutionalized self-extinction, however, the role depends upon the inspirational impact of the vision it conveys, both for its historical efficacy and for its human authority. It is therefore a rather delicate and searching test of the soundness of his programmatic "super-theory" as a whole, just what its effect on the vision of others does prove to be: how plentiful and how ideal the "ideal cadres" actually turn out.

Quite certainly, the ideal cadres will continue to have not merely a plethora of fanatical or backsliding colleagues but also a wide array of political opponents. Some of these colleagues and opponents, naturally, will be simply beneficiaries of privilege, determined to defend their privilege for its own sake. But others will oppose Unger's program because they do not share his vision of the form (or formlessness) of the human good and because they do not trust his political judgment. In the last instance, it is impossible to evade the issue of trust in politics.[57] Why should anyone believe that a belligerently dissident opportunism really makes a benign contribution to human life everywhere? The zest for interminable self-reconstitution appears as febrile at a personal level as it appears unpromising as a collective political project. The hope of doing good through political agency obviously excites Unger more than the fear of doing harm through it unnerves him. This is certainly one dimension to the political opposition today between left and right. But since one can do harm by political action much more easily than one can do good, the left, and especially the foes of subjugation and hierarchy, would be unwise to construe it as the sole or even the most decisive line of division between the two. Unger, like Georges Sorel, believes the politics of human emotion is just as important as, and perhaps even more important than, the politics of consequence.[58] Certainly, history presents human beings with the circumstances they directly encounter. Unger, like Sorel, refuses to believe that humans must accept the circumstances as given. He offers his sophisticated attack on the muddled fatalism of modern social theory, which often echoes Sorel's accents, as a negative spiritual exercise in self-strengthening. Radical intellectuals, plainly in the West but also possibly in the Third World, are likeliest to draw strength from it, since they find their identities at present in such urgent need of reinforcement. The union between radical intellectuals and oppressed masses has been the most turbulent and consequential liaison in modern politics. It is not an easy romance to chronicle justly. But it seems most unlikely that one can describe it more honestly or understand it more clearly simply by restoring the self-confidence of radical intellectuals.

We may be unable in principle ever to know just what we must take

---

56 FALSE NECESSITY at 590; *cf.* J. DUNN (1985), *supra* note 11, at 119–38.

57 Dunn, *Trust and Political Agency,* in TRUST (D. Gambetta ed. forthcoming 1988).

58 *Compare* G. SOREL, REFLECTIONS ON VIOLENCE (1961).

as given in human affairs. But it is a criterion of sanity for every human being to accept very much as always being given. (Compare Thomas Carlyle on the universe.) Even to formulate coherent intentions, we require a human world with very highly interpreted properties. To formulate political intentions with any amount of ambition and determinacy requires a correspondingly sharper degree of causal assessment. The urgency, and on occasion the flair, of Unger's institutional imaginings indicates the limits of the hostility to a strictly political division of labor of even the most modernist of legislators. It does not, however, wholly still the suspicion that this rethinking of the radical project holds more for radical intellectuals than for their indispensable partners, the *malheureux*, who no doubt potentially remain *les puissances de la terre,* but who are usually less preoccupied with self-reconstitution.

With magnificently reckless self-exposure, Unger concludes *False Necessity* by affirming as the goal of his program for radical democracy "a better chance to be both great and sweet."[59] The wish to be both great and sweet is a recognizably modern yearning; the wish to be sweet being, for example, comparatively undeveloped amongst the Roman governing classes. It is a natural goal of a radical program to make a social world fit for radical intellectuals. But perhaps it is less reassuring as a rubric for political action. In particular, this kind of goal gives too little weight to the dangers of political miscalculation by the best intentioned leaders, or to the thoroughly demotic realism with which most human beings still view the hazards and frustrations of ambitious and vague projects for political and social reconstruction. Only a more pedestrianly consequentialist approach could distinguish between wise and foolish instances of such projects. And only the conviction that solid and dependable reasons for undertaking them exist can render these projects exercises in rational cooperation for great masses of human beings rather than exhilarating adventures for the talented, daring, and determined few. This is especially true in light of all the political turbulence, ambiguity, and anxiety which Unger rightly insists will always accompany them. Human fragility does not make social oppression any more forgivable than its radical critics suppose it to be. In fact, it is precisely human fragility that makes social oppression such a clear evil, and the same fragility that makes the burden of judging accurately the central responsibility of anyone who aspires to guide political practice. Human life is too short, too tiresome, too sad, and too beset by danger for Unger's sense of the heroic to furnish a compelling basis for political judgment for mankind at large. Gracchus Babeuf, the precarious bridge between the thought world of classical republicanism and the harsh manipulative adventures of the professional revolutionary tradition, put the case admirably:

The republican is not a man in eternity, he is a man in time. His paradise is

---

[59] FALSE NECESSITY at 595.

on this earth; he deserves to enjoy there liberty and happiness, and to enjoy it for as long as he has being, without postponement, or at least with as little as possible. All the time he spends outside this condition is lost to him, he will never recover it again.[60]

What to do in politics always depends on what we can, and will, cause to come about. Unger correctly insists that we can seldom or never *know* this. Such epistemic opacity, however, merely implies that we must learn to judge it better in practice: an endless task. Over time, and for this purpose, Unger's scepticism and preoccupation with institutional form are likely to prove more instructive than the ardor of his faith.

---

[60] JOURNAL DE LA LIBERTÉ DE LA PRESSE, no. 19 (8 vendé míaire, an III) at 4, *quoted in* R. ROSE, GRACCCHUS BABEUF: THE FIRST REVOLUTIONARY COMMUNIST 161 (1978).

PRACTICAL REASON AND SOCIAL DEMOCRACY: REFLECTIONS ON UNGER'S *PASSION* AND *POLITICS*

Geoffrey Hawthorn

I.

Roberto Mangabeira Unger's project[1] is breathtaking. It is also paradoxical. He is writing what may be the most powerful social theory of the second half of the century and yet wants to stop social theory as it is usually understood. He defends all but the most radical of modernist tenets and yet proposes the "archaic idea of a universal language of self-reflection" that has prescriptive force.[2] I want to pursue this paradox.[3]

I want to suggest that one can come to Unger's project as what he nicely describes as a "modest eclectic," that is, as one who accepts the limitations of existing models of social explanation and political possibility but who suspects "that drastic reconstructive proposals will shatter against limits more unyielding than a mere accumulation of institutional and imaginative biases."[4] I want also to suggest that one may remain more truly skeptical than Unger about other people, and about the possibilities of knowing other people. I want nevertheless to agree that one may, for these reasons and for Unger's, resist the more extremely modernist option, what Unger calls "ultra-theory," because, unlike Unger's own "super-theory," "ultra-theory" sits uneasily between accepting what it pretends to reject and rejecting everything, including the basis for anything it may itself want to accept. I want in short to suggest that one can in these ways reach conclusions which—though perhaps more qualified than Unger's—are not opposed to them. The only difference is that one does so more pragmatically.

---

[1] "Unger's project" refers collectively to three works, FALSE NECESSITY, SOCIAL THEORY, and PASSION.

[2] PASSION at 84.

[3] I first formed most of my thoughts on Unger's arguments in a discussion on political theory and political practice at the Instituto Internacional de Estudios Avanzados in Caracas in December 1985. Luis Castro, who arranged the discussion and whose institute (with help from the British Council) generously supported it, Gloria Carnevali, John Dunn, Teodoro Petkoff, Richard Rorty, Alan Ryan, and Roberto Unger himself have all affected them. *See also infra* note 34.

[4] SOCIAL THEORY at 140.

II.

Insofar as social theory has attempted to connect the concerns of exemplar history with ethics and the scientific method—that is, insofar as it has marshalled examples of how we have lived in order to answer the question how we should live—it has failed.[5] It has done so, Unger himself suggests, in essentially two ways. The first is methodological. Each of the two prevailing modes of analysis, which Unger calls "deep-structure analysis" and "positivist social science and naive historiography," has retreated into spurious naturalism. One has done so by supposing "a closed list of structures"; the other by eliding the distinction between contingent "routines," or unreflective practices, and unavoidable constraints. This arises in part from the fact that European social theorists were "tempted to misunderstand the triumphant European settlements as the necessary form of a stage in world history," and from this to derive a theory of natural and necessary stages.[6]

The second failure is connected to the first. It is a failure of imagination, a failure to think about human possibility. "Positivist social science" and "naive historiography" do not directly concern themselves with possibility. At best, they specify conditions that have been met elsewhere and suggest that if those conditions are repeated, the previous outcomes may recur. But these outcomes may not be desirable, and they will not exhaust the possibilities. "Deep-structure analysis," on the other hand, does consider possibility—Marxism is the most conspicuous case—but both confines it in "false necessity" and is curiously coy about its substance and shape. As in romance, the battles are fought with the loved one. What the love, when lived, looks like remains obscure.

What is possible, Unger suggests, is a question in politics. Indeed, "it's all politics." Not only is the question of what the human future will be self-evidently political. It is also that the eighteenth-century thought that a social world exists that is self-creating and self-governing, to be explained neither by legislation nor by character but by principles that are distinctively its own, has been subverted by events. That thought may have made some sense for those European worlds that in the eighteenth century were already beginning to disappear. It has subsequently made some sense for those societies that Europeans and their anthropologists had begun to discover elsewhere. But it has increasingly been overturned in the ironical outcome, in strong modern states, of the enthusiasm for popular rule which in part inspired it. As Unger argues,

> The triumph of liberal or authoritarian mass politics has weakened the system of fixed social stations that might enable people to seek their essential safety in the performance of a precise social role and in the claims upon

---

[5] This is my characterization, not Unger's; but the conclusion is similar. For a brief elaboration, see G. HAWTHORN, ENLIGHTENMENT AND DESPAIR: A HISTORY OF SOCIAL THEORY 254-75 (1987). I take one or two other reflections in this part of this Article from these pages.

[6] *See* FALSE NECESSITY at 282.

resources and support that may accompany these roles. The experience of world history, with its headlong recombination of institutional practices and ways of life, has forced whole peoples increasingly to disengage their abstract sense of collective identity from their faithfulness to particular customs.[7]

To understand that fact and to think constructively about what to do with it one has now to think of politics and law as something more than the epiphenomenal expressions of other, as it has often been said in social theory, more "fundamental," kinds of event.

The rehabilitation of politics, that is, the disinclination to believe that the answers in theoretical reason are sufficient for questions of practice, is, in the 1970s and 1980s, an increasingly common theme in discussions both of social theory and of politics. Many commentators have reacted to the collapse of practical reasoning in "positivism" or to the theoretically more deliberate attempt to preempt it in "structures." Rawls and Habermas are perhaps the most serious.[8] But even they, dissimilar in other respects though they are, are in important respects, and similarly, insufficient.

Both start with a conception of what people are, and of the most general circumstances in which they find themselves, and argue to a view of what societies that included such persons could be. Both assume that people are committed to live together and to arrive at an agreed form of, or framework for, collective life through a "reflective equilibrium" (Rawls' phrase) or through "self-reflection" (Habermas'). Both further assume—Rawls more clearly than Habermas—that having agreed to a form of collective life, people will agree to explicit principles to maintain it and will decide these principles in an equally explicit procedure. This can be done, they both believe, with the greatest practicable degree of social transparency, as Rawls calls it, with the greatest "publicity." And the society that is to be thus "public" is a society of the kind that we, as distinct from the medieval English or the citizens of modern Zaire, do now inhabit. It is a society in which incomes and wealth are the "all-purpose means," in which there are further constraints in practical life and "discourse," but in which it can make sense to imagine that there exist the will and the means to arrive at a reflective equilibrium between our intuitions and our reasons.

But neither Habermas nor Rawls makes clear how a mere understanding of a common interest—either in justice or in what Habermas calls *Mündigkeit*—might hold such a society together. Nor is it clear in either thinker for whom such a society is an option. Unlike Habermas, Rawls does see that there are innumerably many and particular loves and attachments and thick conceptions of the good. But having consigned

---

[7] FALSE NECESSITY at 524.

[8] *See generally* J. RAWLS, A THEORY OF JUSTICE (1971); J. HABERMAS, COMMUNICATION AND THE THEORY OF SOCIETY (1979).

them to the private realm, as liberal moral philosophers tend usually to do, he, like Habermas, leads us out all too easily to the politically opaque and uninteresting constituency of all the rational agents there are.

In their original impulse and formulation, each of these theories represents a retreat from social theory. Each depends to the least possible extent on any fact about any actual society, and each rests on a conception of persons which is at once thin and prior to any such society. If the theories differ, it is in their respective inclinations to teleology and in their attitudes toward the distinction between the public and the private. Rawls, unlike Habermas, has no telos; he also, unlike Habermas, distinguishes between the good, a private matter, and the right, an object of justice that is accordingly public.[9] But these differences should not obscure the fact that each, as Unger puts it, is an instance of "the disappointing consequences of the modern philosophical attempt to dispense"—Unger should say, as far as one can—"with a view of the self or of society as a basis for normative vision."[10] In reply to false necessity, he complains, they offer only emptiness; or, if they do secrete a substantive conception, they retreat. Having lost the older and putatively universal social theories, we are left with a dilemma: we either have a politics which, as a politics for us, as we are, is insufficient to motivate us; or we have sociologies which are too specific.[11]

Unger's escape from this dilemma is dramatic and clear. "The ulti-

---

[9] T.M. Scanlon's more minimal reformulation of Rawls' already minimal assumption sharpens the difference between the good and the right in a contractualist theory focusing on human motives. *See* T. Scanlon, *Contractualism and Utilitarianism*, in UTILITARIANISM AND BEYOND (A. Sen & B. Williams eds. 1982). Rawls has been characteristically well aware of the problem of motivation: "to establish [the principles of justice] it is necessary to rely on some notion of goodness, for we need assumptions about the parties' motives." J. RAWLS, *supra* note 8, at 396. Rawls adds, however, that, given what he is trying to argue, "these assumptions must not jeopardize the prior place of the concept of right." *Id.* He thus restricts them to the "bare essentials." *Id.* Scanlon proposes, as an alternative to Rawls, that "an act is wrong if its performance under the circumstances would be disallowed by any system of rules for the general regulation of behaviour which no-one could reasonably reject as a basis for unenforced, general agreement." Scanlon, *supra*, at 110-12. This principle, unlike Rawls', rules out self-sacrifice and, in Scanlon's view, "has the abstract character appropriate in an account of the subject matter of morality." *Id.* The question is whether Rawls' bare theory of motive is sufficient. A second question might be whether Scanlon's can be a motive at all.

[10] PASSION at 45.

[11] Interestingly, both Rawls and Habermas return to Kant, that is, to what one might call the formal start of what became "classical" social theory, and to the most powerfully argued instance of the modern origin of (what Unger and I agree is) the mistaken belief that answers to questions in practical reason are formally analogous to answers to questions in theoretical reason. Ironically, Rawls has in recent years withdrawn from his a priori universalism to a more relativized case. *E.g.,* Rawls, *Kantian Constructivism in Moral Theory*, 77 J. PHIL. 515-72 (1980). (Rawls' 1986 Hart Lecture at Oxford University, Judith Shklar kindly explained to me, is an instance.) Habermas has retreated from his more or less unadorned Kantianism, with its pre-Hegelian innocence of the motivating power and moral importance of particular *Sitten*, into a more naturalistic, evolutionary argument of what Unger reasonably could call a "falsely necessitarian" kind. In two very different ways, therefore, both have retreated into what is more recognizably social theory.

mate stakes in politics," he claims, "are the fine texture of personal relations."[12] Politics accordingly requires a conception of human nature that
is both fuller and more firm than that which the Kantians and other
liberals provide, but which stops short of the "metaphysical realism" in
alternative theories like those of Aristotle and Marx: a conception which
steers between the thin and arbitrary character of the one and the thick
but unacceptable preemption, what Unger sees as the causal or teleological false necessity, of the other.[13]

In the first place, the conception must have some initial claim on us
as we think we are. Unger believes that we can profitably start from the
"conceptions and projects supported by the major world religions and
the moral doctrines associated with them."[14] But, he immediately adds,
it does not much matter where we start, since a second and more important condition is that the conceptions which are worth pursuing are those
that are strengthened by criticism, rather than reduced by it. The third
condition is that those conceptions which survive the criticism also, as a
result, converge.[15]

Unger concludes that the two that do survive and converge are the
"Christian-romantic" and the modernist. Each has "two great
themes."[16] In the romantic extension of Christianity, these are "the primacy of personal encounter and of love as its redemptive moment, and
the commitment to a social iconoclasm expressive of man's ineradicable
homelessness in the world."[17] In modernism, they are the belief that
"our dealings with other individuals have primacy over the search for an
impersonal reality or good," and the belief "that no institutional order
and no imaginative vision of the varieties of possible and desirable human
association can fully exhaust the types of practical or passionate human
connection that we may have good reason to desire and a good chance to
establish."[18] Seen in this light, indeed, modernism is no more than a
"moment" in the transformation of the Christian-romantic view. But
although it corrects the Christian-romantic's tendency to locate the good
either in the transcendental or in a fixed set of rules, glossed with senti-

---

[12] FALSE NECESSITY at 518.

[13] *See* PASSION at 44-45.

[14] *Id.* at 50-51.

[15] *Id.*

[16] *Id.* at 24.

[17] *Id.* There is an affinity between Unger's hopes and Hegel's claims that "[t]he right of the
subject's particularity, his right to be satisfied, or in other words the right of subjective freedom, . . .
the pivot and the centre of the difference between antiquity and modern times," is "in its infinity . . .
given expression in Christianity and . . . has become the universal effective principle of a new form of
civilisation;" that "amongst the primary shapes which this right assumes are love, romanticism . . .
etc.," "some of which come into prominence [in Hegel's own philosophy] as the principle of civil
society and as moments in the constitution of the state;" and that the principle of and for civil
society is to be worked out in the concrete settings of concrete *Sitten*. G. HEGEL, PHILOSOPHY OF
RIGHT § 124, at 84 (T. Knox trans. 1967).

[18] PASSION at 35.

ment—the nineteenth-century, call it "bourgeois," view of the good, the view to which the first modernists were reacting—modernism can too readily tip into a self-destructive reflex of resentment, and thus, into nihilism or a fatalism about the possibility of revising the contexts it rejects. In the modernist view, which has as its principled corollary what Unger calls "ultra-theory," there can too easily be no constructive politics at all.

To redress this, Unger argues, the relentlessly particularizing impulse in modernism must be connected to a "universalizing discourse." Unger does not "deny that the categories and commitments of a normative tradition have a historically located origin."[19] Such a tradition "will probably always bear the marks of its specific historical genesis," and, to that extent, it is unrealistic to hope that social theory will be truly "universal."[20] But through the "universalizing discourse," modernism can give "revised sense . . . to the antique ambition of universality in prescriptive theories of human nature."[21] The "universalizing discourse" will "recast our ideas about sociability by diminishing their dependence upon a historically confined sense of associative possibility [and permit us to] imagine the ordering of social life that empowers us more fully by giving freer play to the two great dynamics of empowerment—the dynamics of passion and of practical problem-solving, each of which requires that our relations to one another be kept in a state of heightened plasticity."[22] Of course, this recasting "implies a gamble," but the only alternatives, Unger insists, are radical skepticism or cultural fatalism.[23] The politics that results is accordingly intended to enhance "our practical capability through the openness of social life to the recombinatorial and experimental activities of practical reason," to realize "a more complete and deliberate mastery over the imaginative and institutional contexts of our activities," and thereby to reduce the tension between "our need to participate in group life and our effort to avoid the dangers of dependence and depersonalization that accompany such engagement."[24]

The more immediate concern, "[t]he great political issue before us," is whether the social democrats are right.[25] Social democracy is the "least oppressive" of existing political models; it is the "most respectful of felt human needs, and therefore also most likely to attract the most diverse support of the most thoughtful citizens."[26] But the social-democratic ideal, Unger says, is flawed. The social democrats, he explains,

---

[19] *Id.* at 80-81.

[20] *Id.*

[21] *Id.*

[22] *Id.*

[23] *Id.*

[24] FALSE NECESSITY at 363.

[25] FALSE NECESSITY at 25.

[26] *Id.*

like most other political protagonists in "the late twentieth century North Atlantic countries," still accept a "mutually repellent" but seemingly unavoidable trio:

[A]n ideal of private community, meant to be realized in the life of family and friendship; an ideal of democratic participation and accountability, addressed to the organization of government and the exercise of citizenship; and an amalgam of voluntary contract and impersonal technical hierarchy or coordination, suited to the practical world of work and exchange.[27]

They also are imprisoned in false necessity and accordingly committed, or, as "modest eclectics," simply resigned, to a politics of what is at best limited "empowerment." Unger's program therefore diverges

from the social-democratic ideal in its advocacy of radically revised ways of organizing market economies and democratic governments, in its search for the institutional arrangements that further soften the contrast between context-preserving routine and context-revising conflict, in its preference for the styles of welfare guarantees that presuppose these institutional reforms rather than compensating for their absence, and in its effort systematically to connect involvement in local and workplace self-government with conflict over the basic terms of life.[28]

A sketch such as this cannot do justice to the extraordinary range and subtlety of Unger's argument, although it does indicate the relentless level of generality at which he almost always pursues it. Certainly, no such sketch can do justice to the force of Unger's argument. Nevertheless, among the many questions that his argument raises, one is clearly fundamental. If we accept Unger's criticism of the thinness of the purported universal conceptions of human nature in politics, and also accept that local conceptions are not incorrigible, is Unger's the only alternative? I do not think it is. I want to suggest that an alternative view of the relative importance of the "passions" and the "interests" in politics does not, as Unger says that it does, rule out what a modest eclectic might hope that a social democracy can be.

III.

There is irony, as Albert Hirschman has said, in reintroducing passion into politics:

As soon as capitalism was triumphant and "passion" seemed . . . to be restrained and perhaps even extinguished in the comparatively peaceful, tranquil, and business-minded Europe of the period after the Congress of Vienna, the world suddenly appeared empty, petty and boring . . . . The stage was set for the Romantic critique of the bourgeois order as incredibly impoverished in relation to earlier ages—the new world seemed to lack no-

---

[27] *Id.* at 271.

[28] *Id.* at 586.

bility, grandeur, mystery and above all, passion.[29]

And that critique has continued, in tones sometimes of despair, as in Max Weber, sometimes, as in Marcuse, of anger, sometimes, as in Unger himself, of hope. But whatever their temperament, the model for most of those who have in the twentieth century sought to revive the passions in public life has been the virtuous republic. However much they may have transformed it—as did Gramsci, for instance, deliberately recalling Machiavelli in his description of the revolutionary party as the "Modern Prince"—the model remains one of honor in a perpetually vigilant, and often militant, defense of what used to be thought of as manly *virtus*, Machiavelli's *virtù*.

Unger acknowledges that virtue is the apparent historical source for his own vision of empowerment.[30] "Its characteristic . . . trope," he says, "is the need to recapture the selfless devotion to collective ends that supposedly distinguished the ancient republics. Its ambition is to ensure an equality of material circumstance and to enlist a selfless devotion to the common good."[31] In practice, however, he adds, and rightly, it has been a disaster. It has inhibited practical innovation; where it has not actually encouraged violence, it has, as Aristotle and Hegel said it would, made those who pursue honor in it dependent upon the others, in whose eyes they seek that honor; and it has caused these others to sink into resentment and a diminished self-respect. Civic virtue, Unger and I agree, has been a vice.[32]

The classical idea of virtue also rested on what we might now regard as a philosophical mistake. Those who defended it thought that there were facts of the matter about character, about its nature and tendency in individual and collective life—facts of a holistic and teleological kind—and that these could be known in the way in which we know the facts of the rest of nature. The thought was, in Robert Nozick's recent formulation, that if we believe a fact of character to be true, and it is, and this is more than chance coincidence, so that if the fact in question were not true we would have a different belief, then there is a truth of character to "track."[33] But truths of disposition and character are few and far be-

---

[29] A. HIRSCHMAN, THE PASSIONS AND THE INTERESTS: POLITICAL ARGUMENTS FOR CAPITALISM BEFORE ITS TRIUMPH 132 (1977).

[30] FALSE NECESSITY at 586.

[31] *Id.* at 586-87.

[32] *Cf. id.* at 92-95 (characterizing problems of ancient republics) and 49-51 (characterizing the Soviet dilemma).

But, for an ingenious attempt to defend the compatibility in principle between civic virtue and liberty, see Skinner, *The Idea of Negative Liberty: Philisophical and Historical Perspectives*, in PHILOSOPHY IN HISTORY: ESSAYS ON THE HISTORIOGRAPHY OF PHILOSOPHY 193-221 (R. Rorty, J. Schneewind & Q. Skinner eds. 1984).

[33] R. NOZICK, PHILOSOPHICAL EXPLANATIONS 172-85 (1981). As Nozick says, this leaves "large questions open about how to individuate methods, count them, identify which method is at work, and so on." *Id.* at 184. But the answers to these questions do not affect his account of what it

tween and, even then, insufficient for the purposes of practical reasoning. If there were such truths, they would be theoretical truths, truths *of* human nature which, being true *of* all, would be truths *for* all. If we did not accept them, we would have false beliefs. But if there are such truths, they are few, and thin. They are certainly too few and too thin to be a sufficient basis for any practical reasoning in any actual circumstance. Truths for this, if "truths" they are, are both more complicated and more indeterminate. They are "truths"—if one still wants to use the word—which are truths *from* us as we see ourselves *for* our projects as we see them.[34]

Unger only partially escapes from the stronger of these two theses, and remains ambiguous. He does reject any argument about human nature that is grounded in what he calls "metaphysical realism." But he insists that there is "authority" in his conception and that three sorts of reflection can reveal it. One must ask whether the conception suggests "more readily verifiable or falsifiable ideas."[35] One must ask whether it is compatible with a "powerful social theory." Because the connections between a theory of the self and a theory of society are close, "a view of the self is indefensible if no defensible social theory can deploy or presuppose it."[36] Third, and for Unger most importantly, there is "qualified introspection." Unger suggests that each person consult his experience "and gauge the extent to which the story hits home."[37]

But not all subjective experience counts with the same weight. Having judged the faithfulness of the story to your recollected knowledge of per-

---

means for a proposition to be true. (Nor is the formulation itself affected by Nozick's own further argument, contrary to the one I suggest in this Article, that value, what he calls "bestness," also can be tracked. *Id.* at 317.) Unger prefers to talk about the ancient assumption as an assumption of what Hilary Putnam has called "metaphysical," as distinct from "internal" realism. *See* H. PUTNAM, *Why There Isn't a Ready-Made World*, in 3 REALISM AND REASON: PHILOSOPHICAL PAPERS (1983); H. PUTNAM, MEANING AND THE MORAL SCIENCES 135-36 (1978). However, Unger's characterization of metaphysical realism corresponds rather closely to Putnam's characterization of internal realism: "true or false with respect to a single coherent view of the world." PASSION at 44. For an excellent discussion of how the matters discussed in this note bear upon the natural sciences, see N. JARDINE, THE PROCESS OF INQUIRY (1986). For the best account of the influence of such matters on a human science, see B. WILLIAMS, DESCARTES: THE PROJECT OF PURE INQUIRY 292-302 (1978).

34 This distinction is illustrated by the difference between sexual desire—which is a truth *of* human nature but is alone inadequate for making any decision in one's sexual life—and self-love or compassion, or indeed love itself—which, as truths *of* human nature, are too thin and conditional and too practically and cognitively indeterminate, but which, in practical instances in particular lives, do serve as accessible "truths" *from* us as we are.

This and the following discussion owe much to Bernard Williams' essays and to conversations we had about how these thoughts might bear upon a social democracy. *See* B. WILLIAMS, ETHICS AND THE LIMITS OF PHILOSOPHY (1985) [hereinafter ETHICS]; B. WILLIAMS, MORAL LUCK: PHILISOPHICAL PAPERS (1981) [hereinafter MORAL LUCK].

35 PASSION at 86.

36 *Id.*

37 *Id.*

sonal character and collective association, you must also consider the authority of this knowledge. You must do so by evaluating both the extent to which your experience resists the given order of society and culture and the extent to which this culture and society have overcome the sharp contrast between context-preserving routine and context-revising invention. Thus, an informed reflection draws out the lessons of an accumulated conflict, which enlarge the realm of recognized possibility, and calls on the help of the imagination, which anticipates as vision what conflict has not yet produced as fact.[38]

A view of the self, one might say, is indefensible if a defensible social theory runs against it. There is something to be said for this, and I return to it. But Unger's point is more general. It is that there is a possible "knowledge" of character, that this can be arrived at through reflection, and that the reflection carries authority.

The contrary view, which also is "modernist," is that reflection on character ("character" understood as a set of dispositions and aspirations) can destroy knowledge. Reflection implies alternatives, other possibilities. Reflection on aspects of nature other than character can increase knowledge. If I persist in a belief that does not, as Nozick puts it, track natural facts, I would not have a true belief. If, on reflection, I adjusted my belief to the natural facts, I would. That is why the subjunctively conditional formulation of propositional knowledge is so illuminating.[39] But knowledge can be acquired in this way only to the extent that there is a fact of the matter, a truth to track. Once one contemplates alternative states of affairs for which there is no such fact, alternative possibilities for the ends of life, for instance, or for living a life, one loses the "knowledge" that is inherent in having (only knowing about) one way of living. If there ever were societies in which there was such knowledge—societies in which there could be no reflection on life because no alternative for life occurred to anyone in them—they have disappeared and there is no way back to them.[40] In their place are the societies we now inhabit, in and for which alternatives do exist. In these, reflection is endemic and such "knowledge" has gone.

---

[38] *Id.*

[39] Unger sees something of this. "[T]o understand any part of reality," he writes, "is to conceive it from the standpoint of variation. You discover how this part of reality works by imagining it transformed." SOCIAL THEORY at 43. But this does not quite capture the distinction that I think is important, both in itself and to Unger, between explaining something by "locating its actual connections with other things," and understanding it by locating it "in a network of possibility [and] showing the connections it would have to other non-actual things or processes." R. NOZICK, *supra* note 33, at 12.

[40] Williams invents such a society for purely expository purposes and calls it "hyper-traditional." ETHICS, *supra* note 34, at 142-48. But we have no reason to believe that such a society has ever existed. An exceptionally sensitive account of what some might think is a present-day example reveals, on the contrary, the considerable range of choice for a life, and the remarkable extent to which that choice depends upon character. *See* J. LIZOT, TALES OF THE YANOMAMI: DAILY LIFE IN THE VENEZUELAN FOREST (E. Simon trans. 1985).

One can arrive at this conclusion in another way. One can think of the tracker of facts as impartial. That is, if a fact of the matter exists, the truth of true statements about it does not depend on any further fact about the tracker. Whether the tracker arrives at the truth is an interesting question, but it is a question in the history or sociology of science. It is not a question about truth itself. Its answer does not affect the claim that, if there is a truth to track, reflection can bring a believer to believe it. In this sense, truths about those aspects of the world of which there are truths are truths that can be arrived at impartially.

But it is a mistake to think in the same way of truths about how we might lead our lives. If I ask myself how I should live, I care about the answer. If I did not, I would not have sufficient motive to ask the question. Therefore, I cannot be impartial. The life in question is *mine* and the question comes from me. Someone may think me foolish, even mad, to live as I do, but he cannot show me that I am actually wrong; we have ruled out that argument. He is left either with the claim that I am irrational—which in itself is too thin, since it requires some point of reference—or with arguments about my well-being, which, because they refer to a well-being that purportedly is mine, will only bear upon me if I agree that they are arguments to my well-being as I see it. It follows, as Bernard Williams said, that "the excellence or satisfactoriness of a life does not stand to beliefs involved in that life as premise stands to conclusion. Rather, an agent's excellent life is characterised by *having* those beliefs."[41] If therefore there were to be a convergence in the decision to lead a life in one way rather than another, the convergence would be in practical, not theoretical, reason.

It might nevertheless be said that, even if there are too few determinate truths about human nature, and, in modern societies, almost none about how one should live, practical reason must have some theoretical limits. Human beings and their lives cannot be just anything. The suggestion that they can is the exaggeration of those who claim that we are in some way "constituted" by our language and that, by talking differently, we can change. The more modest view is that people have some lasting quality that makes them who they are. There is some quality, in Richard Wollheim's way of putting it, which gives life its thread,[42] a

---

[41] ETHICS, *supra* note 34, at 154 (emphasis in original). For an earlier and more formal statement, see his *Internal and External Reasons*, in MORAL LUCK, *supra* note 34, at 101-13. Once again, Unger sees something like this, but he says that an attempted detachment would change us, which is not quite to say, as I believe, that if we achieved it, we would have no motive to do anything at all, even, perhaps, science.

[42] R. WOLLHEIM, THE THREAD OF LIFE (1984); *see also infra* note 90. For a more formal argument to a similar conclusion, see D. WIGGINS, SAMENESS AND SUBSTANCE (1980). For Wiggins' conclusions on personal identity and on the implications of alternative—what Wollheim calls "radically constructivist"—views, see *id.* at 179-82. One way of deciding between these views is implied by Judith Shklar: what theory of human nature (apart from the theories of those, like Christians, who dislike that nature) would lead us *not* to "put cruelty first" among the vices? J. SHKLAR,

thread that includes dispositions of character. (In more formal terms, individuations are sortals, and they surely have to sort over something other than one of themselves?) There will of course be moments, moments which are a function of character and circumstance and of reflection on the two, at which one will be able to do only one thing. These will be moments of true practical necessity.[43] In our public lives, however, they will be rare. In most public moments, our dispositions will be an insufficient guide to action. A full theory of disposition could be a basis for ethics and for politics, a set of truths in theoretical reason with determinate implications for practical reason. But no such theory exists, and there is reason to think that it never will. There is an inherent indeterminacy in specifying and explaining mental events.[44] It leaves us with our own indeterminate dispositions, our reflections on those and other things, and the practical reasons we produce from each.

These considerations suggest that the "qualified introspection" that Unger urges us to exercise on his conception of passion is as likely to lead us to dissent as to convince us that his particular conception of human nature and its possibilities match our existing dispositions. It is important to turn skepticism on ourselves. Skepticism about our knowledge of others, as Cavell remarks, has often and unwarrantably gone with complacency about our sense of ourselves.[45] Reflection, whether on Unger's conception of love, hope and faith,[46] or on our own dispositions, beliefs and actions, or, insofar as we can gauge them, on the dispositions, beliefs and actions of others, can only further reduce our knowledge of these things. This is so even though reflection may enhance our practical sense of the life we thereby decide that we want to lead. That life will remain *somebody's* life; if it is ours, it will remain ours. If, on reflection, we prefer some other option, our preference cannot be called a mistake. Beyond minimal limits, we have authority for ourselves.

Nothing in the view I have been proposing suggests that the passions are not important. Quite on the contrary. I merely suggest that

---

ORDINARY VICES 7-44 (1985). For a clever answer to the question, however it is posed, see D. PARFIT, REASONS AND PERSONS (1984). Parfit argues for the substantive sense, conceptual coherence, and liberating implications of a causal view of persons in which the closest and most crucial causal connections may not be those through one life (me now and me as a child) but between lives (me and you) and, given progress in medical science, between actual matter (bits of me joined with bits of you). For him this means that identity does not matter. Parfit's view also licenses utilitarianism by undermining one of the most powerful objections to it, that is, that utilitarianism does not respect people as indivisible and continuing. Nothing in this argument about personal identity applies to institutions, the "thread" of which can at most be interests and the continuity of these interests in convention and codification in law.

[43] MORAL LUCK, *supra* note 34, at 124-31.

[44] Unger comments on this in his remarks about psychiatry, but again seems to resist the most radical implication for explanation. *See* PASSION at 282-85.

[45] S. CAVELL, THE CLAIM OF REASON: WITTGENSTEIN, SKEPTICISM, MORALITY AND TRAGEDY 109 (1979).

[46] *See* PASSION at 220-50, especially 247.

because we cannot determine what the passions are, any conception we have of them can have authority over us only to the extent that it in some way, at some point, fits our existing dispositions. Only if a conception appears to us, from where we are, to have such authority, can it be said to have what Unger calls "prescriptive force." This view certainly leaves the rest of Unger's argument more or less in place. It does not license a simple relativism, or, as I will explain in part IV, the conservatism, cynicism, or simple resignation that Unger fears will follow from it. It does not say that reflection is idle. It merely says that reflection will not produce this kind of knowledge. Admittedly, my view retreats from Unger's occasionally extreme formulations of his own opinion.[47] But nothing in it suggests that any of our dispositions, including our dispositions to what Unger thinks of as passion, are immune to greater social transparency or to practical social involvement. On the contrary, the claim that they were immune would betray my view of our dispositions. It would suggest that our dispositions are natural facts to track and that they are as they are independent of our reflection on them. And the more purely pragmatic part of Unger's pointedly political argument, that "the dynamics of . . . practical problem-solving . . . requires that our relations to one another be kept in a state of heightened plasticity,"[48] still stands.

IV.

Theoretically, the view that I have been outlining may seem to be even more radical than Unger's. One might even think it licenses the license of "ultra-theory." But it does not. It holds on to a thin if indeterminable dispositional thread. Politically, however, my view might be thought, as Unger fears, more conservative. If a proposal for radical change has to sit with my existing dispositions, and my existing disposi-

---

[47] Unger claims, for instance, that "our elementary desires" can "change under the influence," not only "of an altered understanding of society," but also of "personality, of thought and language." FALSE NECESSITY at 367. Unger sometimes comes close to the radical antirealist position that, since everything is "constituted" by thought and language, we cannot know (in Hilary Putnam's joke) that we are not brains in a vat, wired up in such a way as to believe that we are who we are, using language in the way that we are. The antirealist must consider Putnam's reply: concepts are not identical with mental objects of any kind; we cannot simply *say* to ourselves that we are brains in a vat and thereby have sufficient grounds for believing that we understand the world and act in it in the way that we actually do. It follows either that we are brains in a vat with some very different ideas about what we are up to, which we are not, because we do not, or that we are not brains in a vat. If we are not brains in a vat, we are concept-using creatures who, when asked questions about the identity of things other than ourselves, give answers that turn on existence, and who, when asked such questions about ourselves, give answers that turn (at the very least) on what it is to be the kind of thing, for instance a concept-using creature, that a person is. *See* H. PUTNAM, REASON, TRUTH, AND HISTORY 1-21, especially 20-21 (1981); *cf.* S. CAVELL, *supra* note 45, at 207 (starting from a less amusing place, that is, Wittgenstein and J.L. Austin, to "put the human animal back into language and therewith back into philosophy").

[48] PASSION at 80-81.

tions have been formed by my past experiences, including my experiences with others (whose dispositions were formed by experiences that go even further back), then I may not be inclined to accept it. The change might not be a change for me that could be a change *from* me, as and where I now am. "The effect of liberty on individuals," Burke remarked, "is that they may do what they please: We ought to see what it will please them to do, before we risque congratulations, which may soon be turned into complaints."[49]

So if, for example, I cannot envisage personal fulfillment in a world other than one in which there is "private community, meant to be realized in the life of family and friendship," "democratic participation and citizenship," and "an amalgam of voluntary contract and impersonal technical hierarchy or coordination, suited to the practical world of work and exchange," then so be it. My only alternatives are either to reconsider the matter from an impartial standpoint or to accede to someone else's more substantive, perhaps even passionate, conception. Both are moves that, as the "I" that I am, in the circumstances in which I find myself, I am unlikely to be motivated to take. If I do accede, the conception will not be my own, or, at least, certainly will not be something to which I arrived or acceded in a practical, rational fashion.

But of course, the options are not so closed. First, and more generally, experience does not so firmly form anyone's dispositions. In a society for which social democracy has been or remains an option, that is, in a society that is at least moderately open, dispositions will be, at least in part, the product of reflection. And there will always be room for more reflection. In particular, there will always be room for more reflection on how our dispositions were formed. This is the truth in so-called Critical Theory, once one brackets out that theory's pre-modern ambition to show us our "real interest," its nostalgia for the absolute, its mistaken belief that we can know the ends to be pursued in life. Reflection on the causes of one's beliefs, and on the consequences of continuing to hold them, can bring one to change them, and accordingly to embrace a proposal for radical change.[50] Second, reflecting on the origins of one's commitment to a social democracy and on the consequences of maintaining that commitment leads to the conclusion that Unger may be right about it, although, given what I have said previously, he cannot be right for quite his reasons. An important distinction may exist, implicit yet easily

---

49 E. BURKE, REFLECTIONS ON THE REVOLUTION IN FRANCE 91 (C.C. O'Brien ed. 1968).

50 For an excellent distillation of the truth and the falsity—the false claims to cognitive truth—in the stronger versions of Critical Theory, see R. GUESS, THE IDEA OF A CRITICAL THEORY 75-88 (1981). So, for example, someone may reflect, counterfactually or subjunctively, on being where others are and in that sense being them. Having done so, he may be led *from where he is* to agree to principles of justice that only can be agreed to by adopting what I think of as an unintelligible "third-" rather than "first-person" view of the self. But for a defense of double vision, from inside and outside, see T. NAGEL, MORTAL QUESTIONS 196-213 (1978).

overlooked in his seemingly seamless case, between the conditions and practical consequences of such reflection in any particular place and Unger's own more distant goal.

Unger insists throughout his work that how we think and what we think about our attributes and possibilities are affected by the institutions there are and by the ideas there are about them. "To an astonishing degree [our] active belief in the pieties of a social world depends on the quiescence of that world."[51] This is so whether "we" are citizens of the so-called first world, to whom he says his proposals are primarily directed, or citizens of countries like his own Brazil, which prompts his own more immediate hopes.[52]

One such set of experiences and ideas, close—one might almost say intrinsic to—both the liberal impulse in social democracy (its wish to treat all citizens equally) and its impulse to reform, is the administrative style of politics. Formal administration, what the sociologists often call "bureaucracy," is, of course, pervasive. But two arguments, which, as Unger repeatedly hints, are more generally implicit in the conventional defense of liberal social democracy, converge on the conclusion that bureaucracy also is desirable. One argument is Kantian, the other utilitarian. The former is that our conceptions of the good, of the substantive ends of life, are a function of our desires. In Kant's own metaphysics, these conceptions are in the phenomenal self and are heterogeneous and perhaps incompatible. They cannot be the basis of a politics, which must lie in reason, seated in the noumenal self. Reason's condition is a freedom to form rational rules, which, being rational, will secure the assent of all the citizens. These rules will ensure freedom, which is the condition of reason. Hence the priority in politics and law, as Rawls suggests, of the right over the good. And hence institutions for rules.

The utilitarian argument starts in an entirely different place. Individuals are seats of desire and the object of a politics is to maximize those desires. But the desires, utilitarians imply, can be separated from their seats and aggregated or otherwise combined for collective purposes. There is no privileged position except that of the calculator in the ministry, who takes, as best he can, what Henry Sidgwick called "the point of view of the Universe." There are other differences. The Kantians' distinction between the right and the good, for instance, forces a distinction between the public and the private, which utilitarians not only do not need, but cannot coherently concede. Nonetheless, the two arguments converge on the conclusion that a settled politics is and must be essentially an administrative matter.

However, administration is, as Unger would say, "routine." It imposes uniformity and encourages passivity and is notoriously prone to

---

[51] SOCIAL THEORY at 41.
[52] *Id.* at 67-79.

imaginative and practical closure. Accordingly, administration is inimical to the open inquiry and debate required not only by strong theories of the possibility of a pervasive passion, like Unger's, but by theories such as my own. (Contrary to the Kantians, I hold that passion prompts reason; I insist, against the utilitarians, that passion exists in individuals who are in part created by it and continue as discernible persons—in politics and in other things—to be motivated by it; and I insist, with the Critical Theorists, that imaginative reflection is itself essential to politics.)

Practically, however, administration is unavoidable. Even those like Unger, "whose hopes depend upon our further emancipation from false necessity, cannot bypass the state; they must rebuild it."[53] In Unger's own program of radical reconstruction, public administration remains to adjudicate "destabilization rights."[54] Ironically, administration will preserve rights that "protect the citizen's interest in breaking open the large-scale organizations or the extended areas of social practice that remain closed to the destabilizing effects of ordinary conflict."[55] Unger also, one presumes, contemplates a similar institution to adjudicate "immunity rights," rights, he says, which are not just "a last-ditch defense against despotic governments" or, as in the United States, "an ecstatic deviation from the tenor of ordinary social life," but intended to provide protection and welfare.[56]

In a more reforming spirit, Unger envisages administration of a "central capital fund." This is "to draw the limits of variation within which the competing investment funds [that it establishes] must operate." It will do so by setting the outer limits on forms of production and exchange and on the employment and price of capital itself. Its most far-reaching consequence, Unger insists, must be completely to separate all "right" in the society from the right to property.[57] Unger also envisages administration in conceding, if uneasily, that the political body "responsible for systematic interventions . . . should have at [its] disposal the technical, financial, and human resources required by any effort to reorganize major institutions and to pursue the reconstructive effort over time."[58] Although he does not elaborate, Unger also, one supposes, would adopt similar administrations in the organization of foreign affairs and defense and other matters with which modern governments must concern themselves and for which expertise is necessary.

Opinions will differ on the extent to which these institutions are feasible. Several, most particularly the institution that guarantees "destabilization rights," are a considerable distance away from the pro-

---

[53] FALSE NECESSITY at 312.
[54] *See id.* at 530-35.
[55] *Id.* at 530.
[56] *Id.* at 526-27; *see also id.* at 524-30.
[57] *Id.* at 493.
[58] *Id.* at 453.

posals even of Unger's most radical contemporaries in social democracies. Others, however—especially if one includes Japan and Brazil in the list of democracies—are a good deal closer.[59] I discuss these different distances in part V. The more immediate issue is what Unger offers in place of the modest eclectic's acceptance of existing patterns of political competition and representation. To succeed, Unger's alternative must ensure that those who exercise control, and particularly economic control, are not able to hold the state hostage[60] and that a more empowered society does not also become more divided and unstable.

Unger agrees that our existing commitments to representative democracy are among the most entrenched of our ideas. He does not want to undermine them. But he insists that we see how very accidental are the representative procedures to which we are so committed. There have been two such accidents. The first was the invention of liberal constitutions, which, he recalls, "sought to grant rule to a cadre of politically educated and financially secure notables, free from both clientalistic dependence and untrammeled factionalism and fully able to safeguard the polities they governed against mob rule and the seduction by demagogues."[61] The second accident is what, given this fear of mob rule and demagogues, was the "surprise" of universal suffrage and the emergence of once feared and detested factions, now called parties, to compete for the vote.[62]

According to a "mythical history" of democracy, "the trials and errors of modern political experience, and the undoubted failure of many proposed alternatives, have confirmed that the emergent institutional solutions were much more than flukes."[63] Needing to present themselves as something other than gangs of pillagers, and to preserve their contin-

---

[59] The policies of the Ministries of Finance and of International Trade and Industry in Japan are well-known successes. Less recognized are the successful innovations of Geisel's military administration in Brazil, from 1973 to 1979, in contrast to the hesitancies of Figueiredo's civilian regime (1979-85). Nevertheless, it would be too simple to infer that only a government with the powers of Geisel's (or as insulated from pressure from below as Japan's) could be so successful. After all, the technical ingenuity of the Cruzado Plan to reduce inflation in 1986 was matched by corresponding political imagination, both in the way in which the plan was devised and its authority conferred, and in the way in which President Sarney managed to turn it into a popular crusade for shoppers in every street. (The point is not affected, I believe, by the fact that by late 1987, the Plan was in ruins and inflation was once again rising at a worrying rate.) The Plan perhaps provides an example of the "new political spaces," mentioned in part V, which many people are imagining, creating, and deploying in countries that have recently emerged from a period of non-democratic rule. The Plan also confirms (what I take to be) Unger's conviction that the political initiative has now moved away from the older democracies. This is not to say that there are not sad exceptions: more than two years after the death of Sekou Touré, I heard a Guinean journalist remark that he and his countrymen were still "waiting for a text."

[60] FALSE NECESSITY at 368-73.

[61] *Id.* at 209.

[62] *Id.* at 213-21.

[63] *Id.* at 211.

ued credibility, parties adopted and implemented broad and reasonably altruistic programs. They also set out to privatize religion and to make society more fluid and fragmented.[64] But this history must be set against the question why two world wars and a few colonial wars after that were fought before the inevitability of these arrangements (at least in Europe) became apparent. More importantly, it must be set against the error of assuming that the fluidity of a liberal politics is a function of a fluid, liberal society. In fact, Unger argues, such a politics only can work in a society in which social forms, especially the consolidated property right and its consequences, are fairly well fixed. Accordingly, a liberal politics is a politics committed to the fixity of social forms.[65]

This is not to say that an empowered democracy should not start from existing political parties. Those who want a new democracy should start by working through the parties on the left.[66] In countries with a strong statist tradition, they might also work with those in the lower echelons of government. These people, like those in the administration of agrarian programs in Latin America, are more radical and have more room to manuever than one would expect. But there is no principled reason to be committed to existing institutions. Indeed, Unger's argument demands that one should not be so committed. We have every reason eventually to work beyond and in some instances perhaps even to transcend such institutions.

For two reasons, our journey to a new democracy will not be a predictable and "relentless march."[67] First, Unger's argument insists that the most vivid and empowering conceptions of possibility will arise only out of the activities themselves. Second, we cannot now foresee the limits to the possible. There will be messes, with much duplication. We have good reason to encourage such duplication, both to extend and to limit powers. For instance, we should reintroduce the experiments with "dual constitutions." Such experiments were attempted in several European countries in the inter-war period, cut short in the international conditions of that time, and repeated in Iceland in 1944 and Portugal in

---

[64] *Id.* at 218.

[65] In this connection, see A. PRZEWORSKI, CAPITALISM AND SOCIAL DEMOCRACY (1985). Przeworski's work demonstrates, in line with Unger, that "when election results and collective bargaining outcomes have no visible impact upon the material conditions of wage-earners, masses become dissociated from their representatives." *Id.* at 163. Contrary to Unger, Przeworski says that when "the institutional crisis of several advanced capitalist societies" becomes "a crisis of participation," the answer is to renew conventional participation—resorting to "movements" only inflames and antagonizes, and risks resolving nothing—because conventional participation "reduces political activities to material issues, and these can be resolved under capitalism in a cooperative" and predictable manner. *Id.* at 163. Przeworski's is the clearest and most intelligent defense of the more usual, "modestly eclectic," view of its subject. This is not to say that his arguments and conclusions are self-evident or that Przeworski does not also see some of what Unger sees.

[66] *See* FALSE NECESSITY at 542.

[67] *Id.* at 127.

1978.[68] As false necessity reappears as mere contingency, imagination should prevail, and, in Unger's conception of the "ultimate stake," the relations between people should reach a point of irreversible transparency and passion.

A modest eclectic will nevertheless press the question of why those with property should not hold us hostage and why, for this and other reasons, the extending and increasingly passionate democracy should not collapse into the self-destructive conflict that vitiated the older models of virtue and passion in politics. After all, and aside from externally imposed exigencies—one thinks, for instance, of the turbulence of Europe before 1939 and of the horrible, if ironic, effects of the Nixon Doctrine on the internal politics of several American allies after 1969—this skepticism has a foundation in democracy's own history and theory. Democratic theorists have repeatedly insisted "that democratic government will work to full advantage only if all the interests that matter" within the nation "are practically unanimous not only in their allegiance to the country but also in their allegiance to the structural principles of the existing society."[69]

Unger freely concedes that an empowered democracy would destroy certain sorts of security. If, to feel safe, people required a "quiescent polity," that is, the assurance of a consolidated property right, a "lifelong guarantee to occupy a particular job," or—he adds a little tendentiously—to live a life "in the manner customary to a certain caste," they will feel insecure in Unger's democracy.[70] "But," he replies, "if the ideals and understanding underlying this institutional program hold up, people will have reason to change their views of what essential security consists in."[71] They will do so "in part by finding senses and varieties of security compatible with an ever greater jumbling up of distinct styles of life and in part by awakening to a conception of the personality as both dependent upon context and [upon] context smashing."[72]

This is Unger's hope. But he also has an argument. He overturns the more conventional democratic theorists[73] by ingeniously suggesting

---

[68] *Id.* at 447.

[69] J. SCHUMPETER, 3 CAPITALISM, SOCIALISM, AND DEMOCRACY 296 (1950); *cf., e.g.,* R. DAHL, POLYARCHY 203 (1971). For an account of the paradoxes of the Nixon-Kissinger Doctrine—its devolution of responsibility for security against the Soviet Union to regional "middle powers" that it also wanted to "modernize," its equation between international security and the internal security of these regimes, and the elision in turn between that and its toleration of internal repression—see R. LITWAK, DETENTE AND THE NIXON DOCTRINE: AMERICAN FOREIGN POLICY AND THE PURSUIT OF STABILITY, 1969-76 (1984). The most extreme instance of these effects was the Shah's Iran.

[70] FALSE NECESSITY at 514.

[71] *Id.*

[72] *Id.*

[73] Przeworski, who has much the same view as Unger on this issue, is an exception. *See generally* A. PRZEWORSKI, *supra* note 65.

that ideological conflict is not just a disabling condition for liberal politics, but also its consequence:

> The feature of the conflict over the basic arrangements of society that most directly makes it resistant to compromise is, paradoxically, its characteristic vagueness, its elusive and almost dreamlike quality. The less the abstract vision championed by the contending parties is worked into a texture scheme of social life, the flimsier the basis for any compromise. In the absence of a detailed plan for a reordered society, the only sure sign of victory becomes the triumph of an exclusive allegiance: The defeat of the disbelievers and the rise of the orthodox.[74]

Religious dispute will disappear from politics if politics causes it to reappear in a different guise. This would not occur in an empowered democracy, because politics and social life would cease to be so separate. Hopes and realities would converge, and ideology, the function of impotence in distance, would dissolve in a constructive pragmatism. In that respect, but in that respect only, we return to the arguments for capitalism before its triumph.

V.

This also, one might say—as for the early-modern enemies of passion—is hope. But two further things make it difficult in advance to say anything more definite about it. First, if my earlier argument is correct, whether or not ideology dissolves into a constructive pragmatics is a function not only, as Unger insists, of the greater fluidity of the new society, the corresponding increase in personal contact, and of how those changes affect people's sense of possibility; nor is it, as more conventional theorists, like Przeworski, suggest, just a function of a narrowed range of disputes in the new society. It is also and to an unknown and in advance unknowable extent independently of either, a function of the dispositions of the people themselves.

Second, one of Unger's own arguments rules out examples. One can travel through the almost interminable literature on democratic polities and distill from it the conditions for democracy. One can then transfer one's findings to other cases and ask whether the other cases meet the conditions. This seems unexceptionable. But the process also can be fruitless, because mistaken and, thus, in Albert Hirschman's word, "pernicious."[75] At the limit, the process can produce the erroneous and arrogant conclusion—as the political adviser at a British embassy in Latin America put it to me recently—that a country consists of "political children" who need "another three hundred years" of steady social evolution.

The mistake that undermines attempts to test for conditions of de-

---

[74] FALSE NECESSITY at 465.

[75] A. HIRSCHMAN, *Notes on Consolidating Democracy in Latin America*, in RIVAL VIEWS OF MARKET SOCIETY AND OTHER ESSAYS 176 (1986).

mocracy is the mistake that Unger identifies in his critique of "positivist social science." If one had applied one's "findings" in empirical democratic theory to, say, Japan in 1946, or Venezuela in 1956, or Argentina, Brazil or Uruguay in the early 1980s, one would have concluded that democracy in these places was not possible. The traditions in each case were inimical to democracy, the internal divisions too deep, the levels of living and education too low, and the political expertise perhaps insufficient. But each of these places has surprised us. The Japanese accepted the constitution imposed on them in 1947 and have since maintained it, even if not quite in the way that General MacArthur envisioned. The four Latin American countries have moved to what is clearly, if in one or two cases still precariously, an open and democratic politics. Moreover, there are moves in several Latin American countries now also to invent, occupy, and deploy what Latin Americans call the "new spaces" of politics. Confirming Unger's explanation of the causes of ideological divisions in societies with a liberal politics, these countries have turned the tables on the more established democracies. The South now demonstrates (in contrast to several countries in the North, including the United States and Britain) a surprising openness, a refusal to resort to fixed and abstract, as it is sometimes said, "ideological" solutions.

But it still does not follow that Unger's argument, which he presents as an argument *for* us all, is one that can be expected to bite equally *from* where we each are. At one extreme are the more fundamental of the many groups of *Islamiyyoun* in the Middle East, like the *Salafiyyn* in Saudi Arabia, who wish quite literally to return to the society the Prophet left at his death in 632. As they presently see themselves, they must be immune to Unger's argument. Also immune, if less obviously so, might be the "Confucian." In Unger's view, these people are superior, even to "Christian-romantics" and their modernist descendants. Their superiority lies in their "sureness of focus on the relation between the personal and the social," their recognition of "the other person as the ground on which the whole life of passion develops," and their acknowledgement of the "dynamism of the life of passion" and of the "readiness with which apparently different passions change into one another and the rightful subordination of all of them to a central impulse."[76] But, as Unger immediately adds, "[o]n their way to becoming concrete moral and political teachings," these Confucian insights become "combined and contaminated with the implications of the naturalistic view."[77] The disposition to subordinate passions to a "central impulse" can lead to mistaking "a specific system of social division and hierarchy for the scheme of social life that can best reconcile the conflicting conditions of self-assertion."[78] Even where "Confucians" do break out, as they did in

---

[76] PASSION at 66-67.

[77] *Id.* at 67.

[78] *Id.*

the cultural revolution in China from 1966 to 1969, the upshot of the "breakthrough [can be] defined as a return to a clearer version of preexisting institutions."[79] "Surely a background condition [of the cultural revolution]," Unger suggests, "was the tilt toward restabilization" and political demobilization "inherent in the available technologies and organizational forms—the ones that China had largely imbibed from the West."[80] But he might also acknowledge that surely another condition was the "Confucian" disposition that he describes.

At the other extreme, although rather less obviously, is the kind of politics built on a dispersed set of entitlements "against the state and . . . power over others,"[81] in which entitlements are treated as property rights. However these entitlements are justified, by a state-defined legal order, for instance, or unspoken constitutional arrangements, or precepts of natural right, the justifications are an additional level of defense against the transformative powers of the state and the modest surprises of routine politics.[82] The entitlements can moreover coexist "with a severely restricted measure of participation in government—a restriction that may apply even to the groups benefiting most directly from the order of powers and immunities."[83] For societies at this extreme, like Britain since 1979, it may be too simple to say that "the state must be arranged in ways that keep routine politics on this narrow path."[84] The Conservative government in the United Kingdom has rearranged some entitlements, perhaps more radically than any government in recent years. The rearrangements were prompted by exactly that escalation of ideology that Unger explains so well. In inspiration and in practice, the rearrangements have been partial, but they may change the hitherto "routine" terms of debate; even if, in the currently weak and divided opposition to them, the British appear still to have no conception of a politics for themselves beyond trying miserably to restore old immunities.

At one extreme, that is to say, are societies, like those of the Islamic East, in which the conception of politics and of the authority for politics runs entirely against invention, experiment, and an open future. From many otherwise different readings, the Koran is a scripturally authorized collectivism of conception far more closed than anything that now exists in the politics of the West or the European East. At the other extreme, the conception in societies like Britain places supreme importance on institutional autonomies and personal privacy. This conception appears to rule out not only the creation of more openness from below, but also the

---

[79] FALSE NECESSITY at 245.
[80] *Id.* at 246.
[81] *Id.* at 131.
[82] *Id.*
[83] *Id.* at 132.
[84] *Id.* at 133.

sorts of central institutions that Unger imagines, even the seemingly least intrusive one that guarantees "immunity" rights. These extremes clearly are not preemptions of a similar kind, or even preemptions at all. To think that they are is to make the mistake, as Unger would say, that "positivists" make. After all, Middle Eastern states occasionally demonstrate understanding of a conception of politics other than those that their more orthodox subjects find in the holy book. (What might Mossadeq have achieved in Iran?) And Britain and the United States, especially in time of war, have managed hastily to invent directive institutions that prevailing sentiments and justifications should have forbidden. Even more surprising moments of invention have occurred elsewhere.[85] As both Unger and Hirschman insist, much more is possible than our usual ways of thinking lead us to suppose. There are always surprises.

Nevertheless, we would not ourselves be surprised if Unger's argument appealed most directly in societies most like the one in which his own dispositions were formed. These appear to be societies—societies which are also exceptionally self-conscious nations—in which there is a Christian tradition, but in which there is also a sense of the unreality, or magical reality, in any actual political arrangement, which makes them hosts to modernism; societies, in which, because of their Iberian past, there is a conception of strong and perhaps even incorporative central rule; societies, however, in which, in the ideals with which they came to independence, there is an equally deep and now ineradicable sense of what it means freely to combine against such rule. Because of the wildly oscillating political history in the lives and thus the memories of a single generation, people in these societies find it easier to think in a way that is at once radical and not fantastical.

VI.

What I have said suggests three virtually self-evident conclusions and a doubt. The first conclusion is that political surprises are surprises and do occur. As Unger says, we have no reason in principle, that is to say, in imaginable practice, to rule out altogether the possibility of any of the political moves that he suggests. A modified view of the inescapable place of passion in politics requires that one rethink some of the most pervasive and particular presumptions, not least those that derive from existing justifications for the present scope, nature, and naturalness of public administration. Second, the moves that Unger suggests are much

---

[85] One striking instance of these are the short-lived but apparently successful institutions—to collect taxes, run factories, and other things—invented by indigenous Korean Communists in 1945 and 1946, between the effective departure of the Japanese and the consolidation of the Soviet-backed North Korean regime and the establishment of the United States Military Government in the south, each of which soon imposed its pre-given models. The experiments are striking in themselves and because there was nothing in the political history or political "culture" of Korea to lead one to expect them. *See* G. HENDERSON, KOREA: THE POLITICS OF THE VORTEX 321-22 (1968).

more imaginable from some places than from others. Third, if Britain, with its disabling combination of ideological inflammation and lack of imagination, is an example of the North Atlantic democracies to which Unger directs his argument, some of these places may not soon be where he hopes they will.

The doubt is about the compatibility between Unger's proposals and the more immediate end of improving the material conditions of the majority. If one concedes that there is a distance between working to improve these conditions within the existing state of affairs and changing this state of affairs to increase autonomy, then one must ask whether this distinction is merely a distance, as Unger believes, or, as Przeworski argues, a real difference, which, in more effectively using the institutions there are, reduces the desire to change them.[86] The answer may turn, not only on the causes of desire, but also on the question of how far those with an interest in the entitlements and procedures of the status quo are willing to defend them with force. Unger's answer probably would be: "Let us see."

But this uncertainty could take a toll, and, together with my earlier suggestions, it prompts three opposing considerations. The first is that— although one can come to something like Unger's own political conclusions, or at least, not resist them, from an even more radical premise than his—the practical reasoning of the agents from and for whom these might be the conclusions may be a reasoning, in virtue of those agents' dispositions and circumstances, which does not incline them to Unger's own view of the importance of passion in politics. It certainly cannot be said that they would be making a mistake if they were not to be so inclined. Second, even if it were, they may decide that the practical and emotional space which such a politics would take up would inhibit the pursuit of other things that the passion prompts.[87]

A third and deeper, though indeterminate, consideration might follow from this. Cavell observes that Othello, perhaps the most Christian and the most romantic of Shakespeare's heroes, had a need for love and its affirmation that caused a "rage for proof."[88] Othello's "Christian-romanticism," it is true, is not Unger's. Othello could not find that delicate balance to which Unger aspires, the balance that lies between affirmation from a context and the acknowledgement in the other that can prevent dependence on the context.[89] Othello could not live in or out of his new marriage, and I do not think that he could have lived a politics of passion that was not heroic. He was a Christian, and so hated being

---

[86] A. PRZEWORSKI, *supra* note 65, at 247-48.

[87] "Socialism," said Oscar Wilde, "takes too many evenings." A politics of passion—even, or especially, if it lingers on, as Unger hopes that it will, in conversations after the meetings are over—may be thought to take too many evenings away from what passion elsewhere dictates.

[88] S. CAVELL, *supra* note 45, at 495.

[89] PASSION at 247-71.

human. But even if we are not Christians, and do not hate being human, we cannot do without love, and this need can cause for us, as for Othello, the rage for proof. In the impulse to affirmation, the rage for proof also might be caused by a passion in politics, which some of us as we now are could do without, because we have always done without it. If so, our ambition for affirmation and transparency may only be satisfied peaceably and predictably, if not with full passion, in friendship. But friendship, if not "mutually repellent" to either, is nevertheless less than love and not obviously sufficient to politics.[90]

The promise in the conversation that Unger so brilliantly begins, and certainly the promise in a more open politics, is that this may be wrong. My anxious eclectic hopes that it is. But if it is, this will be a truth of practice, and not of theory.

---

[90] This suggests a continuity, if also a distance, between the various states. But this is not uncontested. For Cavell, love is to do with "reciprocity" and "acknowledgement"; for Wollheim, friendship also is to do with "acceptance," "the overcoming of confusion, the abatement of intolerance, and the relinquishment of certain controlling attitudes." R. WOLLHEIM, *supra* note 42, at 279-80. At first sight, these conceptions seem to be similar both to each other, and to what I have said here, and compatible with Unger's position in *Passion*. But Wollheim insists that love and friendship "stand contrasted . . . in the feelings, emotions, and beliefs that they draw upon, and . . . also differ in their characteristic histories." *Id*. The center of the contrast, he suggests, is that in love we involuntarily respond and only later, if at all, aquire the "attitude" of acceptance; in friendship, by contrast, we start with the attitude and only later, if at all, come to love. And the love we have for friends is not exclusive, as is the love we have for lovers. We almost always serially substitute for friendship, but rarely if ever do so for love. *Id*. I do not find Wollheim as persuasive as the others, but I mention his differences from them simply to point out the inherent contestability of the matter. Nevertheless, having begun with Kierkegaard's remark that in saying we have to understand life backwards, the philosophers forget that we have to live it forwards, Wollheim concludes with a view that is consistent with my own: that for much of the time, actually leading a life is, or is mostly, understanding it. We have different lives and, especially after reflection, often have different understandings. I have pursued the question of the continuities and discontinuities of love, friendship and public life before reading Unger in Hawthorn, *Three Ironies in Trust*, in TRUST (D. Gambetta ed. forthcoming 1988).

RADICAL POLITICS IN A NEW KEY?

Tony Judt

In the introduction to *Politics*,[1] Professor Unger notes that the defeat of the radical project has produced an awareness that nothing has to be the way it is, combined with a "conviction that nothing important can be changed by deliberate collective action."[2] This apparently devastating combination of the more pessimistic strands of ethical voluntarism and naturalistic social analysis leaves us, according to Unger, at an impasse. We must somehow break clear of a style of social understanding which explains mankind as helpless puppets of the worlds they inhabit and the forces which made them. The problem, however, is that we must do so without abandoning the insight we have gained into the identity of those forces, without which action, however morally informed, stands in serious risk of proving futile, at best.

Unger's book is a polemic against "deep-structure social analysis."[3] Nonetheless, he admits that the Marxist version of such analysis has indeed provided the tools for remaining faithful to Marx's own anti-naturalistic intentions. Consequently, he retreats to the earlier assertion of radical analysis: everything is contextual and all contexts can be broken. His point is that we should not deny the constraints upon us, but should rather dispel the illusions which prevent us from seeing them as constraints.

Whether there is any more real coherence in this line of argument than in the ancient assertions of Engels and others about men being both free and yet determined ("in the final analysis") by material forces is far from clear. Unger suggests that rather than create another world to realize our dreams, we should do the undreamt of in this world. However, this is a wish that cannot be fulfilled without some further thought along what he would call "old-fashioned" lines. It is not enough to dispel naturalistic illusions in order to create a psychological space in which we can feel free: we still need reasons for believing that our actions will result in outcome A (or, at least, that they will not result in outcome B). Perhaps this was less true in the last century, when such criticisms of the naturalistic fallacies might have been well taken, but recent history enjoins us to be a trifle more cautious about doing the "undreamt of"—at least it

---

[1] SOCIAL THEORY.

[2] *Id.* at 2.

[3] *Id.* at 87-96.

speaks thus to the fortunate residents of Western Europe and North America.

It is not, however, my purpose in this Essay to investigate the practical plausibility of Unger's own "frankly speculative" writings. What interests me is the remarkable extent to which their appearance coincides with certain developments within the radical spectrum of European politics. A closer inspection of these developments may prove more useful as a guide to the real implications of rethinking the radical project in this way.

Ever since 1789, European radical thought has focused upon the ideas and practices associated with protest in France—not just for Marx himself, who built much of his social theory upon his readings and observations of French political conflict, but for anyone who, from 1789 until 1917, proposed to construct a theory in defense of radical political action. Not only did the French Revolution provide a model for radical practice in its organizations, its *journées*, its constitutions, and its very message of what a revolution is, but it also provided the legitimating metalanguage of revolution, the teleological account which made it acceptable in the face of reason and force, derived directly from the story of the French Revolution as a bourgeois revolution—a story already nearly a generation old for French liberal historians when Marx first published his own thoughts on the subject. The Bolshevik Revolution and its own claims for itself are irrelevant, since they too fed parasitically upon a reading of the meaning of modern history which, though it did not derive from the French experience, depended on it for empirical sustenance.[4]

It should not surprise us, therefore, to find that much radical thought in the nineteenth and twentieth centuries not only originated and was structured upon the French experience, but also borrowed its goals, programs and unvoiced assumptions. What other than the French experience can explain the radical obsession with central control, with seizing the state, with *directing* society? These goals were certainly not inherent in the earlier traditions of protest in Britain or Italy. Only in the United States, where the indigenous traditions of dissent parted company with Europe before the onset of French discursive hegemony in these matters, did things develop otherwise.[5]

In the twentieth century, the center of revolutionary discourse and power shifted to Moscow, but only in order to transmit back to Central

---

[4] For a fuller argument along these lines, see T. JUDT, MARXISM AND THE FRENCH LEFT chs. 1 & 2 (1986); *see also* F. FURET, PENSER LA RÉVOLUTION FRANÇAISE (1986); F. FURET, LA GAUCHE ET LA RÉVOLUTION FRANÇAISE AU MILIEU DU XIXE SIÈCLE (1986).

[5] It could be suggested that the Left in Spain did not follow French radical thought, which accorded primacy to the seizure and control of society via the state apparatus, because there were alternative strains of radical thought among the Spanish Left. However, this does not weaken my argument but rather shows the significant impact of the French model of revolutionary organization even in places peculiarly unsuited to it.

and Western Europe a language and a project remarkably similar to earlier French efforts. Witness the contemporary accusation directed at Lenin, that he was peddling *"blanquisme à la sauce tartare,"*[6] hence the easy grafting of communism onto the indigenous French socialist tradition.[7] Elsewhere, the appeal of the Leninist claim—that Bolshevism actually *made* a revolution, a claim not available to anyone else in Europe then or, arguably, since—enabled it to bury for good what remained of syndicalist, cooperative, or regional traditions in most of the rest of the European Left. And thus, via the Bolsheviks, the French radical project, with its Paris-centered, *étatist* goals to be achieved through the single protracted moment of revolutionary action, became the pan-European vision of what it meant to be a member of the nonliberal Left.

Adopted in Russia also, and thus widely disseminated in the years 1920-1968, was the French unconcern with spontaneous action—always unlikely to succeed and anyway doomed to a lack of historical self-consciousness. This rather cavalier dismissal of spontaneity combined in France with an often obsequious admiration for the abstract category of "workers"—and the two are causally related. In France, resulting once again from its precocious experience with revolution, political radicalism and revolutionary ideology long preceded the emergence of anything remotely resembling an industrial proletariat. The latter could thus be ignored in the construction of political theory, but had to be imagined into existence for the purposes of that same theory, since only the supposed interests of this proletariat could provide historical legitimation for the rejection of a liberal polity which most other radical movements were still seeking to construct. Once imagined, the proletariat was soon readily admired.

All of the above made rather limited sense to countries that (1) already had a large and real proletariat with traditions of mass spontaneous action, and (2) lacked a government similar to that of France, with its several centuries of structure and legitimacy, to whose seizure and control the opposition could aspire. But for reasons of circumstance familiar to our own times, domestic and international contexts allowed this rather peculiarly French way of thinking about revolution, with its goals and methods of achieving them, to form the nucleus of radical thought— indeed, to define in large measure what being "radical" meant.

Now, with remarkable speed, this whole edifice of French radicalism

---

6 This criticism came from left-wing opponents of the French communists, who noted that Lenin had borrowed heavily from the insurrectionary and dictatorial strategies of the nineteenth-century French socialist Auguste Blanqui, but adapted it to backward Russian tradition.

7 The vexed question of the relationship of French Communism to the indigenous roots of French Socialism is discussed in J. ROBERT, LA SCISSION SYNDICALE DE 1921 (1980); J. CHARLES, LE CONGRÈS DE TOURS (1980); 1 P. ROBRIEUX, HISTOIRE INTÉRIEURE DU PARTI COMMUNISTE (1980); R. WOHL, FRENCH COMMUNISM IN THE MAKING, 1914-1924 (1966). The *locus classicus* remains A. KRIEGEL, AUX ORIGINES DU COMMUNISME FRANÇAIS (1964).

has all but crumbled. Marxism, whose credibility as a science of the future had been shaken by the steady decline of the French Communist Party and the relatively sturdy performance of postwar capitalism, suffered even more through its identification with regimes in Central and Eastern Europe whose moral credibility collapsed in 1956 and died twelve years later. The social conservatism of the blue-collar proletariat made nonsense of the traditional claims of radical politics to be necessarily associated with the former's interests and actions. Finally, and perhaps most devastating of all, the Left came to power in 1981 with no apparent restrictions upon its power, restrictions of the kind that served to excuse its dismal performance on previous occasions in office. When Mitterand and his government turned in a respectable social democratic performance, the disappointment was, for once, inaudible. There were no alternatives left within the radical lexicon. The state had been "seized." Now what?[8]

The question remains unanswered because a generation of left-wing thinkers, buoyed by 1968 and disillusioned by its aftermath, have taken their revenge upon not only the organizations and programs of their movement, not just upon its moral defects and historical crimes, but upon the very epistemological foundations of French (and thus Western) radical thought. Holistic thinking—in their terms the idea that society could be "conceived" and if conceived, then conceived differently—was blamed for the sins of those who had acted out its commands. This, it will be noted, is a peculiarly French way of seeing the matter (and shows, some might argue, what little hold Marxism really had on the French radical spirit), but the consequences for the future of radical thought are very real. In Unger's terms, everyone is now "anti-naturalistic." But what will fill the vacuum? In principle, nothing. Or, to be fair, nothing beyond ad hoc measures intended to achieve only specific and attainable goals derived from neo-Kantian accounts of the normatively desirable. In practice this means that radical politics in France has ceased to exist in any recognizable form.[9]

It could be argued that something similar has taken place elsewhere in Western Europe, minus the self-serving conversations about the sins of holism. Certainly the Left in Britain is not going anywhere. And in

---

[8] On the fortunes of French Marxism in recent years, see T. JUDT, *supra* note 4, at ch. 4; P. ANDERSON, IN THE TRACKS OF HISTORICAL MATERIALISM (1983); E. MALET, SOCRATE ET LA ROSE: LES INTELLECTUELS FACE AU POUVOIR SOCIALISTE (1983). Sunil Khilnani, of Christ's College, Cambridge, is currently preparing a doctoral thesis on the subject which will be a major contribution to the literature.

[9] Representative writings from this period include A. GLUCKSMANN, LES MAÎTRES PENSEURS (1977); B. LEVY, LA BARBARIE À VISAGE HUMAIN (1977); J. RANCIÈRE, LA LEÇON D'ALTHUSSER (1974). *See generally* S. JAMES, THE CONTENT OF SOCIAL EXPLANATION (1984); J. GUILLEBAUD, LES ANNÉES ORPHELINES 1968-1978 (1978). On the pre-history of disillusion, see L. FERRY & A. RENAUT, LA PENSÉE 68 (1985); LES INTERPRÉTATIONS DU STALINISME (E. Pisier-Kouchner ed. 1983).

Italy, the Socialists in office have no radical project while the Communists have been preoccupied at the ideological level with denying their association with the institutionalized Marxism of the Soviet Union rather than advancing a Marxism of their own.[10] Perhaps all of this is just another way of saying that Marxism, as a political force, is dead and has dragged with it into the grave all the energies and assumptions underlying the progressive spirit in Europe since 1789. In the long run, as Unger points out, this situation is intolerable and a source of acute moral deficiency vis-à-vis the inhabitants of less fortunate lands. But *sub specie temporis* it can endure.

Such is not the case in East-Central Europe, however. There something very interesting is taking place. Until 1968, opposition in Poland, Czechoslovakia, and perhaps also Hungary took the form of "revisionism"—the desire to effect changes within the thinking of a sympathetic minority of the ruling party and thereby engineer changes in the system as a whole. This approach depended upon the suppositions that (1) there was such a sympathetic group within the party, (2) this group could hope to exercise some influence eventually, (3) there was a common language shared by rulers and opposition alike, and (4) this language spoke sufficiently well both to the ideals of the opposition and to the real world whose constraints they faced that it made sense to continue using it.[11]

When the Polish government set in motion the anti-semitic, anti-intelligentsia purges of the late 1960s, and when the Husák regime removed 500,000 people from the Czech and Slovak Communist Parties following the Russian invasion, the four conditions of "revisionism" disappeared. When the Polish government expelled leading revisionist intellectuals like Kolakowski, thereby alienating a generation of young would-be reformers, the very notion of revisionism disappeared almost immediately. In Czechoslovakia, with a much more ingrained socialist tradition and deep collective guilt on the part of a generation of intellectuals for their role in installing the Communist regime, belief in the language of socialism died harder, but it too has now virtually disappeared. In the lands of "real existing socialism," no one is a socialist any more: not for want of a belief in the aspirations of socialism, but because of the impossibility of voicing these beliefs except in the discredited language of

---

10 The differences between Italian and French Communism are too well-known to require documentation. For information discussing the relations between Italy's intellectuals and its Marxists, see N. AJELLO, INTELLETTUALI E PCI, 1944-1958 (1979); G. BEDESCHI, LA PARABOLA DEL MARXISMO IN ITALIA, 1945-1983 (1983). An interesting, though non-critical, recent study of the inner workings of the Party is A. ACCORNERO, L'IDENTITÀ COMMUNISTA: I MILITANTI, LE STRUTTURE, LA CULTURA DEL PCI (1983); *see also* the memoirs of G. C. PAJETTA, LE CRISI CHE HO VISSUTO: BUDAPEST, PRAGA, VARSOVIA (1982).

11 On the revisionist movement in East European dissent, see 3 L. KOLAKOWSKI, MAIN CURRENTS OF MARXISM 460-66 (1978); the contributions by Kolakowski and Gross to EAST-CENTRAL EUROPE: YESTERDAY, TODAY, TOMORROW (M. Drachkovitch ed. 1982); J. CHIAMA & J. SOULET, HISTOIRE DE LA DISSIDENCE (1982); V. MASTNY, EAST EUROPEAN DISSENT 1953-1964 (1972).

the regime. Radicals deliberately avoid the very discourse of radicalism in its traditional European form—this language having been appropriated as the discourse of power.[12]

The result has been the creation of a different language for those who would dissent from the regime. This new language clearly does not apply to those in Poland who oppose Communism in the name of integral Catholicism or Greater Polish nationalism or "Russophobia," nor does it include those Czechs and Slovaks who gripe at the material inadequacies of the way of life they are forced to live. These people, however, would never have considered themselves political radicals. Those who do consider themselves radicals, however, have begun to develop a new radical language untethered to now discredited "Soviet" Marxism.

Take the case of Poland. The Workers Defense Committee (KOR), created in 1976 in the aftermath of the trials of protesting factory workers, set for itself no "systematic" goals. It existed legally and openly, and did not even pretend to be engaged in a debate about how to run the state. As Adam Michnik, one of its moving spirits, wrote in 1982, "The most important question was not 'how should the system of government be changed,' but 'how should we defend ourselves against the system?' "[13] This is significant because Michnik, like others of his generation who had been active in the student movements of the 1960s and who took part in the creation of KOR, had come from deep within the Marxist and revisionist traditions in Poland.[14]

By the time Solidarity emerged in 1980, this perspective had deepened into something more positive. The strategy of the new opposition in Poland (combining the intellectuals clustered around KOR with the newly emerging workers' leaders in Gdansk, Warsaw, Nowa Huta, and elsewhere) was not to advise the government on how to govern but to advise the nation on how to live. The utterly unpretentious nature of this claim arises from the fact that the most serious threat facing the cultures of Eastern Europe was the disappearance of *society*, with all power and

---

[12] For works on Poland between 1956-1980, see N. DAVIES, HEART OF EUROPE chs. 1 & 6 (1984); J. DE WEYDENTHAL, THE COMMUNISTS OF POLAND (1978); P. RAINA, POLITICAL OPPOSITION IN POLAND, 1954-77 (1978). For works on Czechoslovakia, see G. GOLAN, THE CZECHOSLOVAK REFORM MOVEMENT (1973); V. KUSIN, THE INTELLECTUAL ORIGINS OF THE PRAGUE SPRING (1971); H. SKILLING, CZECHOSLOVAKIA'S INTERRUPTED REVOLUTION (1976). On the social structure of Czechoslovakia in the Dubček years, see P. MACHONIN, ČESKOSLOVENSKÁ SPOLEČNOST: SOCIOLOGICKÁ ANALÝSA SOCIÁLNÍ STRATIFIKACE (1969). On the Czech purges, see M. ŠIMEČKA, THE RESTORATION OF ORDER (1984); *Acta Persecutionis* (paper on the purge of historians in Czechoslovakia, presented to the XIVth International Congress of Historical Sciences, San Francisco, August 1975). Works published in the 1970s indicating the enduring faith in socialism of Czech intellectuals include Z. MLYNÁŘ, VOICES OF CZECHOSLOVAK SOCIALISTS (1977); J. PELIKÁN, SOCIALIST OPPOSITION IN EASTERN EUROPE: THE CZECHOSLOVAK EXAMPLE (1976).

[13] A. MICHNIK, LETTERS FROM PRISON AND OTHER ESSAYS 28 (1986).

[14] *See id.* On KOR, see J. LIPSKI, KOR (1986). After the emergence of Solidarity, KOR dissolved itself. *See also* A. MICHNIK, PENSER LA POLOGNE (1983).

language and initiative drawn into the black hole of the increasingly incompetent party-state.

It is undoubtedly true that in Poland things were complicated by the religious devotion of the working-class and its apparent lack of desire to take over the state, which eased the path of the leadership of the opposition in creating their "self-limiting" revolution. The state, after all, was not available for the taking, and the genius of the new opposition lay in recognizing this. Hitherto, opponents of Communist regimes had seen no choice but to try and negotiate the terms of government with the rulers—either accepting the ground rules, as it were, or placing themselves in futile, open opposition to that government. For Polish radicals, the Communist state today is not there for the taking—but society is. This was not a completely original insight—Leszek Kolakowski, the spiritual guide to a generation of young Polish intellectuals, had noted as early as 1971 that hope for change in this part of Europe came in the form of pressure on the bureaucratic structure *from below*.[15] But even this does not adequately describe what was proposed by Michnik and others. Their objectives are best captured in the idea of "as if": We shall live in society as if we were free, rather than expending fruitless efforts trying to construct a formally free society.[16]

These were not uncontentious proposals. Solidarity was deeply divided over what, if anything, it ought to propose by way of economic reforms, political liberalization, or civic freedoms. But while the specter of millions of workers organized in an independent union was undoubtedly disturbing to the monopoly party, the deeper threat lay in the propagation of the more subtle idea that merely living as though you were free made you so. This was a rare case of thought making reality. It enabled the more mundane forms of opposition, such as union organization, to endure since it gave them a vocabulary and a sense of purpose independent of specific achievements or setbacks.

The experience of Charter 77 in Czechoslovakia exhibits some remarkable parallels. Formed with a view to publicizing the government's response (or lack thereof) to the Helsinki agreements, it was galvanized into action by the drive to defend a small group of rock musicians (The Plastic People of the Universe) persecuted by the authorities. Like KOR, Charter 77 was largely a movement of intellectuals and, even more than KOR, it has avoided political stances. Its strengths, despite constant harassment and occasional imprisonment, have lain in the fact of its open existence. Its organizers periodically sign their names to its documents, thus behaving as if Czechoslovakia were a *Rechtstaat*. In short, merely

---

[15] Kolakowski, *Hope and Hopelessness*, SURVEY, Summer 1971, at 37.

[16] On the history and ideas of the Solidarity period, see T. GARTON ASH, THE POLISH REVOLUTION (1981); J. STANISZKIS, POLAND'S SELF-LIMITING REVOLUTION (1984); M. ZALEWSKA, SOLIDARITY UNDERGROUND (1983).

by existing it has introduced pluralism into Czech political life.[17]

But, as its best known signatory Václav Havel has insistently noted, Charter 77 was above all an "existential revolution."[18] It was, and remains, a declaration of a fact—that the intelligentsia, which the Husák regime has quite deliberately set out to eliminate, still exists. And, in existing and behaving like an intelligentsia (the Czech understanding of the role of intellectuals is close to that of the French, with the same over-extended sense of responsibility), Charter 77 denies the party-state its most important claim, that of monopoly.[19]

For this reason, the success or failure of Charter 77 (and VONS, the Committee for the Unjustly Persecuted, founded shortly after Charter 77) is not easily measured. Clearly, its very survival is an achievement. But there is a risk in these circumstances that the validity of radical opposition is reduced to the fact of its own existence, which can hardly be satisfactory. So what is the project of the Czech opposition today?

According to Havel, it is to "behave responsibly," by which he means to act as free moral agents. In Havel's hands this notion of responsibility acquires an almost religious bent—each individual is personally responsible for the world.[20] Clearly this is a reaction against the cynicism, low-level corruption, and totalitarian routinization of post-Dubček Czechoslovakia, but it is accompanied by a rising tone of anger at the apparent ease with which Central Europe's most advanced and politicized culture has been "bought off" with consumer goods and intimidated by threats. There is a hint of scorn for the "modern" and the "comfortable" that harks back to the radicalism of a much earlier epoch and that finds little trace in the Polish movement. One reason for this may be that the mystical note in Havel's essays is provided in Poland by the practices and ceremonies of the Catholic Church. Another observation is that scorn for consumerism would ring false in Poland, whose economy is moribund. Contact with reality, with the daily experience of the factory worker, is far more widespread among the Polish intellectual

---

[17] On Charter 77, see H.G. SKILLING, CHARTER 77 AND HUMAN RIGHTS IN CZECHOSLOVAKIA (1981); A BESEIGED CULTURE: CZECHOSLOVAKIA TEN YEARS AFTER HELSINKI (1985); BÜRGER-INITIATIVE FÜR DIE MENSCHENRECHTE: DIE TSCHECHOSLOWAKISCHE OPPOSITION ZWISCHEN DEM 'PRAGUR FRÜHLING' UND DER CHARTA 77 (H. Riese ed. 1977).

[18] Havel, *O Lidskou Identitu*, in O LIDSKOU IDENTITU 260 (V. Havel ed. 1984).

[19] On the peculiarities of the Czech intelligentsia, a subject much discussed among the opposition (not to mention in the novels of Milan Kundera), see A. LIEHM, THE POLITICS OF CULTURE (1968); B. MICHEL, LA MÉMOIRE DE PRAGUE: CONSCIENCE NATIONALE ET INTELLIGENTSIA DANS L'HISTOIRE TCHÈQUE ET SLOVAQUE (1986); *see also* the essays by Vaculík and Kliment in HODINA NADĚJE (1980).

On the links and common concerns of intellectuals in Prague and Paris, see P. GRÉMION, PARIS/PRAGUE (1985), and on the journey of structuralism from Central to Western Europe, see J. MERQUIOR, FROM PRAGUE TO PARIS (1986).

[20] Havel, *Krize Identity*, in O LIDSKOU IDENTITU 349-51 (1984); *see also Kdo je Václav Havel*, Lidová Demokracie, Mar. 10, 1977, *reprinted in* O LIDSKOU IDENTITU 392-94 (1984); Havel, *Six Asides About Culture* (pts. 1 & 2), 3 KOSMAS no.2 (1984), 4 KOSMAS no.1 (1985).

opposition. In this respect, too, the Czech intellectuals are the Parisians of Central Europe.

Not everyone, of course, agrees with Havel. In 1978, Ludvik Vaculík argued that the people should be asked only for unheroic, realistic deeds[21]—anticipating the prison letters of Michnik, who is politely dismissive of those who would ask too much of their followers and who see compromise as an unmitigated evil.[22] For Michnik, as for Vaculík, compromise in matters of economic and political arrangements (assuming such compromises are possible and do not involve "compromises" in the other sense—a difficult path to follow as Michnik readily admits) need not impeach the integrity of the opposition, precisely because (and here lies the originality) it is not a matter of competing projects. In totalitarian systems, men and women who openly ignore (rather than defy) the regime are a de facto (and perhaps even de jure) denial of the regime's monopoly of power and knowledge. In this denial lies their fundamental radicalism.

In Hungary things are different. While the Polish and Czech situations had only a few points in common, these similarities have served to bring a certain common sense to the undertaking.[23] The Hungarians have, in recent years, been faced with the rather odd situation in which the Kadar regime gives a reasonably wide field of maneuvers to its opponents on condition that they do not claim the territory as of right! Consequently, the exact bounds of the permissible are unclear, and it has been suggested that Hungarian dissent tends to oscillate between a sense of cynical frustration ("we can say anything we like so long as it has no impact, so why bother?") and an element of self-censorship (in the absence of clear censorship rules from above). Nonetheless, there is an identifiable Hungarian opposition, and it is recognizably related to those in Poland and Czechoslovakia in the respects that concern us here.[24]

For the Hungarian opposition, living "as if in a free society" is, of course, a necessary condition but it is no longer sufficient. They already have the public space that Solidarity fought for in Poland, and many of the smaller freedoms which the Czechs seek in economic and social af-

---

[21] Vaculík, *Poznámky o Statečnosti*, in O LIDSKOU IDENTITU 203-04 (1984)

[22] *Id.* at 201-03; *Maggots and Angels*, in A. MICHNIK, *supra* note 13.

[23] Since 1980, the intellectual initiative has perhaps been with the Poles but they, in turn, would argue that the experience of the Prague Spring and its aftermath was what finally laid to rest the hopes for revisionism in their own country.

[24] On the opposition in Hungary, see F. FEHÉR & A. HELLER, HUNGARY 1956 REVISITED 154 (1983); Ash, *Does Central Europe Exist?*, NEW YORK REVIEW OF BOOKS, Oct. 9, 1986; Bence & Kiš, *After the Break*, in COMMUNISM AND EASTERN EUROPE (F. Silnitsky ed. 1979); Schöpflin, *Opposition in Hungary: 1956 and Beyond*, in DISSENT IN EASTERN EUROPE 69 (J. Curry ed. 1983). Works of interest by members of the opposition include M. HARASZTI, A WORKER IN A WORKER'S STATE (1978); OPPOSITION=0.1% (M. Haraszti ed. 1979); Haraszti, *Il Dissenso Come Professione*, in 1 MICRO MEGA 242-49 (1986); *see also* A. HEGEDÜS, THE STRUCTURE OF SOCIALIST SOCIETY (1977). A useful source for material on this subject is the journal EAST EUROPEAN REPORTER.

fairs already exist in Hungary—though in very fragile form and with no guarantees of survival. Not surprisingly, therefore, Hungarians think more tangibly about traditional politics as a possible sphere of engagement; there has been much discussion whether the opposition should *want* to constitute itself as a political force.[25] But such discussions always encounter the same difficulty facing Poles and Czechs even as they avoid the question: What does it *mean* to be a political force in a land without politics? If a political opposition were attempted, the predictable result would be, at best, that the conservative elements within the Party and state apparatus would unite and react by restricting the social sphere; at worst, 1956 could be repeated.[26]

In practice, therefore, Hungarian opposition has concerned itself with what one might anachronistically call "single-issue" politics. Ostensibly unpolitical groups arise to discuss and publicize particular problems. The Danube Circle, which concerns itself with the ecological threats arising from projects diverting river water for hydroelectric purposes, is one such example. But, while the government might be willing to recognize the legitimacy of this debate (it is, in fact, embarrassed by its own actions on this front), it cannot accept the form it has taken—that is, spontaneous action outside official control and sponsorship. Thus, the Danube Circle and other similar initiatives become acts of political opposition and dissent.[27]

Groups and individuals who have attempted to discuss the mistreatment of Hungarian minorities in Romania or Czechoslovakia have met similiar outcomes. Here the unacceptable form of such discussions is compounded by the danger to the government of allowing any discussion that might arouse national feeling against other communist states. While the government could benefit from indicating its sympathy for the Transylvanians or the Hungarian minority in Slovakia, the risks of opening up nationalist resentment against the true foreign occupier are too great. Here too, then, simple discussion of an apparently nonpolitical issue is a de facto assault on the legitimacy of the wider system of political ar-

---

[25] *See* F. CLAUDIN, LA OPOSICIÓN EN EL 'SOCIALISMO REAL' 237 (1983). There is a complex and suggestive discussion of the nature of political power in Eastern Europe and particularly Hungary in F. FEHÉR, A. HELLER & G. MARKUS, DICTATORSHIP OVER NEEDS (1983).

[26] On the 1956 Hungarian uprising, see W. LOMAX, HUNGARY 1956 (1976). The continuing sensitivity of the subject is brought out in a recent book by J. Berecz, one of the likely contenders for power in the post-Kadar era. He outlines, somewhat incompetently, the "hard" interpretation of the uprising. J. BERECZ, COUNTER-REVOLUTION IN HUNGARY: WORDS AND WEAPONS (1986).

[27] On the Danube Circle and other ecological groups such as Danube Blues and Friends of the Danube, see 1 EAST EUROPEAN REPORTER (1986) and 2 EAST EUROPEAN REPORTER (1987). The central issue is the proposal to build a joint Czech/Hungarian hydroelectric dam on the Danube at Gabčikovo-Nagymaros, an agreement that Hungary would be happy to see dissolved. The ecological question has been widely discussed in the literature in this region. *See* M. KIRKPATRICK, ENVIRONMENTAL PROBLEMS AND POLICIES IN EASTERN EUROPE AND THE USSR (1978); Kramer, *The Environmental Crisis in Eastern Europe*, 42 SLAVIC REVIEW 204 (1983); Zrosec, *Environmental Deterioration in Eastern Europe*, SURVEY, Winter 1984, at 117.

rangements of which Hungary is a part.[28]

It is in Hungary, too, that the most sensitive of all "nonpolitical" discussions is emerging as a form of silent politics. As in the Czechoslovakia of the 1960s, the question of economic reform is the lever that can open debate on the very premise of socialist political arrangements. Sooner or later the Hungarian "economic miracle" must either collapse under the weight of foreign debt and internal contradiction or lead to changes of investment and industrial organization similar to those that have occurred in the arenas of consumer goods and market-farming. But any such changes would threaten the control exercised by the ministries and economic agencies. This would undermine the only social group (bureaucrats, managers, state employees) who, in Hungary, have retained an interest in the survival of the regime. Everyone knows this—and they also know that the problem cannot be avoided. The difference now is that very few of the critics of the system spend any time trying to link economic reforms with socialism. This relieves the opposition of the burden of imagining utopian scenarios but also reduces them to a condition of virtual impotence since they know that all rational projects, whether economic or ecological, are going to succeed only to the extent that they are compatible with a political arrangement that derives its rationality from quite different criteria.[29]

Perhaps unsurprisingly, therefore, the Hungarian opposition, though blessed with no less a number of gifted thinkers and writers than the other captured countries, has not produced anything approaching a theory of its behavior comparable to those which Michnik or Havel have constructed for their countries. On the other hand, much of what the Hungarian opposition actually does could be seen as radical politics in a

---

[28] On the nationality question in Hungary, see TRANSYLVANIA AND THE HUNGARIAN-ROMANIAN PROBLEM: A SYMPOSIUM (A. Sanborn ed. 1979). Two critical pieces from the opposition are Kenedi, *Why is the Gypsy the Scapegoat?*, 2 EAST EUROPEAN REPORTER i (1986); Kovács, *La Question juive dans la Hongrie Contemporaine*, in ACTES DE LA RECHERCHE EN SCIENCES SOCIALES 45-58 (1985).

In Poland, the nationality questions were "solved" during and immediately after the war. In Czechoslovakia, the Czech-Slovak and Slovak-Hungarian antagonisms live on. For discussions on the region as a whole, see ETHNIC DIVERSITY AND CONFLICT IN EASTERN EUROPE (P. Sugar ed. 1980); NATIONALITÄTEN PROBLEME IN DER SOWJETUNION UND OSTEUROPA (1982); THE POLITICS OF ETHNICITY IN EASTERN EUROPE (G. Klein & M. Reban eds. 1981). The official view from Romania is given in HUNGARIANS AND GERMANS IN ROMANIA TODAY (1978).

[29] On these matters, see W. BRUS, THE MARKET IN A SOCIALIST ECONOMY (1972); SOCIALIST OWNERSHIP AND POLITICAL SYSTEMS (1975); *see also* Brus, *The East European Reforms: What Happened to Them?*, 2 SOVIET STUDIES 31 (1979). For discussion of Hungary in particular, see A. ASHLUND, PRIVATE ENTERPRISE IN EASTERN EUROPE (1985); J. KORNAI, CONTRADICTIONS AND DILEMMAS (1985); *A Programme for Democratic Renewal*, 2 EAST EUROPEAN REPORTER i (1987). A particularly interesting paper was delivered by Kálmán Mizsei of the Hungarian Institute for World Economics entitled Totalitarianism, Reforms, Second Economy: Logic of Changes in the East European Economic Systems, at the Conference on the Effects of Communism on Social and Economic Change in Bologna, Italy, June 23-28, 1986.

new form—an opposition in a condition of permanent *autogestion*, which—like the Polish opposition—engages directly with the regime only when the regime chooses to engage with it.

It would be a profound mistake, and one that could at least in some part derive from the sort of perspective Unger proposes, to suppose that these situations I have described above are satisfactory. This is true in the obvious sense that all of the groups I described would be happier if they could exchange their situation for that of the Austrian, Swedish, or even French radicals. What matters more, however, is that this politics of the nonpolitical (Havel's "power of the powerless"[30]) is itself a reaction to circumstance rather than a positive choice. It is a choice, of course, in that it represents a departure from the old politics of engagement with the problem of government and the state. And it is important in that it is a decision to emphasize form rather than content, and new content over old. But it is a choice forced upon the present generation and it has unhappy side effects. In Czechoslovakia, for example, the effort to avoid engaging in the mendacious and devalued language of the regime has led most recently to a growing religiosity.[31] The drive to rediscover a vocabulary for the expression of truth and opinion, to find a language capable of distinguishing between good and evil, right and wrong, has sent some Czech intellectuals back beyond an Enlightenment whose benefits they question to an obscurantist and integral Catholicism (ironic in the land of Hus and Comenius). Even worse, those who still seek to retain something of the language and purpose of the Central European social democratic tradition find themselves in an untenable condition when asked to show why what they believe is true, but true for reasons different than those adduced by the regime on its own behalf.[32]

It might be argued in reply that East-Central Europe is a most inappropriate context in which to require new political ideas and forms to be consistent or optimistic; this applies with particular force in Czechoslovakia, where the high hopes of the 1960s combine with the repression of the past half generation in an especially devastating way. But this argument is flawed. If there is to be a new departure in the radical discourse, then it can only come about after the old expectations and habits have been completely discredited. It is clear that this discrediting process has gone further among the intellectuals of East-Central Europe than any-

---

[30] *See* V. HAVEL, *The Power of the Powerless*, in THE POWER OF THE POWERLESS (1985).

[31] *See supra* note 20 and accompanying text.

[32] For the history regarding the emergence of religion as a force in East-Central Europe, see CHURCHES IN SOCIALIST SOCIETIES OF EASTERN EUROPE (N. Greinacher & V. Elizordo eds. 1982); RELIGION AND NATIONALISM IN SOVIET AND EAST EUROPEAN POLITICS (P. Ramet ed. 1984); TOLERANCE AND MOVEMENTS OF RELIGIOUS DISSENT IN EASTERN EUROPE (B. Kiraly ed. 1975).

Among many works on the church in Poland, see G. BARBERINI, STATO SOCIALISTA E CHIESA CATTOLICA IN POLONIA (1983); M. POMIAN-SRZEDNICKI, RELIGIOUS CHANGE IN CONTEMPORARY POLAND (1982).

where else in the world. Yet even there the same set of doubts as to the possibility of rethinking the political world necessarily arises.

Take again the case of Poland. In order to secure the survival of Polish society, it was necessary to think and act as though the institutional constraints did not operate. Yet having achieved some success in this goal, the leaders of the opposition found themselves confronted with the practical demands of an ailing economy and the fact that the state does exist—the real limitations upon existing "as if." Behaving "responsibly," for Havel, means being and writing as a moral man. But in Prague today that is all he can do—and as a playwright, moreover, it is all he seeks to achieve.[33] In Warsaw, amnestied and faced with a government that is beginning to behave "as if" it sought to resolve its dilemmas, Michnik is seriously troubled at the disaster facing his country's economy: the collapse of the work ethic ("we pretend to work and the government pretends to pay us") and a complete divorce between the society and those who direct its institutions. These are not characteristics of a system undergoing revival, and behaving responsibly means taking these matters seriously.[34]

How do you take seriously the troubles facing a modern social organism? You try to advance solutions to its problems, solutions that, in the real world of Eastern Europe, entail imagining how the government might better order its citizens' affairs. And so we are back to projects, however modest, which engage the problem of organization and the state. This is not news to the more imaginative and honest of Poland's leading dissidents (nor those of Hungary), but they have not yet produced any answer beyond confirming through their actions the desirability of those aspects of a liberal pluralism whose wider forms are unavailable to them now and which are likely to remain so indefinitely.

Which returns us, in a way, to France. The radical project in France (that is, socialism in one form or another) was defined by its opposition to the existing set of arrangements. The same was true of the varieties of left-wing thought and action elsewhere in Western Europe. But, deprived of the promise of the future by the advent of that future in the form of political power, socialism loses the larger charm which gave meaning to its lesser achievements. Once these achievements cease to be part of a greater dream, they lose much of their appeal. Either they must

---

[33] On language and culture in Czechoslovakia, see M. GOETZ-STANKIEWICZ, THE SILENCED THEATRE: CZECH PLAYWRIGHTS WITHOUT A STAGE (1979); D. HAMŠÍK, WRITERS AGAINST RULERS (1971) (the role of writers and artists in the prelude to the Dubček era); THE WRITING ON THE WALL: AN ANTHOLOGY OF CONTEMPORARY CZECH LITERATURE (A. Liehm & P. Kussi eds. 1983).

[34] Similiarly, in Czechoslovakia the ecological disaster now facing northern Bohemia has led some opponents of the regime to give priority in their writings to constructive proposals for control of industrial emissions and effluent—a subject also beginning to receive official press coverage. The problem in an economy characterized by production targets and "soft budget constraints" is that no one, manager or minister, has a compelling incentive to act.

be recast to derive their justification from other moral and political traditions, including those against which socialism was itself defined, or they
simply cease to be "politics." Of course, a sense of moral and political
purpose can be reborn in conditions of oppression—which is what happened in France in certain circles of the wartime Resistance and is part of
the story of contemporary East-Central Europe—but this hardly justifies
seeking out such conditions to resolve these dilemmas.

Hence the paradox of the present lesson of Poland and its neighbors.[35] It is possible, at least occasionally, to rethink the meaning of
political radicalism and intelligently to engage the state and its institutions on your own terms. But this cannot be a political project in itself
because it is, above all, merely a response to the impossibility of creating
such a project. In its most pessimistic form it amounts to asking for
bravery and honesty of oneself and one's friends. And should it be fortunate enough to succeed (and most Poles readily concede that the "success" of the opposition has always hinged in part on external
developments), it must inevitably face the choice of either returning to
"normal" political discourse (or as normal as circumstances permit) or
betraying its purposes. Perhaps it has to betray itself anyway.

Political thinkers living and writing in the West have generally been
spared such dilemmas. But they should not have too much difficulty
recognizing the larger message. Unger's vision of "alternative institutional forms" is not very different from the vision traditionally entailed in
the radical politics of post-Enlightenment societies. Unger's claim that
things do not have to be as they are, while not being (or being capable of
becoming) just anything, is not original. It bears repetition, however,
though the message is less urgent now, in the West at least, than it might
have been had it been suggested twenty years ago. And of course, his
search for some sort of social experimentalism with its center of gravity
firmly placed on the individual is as desirable an undertaking as it has
ever been. But it is still worth recalling that the space in which we are
invited to undertake such experiments is constrained by very real institutions and persons. The importance of the experiments to their participants thus probably varies in inverse proportion to the freedom their
participants have to undertake them.

I do not believe that it follows from this that we should define our
present projects negatively—as though we should confine our efforts to

---

[35] Things have until very recently been quite different in the German Democratic Republic.
There the dominant figures in the opposition remained well within the terms of socialist discourse
even to the extent of casting doubt on the virtues of political pluralism and its attendant economic
forms. *See, e.g.*, R. BAHRO, THE ALTERNATIVE IN EASTERN EUROPE (1984); R. BAHRO, FROM
RED TO GREEN (1984); RUDOLF BAHRO: CRITICAL RESPONSES (U. Wolter ed. 1980). In this last
collection, see especially the article written by Jiří Pelikán, who notes that Bahro's neo-Marxist
terminology is "remote from reality" and quite without appeal in Eastern Europe. This criticism has
been picked up, predictably, in West Germany. *See, e.g.*, SOLIDARITÄT MIT RUDOLF BAHRO:
BRIEFS IN D. DDR (H. Schwerger ed. 1978).

defending our present good fortune. That is not the message from Warsaw or Prague and, even if it were, it would be wrong.[36] Nor is it really a
matter of choice—radical politics is by definition a critical undertaking.
But it need not be a naive one. *Pace* Unger, not all contexts can be broken, even though it may be necessary to pretend otherwise in order to
break any given context. The reminder we have received from East-Central Europe is one of paradox—that single-issue discussions can be the
stuff of national opposition,[37] that obscurantist organizations of doubtful
pedigree (for example, the Catholic Church in Poland) can play powerful
roles as intermediate institutions in alliance with a generation that once
scorned them as reactionary and dangerous,[38] and that denial of the very
claims of the party-state may be the way to create a framework in which
you can work with that same state.

But it is a paradox within facts: the fact of the Soviet Union, its
army, and its interests. It is surrounded by lesser facts: economic crisis
and the need for a stable state apparatus. The view from nowhere may
suggest that these are passing contexts. But radical politics are always
somewhere and it is as true now as it was in 1789 that you cannot hope to
change anything without acknowledging this. Of course, acknowledging
it to excess precludes changing anything at all—but this is a psychological observation rather than an historical one. The revolutionary tradition bequeathed us by the Jacobins may have helped generate Husák and
Jaruselski,[39] but it has also taught us much more. Perhaps we should not
too readily acclaim its demise.

---

[36] Misunderstandings nevertheless arise. In Czechoslovakia, the English neo-conservative writer,
Roger Scruton, is a venerated figure, while Western liberals and conservatives alike have fallen over
one another to recognize and acclaim Adam Michnik and his fellow radicals. Necessity and circumstance notwithstanding, these are very odd matchings. The majority of the Czech dissidents are ex-
socialists with a very clear-headed view of the distinction between the desirable and the possible,
while Scruton probably genuinely believes in the need to reestablish the Austro-Hungarian Empire,
mistaking Czech *litost* in this matter for a program. As to Michnik, it is all but certain that, under
almost any other circumstance, he would be a figure of some disrepute and distaste to *bien pensant*
politicians from Paris to Washington.

[37] Witness the force of the protests against the persecution of the Jazz Section in Czechoslovakia,
or the energy generated by the Danube issue in Budapest. In Poland today the Peace and Freedom
movement, an organization of young persons aroused by the nuclear question, has taken off in a
number of directions including ecology, conscientious objection to military service, regional disarma-
ment, and capital punishment. All of these, of course, return it of necessity to the question of political and civil rights, as the necessary general conditions for the voicing of such concerns.

[38] *See, e.g.*, A. MICHNIK, L'EGLISE ET LA GAUCHE (1979).

[39] Limitations of space deter me from elucidating with greater precision the causal relationship
at work here.

WHEN THE OWL OF MINERVA TAKES FLIGHT AT DAWN: RADICAL CONSTRUCTIVISM IN SOCIAL THEORY

Robert P. Burns

I. INTRODUCTION

In this essay I first make some observations on the rhetoric of Unger's work. I then try to identify Unger's philosophical method (his warrant for moving from proposition to proposition) and his interpretation (the ontological status he assigns his theory) as more or less permanent philosophical possibilities and argue that this theoretical choice determines many of the most striking features of the theory. I then show how Unger's theory is designed in part to meet the problems that Rawls faces in his attempt to invent norms and institutions for the "basic structure" of society. Unger does this by creating what Kant, Hegel and Marx agreed could not be created, a normative *speculative* theory. I then focus on his basic metaphors and offer a critique, following Hannah Arendt, of the vision of politics embedded in them. Finally, I suggest that Unger joins to his basic metaphors a violent reinterpretation of Christianity that accomplishes a transvaluation of values that is modernist, univocal, and aestheticized.

II. THE RHETORIC OF THEORY

Unger understands well that his project is ridiculously ambitious. It requires a vast reconstruction of social, economic, legal, moral, political, and constitutional worlds, guided by a theory superior to every other theory, self-conscious about its own ontological and epistemological status, informed by a close analogy to scientific method as interpreted by the radical vanguard in the philosophy of science, advancing a "modernist project" embodied in the work of the great literary geniuses of the twentieth century, interpreted as containing a vast world-historical correction of the (!) "Christian-romantic" vision. The theory generates a concrete constitutional, political, and economic program—concerned not only about epistemological status, but also about how to indoctrinate and organize cadres of "revolutionary reformers" and where to look for constituents. Unger argues that the explanatory and prescriptive aspects of the theory are applicable to the "rich North Atlantic countries," the communist world, and the so-called Third World. Is the theory ridiculous in the sense that the sages and saints always seem ridiculous to their own age, or in the special sense that Promethean acts always are? Tihar to Stavrogin in *The Possessed*.

Unger knows it's ridiculous. In fact, he is most like Hegel in that he knows everything. There is hardly an objection he does not clearly state. He is a master rhetorician in this at least: that he so fairly states the objections against himself. Is this the fairness of a genuine intellectual *libertas ad opposita* or is it the characteristic of the deftest rhetoricians, who always state the opponent's case better than he could himself?[1] The theory has a drive, a thrust, that pushes past all objections. The willfulness is evident for example in its astounding generality.

Almost all of *Passion* and a good deal of the trilogy stems from a phenomenological description of certain personal and political experiences. This is a "storytelling with the austerity of discursive thought rather than the lush particularism of literary art, a storytelling about the exemplary individual caught in the mesh of personal dependencies and encounters, a storytelling that draws its chief inspiration from the experiences of context-breaking . . ."[2] This austerity, however, deprives the reader of the ability to make his or her own mind up about the basis of the universal in the concrete, whether his or her particular story is an "objective correlative" to his or her universal. My fear throughout was that Unger's truth is abstract and willful, that he is himself one of those "fancy rhetoricians" he describes, that he has no *principle* that would allow his own theorizing to be anything but his "ideological seduction." Can I trust you, writer, when you enlist my aid as your "reader": or is this Ben Franklin's borrowing a book from a political opponent to break down his vigilance? Clever and utterly manipulative. If politics is just fighting, and theory and practice are so closely intertwined. . . .

The thrust of the theory lies in the controlling metaphors and programmatic slogans. They are the engines of the enormous act of will and energy that lies in this work. It is, therefore, worth focusing precisely on the implications of these basic images and slogans.[3] What are they? "Everything is politics," and its entailments, "man as maker," "society as artifact," "conflict as tool."[4]

Unger's rhetoric is likely to be alien to American academics, and especially legal academics, because he is critically addressing Marxist

---

[1] The characteristic refutations are that the objection involves a false prediction or embodies a sentimental archaism long since sacrificed on the butcher block of history.

[2] PASSION at 84.

[3] See *infra* notes 27 through 55.

[4] SOCIAL THEORY at 166.

scholasticism. Indeed, his efforts are prompted specifically by his disgust at the ease with which leftist intellectuals in his native Brazil were misled by that scholasticism about the real possibilities inherent in that country's recent turmoil. To the American legal academic Unger may seem to emerge like Melchizedek without intellectual parentage, so vast is his erudition and so little domesticated in the strains of Anglo-American political and legal philosophy to which we tend to turn when we seek a philosophical compass in legal matters. Our open ocean sailing is the most timid hugging the shore for him. One example: Though he and Rawls both begin from a short list of alternative moral positions, Rawls's list comprises only those moral theories recently championed in American or British philosophy departments. Sidgwick provides the list. Unger reaches for much more basic *Weltanschauungen* embodied in the world religions. Both philosophers are convinced that the battle among rival prescriptive theories is not likely to be won on the level of "meta-theory" and theory of knowledge (though both give great attention to the sorts of epistemological problems generated by the overlapping traditions to which each feels accountable). Both understand the need to "get on with" the task of generating concrete norms and specific institutions—something that has, in Rawls's view, been utilitarianism's great strength.

Unger has chosen to construct a theory to motivate those possessed of a "transformative vocation." Its abstractions seem, every one of them, a war plan.[5] Indeed, another image that I could not escape in reading this long, often loosely structured and frequently repetitious trilogy, as it flowed around the many theoretical, practical, and historical obstacles in its path, was that of a kind of huge intellectual ancient Persian Army.[6] Is the theory a gigantic rhetorical exercise, whose very comprehensiveness creates its own truth, so vast in its generalizations that by the time specialists here and there have shown its limitations, the sheer power of the wave has passed them by? More troubling, on Unger's own principles, why shouldn't it be? Utilitarianism succeeded largely because it appeared to generate specific institutional and moral consequences. Unger knows that too.

Unger argues that the line between a truly predictive theory and a self-fulfilling myth is murky, then spends over a thousand pages proposing one such myth. In his essay on psychiatry, he defines the success of a psychotherapy by the extent to which it "shared in the power of art to

---

[5] Even what appears not to be—his rejection of an early Sartrean existentialism—really is. Since an existentialism so extreme could not seriously be constructive, it tends to be bohemian and privatistic. No wars there.

[6] Kolakowski writes that, "Since Lenin was interested only in the political effect of his writings, they are full of repetitions. He was not afraid to repeat the same ideas again and again: he had no stylistic ambitions. . . . " L. KOLAKOWSKI, MAIN CURRENTS OF MARXISM: II THE GOLDEN AGE 523 (1978).

emancipate the imagination and the will."[7] Under current conditions in a "society in which public and private life are felt to be more or less starkly separated and in which the most probing experiences are, for most people, reserved to the intimate realm of private experience," the explanatory story that psychiatry employs "with the best chance of success . . . is the one that combines a truth with a lie." The truth is the metaphorical connection of the story with the life of passion. "The lie is the passage of this true insight through a prism that filters out whatever understandings of the history of passion and perception would be most likely to subvert willing participation in established society and culture."[8] He proposes to eliminate the "alloy of falsehood in explanatory stories" in psychiatry in order to "drive home the contingent and transformable character of the social and cultural settings of personal experience" and thus "to enlarge his realm of possible understanding and experience, to enlarge it even beyond what his society and culture could readily countenance" at the price of personal happiness, stability, and resignation.[9]

But has he moved the theory that combines truth with a lie to the level of social theory? "[W]e cannot separate, clearly and definitively, the part of a speculative social theory that represents a successful attempt at a more detached understanding and the part that can succeed only as a self-fulfilling myth, even a myth of emancipation and enlightenment."[10] Columbus "succeeded" from the perspective of world history (though not from his own) because he was in error about geographical fact. Lenin "succeeded," Kolakowski argues, because he consistently failed to understand his situation and failed to predict even the near future, but always did so in the willful direction of the immanence of the revolution:

> His mistakes enabled him to exploit the possibilities of revolution to the full [to the hilt!], and were thus the cause of his success. Lenin's genius was not that of foresight, but of concentrating at a given moment all the social energies that could be used to seize power, and subordinating all his efforts and those of his party to this one aim. Without Lenin's firmness of purpose, it is unthinkable that the Bolsheviks could have succeeded. . . . In critical situations Lenin committed violence on the party, and his cause prevailed as a result. World communism as we know it today is truly his work.[11]

Unger tells us that his own theory is the "work of a mind anxious about the realism of the radical cause."[12] His assertions are "conten-

---

[7] *Passion* at 291.
[8] *Id.* at 292–93.
[9] *Id.* at 292–93.
[10] FALSE NECESSITY at 324.
[11] KOLAKOWSKI, *supra* note 6, at 526.
[12] FALSE NECESSITY at 305.

tious but defensible grounds for argument rather than knockdown proofs."[13] By abandoning a futile quest for certainty he hopes to "gain the countervailing explanatory advantages suited to its character."[14] Yes, but what is the character of the "self-fulfilling myth" of this "anxious" mind?

Unger's theory does not then *have* a rhetoric: it *is* a rhetoric. The modern political and social theories that most clearly distinguish formative contexts from routine or ordinary practice are unthinkable without a modern concept of science which sharply contrasts theoretical knowledge from commonsense knowledge. Formative contexts are what is known by a science of society, just as common sense knows ordinary "routine" practice. Ordinary morality governs the latter. What norm governs the formative contexts? Adam Smith, who sharply distinguished a scientific and commonsense knowledge of society and strongly influenced Marx, never faced the question. For him a deistic god had set in motion a deterministic history of formative contexts for man's utilitarian good. Science could know this history, but the only normative bite of this knowledge was negative: In making legal judgments, for example, one should be careful to rely solely on one's moral sentiments and not try directly the Promethean task of pursuing that utilitarian goal. As with happiness in traditional moral learning, the end cannot be reached by aiming at it. (There is of course a scholasticism concerning the impossible relationship between the explanatory and the prescriptive in Marx.) In any case, *the nature of the formative context or basic structure each theory knows is determined by the self-understanding the theory has of its own ideal of theoretical or "scientific" knowledge.* For a rhetorical theory, operationalist, and existentialist, a formative context *must* be the result of past arbitrary determinations. Taken "to the hilt," all determinations *must* be the results of the most morally arbitrary of actions, "fighting."

Unger chooses, and on his own principles it must be pure choice, one of the perennial philosophical options as to method and interpretation of his own theorizing. It's represented in ancient philosophy by the Sophists and by Cicero. Unger rejects all modes of thought in which simple parts are put together (logistic methods), universal truths are approximated (dialectical methods), or problems solved (problematic methods). Instead he adheres to a self-understanding of method in which arbitrary formulations are interpreted (operational methods).[15]

---

[13] FALSE NECESSITY 340.

[14] *Id.*

[15] I follow Richard McKeon's account of "philosophical semantics" here. Philosophical Semantics and Philosophical Inquiry (unpublished paper on file at the University of Chicago). *See also* R. MCKEON, FREEDOM AND HISTORY: THE SEMANTICS OF PHILOSOPHICAL CONTROVERSIES AND IDEOLOGICAL CONFLICTS (1952); M. BUCKLEY, MOTION AND MOTION'S GOD (1971). It may be that these possibilities are exhaustive: "The assumption of least parts, but no whole except by composi-

For operational or rhetorical methods, such as the one Unger embraces, freedom is "achieved and retained operationally by the acquisition and use of power and of knowledge which is power."[16] For the existentialist interpretations, "freedom is spontaneous or undetermined activity, and external impediments include psychological as well as physical hindrances and the fixities of automatic and habitual responses . . ."[17]

Unger says that no one has ever taken the notion of society as an artifact to the hilt, not even Vico, who is most closely associated with the notion that we can know society only because we make it. Vico was a professor of rhetoric who sought to revive rhetorical modes of thought in the face of Cartesian ideals of science. Unger is himself very much in this tradition: He stands with the rhetoricians against the grammarians (structuralists, for example) and logicians (micro-economists). He is right that his position is extreme: It does take one mode of thought to the hilt, that represented by the sophistical or rhetorical tradition.

For a pure rhetorician, facts are purposes and purposes are arbitrary. His assertion then that problem solving and interest accommodation are decisively shaped by unique institutional and imaginative contexts that cannot be explained as the mere residues of past exercises in problem solving and interest accommodation is a pure expression of an operationalism against a problematic method. But, as Hegel said, one bald assertion is as good as another. My suspicion is that a problematic method can just as consistently interpret history and the current contexts of problem solving as the results of the residues of past exercises in problem solving. John Dewey does, in the main, do just that. And it is difficult to see how Unger can, *from within his theory,* simply reply, "History just doesn't happen that way."

I will argue that many of the problems his theory suffers from are more or less directly related to the extremism of his operational ideal of the truth of this theory.

III. UNGER'S CRITIQUE OF RAWLS AND THE NEED FOR AN EXPLANATORY THEORY

Unger criticizes what he takes to be one of the most influential lines of normative social and political theory abroad in the Anglo-Saxon world, that associated with Rawls in social theory and Dworkin in legal theory. My purpose here is simple and thus my sketch of Rawlsian method is oversimplified. Unger criticizes Rawls's approach,

---

tion; the assumption of an ontological unifying principle but no absolute least parts; the rejection of least parts and separated wholes and the assumption of problems and natures encountered in the middle region; and the assumption that all distinctions are initially arbitrary." PHILOSOPHICAL SEMANTICS at 4.

[16] *Id.* at 8.
[17] *Id.* at 7.

representative of the "liberal center" as he puts it, in quite specific terms. I believe that his criticisms are telling, though a full description of my convictions here would take me too far afield. Unger's *constructive* attempt can well be understood to provide exactly the kind of explanatory-prescriptive theory that Rawls' "failure" mandates, *if* one is to move beyond Rawls on the left with a robust normative general theory applicable to, indeed determinative of, the basic structure of society, or for formative contexts. My strong misgivings about Unger's project expresses my own "Kantian" willingness to pay the price of theoretical sterility to avoid the imposition of enormously abstract romantic and aesthetic norms in politics.

The key subject of justice for Rawls is the basic structure of society, a notion akin to Unger's concept of formative context. The basic structure provides the background institutions within which we may pursue our individual interests and live our personal moral lives. The morality of human action is not measured by the goals we pursue but by the conditions and constraints we impose on their pursuit. This rests on an acceptance of the thoroughly Kantian notion that the (noumenal, practically reasonable) self is prior to the ends it pursues. Of course, Rawls tries to shed from his theory as much of the Kantian metaphysical "baggage" as he can manage, a maneuver that causes many of the strains in the theory, as Sandel has pointed out.

The problem is to evolve norms to govern this basic structure. Ordinary morality, which always operates within a basic structure, is of no use here. On this Rawls agrees with Adam Smith, Kant, Hegel, and Marx. The key constructive device for Rawls is the notion of reflective equilibrium. It is through reflective equilibrium that the shape of the original position is determined. Since the original position is created "so as to lead" to a particular set of principles and institutions, the fact that the occupants of the original position, proceeding strictly according to the principles of rational choice, choose this or that institutional structure is philosophically trivial. Whether or not the "representative men" would choose Rawls' principles presents only secondary logical questions (within the aspiration to "moral geometry"), or questions in game theory as to whether the "rational" degree of risk aversion can be specified within a game-theoretical framework.

Rawls describes his construction of the original position and notion of reflective equilibrium in the following terms:

> In searching for the most favored description of this situation [the original position] we work from both ends. We begin by describing it so that it represents generally shared and preferably weak conditions. We then see if these conditions are strong enough to yield a significant set of principles. If not, we look for further premises equally reasonable. But if so, and these principles match our considered convictions of justice, then so far well and good. But presumably there will be discrepanices. In

this case we have a choice. We can either modify the account of the initial situation or we can revise our existing judgments, for even the judgments we take provisionally as fixed points are liable to revision. By going back and forth, sometimes altering the conditions of the contractual circumstances, at others withdrawing our judgments and conforming them to principle, I assume that eventually we shall find a description of the initial situation that both expresses reasonable conditions and yields principles which match our considered judgments duly pruned and adjusted. This state of affairs I refer to as reflective equilibrium.[18]

The generally shared conditions express our respect for one another as moral persons and spring from the most formal or "Kantian" moment in the theory. Since "we" do not normally have elaborate convictions about principles of justice, reflective equilibrium is plausible only if one can derive from the principles a set of institutions which actually do embody those convictions. Rawls proceeds to do just that in the "four stage sequence." A "back-and-forth" then becomes possible between the formal structure of the original position and those aspects of the institutional framework—constitutional, legislative, and socioeconomic—that embody our settled convictions of justice.

This is where Rawls faces his problems.[19] Some of the economic institutions he "derives" are too indeterminate to compare to settled existing institutions. Some purchase similarity to existing institutions at the price of deviation from the fairest reading of the demands of his actual principles. On the other hand, if his principles are taken seriously, especially the lexically prior opportunity principle, one derives institutions that are strikingly different from existing American institutions, often in odd ways that seem more the artifacts of the simplifying devices of his theory. If this is so, then his attempt to escape Kantian formalism in constructing principles "so as to lead" to particular principles and institutional consequences involves either an act of will or an act of judgment. As an act of will it is ideology. Judgment, in any coherent meaning of that term,[20] simply functions without object at this level of generality. The difficulty with simply "finding" our settled judgments of justice in our institutions and then extending them is that these institutions embody multiple lower level conceptions of justice that are incompatible with each other and in tension: to each according to his marginal contribution, to each according to his legal rights, to each according to his need.[21] Each of these principles if ruthlessly universalized can generate a "utopia" and can be found in relatively pure form in one or other thinker and society. But there is no obvious way in which any one of

---

[18] J. RAWLS, A THEORY OF JUSTICE 20–21 (1971).

[19] I argue this at length in Burns, *Rawls and the Principles of Welfare Law,* 83 NORTHWESTERN UNIVERSITY LAW REVIEW (1989) at 184.

[20] R. BEINER, POLITICAL JUDGMENT (1983).

[21] The most acute statement of this principle is D. MILLER, SOCIAL JUSTICE (1976).

them "more fully" embodies the master principle of respect for human beings as moral persons or ends in themselves.

Rawls wants to give his theory genuine normative power, and so cannot allow his most general principles to sink back into the swamp of existing institutions and the lower level conceptions of justice with which they are intertwined. If the real is the rational, period, there is no place for general normative theory applicable to the basic structure.

Now even conservative thinkers can allow for the extension of a particular ideal or concept already implicit in the legal or political system to new areas in order to resolve a particular "crisis" or "problematic situation" that has developed as a result of the internal dynamics of a legal-economic institution in all its concreteness. Rawls's goal is much more ambitious and the reach of concepts which we may properly call "moral" is much vaster. In order to give concreteness to the moral imperative within his theory, he projects out first principles and then the institutions toward which legislators and judges are *obliged* to move their societies. To a Burke, Hegel, Arendt, or Oakeshott it will seem that this places impossible burdens upon strictly moral concepts and moral arguments. One must be content with a much less normatively ambitious (though not necessarily theoretically ambitious) theory.

To travel down the more normatively ambitious road, it would apparently be necessary to field an explanatory-prescriptive theory which would allow the theorist to distinguish between those aspects of existing institutions that had normative weight and those that are without such weight. This would require a theory of contemporary social and economic realities in order to discern "what is practically necessary and at the same time objectively possible."[22] It would show that aspects of those realities arose contingently (Dewey) or more or less necessarily (Marx) under social conditions that no longer obtain, and would contain something like Dewey's account of the imprisonment of practices in obsolete but inertial social institutions or Marx's theory of false consciousness.[23] Without such a theory, a normative structure, such as the one that Rawls elaborates, in which the theorist "chooses" to create this or that variant of the original position "so as to lead" to

---

[22] J. HABERMAS, THEORY AND PRACTICE (1973) at 44.

[23] J. DEWEY, LOGIC: THE THEORY OF INQUIRY 487–513 (1938). L. KOLAKOWSKI, MAIN CURRENTS OF MARXISM: THE FOUNDERS, 174–76 (1978). Social conflict between or among groups is obviously a much less central category in Dewey's thought than in Marx's, though there are many significant convergences; R. BERNSTEIN, PRAXIS AND ACTION: CONTEMPORARY PHILOSOPHIES OF HUMAN ACTIVITY 11–83, 165–229 (1971). Unger finds the "false consciousness" explanation of the stability of prevailing economic institutions in the era of universal suffrage to be limited. "False consciousness" does describe the "second-order necessity" of the routines which a formative context shapes between periods of conflict. The people's assumptions about the necessity of those routines "is never stronger than the framework of institutions, practices, and preconceptions on whose continued stability it depends." Small scale conflict can, he argues, quickly escalate and undermine the "pieties that until then had seemed to bewitch" people. FALSE NECESSITY at 215.

this or that set of basic institutions would remain only a choice, an exercise of freedom beyond explanation.

Enter Unger. One of his points of departure for social theory is the failure of the Rawlsian project to generate credible ideals for and transformative insight into the basic structure or formative contexts of society.[24] He accuses the theory of a "fatal vacillation" between principle and intuition. But rather than introducing a theoretical device for distinguishing those aspects of the existing order that have normative force and those that do not, he eliminates the problem by constructing a theory in which existing "institutions, practices, and preconceptions" are both infinitely plastic, a kind of *materia prima* for the will of those with a transformative vocation, and totally bereft of normative significance, embodying nothing like a "considered judgment" or a *Sittlichkeit*. To do this he combines the master metaphor of society as artifact which is consistent with his "rhetorical" theory with his reinterpretation of the Christian vision. It is to his master metaphor that I now turn.

IV. *Homo Faber* and Political Life

Unger's transformative man is radically worldless. His goal is to follow this theory to create a social world in which everybody is as worldless as possible—a world in which "negative capability" is given the fullest possible play. In that sense it's a maximizing theory. Unger's utopia is not a world in which some degree of alienation is encouraged in the interests of criticism and to embody the modern principle of subjectivity, the legacy of Christianity's vision of the unique value of the person that forever bars the return to the fully integrated societies of antiquity. Although Unger's volume on personal relations is not yet published, the theory clearly rejects the "critical" strategy of bowing to human finitude by partitioning the intellectual and practical worlds, and assigning to each its own principle. In the more "progressive" version of this kind of critical or, broadly, Kantian theory, principles from one sphere may be allowed to penetrate another. This penetration is, however, a difficult, "unprincipled" matter, dependent upon an intermixture of prophecy and wisdom, moral or religious proclamation, and political judgment.

The latter process is wholly different from the politics of fabrication that Unger endorses. For Rawls, existing society is not an artifact. It is rather the sediment of earlier considered moral judgments embodying conceptions of justice. It has moral force, a force that reflective equilibrium honors. It is not the result of so morally arbitrary an activity as

---

[24] Social Theory 37–39. *See also* The Critical Legal Studies Movement 13 where his criticism is extended to the Rawls-inspired rights and principles school of legal philosophy.

"fighting." There is no perfect fit between our current moral judgments and the principles of justice embedded in those institutions, a fact that provides the opening for normative theory, but there is considerable overlap. Now, a human artifact is *for* something. For Kant politics is for morals: Politics is for law and law guarantees the purely negative conditions that make respect for the dignity of persons as ends in themselves more nearly possible.[25] The moral life is "the Good," because the good will is the only thing of absolute value, that which transcends the meaningless Newtonian natural mechanism and the depressing and morally destructive tale of foolish ambition, greed, and chance that was human history. Only the unique spontaneity (*Wille*), which a person exercises when he acts morally (with practical reasonableness), frees him from meaningless natural mechanism (and its psychological manifestation, arbitrary will, *Willkür*). The discontinuities between the modes of political, legal, and moral action and the problems of their interrelations that plague Kantian thought are themselves the marks of our *finitude,* the senses in which the human condition must be "broken" in order to provide its various spaces: domestic, moral, political, legal, religious, always a scandal to speculative thought's drive to unify.[26]

The fundamental basis of Kant's belief that there must be a noumenal world in which moral willing participated was just this: Without such a world, "it becomes impossible to distinguish between an aesthetic and a moral praxis."[27] The former would "consist in determining a future state of affairs—an ideal—as the good, and therefore as the end to which our action ought to be the means."[28] All we would need was a science, an explanatory theory, that would allow us to get there from here. Kant's objection, against the romantics, is that the "determination of the good as an object in time is necessarily aesthetic," resting on an inner conviction beyond proof:

> Conceptual thought could at most tell us that such a state of affairs is possible, and how we can realize it—but not that it is the good. If we are none the less convinced that it is, this can only mean that we have represented to our minds an imaginative synthesis which we feel to be fully satisfactory. The hall-mark of the aesthetic standpoint is that it defines both the true and the good as 'that which satisfies the mind.' This is the proper definition of the beautiful, and the satisfaction is a disinterested satisfaction. But if we confuse this with the morally good, then our Utopia takes on the character of a moral determination. It becomes universally obligatory as the objective of action.[29]

---

[25] P. RILEY, KANT'S POLITICAL PHILOSOPHY 12 (1983).

[26] R. KRONER, KANT'S WELTANSCHAUUNG (1956).

[27] J. MACMURRAY, THE SELF AS AGENT 55 (1957).

[28] *Id.*

[29] *Id.*

A person with such a vision, and with requisite power, is not only permitted but morally obligated to coerce others into conformity. It is the fear of romantic totalitarianism that convinces Kant that the "Kingdom of God is within."

For Arendt, too, fabrication, the creation of human artifacts, including legal artifacts, first the constitution and then the laws, is for something. It is for politics, the mode of human action that, in her vision, overcomes meaninglessness. Constitutional and legal fabrication creates the conventional public identities or masks that are discontinuous with the truly unique and differentiated self, a self that can only be fully revealed to "friendship and sympathy, and to the great and incalculable grace of love,"[30] not to the formal, constructed equality of the *nomoi*. But Arendt remains a critical thinker in the Kantian sense in that each mode of activity is "redeemed" by another, and thus must be kept distinct from the others:

> We have seen that the *animal laborans* could be redeemed from its predicaments of imprisonment in the ever-recurring cycle of the life process, of being forever subject to the necessity of labor and consumption, only through the mobilization of another human capacity, the capacity for making, fabricating, and producing of *homo faber,* who as a toolmaker not only eases the pain and trouble of laboring, but also erects a world of durability. The redemption of life, which is sustained by labor, is worldliness, which is sustained by fabrication. We saw furthermore that *homo faber* could be redeemed from his predicament of meaninglessness, the "devaluations of all values," and the impossibility of finding valid standards in a world determined by the category of means and ends, only through the interrelated faculties of action and speech, which produce meaningful stories as naturally as fabrication produces use objects. If it were not outside the scope of these considerations, one could add the predicament of thought to these instances; for thought, too, is unable to "think itself" out of the predicaments which the very activity of thinking engenders. What in each of these instances saves man—man *qua animal laborans, qua homo faber, qua* thinker, is something altogether different; it comes from the outside—not to be sure, outside of man but outside of each of the respective activities. From the viewpoint of the *animal laborans,* it is like a miracle that it is also a being which knows of and inhabits a world; from the viewpoint of *homo faber,* it is like a miracle, like the revelation of divinity, that meaning should have a place in this world.[31]

With action it is different. Action's first existential limitation stems from the irreversibility of the processes it puts into motion. Its redemption is itself an action, that of forgiveness.[32] Its other limitation stems from its unpredictability, "for the chaotic uncertainty of the future,"

---

[30] H. Arendt, The Origins of Totalitarianism 301 (1973).
[31] H. Arendt, The Human Condition 236 (1958).
[32] *Id.* at 237.

which the capacity for action itself ensures. Its redemption is through an action, the faculty to make and keep promises.

Recall Unger's basic metaphors: "man as maker," "society as artifact," "conflict as tool."[33] For Arendt, this set of metaphors gives over the political realm into the hands of *homo faber,* but in a way that robs that mode of human activity of its special contribution to the human condition. Unger's normative principle for evaluating constitutional and economic arrangements is the maximizing of negative capability, the ability to remake the formative contexts in the process of everyday life. For Arendt, *homo faber* contributes to the world its durability and stability. Durability in artifacts and institutions stand against the Heraclitean flow of physical nature and psychic nature, the "voracious needs and wants of their living makers and users."[34] Human identity is constituted by tangible worldly objects: "being related to the same chair and the same table"[35] and living within a stable "constructed" constitutional and legal framework that is no more expressive of the "will" of the people than is a house expressive of the will of those who live in it.

Man, insofar as he is *homo faber,* instrumentalizes: The end does more than justify the means; it "produces and organizes them."[36] It is the end that justifies the necessary violence done to nature to get the wood, and making the cabinet justifies reshaping the wood often beyond recognition. The experience of fabricating has a certain Promethian pleasure about it: The "experience of this violence is the most elemental experience of human strength . . . [and] can provide self-assurance and satisfaction, and can even become a source of self-confidence throughout life."[37] What Unger seeks to do is to freeze *homo faber* in his Promethean moment of destruction ("context smashing"). What he creates is measured solely by the degree to which it lends itself to continuous smashing. Both of Unger's varieties of empowerment "require not only that social relations be jumbled up but that they be kept in a state of heightened plasticity."[38] Heightened plasticity "is itself a mode of empowerment . . . for it gives us mastery over the social settings of action."[39]

There exists a problem for modern utopias that is especially poignant for Unger whose modernism is taken "to the hilt." It is true that even for Plato, the philosopher-king "makes" his artifact, his city, as the sculptor makes his statue. Before the modern age, however, both

---

[33] SOCIAL THEORY at 166.
[34] H. ARENDT, *supra* note 31, at 137.
[35] *Id.*
[36] *Id.* at 153.
[37] *Id.* at 140.
[38] PASSION at 188.
[39] *Id.*

fabrication and political action were viewed as limited by reason, a faculty whose knowledge, which was a vision of or participation in the Good, imposed limits. "Only the modern age's conviction that man can know only what he makes, that his allegedly higher capacities depend upon making and that he therefore is primarily *homo faber* and not an *animal rationale,* brought forth the much older implications of violence inherent in all interpretations of the realm of human affairs as a sphere of making."[40] Marx's acceptance of the necessity of violence as the means of significant social change "only sums up the conviction of the modern age and draws the consequences of its innermost belief that history is 'made' by men as nature is 'made' by God."[41] After all, what *is* a hilt?

Unger fabricates a theory in which the standard for success of the constitutional framework is nothing but the maximum possibility of endless refabrication of "formative contexts" and, necessarily, of the constitution itself. As he recognizes, this is modernism taken to an extreme. Kant, as a modern thinker, attempted to solve this problem of infinite regress or "bad infinite" within the framework of *homo faber,* the framework of ends and means, by transcending it through his doctrine of man, and the good will, as an end in itself, something that would confer *meaning* on an otherwise meaningless endless sequence of ends and means. The good will is bedrock, the noumenal world, a foundation, though its absoluteness poses enormously difficult problems addressed with the greatest delicacy in the critical philosophy.

Unger will, of course, have none of that. Unger attempts to find meaning in the endless remaking of the human "artifact." Herein lies the problem: "While only fabrication with its instrumentality is capable of building a world, this same world becomes as worthless as the employed material, a mere means for further ends, if the standards which governed its coming into being are permitted to rule it after its establishment."[42] One of the consequences of conceiving political action as making, as fabrication, the means to producing an object, is that its distinctive form of speech, political rhetoric, becomes an instrument of war ("fighting"), "mere talk," simply one more means toward the end, "whether it serves to deceive the enemy or to dazzle everyone with propaganda."[43] Unger's own description of a politicized environment riddled with meetings where one finds only "manipulation and boredom" comes to mind. His own assurance that the typical forum for politics in an empowered democracy will be "conversation" seems both

---

[40] *Id.* at 228.
[41] *Id.*
[42] *Id.* at 156.
[43] *Id.* at 180.

unlikely and not very reassuring. After all, there is an entire industry devoted to teaching the "art" of manipulative conversation.

Unger's actual constitutional arrangements provide for a set of rights that provide traditional civil rights and physical security, minimal material welfare, protection against subjugation by any public and private power.[44] He combines this with a structure in which ideological political parties can enact their programs with relative ease, even programs, as he recognizes, that would involve the dismantling of his constitutional structure. Practically, however, ideological parties on the right have always taken aim at many of the social and economic immunity rights that Unger wants to provide. They view the elimination or scaling back of those rights as an important element of their programs: The recent actions of a relatively nonideological party in the United States should be proof enough of that. How are the petty-bourgeois commodity producers, who would probably dominate Unger's government, likely to view these immunity rights? Recall that the texture of their routine practices are subject to "the most unforgiving versions of nineteenth-century private law" and that they will live in a society where the norms of mutuality that protect the weak from the strong "can be pretty well dispensed with."[45]

Moreover, on the level of theory, Unger seems to be subject to exactly the same kind of criticism that he levels at Rawls and the Rights and Principles school, only in a more disguised way. To say that Unger's constitution would provide "physical security, minimal material welfare, protection against subjugation by any public or private power" says almost nothing about the many normative policy decisions (about the relation between adequacy and work incentive, equality and equality of opportunity, for example) that are the hard questions in social welfare policy. Rawls does seem to be guilty of a "fatal vacillation between principle and intuition" in these matters. For Unger intuition is stripped of normative significance completely, and principle is too abstract to answer the important questions. He forsakes such questions and trusts in the endless process of refabrication. What is to stop his ideological parties, imbued with an instrumental spirit of the laws, from vastly scaling back or eliminating those rights? For he has neither authority, tradition, nor the conviction, without metaphysical realism, that those rights are . . . well, real.

George Grant—a student of Nietzsche and Heidegger—argues that the most decent constitutionalism is wholly discontinuous with the modernist philosophy of the twentieth century to which Unger appeals. "Contemporary" philosophy can't provide the justification we need for the most basic human rights. In his view, contemporary thought is

---

[44] FALSE NECESSITY at 513–20.

[45] *Id.* at 517, 522.

beset with "darknesses" that prevent modernist reason from giving any account or legitimation of the premises of our constitutionalism, especially of individual rights. Under these circumstances, it would be disastrous, Grant argues, to let any specifically "modernist" philosophy, especially one would think, a philosophy that took modernist thought about society "to the hilt," to inform constitutional thought. It's no accident, Grant repeats, that Heidegger, "the greatest contemporary philosopher," was drawn to national socialism, whose "inner truth and greatness" he perceived as "the encounter between global technology and modern man," words that Heidegger published eight years after the Reich's end. Grant recalls that "[o]ne theoretical part of that encounter was the development of a new jurisprudence, which explicitly distinguished itself from our jurisprudence of rights, because the latter belonged to an era of plutocratic democracy which needed to be transcended in that encounter. Such arguments must make one extremely careful of the ontological questioning of our jurisprudence. . . ."[46] I assume that it would make one even more careful about the restructuring of our jurisprudence on modernist lines, and perhaps especially about a constitution where the "whole life of society is in fact arranged so as to multiply the transformative practical and imaginative activities that bring every aspect of society's order into question and open that order up to conflict."[47]

Arendt is in substantial agreement.[48] "Tradition transforms truth into wisdom, and wisdom is the consistence of transmissible truth."[49] For her, the medieval and early modern tradition of natural rights has not survived the political catastrophes and intellectual developments of the twentieth century. The treasured inheritance of American constitutional rights thrives as an historical inheritance from the common law rights of Englishmen and by an achievement absolutely unique in the history of all modern revolutions, including the French and Russian Revolutions. This was the establishment of authority and tradition in the Supreme Court. For her, this is the *only* specifically modern in-

---

[46] G. GRANT, ENGLISH-SPEAKING JUSTICE 103–4 (1985). Grant's conclusions are consistent with the relative ease with which John Courtney Murray could ground American constitutionalism on premodern modes of thought in J. MURRAY, WE HOLD THESE TRUTHS; CATHOLIC REFLECTIONS ON THE AMERICAN PROPOSITION (1960), though those were not the modes of thought in which the Founders themselves defended their project. *See* Burns, *The Federalist Rhetoric of Rights and the Instrumental Conception of Law,* 79 NORTHWESTERN LAW REVIEW 949–66 (1985). It is also consistent with Arendt's assessment that the American Founders solved in practice but not in theory the problem of the legitimacy of fundamental law in a secular state, a practical solution that saved the American republic precisely from "the onslaught of modernity." H. ARENDT, ON REVOLUTION 196 (1965).

[47] FALSE NECESSITY at 134.

[48] *Burns, Hannah Arendt's Constitutional Thought* in AMOR MUNDI: EXPLORATIONS IN THE FAITH AND THOUGHT OF HANNAH ARENDT 157–85 (J. Bernauer ed. 1987).

[49] Arendt, *Walter Benjamin* in H. ARENDT, MEN IN DARK TIMES 196 (1968).

stance of such authority and tradition, which consists in our civil religion, our being tied back (*religare*) to the foundation, a tie which Unger would seek to cut. "Memory and depth are the same, or rather, depth cannot be reached by man except through remembrance."[50] The following description of the risk Unger is prepared to take makes hugging the shore of tradition rather more appealing:

> The movement in this direction is subject, by its very nature, to a catastrophic detour from which there is no guaranteed automatic return. The system of powers and immunities may be followed by the overthrow of all the citizen's defense against the state, a state whose structure of right need be no more than its own dream of absolute power. . . .This terror can occur only as an interlude, though a repeated and savage one . . .[51]

Does Unger fail to appreciate, as Robespierre came to understand, how difficult, indeed impossible on modernist premises, it is to "put the law above man"? Without either a "higher source" or genuine authority, law could follow law with dizzying speed and fatal consequences, each one swept away by the higher law of the Revolution itself.[52] "In theory as in practice, only a counter-movement, a *contre-revolution,* could stop a revolutionary process which had become a law unto itself."[53]

In sum, Unger proposes to remedy Rawls' "fatal vacillation" between principle and intuition. Rawls' principles and intuitions are "result oriented": they embody convictions about the just distributions of the benefits of social cooperation. Unger eliminates the possibility of the conflict by invoking a set of slogans and metaphors that elevate the *process* of political action above any particular result. All its laws are "laws of movement."[54] His metaphorical understanding of politics is distinctive: Politics is the use of the tool of conflict to refabricate an artifact endlessly. He appeals to the Promethean joy of *homo faber* as an end in itself; it is to serve this end and not to establish any particular result that the entire utopia is constructed. It provides neither a substantive moral ideal of justice that includes a basis for human rights, as Rawls attempts, nor a critical philosophy that places meaningful action outside the endlessly accelerating process of refabrication, as Arendt provides.

I will argue in the next section that Unger's aggrandizement of the sphere of the political, understood in his particular sense, is at the expense of the moral sphere of human interaction. I suggest that his invocation of Christianity to move beyond good and evil in a prescrip-

---

[50] Arendt, *What is Authority?* in H. ARENDT, BETWEEN PAST AND FUTURE 140 (1977).

[51] *Id.*

[52] H. ARENDT, ON REVOLUTION 183 (1963).

[53] *Id.*

[54] H. ARENDT, *supra* note 30, at 463.

tive theory involves a violent transvaluation of values both for Christianity and for politics.

V. REFLECTIONS ON MODERNISM AND THE MORAL LIFE

Unger, as a normative revolutionary thinker, rejects the doctrine that a substantive social philosophy merely mirrors the society of which it is a part. He cannot echo the words of Hegel's mature philosophy: "So much for philosophy telling the world how it should be. . . . " On Hegelian principles the creation of *Politics* would be possible in, and an expression of, a mode of modernism that was ready to die. Of course, that is what a "traditionalist" author such as MacIntyre suggests. Indeed that focus of MacIntyre's work is the restoration of the possibility of moral life[55]—the life that man was made for and which answers the question, "What kind of man shall I become?" MacIntyre's project demonstrates the sense in which Unger's is a choice and, on his own principles, an arbitrary choice.[56]

What is necessary for that kind of life is the existence of authoritative practices, which must be projected from modernist influences. MacIntyre projects communities discontinuous with modernity to recreate the possibility for moral life. Unger, on the other hand, radicalizes what MacIntyre takes to be the worst aspects of modernity. Unger seems to think that traditional notions of morality—that is, Austin tells us,[57] morality itself—are too tightly intertwined with an acceptance of existing institutions. But genuine practices require the existence of genuine authority. Authority is grounded in an acknowledged superior assimilation of the powers that make for an effective practice. It is an example of *justified* hierarchy and roles. (Unger's "unjustified" hierarchy and "rigid" roles hedges: He doesn't tell us straight out what makes a hierarchy justified and what makes a role not rigid.)

I practice a very modest craft, the practice of trial law. In some ways I am critical of these institutions and practices. Participants often try, largely for moral reasons, to change those "formative contexts" if that is not too broad a term for a relatively limited set of institutions and practices.[58] But that is only part of the experience of participation

---

[55] A. MacIntyre, After Virtue (1981).

[56] Ironically, he hurls at a morality of the virtues the same charge that Marx hurled at the petty-bourgeois economy Unger himself espouses: Sentimentality, failing to cast a cold, clear gaze on existing conditions and failing to appreciate that you can't go home again. Unger concedes Marx's argument, but then sets about to change the formative contexts that Marx's deep logic theory took to be determined and impervious to a wave of the theorist's wand. MacIntyre, who has a criticism of deterministic social science that in may ways parallels Unger's, would seek to change the formative contexts of modernity so as to make more traditionally *moral* life possible.

[57] Austin, *A Plea for Excuses*, 57 Proc. of the Aristotelian Soc'y 8 (1956).

[58] M. Frankel, Partisan Justice (1978).

in this practice, which is a contemporary practice of rhetoric, one of the traditionally most morally complex of the practices. Often I feel judged by the practice, inadequate to it and to my role within it. These are not simply technical inadequacies, but moral inadequacies: inability to overcome fear or self-consciousness or, more subtlely, inability to "see" the moral truth of a human situation so as to construct an examination or argument around it[59] or tell a minimally acceptable story to allow the truth of a situation to appear. As Arendt has reminded us, only the pure of heart can tell a story that says the thing.[60] Just as the person transcends the role, the role transcends the person. This is a truth that Unger's methods and principles seem not to allow.

Ordinary moral norms were developed to meet human needs. These moralities constrain the individual's propensity, whose classic statement is Kierkegaard's aesthetic pattern, to view the entire world as a function of his or her material and erotic possibilities. The amazing thing, noted by the great spiritualities and moralities, including Christian moralities, is that a person's acceptance of moral norms effect a kind of pedagogy in seeing the other as other than can in turn effect a basic transformation of the soul—call it a conversion, as Bernard Lonergan still does.[61] What seemed like an alien doom *ab extra* turns out to be a step on the *intinerarium mentis ad deum.*[62]

Unger would call this morality "routine." The highly rhetorical choice of words deprecates the insight, effort, and heroism that ordinary people exhibit in living according to these norms. Kant found the ordinary man living morally to be as sublime as the starry heavens above and indeed found his "good will" to be the eternity in a grain of sand—the peculiarly human form of the reconciliation of the infinite and the finite in man—that made meaningful the otherwise meaningless and mechanical course of world history. Unger follows not Kant

---

[59] *See* J.N. Findlay, Kant and the Transcendental Object: A Hermeneutical Study *ix* (1981):

> "My own thought-relations to Kant have continued throughout my philosophical life. While I began interpreting Kant in terms of an idealism which saw all knowledge as springing from the spontaneous thought-acts of the pure subject into which there could be no external intrusion—the Thing-in-itself being a merely senseless survival—I was led to see and feel the many absurdities of trying to account the content of knowledge, and for agreement among knowers, on such a purely constructive basis, and was also deeply influenced by Prichard's book, *Kant's Theory of Knowledge* (1911), in my perception of profound error in any opinions which assimilated knowledge to making. I see moral as well as intellectual error in such opinions, since they tend to destroy the deep respect for existent fact and being without which men cannot be decent or courageous."

[60] H. Arendt, Eichmann in Jerusalem 229 (1963).

[61] B. Lonergan, Method in Theology, 238–39 (1981); *See* I. Murdoch, The Sovereignty of the Good (1971).

[62] "Fighting" can be a step on this way: as an experience of freedom, discipline, and "selflessness" as many aristocratic moralities, from Platonic to chivalric to Prussian to Edwardian, promise. But it's only a step.

but Marx. When asked by his daughter his definition of happiness, he responded directly: "Fighting!" It seems to me that *Passion* effects a transvaluation of values for a thinker who now realizes that traditional Christian morality is in many ways profoundly antipolitical.[63]

We know that politics are necessary and we struggle to understand the relationship between the "political virtues" and "moral virtues." Unger eliminates this tension by eliminating one side of it. He writes and theorizes relentlessly from the perspective of the political actor, the fighter, the prophet. He ignores Weber's stern advice about the necessary corruption of ends by means for the persons who are politicians in the modern world. And, I fear, he ignores the conclusion drawn by perhaps the most zealous advocate of political life:

> This whole [political] sphere, its greatness notwithstanding, is limited. . . . [I]t does not encompass the whole or man's and the world's existence. It is limited by those things which men cannot change at will. And it is only by respecting its own borders that this realm, where we are free to act and to change, can remain intact.[64]

Everything in the public world may be frozen politics in the sense that nothing could appear in the world of power save through political means: no rights of Englishmen without the threat of fighting at Runnymede. Unger characterizes this process in the following terms:

> An institutional or imaginative framework of social life arises through the containment and interruption of conflict. Defeated or exhausted, people stop fighting. They accept arrangements and preconceptions that define the terms of their practical and passionate relations to one another.
>
> These terms are then continuously recast as an intelligible and defensible scheme of human association: a set of models of sociability to be realized in different areas of social life. This reconstruction is more than an imperative of justification. It is an aspect of what it means to settle down in a social world and to make out of it a home. People then no longer need to understand the organization of society as merely the truce lines and trophies of an ongoing social warfare.[65]

This is what Unger calls the "spiritualization of violence." There is, however, a point to what an older rhetoric called the "genetic fallacy." Political means may be used to create "spaces" where religious and moral practices discontinuous with those means may flourish. The linguistic turn prefers to speak of different "discourses" and a linguistic

---

[63] *See e.g.,* K. POLANYI, THE GREAT TRANSFORMATION 249–58 (1957); H. ARENDT, *supra* note 52, at 33, 36.

[64] Arendt, *Truth in Politics* in 263–64 in *supra* note 50.

[65] SOCIAL THEORY at 151. Recall the words of one of Unger's "heretical modernists":

> The real dwelling plight lies in this, that mortals ever search anew for the nature of dwelling, that they must ever learn to dwell. What if man's homelessness consisted in this, that man still does even think of the real plight as the plight.

M. TAYLOR, JOURNEY TO SELFHOOD, HEGEL AND KIERKEGAARD *i* (1980), quoting Heidegger.

phenomenology reveals very different styles of speaking in religious life, moral conversations, deliberative political argument, and a great plurality even within legal discourse.[66] Unless reality is flattened out by a universal operationalism it would seem that forms of life may embody values discontinuous with those embodied in the means by which they in part fought their way into the political world. And hasn't some of their coming to be been through a kind of moral persuasion that can't be reduced to "fighting"? If politics is fighting, then everything is not politics.

If everything *is* politics what happens to the moral space? Lenin is again a good teacher here:

> We say that our morality is entirely subordinated to the interests of the proletariat's class struggle . . . Morality is what serves to destroy the old exploiting society and to unite all the working people around the proletariat, which is building a new, a communist society. . . . To a communist all morality lies in this united discipline and conscious mass struggle against the exploiters. We do not believe in an eternal morality, and we expose the falseness of all the fables about morality.[67]

So in his essays on Tolstoi, Lenin dismissed as "reactionary" that aspect of the great thinker's work that espoused moral perfection, universal charity, and nonresistance, but praised as progressive and "useful material" his criticism of the peasants' suffering and the hypocrisy of the Church.[68]

Some of the "apolitical" features of these other discourses are conservative: They seek, at least in their own self-understanding, to preserve the institutionally embodied results of past prophecy and liberation. I don't think that Unger would claim that his ideal is neutral as to preservation or change, that it embodies merely an ideal of disinterested intelligence and criticism in these matters, that it merely seeks to open areas previously immune to criticism.

---

[66] I argue this at greater length in Burns, *Hannah Arendt's Constitutional Thought* 157, 175–79 *supra* note 48.

[67] LENIN, WORKS, 31 at 291–94 quoted in KOLASKOWSKI, *supra* note 6, at 516.

[68] Kolaskowski identified three main currents in Marx's thought. They exist in a complicated mix and there are strong tensions among them. The first is that most were influenced by nineteenth-century deterministic physical science. This is the strand that Unger jettisons. More dangerous, in Kolakowski's view, are the romantic and Promethean strands in Marx's thought, which Unger intensifies. Marx's romanticism, like Unger's, counselled not a return to the past, but a quickening of the most distinctive features of the present order and an elimination of "mediating structures." Marx's "Faust-Promethean motif" manifested itself in his "faith in man's unlimited powers as self-creator, contempt for tradition and worship of the past," his emphasis on the collective mastery over first the natural conditions, then the social conditions of progress. It was this last, Promethean motif, which served as much of the justification for the elimination of democratic institutions under Lenin, when "Prometheus awakens from his dream of power, as ignominiously as Gregor Samsa in Kafka's *Metamorphosis.*" *Id.*, Vol. I, 408–16, 420.

His theory seeks in principle to accelerate change through political practice understood as fighting. The theory is not rooted in any sort of transcendental reflection on the conditions of possibility of acting intelligently at all. It involves a choice. But without something like a trancendental method, Rawls' problem returns in an even sharper way. Why should one choose this very particular theoretical stance among other possible theoretical stances? What criteria of judgment could you possibly use?

The identification of the actual with the possible is no less "hallucinatory" than the identification of the actual with the necessary.[69] Unger "solves" the problem of developing norms for the basic structure of society in a most extraordinary way. He reinterprets the Christian vision to radicalize one of its themes, that of man as *homo viator*. This allows him to interpret modernism as a development of this Christian vision. But this does not allow him, in the manner of Rawls, to describe a regime which embodies the right in a stable manner. Indeed the criterion he takes from his modernist Christianity is a kind of procedural one: The exilic religious ideal requires incarnation in a constitutional regime that is endlessly remade, in which homelessness is actively sought.

In his little classic, *Christ and Apollo*, William Lynch argues for the profound discontinuity between Christianity and precisely the kind of modernism that Unger espouses. He argues that modernist drama is inferior to classical and Shakespearean drama specifically in the quasi-theological exaltation of its heroes:

> [T]he "tragic figures" of the modern stage are usually doing very nicely indeed in our last acts in point of strength, energy, and exaltation. Up to the very last act the new theatre was able to look at the truth like an eagle. But in the last act, it became incurably romantic, abandoned the finite, and grasped at any kind of infinite. . . . [70]

Lynch's complaint is that these endings did not emerge from the true logic of the dramatic motion, but were just tacked on. These typical paeans to the immortal greatness of man were "nonevidential statements, attitudes which were blind assertions and thrust of the will."[71] Modernist drama is blind to the deepest level of human existence, "a place where the human spirit dies in frequently real helplessness." Here is the authentic place of faith: where the soul "realizes that it is no match for the full mystery of existence, where, therefore, it suffers a death" that is the prerequisite to new life.[72]

---

[69] FALSE NECESSITY at 291.
[70] WILLIAM LYNCH, CHRIST AND APOLLO 81 (1960).
[71] *Id.*
[72] *Id.* at 88–89.

The key to great literature is, as Goethe said, the vision of the universal in the particular, truly *in* the particular. Since the universal is in different particulars in different ways, this requires what Lynch calls the analogical imagination. This is in sharp contrast to the allegorical imagination which is an exercise in the *will*. Since modernism often conceded the order of cognition to science, it was easy for it to turn literature into "an instrument of power," which could "at least use reality in the effort of the will, through vague thrusts. . . . "[73] "The will of itself wishes only to get to its goals; nor will it be very discriminating about the means, and will in fact reduce everything to a means, never caring cognitively for the thing in itself but always using it as an instrument."[74] Lynch finds a good deal of the "imagination of the will" in the exploitive "univocality of the mechanically allegorical imagination."[75] One thinks of the plays of Sartre. And one thinks of Unger's histories in his third volume.

Lynch argues that great literature has a moral dimension[76] and draws on Thomistic metaphysics and Kierkegaard's dialectics to argue that the "ethical is like reality itself in that it is *articulated*."[77] It involves one family, not the idea of family, one set of specific concrete obligations that spring from talents and obligations. "It forces choices of the actual over the actual, the concrete over the concrete; it compels a man to choose *his* concrete."[78] Each thing is what it is and no other and "there are profound sources of differentiation which we call good and evil."[79] It may be true *speculatively* that each thing is what it is and everything else but not *morally*. Kierkegaard's aesthetic man will, of course, have none of that:

> This man imposes a blanket of "the beautiful" over this field of articulation, thus wiping out the lines and situation of the latter in one magnificent stroke. Given the right techniques, the right moment, the right magic, "beauty" can equalize or abolish good and evil, can eliminate the necessity of choice, can smash the Ixion wheel of struggle. . . .
> In the name of infinite possibility one must be cautious not to commit oneself to the finite. To do so is unscientific, vulgar, and actual. It is a violation and a loss of freedom. The actual is a narrow gate, and who ever heard of entering heaven by a narrow gate?[80]

---

[73] *Id.* at 128.

[74] *Id.*

[75] *Id.*

[76] See also I. Murdoch, *supra* note 61.

[77] *Id.* at 129. *See* M. Taylor, Journeys to Selfhood: Hegel and Kierkegaard 241–52 (1980). For Unger the "original truth" of art is *in*definition and its quest is for the unlimited. False Necessity at 574.

[78] *Id.*

[79] *Id.*

[80] *Id.* at 129.

I am myself no theologian, but the reference to the narrow gate is, of course, to Matthew 7: 13–14.[81] The saying summarizes the life of the Golden Rule and the entire Sermon on the Mount and echoes the first of the Beatitudes, "Blessed are the poor in spirit." "The implication of this claim is that when we approach the gate, our fulness must contract into emptiness if God is to give us access to divine happiness."[82] The narrow gate can only be entered alone and we must bend our natural consciousness to get through. "The pathway he asks us to follow leads us to the freedom of a disciplined life, and it is life of this kind that will finally allow us to express divine perfection."[83]

> Freedom is not to be identified with the apparent spontaneity and with the sheer diversity of a broad pathway, but with the focused and the orderly existence of the narrow way. . . . The alternative to such a life, where the erotic consciousness seeks to express itself freely along a broad path, will never lead to the fulness it seeks. Jesus tells us that the wide gate and the broad pathway lead to destruction and that *they do so as a natural result of the human quest for perfection.* If we miss the narrow gate and the narrow path, we will be destroyed, not by divine vengeance, but by our insistence upon following a pathway of our own.[84]

The asking and seeking that Jesus demands no doubt involve a great deal of psychological intensity. The danger is that "God is not lost but simply displaced by our own infinite demands to achieve divine perfection for ourselves."[85] Vaught continues in a manner strongly reminiscent of Unger, but reaching a conclusion for religious life far more consistent with the view of Kant in morals and Lynch in aesthetics:

> The only self-defining being is a divine being, and this fact becomes a human problem because we are not only finite . . . but infinite as well. We are both finite and infinite at once. Because we are not simply finite but infinite as well, the natural consciousness attempts to explode beyond its finite limits, displacing our finitude with an infinite power of its own.[86]

For Unger, the religious consciousness' infinity is made an infinity of discontent. Though he tells us that the transformative vocation will produce anxiety when it does not have means and opportunity, it appears that such vocation will be permanently anxious. It will always be hunting down something to push against. The self's sense of its own reality can come only where it feels resistance. But Unger's social world is an infinitely plastic world—and it is infinitely plastic in conception to

---

[81] "Enter by the narrow gate; for the gate is wide, and the way is broad that leads to destruction, and many are those who enter by it. For the gate is small, and the way is narrow that leads to life, and few those who find it."

[82] C. Vaught, The Sermon on the Mount: A Theological Interpretation 178 (1986).

[83] *Id.* at 180.

[84] *Id.*

[85] *Id.* at 172.

[86] *Id.* at 172.

Unger's transformer, though the slightest attempt actually to transform even a small part of it will demonstrate how little plastic it is.[87] The world's resistance will inevitably be conceived as an irritant, a technical problem for the politician-as-builder or a tactical problem for the politician-as-fighter, an irritant to the infinite advance of will. No wonder that technical and tactical metaphors often seem most appropriate for comprehending rhetoric, his chosen medium, *when politics is conceived so tactically.* A vision of the social world (and as in Marx, there is no real vision of the natural world as having even relative independence) as infinitely plastic will never satisfy the self because one can never reach the other, the "absolute" in any part of it. Unger notes that a kind of madness ensues where the conditions for self-assertion do not prevail. I believe that the vision of the social and political world as infinitely plastic, as "prime matter" as the Thomists say, for the transforming will is a kind of madness. It should be only a kind of "methodological postulate" for a certain limited kind of practice and must be subject to critique in the pre-Marxist sense of limitation of spheres.

There is all the difference between refusing to conspire in murder, as in the philosophical conscientious refusal of Socrates and the Christian conscientious refusal of Jaegerstaeter, and even in a willingness to fight physically or verbally for the real needs of the other, and a vocation that simply looks for a fight. Unger's rejection of the "moderate Aristotelian city" is in the name of the modernist depiction of the contextless subject which he takes to be continuous with Christian notions of the world as exile.[88] But it seems an idealistic wave of the theorist's wand that attempts to reconcile Christian practice that has given preeminence to the peacemaker and the suffering servant with that of the modernist transformative vocation's focus on successful fighting. It does serve the needs of the system for a source of normative energy. Was it Nietzsche who said, "The will to system is the will to lie"? Christ says: "Don't let the left hand know what the right hand is doing." "When you pray go into your room and close the door." The transformer, Unger admits, wants to shine and lord it over the other all in the stated interests of service.

The Kantian elevation of the moral point of view necessarily implies that much more of the political and social world has to be taken as just "given," as subject to "natural" forces, of physical nature (recall Montesquieu), or of human psychology. The praxis unconstrained by the moral point of view that would imply successful "acting into na-

---

[87] Recall Mitya's argument in *The Brothers Karamazov* that the doing of a modest but real good, like keeping down the price of meat, rather than building ideological crystal palaces of possibility, is a moral act that only a real faith will sustain. F. DOSTOYEVSKY, THE BROTHERS KARAMOZOV 721 (modern Library College Edition 1950).

[88] He also says that mass politics, world history, and international military competition accomplish "what the great religions never could." I do have to suspect these vast equivalencies.

ture" here would inevitably be a Promethean exercise "beyond good and evil." Indeed the virtue that Unger consistently recognizes is put most in jeopardy of his mode of praxis is precisely "loyalty." Recall the words of a Christian statesman of great experience and depth:

> To separate himself from the society of which he was born a member will lead the revolutionary, not to life but to death, unless, in his very revolt, he is driven by a love of what, seemingly, must be rejected, and, therefore, at the profoundest level, remains faithful to that society.[89]

As Royce argued, loyalty is not just one virtue among others. There is an ideal relationship between the moral point of view and the virtue of loyalty. Murdoch writes that "all is vanity" is the first lesson of ethics: For the moral point of view the great enemy is willfulness in conceiving reality and in pursuing one's own projects ruthlessly. It blinds a person to the "central insight of Kantian ethics," that the more the separateness and differences of other people are realized, and the fact that others have needs and wishes as demanding as one's own is appreciated, the harder it is to treat another person as a thing.[90] For the concrete individual a critical loyalty to a joint enterprise that "balances" the needs and wishes of many persons embodies this loyalty. Unger knows that loyalty will be a very difficult virtue in his regime.

CONCLUSION

Heidegger compared Kant's theoretical philosophy to a fortress which many have passed by without storming and which thus still dominates the landscape. In that sense, many philosophies that have come after Kant are pre-Kantian. Kant sharply divided the aesthetic from the moral, the realm of the artistic artifact from that of the imperatives for action. Great art is recognized because it occasions the "subjective" pleasure in the harmony of our faculties, the infinites of reason and the finites of sense, imagination, and understanding. Romanticism effaces the distinction.

But Unger knows this too. He makes no claim that his "rainbow bridge of concepts" mirrors the real world. He does tell us that theory should aspire to art in its revelation of possibility. Is the theory then an aesthetic object? Or does it have genuine normative force? I recall what Edmund Wilson wrote about Lassalle:

> Lassalle, with a pride that like Swift's always took the form of insolence, was driven, for all his princely tastes, to fight for the dispossessed proletariat just as surely as Swift, for all his worldly ambitions, was driven to fight for the impoverished Irish. Such a man can never figure as a prince save in the realm of art, morals, and thought; and he

---

[89] D. HAMMARSKJOLD, MARKINGS 79 (1964).

[90] I. MURDOCH, *supra* note 61, at 66 (1970).

can never make deals and alliances—in this Lassalle is quite unlike Disraeli—with the princes of this world . . . ."[91]

Unger is a prince in the world of thought at least in Machiavelli's sense: He wants to teach us how not to be good. He knows that too. He is aware that he is attempting a transvaluation of the traditional tie between Christian self-understanding and the moral point of view. He seems convinced that this is the price of the "repoliticization of the biblical inheritance."[92]

Why pursue Unger's possibility, with all the dangers he warns us of? Why accept the robustness of this kind of theoretical willfulness when so many millions have given their lives for the doctrines of "clever and bookish militants who [often hypocritically, Unger tells us] saw themselves as friends of the people." Not in the interest of reason, or universal morality, nor to further the interests of a universal class. Because it is likely to be more successful? He argues that way, and indeed devotes his third volume to that argument. I suspect, though, that the "success" is a subordinate argument. As he says, a secular normative argument will root itself in a concept of the personality, of activity, or personal encounter. His is rooted in the notion of personality and personal encounter described in *Passion*.

Without a transcendental perspective can he claim any more for his theory than that it is the "ideological seduction" of a particularly able, ambitious and clever rhetorician? But why does he give us such hostage words by which to describe his own theory? Why is he honest about the transvaluation of values that his theory implies? In what interest does he tell his reader about the dangers for our most cherished rights and practices his theory holds? Is it only because it is the way of a good rhetorician? Or does his honesty on this score embody older ideals of truthfulness that a purely operational method cannot make sense of? Should he have this insight into his own honesty, would it be one of those whose truth requires a new context, a notion of a theory that aspires to more than a call to arms?

The content of the theory and the philosophical claims for the theory are closely related. The Thomist can speak robustly and without theoretical embarrassment of the analogous structure of reality. His world is filled with finite beings and one sort of being—the human—which is an infinite in the finite, though not "caught" in the finite. He "becomes who he is" by thinking, acting, and making in ways that respect natural limits. God is the "principle of concretion" who defines all finite beings, who *can* create the not-God only by a negation of his own Infinity. The Thomist too holds that, with the one exception of

---

[91] E. Wilson, To the Finland Station: A Study in the Writing and Acting of History 252 (1940).

[92] J. Habermas, Legitimation Crisis 212 (1973).

God, *omnis determinatio est negatio.*[93] Since everything is what it is by a communication of necessarily finite being, God is at the center of every being and at its borders, because its borders are its center. The self-limitation of ethics feels sacrificial, but the dismemberment of the the "old self" that comes in the main from surrendering possibility opens the self to Being itself. This carries over into social philosophy: The "imperatives of political and social morality derive from the inherent ['natural'] order of political and social reality itself, as the architectonic moral reason conceives this necessary order in the light of the fivefold structure of obligatory political ends—justice, freedom, security, the general welfare, and civil unity or peace. . . . "[94] These ends are "public not private. They are therefore strictly limited."[95]

Modern philosophy developed largely in reaction to Galilean science's claim to be the organon of truth about reality. A fully "mathematicized" nature,[96] including human nature, of course, simply could not be understood as containing morally significant "articulations." Kant's critical philosophy, the philosophy of limits, was developed in response to the intellectual crisis caused by modern science's truth claims. It preserved the Platonism in morals (the categorical imperative is the only "fact of reason") that could limit the political realm and could limit the rule of *homo faber* in politics. The political was in the service of the moral. There was something to find and to respect; everything was not fabricated: "[E]verything . . . cannot be reduced to an instrument of policy in the quest for empty success."[97] A critical thinker like Arendt abandons the Platonism but remains a thinker of the limit. She bears the theoretical tensions of unresolved questions about the interrelations of the critically differentiated spheres in the interest of practical decency or meaningful action.[98] The will drives the

---

[93] In different ways, Hegelians and Process thinkers hold that this metaphysical principle applies to God as well.

[94] J. MURRAY, WE HOLD THESE TRUTHS 272 (1960).

[95] *Id.*

[96] E. HUSSERL, THE CRISIS OF EUROPEAN SCIENCES AND TRANSCENDENTAL PHENOMENOLOGY 23 (1970).

[97] Traversi, *Henry the Fourth, Part I,* 15 SCRUTINY 15 (1947–48), quoted in A. DONAGAN, THE THEORY OF MORALITY 240 (1977).

[98] Thus a great neo-Kantian thinker like Max Weber will argue, in effect, that the political vocation is absolutely antithetical to the absolute ethics of Jesus and yet that there is a relationship in the purely spontaneous act of conscience ("Here I stand. I can do no other.") of a "mature man." Weber's classic description of the political vocation and of the Christian vision bear a comparison with Unger's "transformative" vocation that I cannot undertake here. Weber's descriptions of both religious and political life seem to me less willful than Unger's. He is unwilling to dissolve strong contraries by the "transvaluation of values," political and religious, that can be achieved by an idealistic wave of the theoretical wand. The theoretical temptation to elude such tensions may stem from a will or a felt "responsibility" to . . . well, make world history come out right. That *is* ridiculous. It is also dangerously Promethean. Weber, *Politics as a Vocation* in FROM MAX WEBER: ESSAYS IN SOCIOLOGY (H.H. Gerth and C.W. Mills eds. 1964).

theoretical intellect to quest for the One. As Plato said, one should not go from the many to the One too quickly.

Unger's theory cannot *in principle* find or recognize value, limited and situated, in existing institutions or practices, or see some such institutions as instrumental in preserving the conditions of moral life. All of its laws are "laws of movement."[99] It aims only at the acceleration of the process of destruction and reconstruction.[100] Rawls has called his method "Kantian constructivism." Unger's is best described as "Sophistic constructivism."

Some may actually modify their practice in light of this theory. But others will prefer to wait for another theory:

> There may be new revolutions and new Napoleons; there may be new heroes and new martyrs for conscience, but it is not the business of philosophy to prohesy their advent or, most certainly, to encourage and assist in their birth. For better, but probably for worse, they may come about, but 'philosophy is the exploration of the rational, it is for that very reason the apprehension of the present and the actual, not the erection of a beyond, supposed to exist, God knows where, or rather which exists, and we can perfectly well say where, namely in the error of one-sided, empty, ratiocination.'[101]

---

[99] A. ARENDT, *supra* note 30 at 463 (1973).

[100] *Id.* at 467.

[101] J. ROBINSON, DUTY AND HYPOCRISY IN HEGEL'S PHENOMENOLOGY OF MIND: AN ESSAY IN THE REAL AND IDEAL 130 (1977), quoting G. HEGEL, PHILOSOPHY OF RIGHT 10.

COMMONSENSE REASONING, SOCIAL CHANGE, AND THE LAW

David E. Van Zandt

Social theories are not of much use unless they advance in some respect our understanding of the social world. In striving for such insights, social theories come in two types. Some attempt to construct admittedly simplified models of social relations from a few specified principles. In using a limited set of principles, such theories risk producing models that are not descriptively comprehensive or even plausible.[1] In fact, they may only describe and explain a limited region of social behavior.[2] The payoff for taking this risk, however, is that such models are better able to predict specific patterns and behaviors. Observation of actual social relations can then be used to test those predictions. Through such prediction and observation, these theories provide insights into the operation of actual social relations.

The other type of social theory has a more grandiose aim. Its goal is to provide a complete or comprehensive description and explanation of social relations—a story[3]—that is superior to any other explanation. Such theories are often intended to be normative as well as positive; that

---

[1] "[A] model, persuasively to present an idea-structure as a possible linkage-format for descriptions of a given subject matter, *must* differ from the subject matter. If it were not different, the original structure would itself be observationally obvious to everyone who confronted the descriptions, or at least as obvious as in the model." N. HANSON, OBSERVATION AND EXPLANATION 79 (1971). "[B]y completely eliminating *all* differences between the model and the original state of affairs one ends up destroying the very thing the model was meant to achieve—namely, the provision of an 'awareness of structure' absent from the original confrontation with a complex of phenomena." *Id.* at 81.

[2] Robert Merton's idea of social theory of the middle range sacrifices comprehensiveness for explanatory power. *See* R. MERTON, *On Sociological Theories of the Middle Range*, in ON THEORETICAL SOCIOLOGY 39, 51-52 (1967); R. MERTON, SOCIAL THEORY AND SOCIAL STRUCTURE 3, 9 (1949).

[3] I am tempted to say "myth" in the anthropological sense of a story that presents both a "model of" and a "model for" society. *See* Geertz, *Religion as a Cultural System*, in ANTHROPOLOGICAL APPROACHES TO THE STUDY OF RELIGION 1, 3-4 (M. Banton ed. 1965) (culture as whole performs normative and explanatory functions). *Politics* has many of the aspects of a cultural symbol system: it not only provides its readers with a description and explanation of the world, but also presents a world toward which readers should strive. *Cf.* K. MANNHEIM, IDEOLOGY AND UTOPIA 56, 59 (L. Wirth & E. Shils trans. 1936) (total conception of ideology: "reconstruction of the systematic theoretical basis underlying the single judgments of the individual" in particular social grouping).

is, in addition to explaining the world, they suggest how the world should be reconstructed. They strive to describe and explain every facet of social life in order to present a new and attractive view of social relations that will educate the reader.[4]

Obviously, the complexity of social life alone makes the complete achievement of this ambition impossible. Theories of this second type, however, assert that their outlines of the description and explanation are complete and that filling out the theory is a noncontroversial, ministerial task. The measure of the success of such theories is not their preciseness or predictive power, or the specific insights they provide, but rather their overall plausibility or persuasiveness as comprehensive pictures of the social world.

Roberto Unger's *Politics* is clearly a theory of this latter type.[5] A magisterial sweep through a vision of a new world that seeks to fulfill human potential and desire, it attempts to blend a positive analysis of society with a normative program for social change. Its purpose is to persuade and prompt.[6] Because any study of such ambitious scope must of necessity treat numerous difficult issues with extremely broad strokes,[7] it is easy to criticize any number of Unger's propositions for their lack of

---

[4] Critical theory, as described by some, has these characteristics. *See* Balkin, *Deconstructive Practice and Legal Theory*, 96 YALE L.J. 743, 765 (1987) (critical theory has goal of enlightenment and emancipation, not development of series of true propositions; is self-referential; and is confirmed by self-reflection) (citing R. GEUSS, THE IDEA OF A CRITICAL THEORY 55-95 (1981)).

[5] The three volumes of *Politics* are the culmination—for now—of Unger's developing social theory and of his practical experience in Brazilian politics and reform. *See also* PASSION; *The Critical Legal Studies Movement. Politics* is a development of the themes outlined by Unger in his address to the Conference on Critical Legal Studies in March 1982 held at the Harvard Law School and published in revised form as *The Critical Legal Studies Movement*. Unger's earlier work has the same transformative inspiration. KNOWLEDGE AND POLITICS at 15-16.

[6] *See, e.g.,* SOCIAL THEORY at 9 ("A final aim of [*Social Theory*] is to enlist the reader's help in the theoretical campaign this work initiates.").

[7] In producing a study of this type, Unger seems to ignore the import of one of his own aphorisms: "Any complete story about nature and society lacks the compelling character of the most compelling local narratives." SOCIAL THEORY at 83. A significant strain of thought within the critical legal studies movement shares this concern. *See, e.g.,* Boyle, *The Politics of Reason: Critical Legal Theory and Local Social Thought,* 133 U. PA. L. REV. 685, 773 (1985) (local critiques to be preferred); Gordon, *New Developments in Legal Theory,* in THE POLITICS OF LAW 281, 290 (D. Kairys ed. 1982) (social analyst should work not at level of large-scale social theory but in smallest routine interactions of daily life); Note, *'Round and 'Round the Bramble Bush: From Legal Realism to Critical Legal Scholarship,* 95 HARV. L. REV. 1669, 1684 (1982) ("Speculative inquiry, however, is prey to ensnarement in historical circumstance, an ensnarement that destines most theory to oscillate between phantasmic utopia and peregrine detail."); D. Trubek, "Critical Empiricism" in American Legal Studies: Paradox, Program, or Pandora's Box? 37 (July 1986) (unpublished paper presented at Cardozo School of Law summer workshop and at Conference on American and German Traditions of Sociological Jurisprudence and Critical Legal Thought, July 10-12, 1986) (on file with *Northwestern University Law Review*) ("[O]ne gets a better, more complete understanding of social life if one tells thick stories about something concrete than if one seeks to make broad generalizations, or seek for deep, determining forces.").

development, their vagueness, or their arguable inaccuracy.[8] Moreover, *Politics'* internal logic may not be as tight as we would wish.[9]

Taken as a whole, however, *Politics* presents a possible and even attractive story of a better social and political life. Such a theory should be judged by its overall plausibility and persuasiveness, rather than by a standard that requires precise modeling and the generation of falsifiable predictions.[10] The appropriate question, in my view, is whether *Politics* presents a view of the world that comports with our present understanding of the way that world operates, while at the same time providing us with new insights into social relations.[11] I will evaluate *Politics* using this standard.

I do this by prising out and examining one of the central concepts on which Unger's story rests. That concept is the idea of "formative context." A formative context, Unger's version of social structure, is vaguely and functionally defined as the "set of basic institutional arrangements and shared preconceptions"[12] within which routine or every-

---

[8] For example, Unger does not explain his preference for democratic control of the shifting of resources over an entitlement or rights approach such as the one offered by Richard Epstein. *See* R. EPSTEIN, TAKINGS 12-14 (1985). Moreover, Unger is extremely vague about the criteria for the allocation of shares of the revolving capital fund among entrepreneurs. *See* FALSE NECESSITY at 493-95; *see also infra* note 143. Although I did not comb the three volumes of *Politics* for arguable inaccuracies, the work is bound to have a few, although probably fewer than this article.

[9] *Politics* is certainly subject to the same types of criticisms that reviewers have leveled at *Passion. See, e.g.*, Boyle, *Modernist Social Theory: Roberto Unger's* Passion (Book Review), 98 HARV. L. REV. 1066, 1077 (1985) (Unger's use of "convergence" concept unable to bridge Humean fact/value dichotomy: "Unger is simply more convincing when he concentrates on experience and on the politics of everyday life, rather than on the formal logical categories for producing truth."); Weinrib, *Enduring* Passion (Book Review), 94 YALE L.J. 1825, 1835 (1985) (circularity in idea of revisable contexts).

[10] In fact, if the latter were the standard, *Politics* does not get out of the starting gate. I am sure that many will dismiss *Politics* under this latter standard as another general, vague, unhelpful, and long-winded social theory that presents only the writer's musing and dreams of a better world. I prefer to suggest where I think the theory goes astray even as a theory of the second type.

[11] *See* Boyle, *supra* note 7, at 736 ("[T]hese theoretical problems and philosophical contradictions are only relevant in so far as they reflect (and reflect back upon) our basic experiences of social life.").

[12] SOCIAL THEORY at 62. The institutional arrangements are organized according to more or less explicit or articulated norms. FALSE NECESSITY at 58. The shared preconceptions are the models of "what relations among people should be like in different domains of social existence." *Id.* A formative context is neither a natural object nor a mere mental prejudice: instead, Unger asserts, "The primary sense in which a social structure exists is practical. It exists both because and in the sense that people cannot easily disturb it in the course of their ordinary activities." FALSE NECESSITY at 61.

Unfortunately, this is as precise as Unger ever gets in defining his central concept. His later analysis of general social and economic structures such as petty commodity production and empowered democracy as formative contexts suggests that formative contexts are society-wide social structures. However, he never attempts a more specific definition.

The oft-noted lack of clarity in the writing of scholars such as Unger who are schooled in the continental tradition has been explained as a politically motivated reaction against the prevailing "paradigm of 'proper' philosophical expression." Balkin, *supra* note 4, at 745 n.6 (citing Sturrock,

day social disputes are waged and settled.[13] His positive claim about formative contexts is that they vary in their resistance to change. The normative counterpart to this descriptive proposition is that those formative contexts which are more open to change should be preferred. Unger thinks that through this concept, *Politics* presents a new and more promising version of the traditional social theoretic concept of social structure, a version that in turn provides a blueprint for a better society.

I find that Unger's analysis of formative contexts and the implications of that analysis for understanding social change lack plausibility and provide little insight into social life. While the concept of formative contexts can be criticized from a number of angles,[14] my criticism is that Unger's concept of formative contexts rests on an inadequate or implausible microsociological theory—that is, a theory of the relations among individuals within a society. My central thesis is that Unger's microsociological theory cannot support his program because it causes him to underestimate the immutability of formative contexts. In making this argument, I elaborate Unger's idea of formative contexts first by tracing the problem it is designed to solve, and then by illuminating the microsociological theory that animates it. Finally, I suggest an alternative microsociological theory and use it to draw some conclusions both for the overall prospects of Unger's program and for law.

I. FORMATIVE CONTEXTS: REVISABLE SOCIAL STRUCTURES

The concept of formative contexts is Unger's preferred conceptualization of social structure. Because every social theory includes some

---

Introduction to STRUCTURALISM AND SINCE 16-17 (J. Sturrock ed. 1979)). Unger's lack of precision, however, may be epistemologically based. Unger may believe that any more definitive statement would be a distorted description of this essentially protean idea. A detailed definition would give the reader a false sense of stability. To the extent that Unger's theory is intended as a comprehensive explanation, this point has some validity. However, his failure to specify the meaning of formative context certainly makes his theory less useful as a social theory in the first sense I identified above.

[13] For some time, Unger has been approaching social theory through the somewhat amorphous concept of "context." Both *Passion* and *The Critical Legal Studies Movement* essays rely on the concept as the centerpiece of their analyses. *See The Critical Legal Studies Movement* at 649 ("Formative contexts . . . represent frozen politics: they arise and subsist through the interruption and containment of fighting over the basic terms of collective life."); *id.* at 665 ("[T]here are practical and imaginative structures that help shape ordinary political and economic activity while remaining stable in the midst of the normal disturbances that this activity causes."); PASSION at 5-15 (definition of context).

[14] The use of the concept has been criticized as vacuous and chameleon-like. *See* Weinrib, *supra* note 9, at 1840-41; Note, *Roberto Unger's Theory of Personality, Law, and Society: Critique and Prospect for a Revised Methodology,* 35 CINN. L. REV. 423, 433 (1986); R. Garet, Human Nature as Self-Transformability 78-92 (Sept. 1986) (unpublished paper presented at Columbia Law School Legal Theory Workshop) (on file with *Northwestern University Law Review*). Unger speaks about contextualism, but rejects the Wittgensteinian idea of context. PASSION at 11; *see* Yablon, *Law and Metaphysics* (Book Review), 96 YALE L.J. 613, 623-24, 631 (1987).

idea of social structure[15]—whether it is system, social habit, institutional structure, mode of production, or social role—different theories often compete over the definition, description, and precise contours of the idea. A particular theory's position on the nature of social structures depends on which of two great meta-issues the theory focuses upon. Very often, a particular theory addresses one issue to the relative exclusion of the other.

The first meta-issue is the question, "How is social order possible?"[16] For theorists concerned with this issue, social order is produced by identifiable or discoverable processes that hold society together. Social structure is either the skeleton that provides social order with its cohesion or the persistent result of cohesive forces. Some thinkers in this group see an inherent conflict between human nature and social structure or order.[17] Others are more agnostic about the existence of this conflict

---

[15] The term "social structure" has had as many meanings as there have been sociologists and anthropologists to use it. The heyday of the term was the late nineteenth and early twentieth centuries, when sociologists analyzed societies using an analogy to the morphological structures of living things or, later, the organic functions of biological entities. *See* L. COSER, MASTERS OF SOCIOLOGICAL THOUGHT 28, 91 (1971) (Auguste Comte sought social physics, while Herbert Spencer examined progressive differentiation of structures and functions); A. RADCLIFFE-BROWN, *On the Concept of Function in Social Science*, in STRUCTURE AND FUNCTION IN PRIMITIVE SOCIETY 178, 178 (1952) ("The concept of function applied to human societies is based on an analogy between social life and organic life."); *id.* at 179 (structure is distinguished from functioning of structure). *See generally* E. EVANS-PRITCHARD, SOCIAL ANTHROPOLOGY 50 (1951) (idea of structure and function can be traced back to Montesquieu: "he speaks of the *structure* of a society and the *rapports* between its parts"). More recently, sociologists relying on the early work of Durkheim and Mauss on social classification, E. DURKHEIM & M. MAUSS, PRIMITIVE CLASSIFICATION (R. Needham trans. 1963) (originally published in 1903), and on the structural linguist Ferdinand de Saussure, F. DE SAUSSURE, COURSE IN GENERAL LINGUISTICS (C. Bally & A. Sechehaye eds., W. Baskin trans. 3d ed. 1966), have called on the idea of linguistic structure to provide content to the term. *See, e.g.*, C. LEVI-STRAUSS, *Structural Analysis in Linguistics and in Anthropology*, in STRUCTURAL ANTHROPOLOGY 31 (C. Jacobson & B. Schoepf trans. 1963).

[16] *E.g.*, E. DURKHEIM, THE DIVISION OF LABOR IN SOCIETY 61 (G. Simpson trans. 1933) (role of division of labor "is not simply to embellish or ameliorate existing societies, but to render societies possible which, without it, would not exist"); G. HOMANS, THE HUMAN GROUP 90-91 (1950) (adaptation of social group to external environment); Parsons & Shils, *Values, Motives, and Systems of Action*, in TOWARD A GENERAL THEORY OF ACTION 47, 197 (T. Parsons & E. Shils eds. 1951) ("Internal differentiation, which is a fundamental property of all systems, requires integration. It is a condition of the existence of the system that the differentiated roles must be coördinated either negatively, in the sense of avoidance of disruptive interference with each other, or positively, in the sense of contributing to the realization of certain shared collective goals through collaborated activity."); *see* Wallace, *Overview of Contemporary Sociological Theory*, in SOCIOLOGICAL THEORY 1, 41 (W. Wallace ed. 1969) (functional imperativist social theories directed to explaining how social systems persist). The more modern and microsociological schools of social choice and ethnomethodology are preoccupied with the same question: How is collective action or a social sense of order produced? *E.g.*, H. GARFINKEL, STUDIES IN ETHNOMETHODOLOGY (1967); R. HARDIN, COLLECTIVE ACTION (1982); J. MITCHELL, SOCIAL EXCHANGE, DRAMATURGY AND ETHNOMETHODOLOGY (1978).

[17] *See, e.g.*, T. HOBBES, THE LEVIATHAN 63-65 (M. Oakshott ed. 1955) (London 1651); S. FREUD, CIVILIZATION AND ITS DISCONTENTS 44 (J. Strachey trans. & ed. 1961) ("it is impossible

and the source of social strains.

Theorists addressing the second meta-issue ask what is the basis of social change. They focus on the relation between the individual and the social order in their search for that basis.[18] Although the reasons for the existence of the social order are not always self-evident, they are considered to be unproblematic once they have been isolated; the real focus of interest is on how that order affects—usually negatively—the individual, and on how that effect can be altered.[19]

Although it seems obvious that both questions should be central to any adequate social theory, few theorists have expressly addressed, much less answered, the questions together in a convincing fashion. Unger is not an exception: for him, the idea of social order once it is understood is unproblematic, almost self-evident. The predominant thrust of *Politics* is to answer the second question: What is the nature of the relation between the social order and the individual, and how can it change? That answer, however, rests on an implicit theory of the nature of social order.

A. The Nature of Social Order: The Naturalistic Premise and Modern Social Theory

In *Social Theory*, the first volume of *Politics*, Unger locates his idea of formative contexts in the modern history of social thought. He introduces the concept to criticize two variants of the social theory that he finds prevalent in modern (post-Enlightenment) thought. Modern social theory is defined, according to Unger, by its rebellion against the "naturalistic premise"—the idea that social worlds are neither conditional nor subject to revision by acts of will.[20] The modernist insight,[21] according to Unger, was to realize that social worlds not only constrain individual members of society, but also are created by them and thus are malleable.[22] In Unger's view, however, neither version of modern social theory carries this insight far enough:[23] in fact, both actually regress to quasi-naturalist positions.

Under one variant, which Unger identifies as "positivist social sci-

---

to overlook the extent to which civilization is built up upon a renunciation of instinct"); M. OLSON, THE LOGIC OF COLLECTIVE ACTION 1-2 (1971) (conflict of self-interest and achievement of social good causes only small groups to emerge).

[18] *See, e.g.,* 1 & 2 M. WEBER, ECONOMY AND SOCIETY (G. Roth & C. Wittich eds. 1978); A. GIDDENS, THE CONSTITUTION OF SOCIETY (1984).

[19] *See, e.g.,* J. ROUSSEAU, THE SOCIAL CONTRACT 49 (M. Cranston trans. 1968) (Paris 1762) ("Man was born free, and he is everywhere in chains. . . . How did this transformation come about? I do not know. How can it be made legitimate? That question I believe I can answer.").

[20] SOCIAL THEORY at 19-23.

[21] Unger previously analyzed "modernist" theory in PASSION at 33-36.

[22] SOCIAL THEORY at 1 ("Modern social thought was born proclaiming that society is made and imagined, that it is a human artifact rather than the expression of an underlying natural order.").

[23] *See id.* at 23-24, 87.

ence,"[24] the predominant problem is the first meta-issue: how is social order possible. In Unger's account of positivist social science, social order is constituted by an endless stream of problem solving or interest accommodation activity.[25] Particular results of this activity, when viewed in the aggregate, make up the social order. Some positivist explanations tend to downplay the constraining influence of the social order and reinforce familiar, almost naturalistic, beliefs about society.[26] The social and institutional background to human activity is rarely brought under critical light. In other positivist accounts, the number of possible outcomes of problem solving or interest accommodation is thought to be limited by "[i]nflexible economic, technological, or psychological imperatives."[27] This version of positivist social science presents the world as constituted by an a priori set of features from which individuals cannot escape.

The second variant of modern social theory, which Unger labels "deep-logic theories,"[28] addresses more directly the relation between the individual and society and the problem of social change. It expressly acknowledges that constraining social contexts exist and goes on to argue that they change through history. These social contexts, according to Unger's exposition of deep-logic theories, stand apart from and order the routines of everyday social life. Each social context has an internal coherence in which each element is inseparable from each other element.[29] Deep-logic theories seek meta-principles to explain the transformation between one social context and another. These principles either define a limited set of possible social contexts or describe the necessary evolutionary progression of such contexts.[30]

Both versions, according to Unger, hedge on their rejection of the naturalistic premise.[31] Versions of positivist social science that refuse to

---

[24] Unger cites the following as representative: D. EASTON, THE POLITICAL SYSTEM: AN INQUIRY INTO THE STATE OF POLITICAL SCIENCE (1953); M. FRIEDMAN, CAPITALISM AND FREEDOM (1962); D. NORTH & R. THOMAS, THE RISE OF THE WESTERN WORLD: A NEW ECONOMIC HISTORY (1978); Solow, *Alternative Approaches to Macro-Economic Theory: A Partial View*, 12 CAN. J. ECON. 339 (1979). SOCIAL THEORY at 235-36. Unger's broad-brushed descriptions of these two variants are, of course, open to challenges of both miscategorization and misunderstanding. I recount them because of the light they shed on Unger's own views.

[25] SOCIAL THEORY at 130.

[26] *Id.* at 131.

[27] *Id.* at 135.

[28] Unger cites the following as representative: M. WEBER, *supra* note 18; M. WEBER, THE PROTESTANT ETHIC AND THE SPIRIT OF CAPITALISM (T. Parsons ed. 1958); K. MARX, THE GERMAN IDEOLOGY (C. Arthur ed. 1970); K. MARX, *Introduction to a Critique of Political Economy*, in THE GERMAN IDEOLOGY 124 (C. Arthur ed. 1970). SOCIAL THEORY at 229-30.

[29] Unger gives as an example Marx's idea that each mode of production is an indivisible and repeatable type. SOCIAL THEORY at 90-91.

[30] *Id.* at 91-92.

[31] *Id.* at 93 ("In all these ways the deep-structure tradition hedges on the repudiation of the naturalistic premise.").

examine the institutional background implicitly take that background as natural and given. Other versions of positivism more expressly point to naturalistic limitations located in biological or psychological traits. The quasi-naturalism of the deep-logic theories is more subtle. It rests on the idea that there is some natural logical progression or natural set of types of social order.

B.   The Idea of Formative Context

Unger wants to "take the antinaturalistic idea of society to the extreme,"[32] by developing his notion of formative context. A formative context or an "institutional and imaginative structure of social life," as he sometimes describes it, produces and sustains "a system of social roles and ranks" for members of the society. Formative contexts also yield "a detailed set of practical and discursive routines,"[33] which put in place "a particular version of society."[34] Unger relies on the concept of formative context to perform the yeoman's work in his theory.

1.   *The Descriptive Function.*—First, the concept is intended to provide an adequate descriptive device. In constructing his concept of formative context, Unger accepts the deep-logic theories' distinction between formative context and everyday routines of conflict that occur within the boundaries of a formative context. The formative context defines the nature and limits of the routine activities of daily life.[35] These routines are recurrent patterns of economic, political, and governmental activities and disputes that make up the stuff of everyday life, the most important of which are the conflicts over the allocation and control of resources and other people.[36] Although these activities and disputes are often turbulent, they are "structure-preserving routines"[37] that rarely challenge the validity of the formative context itself. To a great extent, the formative contexts are "the hardest of social facts . . . in the sense that they are both the most resistant to transformation and the richest in the range of their

---

[32] *Id.* at 86; *cf.* KNOWLEDGE AND POLITICS at 1-3 (seeking total critique).

[33] FALSE NECESSITY at 59.

[34] *Id.* at 58.

[35] "All sustained practical activity takes for granted certain terms of the access that people have to one another: material, cognitive, emotional. These assumed terms appear most decisively as established powers and rights. Such rights and powers draw the outline within which people can make claims upon one another's help." SOCIAL THEORY at 19.

[36] FALSE NECESSITY at 58 ("By far the most important of the routines it shapes are the conflicts over the possession and mastery of the resources that establish the terms of people's access to one another's labor and loyalty and that enable the occupants of some social stations to control the activities of the occupants of other social stations."); *see The Critical Legal Studies Movement* at 586 ("The ultimate stakes in politics are always the direct practical or passionate dealings among people. The institutional order constrains, when it does not actively shape, this microstructure of social life.").

[37] FALSE NECESSITY at 60.

effects."[38]

Unger departs from the deep-logic theories, however, in his view that a formative context has no indivisible or repeatable identity as does a Marxian mode of production. Everything in the social order is malleable, or in his oft-employed and colorful phrase, "up for grabs." Certain elements of the order can change without concomitant changes in other elements.[39] In fact, Unger views this path of change as a formative context's normal mode of change.[40]

The path also does not follow any preordained route. Unger rejects the view of deep-logic theories that there are meta-principles governing how formative contexts change. Societies do not proceed along a predetermined evolutionary scale of types nor are they selected by some master principle from a limited list of types. Societies move both up and down any scale one can put together; through mixture and cross-fertilization, the number of possible types of social order is limitless.

This is not to say that social change is a completely stochastic process. Unger asserts that some changes are more likely to occur to a particular formative context than others.[41] Each formative context "results from a particular, unique history of practical and imaginative struggles."[42] A move from formative context A to formative context B may be more probable than a move from A to formative context C. Still, such changes are not predetermined, and more importantly, there is no guarantee that any particular societal change will be for the better. In the end, there is no social teleology.

2. *The Normative Function.*—This lack of teleology does not mean that one formative context is no better than another for Unger. In fact, the whole normative effect of Unger's theory rests on the denial of this type of social-order relativity.[43] Formative contexts differ in terms of their relative entrenchment: that is, they differ in the extent to which they "resist challenge, revision, and even identification in the course of

---

[38] *Id.*

[39] *Id.* at 64 ("[F]ormative contexts can be changed piece by piece. They need not be dealt with on a take-it-or-leave-it basis and replaced as indivisible units, in the fashion of modes of production in Marxist theory.").

[40] He calls this type of change "revolutionary reform":

Such partial substitutions amount to revolutionary reforms as opposed to either reformist tinkering within a formative context (e.g., one more move in a well-established reform cycle) or the revolutionary substitution of an entire social framework (a limiting case never more than approximated by any real-world situation). The view developed in this book sees revolutionary reform as the normal mode of context change.

Id.

[41] *Id.* at 36 ("Each formative context not only reproduces certain routines but also makes certain trajectories of context change more accessible than others."); *see* PASSION at 10 ("[C]ontexts of representation or relationship differ in the severity of the limits they impose upon our activity.").

[42] FALSE NECESSITY at 34.

[43] *Cf.* Weinrib, *supra* note 9, at 1825-26 (prescriptive role of contextuality in *Passion*).

practical and argumentative routines."[44]

Those differences, for Unger, separate the more from the less preferred forms of social life. The formative contexts to be preferred are those that are most open to change, those that will permit individuals full freedom to make a better society.[45] Such formative contexts have the most "negative capability," which he defines as the softening of the contrast between context-preserving and context-transforming activities.[46] Individuals should strive to establish formative contexts that are easily revisable and that will not imprison them in their own creations. *Politics* presents and argues for the best model of formative contexts—empowered democracy—in order to cause its general acceptance.[47]

C. *Microsociological Foundations*

The engine behind the move from an inferior to a superior formative context is the activity of the individual. That activity is also the locus of the normative preference for formative contexts with more negative capability. According to Unger, formative contexts change when the routine conflicts among individuals over the control and allocation of resources escalate into conflicts that challenge the very framework of the disputes.[48] Those escalations arise when members of society break out of normal and routine limits that the existing formative context imposes on ways of perceiving the world and on the scope and extent of acceptable conflict.

This conception of change in formative contexts rests on a particular microsociological theory. By microsociological theory, I mean a theory

---

[44] FALSE NECESSITY at 59; *see* PASSION at 10 ("But it may be loosened. For contexts of representation or relationship differ in the severity of the limits they impose upon our activity.").

[45] *See* PASSION at 9-11, 27, 264-66.

[46] FALSE NECESSITY at 35-37.

[47] Substantial portions of *Politics* are dedicated to presenting the formative context of empowered democracy from a variety of perspectives. *See* FALSE NECESSITY at 395-570. Empowered democracy is a revision of an historical formative context of petty commodity production.

[48] A serious question that Unger never addresses, much less answers, is, what is the test of the difference between context-reproducing and context-transforming disputes? Context-reproducing activities are "certain practical activities or conceptual activities" that "go all the way from group rivalry and party politics to moral and legal controversy" and that "constitute the most important of the routines shaped by a formative context; they renew its life and connect it with the concerns of everyday life." *Id.* at 34. Unger acknowledges that most routine conflicts take "[t]he ordinary modes of exchange and attachment, dependence and dominion . . . as given" terms of the formative context. SOCIAL THEORY at 19. He states, however, that "[a]t any moment people may think or associate with one another in ways that overstep the boundaries of the conditional worlds in which they had moved till then." *Id.* at 20. Of course, to the extent that formative contexts have high levels of negative capability, the difference between context-reproducing and context-transforming disputes is imperceptible. *See* FALSE NECESSITY at 36. "No stable, clearcut, and rigid line separates the routine from the subversive." *Id.* at 34. At some level of negative capability, the isolatability of a formative context would evaporate. Unger, of course, given his theoretical method, *see supra* text accompanying notes 4-6, has little need to provide distinguishing criteria as long as this description is persuasive.

that answers the first meta-issue of social theory, a theory of the production of social order.[49] Although most social theories concerned with macrosociological issues such as the allocation of political power and economic rights simply assume such a theory, Unger's microsociological theory is reasonably explicit. Throughout *Politics*, he frequently refers to the microsociological elements underpinning his concept of formative contexts, some of which were developed in *Passion*.

    1. *The Opposition Between the Social and the Individual.*—Unger's microsociological theory posits a stark opposition between individuals interacting with each other and formative contexts. Although all human activity necessarily takes place in a social context[50] and "[c]onditionality is never overcome,"[51] formative contexts essentially constrain individuals and their activities.[52] They coerce individuals, reduce their options, direct their activity, and even determine their perception of the social world.[53] Much of the activity that takes place within a formative context

---

    [49] Here, microsociological refers to the level of analysis rather than to a particular theory. The reference is to the behavior of entities such as the individual or a member of a society rather than to the behavior of larger institutional entities such as firms, the state, voluntary associations, or social class. Unger's formative context is a type of institutional entity or a set of discernibly similar social practices that exist across a span of time and space and that has a systemic form. A. GIDDENS, *supra* note 18, at 24. In much social theory, "society" is the institution that is the focus of attention. G. SIMMEL, THE SOCIOLOGY OF GEORG SIMMEL 9 (K. Wolff trans. & ed. 1950) ("[T]he interactions we have in mind when we talk about 'society' are crystallized as definable, consistent structures such as the state and the family, the guild and the church, social class and organizations based on common interest."). Underlying that institution is the interaction of individuals in that institution which both determines and is determined by the institution. *Id.* at 9-10.

    In order to define the objects of study, I employ a version of methodological individualism. The version, however, is extremely formal and takes no position on the substantive content of the concept of an individual. It brackets off any resolution of the question of whether the individual or the social is prior to the other. Its function is to provide an ostensive definition of the subject matter under study. Of course, discrete microsociological theories supply the substantive content. Utilitarians see the individual as a bundle of preferences and a utility-maximizing drive that implements the preferences. Freudians view the individual as the locus of several psychodynamic structures and drives. Other theorists assert the priority of the social and treat the individual as the product of intersubjectivity. *See* Schutz, *Scheler's Theory of Intersubjectivity and the General Thesis of the Alter Ego*, 2 PHIL. & PHENOMENOLOGICAL RES. 323 (1942).

    [50] *See* PASSION at 7-8 ("Nor, contrary to those who dismiss the seriousness of contextuality, can any activity go forward without selecting from the indefinitely large range of possible frameworks the one that it will tentatively take for granted.").

    [51] *Id.* at 10; *see* SOCIAL THEORY at 18.

    [52] In this respect, they bear affinity to Durkheimian social facts. *See* Brubaker, *Rethinking Classical Theory: The Sociological Vision of Pierre Bourdieu*, 14 THEORY & SOCIETY 745, 752 (1985). Durkheim identified social facts as phenomena separate from psychological facts or physical facts. Social facts are akin to moral facts: they coerce and constrain individuals in society. E. DURKHEIM, THE RULES OF THE SOCIOLOGICAL METHOD 10, 14 (S. Solovay & J. Mueller trans., G. Catlin ed. 1966). Durkheim's stark characterization of social facts may in part be due to the entrepreneurial goal of establishing a new and separate science of society on positivist grounds. *Id.* at xlix.

    [53] This insight is not new, and has a great deal of currency within Unger's own critical legal

"can be explained as the product of the institutional and imaginative context (order, structure, or framework) within which routine activities and conflicts occur."[54] Formative contexts are external to and alien from individual interaction.

2. *The Presocial Element.*—Because of this, formative contexts are never adequate to the possibilities of the individuals who reside in them. For Unger, there is always some human activity and interaction that is prior to and independent of any particular context. Human activity can never be completely bound by any particular social context, and no social context is ever an adequate expressive vehicle for all human activity.[55] The individual is never completely defined by or at home in any social order.[56] "Nothing can entirely reduce us to the condition of puppets of a formative context or of the laws and constraints that might generate a limited set or a compulsive sequence of such contexts."[57] There is an element of irreducible human freedom.[58]

This radical disjunction between interaction among individuals and the coercive formative context is the source of the distinction between "context-preserving" and "context-transforming" interactions among individuals. Most human activity is of the context-preserving type. It is routine and largely determined and constrained by the formative context. Because of its derivative stature, it is artificial and less authentic, although necessary.[59]

---

studies movement. James Boyle points to the basic tension that runs through all critical legal studies movement work: the tension between structuralist and subjectivist perspectives. Boyle, *supra* note 7, at 766-68. Duncan Kennedy's concept of fundamental contradiction, which he claims animates liberal legal consciousness, is a version of this way of looking at the world. Kennedy, *The Structure of Blackstone's Commentaries*, 28 BUFFALO L. REV. 205, 211 (1979). Peter Gabel is probably the most articulate spokesperson for the view that social structure coerces and represses individual activity. Gabel, *Reification in Legal Reasoning*, 3 RES. L. & SOC. 25, 28-29 (1980).

[54] FALSE NECESSITY at 4.

[55] *See* PASSION at 9 ("There is no past, existent, or statable catalogue of social worlds that can incorporate all the practical or passionate relationships that people might reasonably, realistically, and rightly want to strike up.").

[56] *See id.* at 26 ("the idea that man is never at home in the world: that nothing but another homeless person can satisfy the unlimited demands of his spirit.").

[57] FALSE NECESSITY at 34-35; *see* Note, *supra* note 14, at 433.

[58] If Unger is serious about taking "the antinaturalist idea of society to the extreme," SOCIAL THEORY at 86, this assertion of an apparently natural element of human freedom that exists apart from any particular social context is puzzling. My analysis below is an attempt to suggest that even individuals' sense of human freedom is a social product that can be explained and understood only by reference to social factors.

[59] Unger does not at any point refer to the alienated nature of this routine interaction, although that theme is implicit. Peter Gabel's work develops this theme explicitly. *See* Gabel, *supra* note 53, at 27 ("[T]he social body of a collectivity becomes the expression of a *gap* that gives reality the feel of pseudo-reality . . . .") ; *cf.* P. Gabel, Ontological Passivity and the Constitution of Otherness Within Large-Scale Social Networks (unpublished paper presented to Columbia Legal Theory Workshop, Mar. 17, 1986) (on file with *Northwestern University Law Review*) (all interaction based on role or social structural position is alienated).

Incidents of context-transforming interaction occasionally irrupt into this mundane and routine world. Such irruptions are "both exceptional and transitory."[60] Human activity of this type, as one would expect given Unger's views on the path of formative context change, "is not itself governed by a system of lawlike constraints and tendencies."[61] Unlike routine activity, it is free from and outside the system, and takes its cue from no particular formative context. There is always this presocial element in human activity. In Unger's scheme, this interaction among individuals is prior to the formative context.[62]

The actual source and nature of this activity is obscure.[63] In *Passion*, Unger suggests that such activity arises out of the practical and passionate dealings and associations of individuals with each other outside of or apart from routine, context-determined activity.[64] These insights or visions of new forms of human association are generated by a type of presocial interaction among free individuals.[65] Because they are presocial, they are unmediated and unconstrained by formative contexts. Although transitory, they are the sources of true creativity and human fulfillment.[66] They are most often expressed in direct and unmediated social interaction such as in love and other close interpersonal

---

[60] SOCIAL THEORY at 21. Individuals cannot operate for long outside of a formative context. "Either [the context-transcending activity] fails and leaves the preestablished context in place, or it generates another context that can sustain it together with the beliefs or relationships allied to it." *Id.*

[61] FALSE NECESSITY at 4. Unger eschews entanglement with ultimate metaphysical controversies about free will and determinism. *Id.* Although his "framework-revising freedom" may be "illusory" from some philosophical perspective, such a perspective, he suggests, does not respect the freedom that is our "everyday experience." *Id.* at 5. The puzzle posed by these perspectives, he asserts, "represent[s] a permanent insult to societies whose official culture claims to base fundamental social arrangements upon the wills of free and relatively equal citizens and rightholders rather than upon blind drift or coercive authority." *Id.* So much for the relevance of philosophical "puzzles."

[62] *See* PASSION at 95-96, 267.

[63] *See supra* note 48 (Unger never explains how to distinguish this activity from context-reproducing activity).

[64] He refers to "the experience of mutual longing rather than that of participation in a division of labor or a tradition of shared discourse." *See* PASSION at 22.

[65] *See id.* at 24. This is akin to the idea of undistorted communication or ideal speech employed by Habermas. Habermas, *Toward a Theory of Communicative Competence*, in RECENT SOCIOLOGY NO. 2: PATTERNS OF COMMUNICATIVE BEHAVIOR 115, 143 (H. Dreitzel ed. 1970) ("a number of symmetrical relations for the ideal speech situation. Pure intersubjectivity is determined by a symmetrical relation between I and You (We and You), I and He (We and They)."); *see* Boyle, *supra* note 7, at 753 ("Habermas uses this meta-epistemology to justify political choices *between* alternative types of rationality.").

[66] *See* PASSION at 268 ("Our most credible experience of a foundational reality is our experience of the quality of the personal."). This romanticization of pure intersubjectivity is a theme in other critical legal studies movement writings. Gabel & Kennedy, *Roll Over Beethoven*, 36 STAN. L. REV. 1, 3-4 (1984) ("unalienated relatedness" and "intersubjective zap"); Gabel, *supra* note 53, at 26-27; P. Gabel, *supra* note 59, at 143.

encounters.[67]

3. *Maps for Social Change.*—When these irruptions of pure inter-personal interaction disrupt the course of ongoing routine and practical activity in a formative context, they cast a new light on existing formative contexts. Through this context-transcending activity, individuals[68] press against the limits imposed by formative contexts.[69] In Unger's view, "[a]t any moment people may think or associate with one another in ways that overstep the boundaries of the conditional worlds in which they had moved till then."[70] Context-transforming activity apparently involves a heavy conceptual element: it is the capacity of individuals to think of new worlds or formative contexts before they exist. "[T]he power of insight outreaches all the statable contexts of thought."[71]

Whether Unger refers to such irruptions as visionary[72] or as internal developments,[73] they provide the needed Archimedean point from which to criticize the existing formative context and to define objective criteria

---

[67] *See* PASSION at 95-100, 221-24; *see* Note, *supra* note 14, at 440.

[68] At times, Unger seems to suggest that formative contexts may revise themselves. For example, he suggests that "each of these context-reproducing activities can escalate under favorable circumstances into context-disturbing conflicts." FALSE NECESSITY at 72. However, I believe that such talk is simply a feature of the undefined character of his notion of the nature of the agency of social change.

[69] *See* PASSION at 53-57 (heroic ethic); *cf.* Rosen, *Intentionality and the Concept of the Person*, in NOMOS XXVII: CRIMINAL JUSTICE 52, 69-70 (J. Pennock & J. Chapman eds. 1985) (romantic image of self: "This romantic self may be seen as given its greatest chance for development if freed from the oppression of civilization, inhibitions, or social convention . . . .").

[70] SOCIAL THEORY at 20; *see* PASSION at 9.

[71] SOCIAL THEORY at 20; *see* PASSION at 35 (second element in modernism is "the belief that no institutional order and no imaginative vision of the varieties of possible and desirable human association can fully exhaust the types of practical or passionate human connection that we may have good reason to desire and a good chance to establish."). This idea is akin to the proposition that human language is never completely adequate to express human experience. *See* M. MERLEAU-PONTY, *Indirect Language and the Voices of Silence*, in SIGNS 39, 43 (R. McCleary trans. 1964) ("[T]he idea of *complete* expression is nonsensical.").

[72] FALSE NECESSITY at 359-60. "Our thinking about ideals becomes visionary or external to the extent that it holds up a picture, however partial or fragmentary, of a radically altered scheme of social life and appeals to justifications that do not stick close to familiar and established models of human association." *Id.* at 359. Visionary thought can come from either "the philosopher who ascribes normative force to a conception of personality or society, to a method of choice that supposedly relies on no such conception, or even to an entire metaphysical or religious picture of the world," or "the political prophet who evokes a reordered social world in which all major forms of individual and collective self-assertion may be promoted and all our practical and passionate connections may be cleansed of some of the perils that make us shrink from them." *Id.*; *see The Critical Legal Studies Movement* at 580.

[73] FALSE NECESSITY at 355-58.
Internal argument forswears the search for ultimates. It takes place within a tradition of accepted moral and political ideas largely defined by a scheme of models of human coexistence, made actual by institutional arrangements and social practices . . . . The interlocutors in an internal controversy probe the uncertainties, the ambiguities, and the tensions in the imaginative world defined by their shared points of departures. . . . Such disagreements over the scope and the practical form of received models of association expose tensions within these models

for the selection and implementation of better formative contexts. Such activity is the source of genius or the divine inspiration that provides the possibility of a better social order:[74] for Unger, it is an irruption of the sacred into the profane.[75]

What does this privileged vantage point prescribe? Although the precise contours of a particular formative context cannot be stated a priori, the best formative context, according to Unger, is one that is consistent with this interpersonal subjectivity.[76] The formative context that allows this subjectivity to flourish and that is least resistant to changes demanded by this subjectivity is to be preferred over all others. "The vision offered by this program is that of a society in which people are more fully empowered through the development of institutional arrangements that both diminish the gap between framework-preserving routine and framework-transforming conflict and weaken the established forms of social division and hierarchy."[77] Such a formative context would be the next best thing to a purely "natural context."[78]

The microsociological theory underlying Unger's idea of formative contexts is distinctly charismatic.[79] It rests on the ability of certain indi-

---

that may previously have been concealed and force us to choose the direction in which we want to develop each model.

Id. at 356; *see The Critical Legal Studies Movement* at 580.

[74] *Cf.* Boyle, *supra* note 7, at 737 (doing social theory leads to feeling of empowerment).

[75] The microsociological model employed by Unger is similar to that used by so-called "phenomenologists of religion." Such "phenomenologists" view religion as the irruption of the sacred through the fabric of a profane world, causing a reordering of that world. M. ELIADE, THE SACRED AND THE PROFANE 21 (1957) (religious experience involves "hierophany" or "the break effected in [homogeneous] space that allows the world to be constituted, because it reveals the fixed point, the central axis for all future orientation"); *see also* P. BERGER, A RUMOUR OF ANGELS (1969); R. OTTO, THE IDEA OF THE HOLY (2d ed. 1952); Bellah, *Christianity and Symbolic Realism*, 9 J. SCI. STUDY RELIGION 89 (1970). Unger's description in *Passion* of the heroic ethic contains this same idea of context-breaking. PASSION at 53-57.

[76] *See* PASSION at 192-93 ("An order must be invented that, considered from one standpoint, minimizes the obstacles to our experiments in problem-solving and in accepted vulnerability and, viewed from another perspective, multiplies the instruments and opportunities for its own revision.").

[77] FALSE NECESSITY at 362. Empowerment, according to Unger, comes in three varieties: the first is "the development of our practical capability through the openness of social life to the recombinational and experimental activities of practical reason"; the second is "more complete and deliberate mastery over the imaginative and institutional contexts of our activities"; and the third is "our success at escaping both submission and isolation and in diminishing the conflict between . . . our need to participate in group life and our effort to avoid the dangers of dependence and depersonalization that accompany such engagement." *Id.* at 363.

[78] *Id.* at 362.

[79] According to Weber, charisma is

a certain quality of an individual personality by virtue of which he is considered extraordinary and treated as endowed with supernatural, superhuman, or at least specifically exceptional powers or qualities. These are such as are not accessible to the ordinary person, but are regarded as of divine origin or as exemplary, and on the basis of them the individual concerned is treated as a "leader."

1 M. WEBER, *supra* note 18, at 241. Weber's conception of charisma has been viewed as psychologi-

viduals to break through the existing formative context and thus revise it. The source of changes in formative contexts is the moments of interpersonal subjectivity that are presocial. In sum, the microsociological paradigm of *Politics* posits a presocial force rooted in intimate interpersonal relations that is directed and constrained by social structure, but that is not constituted by it and that periodically irrupts to revise it. This quasi-religious force presents to the world new models of human association or of formative contexts. It is the core of his answer to the second meta-issue of social theory: the problem of social change.

D.   Social Change Through Rational Persuasion

Unger never explicitly discusses how the new models suggested by these irruptions are to be implemented in social relations. Although copious pages are spent discussing vague outlines of his idea of empowered democracy as a desirable formative context,[80] he is strangely silent[81] on the actual mechanisms of social change.[82] Unger, however, does seem to have a model of implementation in mind. His extensive statements about the programmatic nature of *Politics* and his attempt to outline and justify his preferred formative context—empowered democracy—suggest that his is a model predicated on rational persuasion.[83]

The model has its roots in the microsociological theory I outlined

---

cal. Shils, *Charisma, Order, and Status*, 30 AM. Soc. REV. 199, 201 (1965). In fact, it is actually a thoroughly sociological concept. As he carefully illustrates, charisma is an artifact of a social reaction to an individual. "It is recognition on the part of those subject to authority which is decisive for the validity of charisma." 1 M. WEBER, *supra* note 18, at 242. And "[i]f proof and success elude the leader for long, if he appears deserted by his god or his magical or heroic powers, above all, if his leadership fails to benefit his followers, it is likely that his charismatic authority will disappear." *Id.*

[80] FALSE NECESSITY at 395-570.

[81] Unger is very good at explaining how attempted programmatic social changes have failed. In doing so, he appeals to structural constraints on both action and understanding. *See* SOCIAL THE-ORY at 67-79 (1985 Brazilian example). The same reasons that Brazilian experiments failed, however, may adversely affect the experiment he proposes.

[82] One model that could be derived from his microsociological ideas is that the new social order will be put into place by some type of Weberian charismatic leader. That leader will provide the blueprint for the new world that will be accepted by the populace as a visionary and divine pronouncement.

> In traditionalist periods, charisma is *the* great revolutionary force. . . . Charisma . . . *may* effect a subjective or *internal* reorientation born out of suffering, conflicts, or enthusiasm. It may then result in a radical alteration of the central attitudes and directions of action with a completely new orientation of all attitudes toward the different problems of the "world."

1 M. WEBER, *supra* note 18, at 245. The new world will be implemented simply because it is an irruption of the presocial. Unger's view, if I have successfully described it, is more complex. It requires members of society not simply to accept the visionary's views as correct, but to undergo a similar visionary process.

[83] It could be that, despite his statements to the contrary, Unger is not actually concerned with changing minds. *Politics* often seems to take the form of "church chat": "[l]ike most other CLS people when talking utopia, Unger seems to be preaching to the converted." R. Bossert, The Uto-pian Promise of Critical Theory in Legal Studies 21 (unpublished paper, Jan. 13, 1987 draft) (on file with *Northwestern University Law Review*).

above. According to this model, *Politics* is the first and most difficult step in accomplishing the transformation of society. It takes a visionary to step outside of his or her current formative context and create a picture of a better way to organize social relations, a better formative context. All that is apparently required is that a few gifted individuals attain those moments of vision. Clearly, *Politics* is intended to be such a vision.

Once this is done, the resulting picture will offer a rationally persuasive critique of the current formative context, prompting the other individual members of society to step outside of their formative context into the presocial and pure realm of authentic interaction among free individuals.[84] In that realm of interaction and communication undistorted by the current formative context, the desirability and correctness of the new model will be obvious. The preferred formative context will be accepted by society quickly and without extensive controversy.[85]

The essential assumption behind this model of implementation is that a new vision of formative contexts can be persuasively transmitted through rational argumentation and demonstration.[86] The necessary and sufficient condition for social change is a type of consciousness-raising or liberation from social conditions that thwart adequate rationality. "We can change our situation in the course of trying to understand it."[87] At the heart of Unger's extremely optimistic view of radical social change[88] is the idea that we are all philosophers who can and must bracket off or stand back from the current formative context and our participation in it,

---

[84] This presumably is the power of criticism to alter lives that members of the critical legal studies movement claim for their work. *See, e.g.,* Boyle, *supra* note 7, at 715, 737 (Unger's work is extraordinarily powerful despite its flaws). Although Unger has stated that a doctrinal breakthrough will not produce revolution in social life, *The Critical Legal Studies Movement* at 646; *see* KNOWLEDGE AND POLITICS at 103 (revision of ideas does not give them force), the overall thrust of his approach, as I understand it, is that such a breakthrough will play a central role.

[85] Behind this idea is the psychoanalytic notion that analysis can remove the layers of distortion imposed through psychosocial development. Boyle, *supra* note 7, at 753 (Habermas and analogy to psychotherapy); Habermas, *supra* note 65, at 143-44; Trubek, *Where the Action Is: Critical Legal Studies and Empiricism*, 36 STAN. L. REV. 575, 610 (1984) (psychoanalytic lifting of delusion in grand theory). However, rational analysis in the Freudian sense is never the ultimate victor. In much modern liberal theory, there is a similar notion of the possibility of undistorted dialogue or communication that can provide a moral foundation for the liberal state. B. ACKERMAN, SOCIAL JUSTICE (1982); M. PERRY, MORALITY, POLITICS, AND LAW (forthcoming 1989).

[86] Boyle, *supra* note 7, at 746 (*Verfremdung* or exegesis can make belief structure visible and thereby destroy it); *cf.* Gabel, *supra* note 53, at 30 (through stating law, judges are able to restore equilibration in popular but false consciousness). *But cf.* KNOWLEDGE AND POLITICS at 103 (revision of ideas does not give them force).

[87] PASSION at 52.

[88] Unger is not alone in this optimism. Many more mainstream liberal thinkers express the idea that it is simply the existence of removable obstacles that prevents correct and true positions on social issues. *See supra* note 85 (possibility of undistorted deliberation). This position is shared by republican and deliberative liberals searching for a moral Archimedean point. *Cf.* Sunstein, *Legal Interference with Private Preferences*, 53 U. CHI. L. REV. 1129, 1155 (1986) ("This understanding is extremely optimistic about the effects of public deliberation.").

and examine it with help from his social theory.[89]

Once a member of society has reached this Archimedean point of undistorted communication and understanding, Unger assumes that the correctness and desirability of the new formative context will be apodictically clear, or at least will become apparent after a period of democratic deliberation. A proper understanding of society leads naturally and effortlessly to changes in society.[90] No coercion or force will be needed to bring about the new world. Indeed, a striking feature of *Politics* is the lack of any discussion of the role of violence or coercion in social change, even though *Politics* recognizes the role of violence in maintaining formative contexts.[91] Unger's thesis regarding social change comes down to a form of moral rationalism: he believes that it is possible under the proper conditions to convince others of the correctness of a moral position through rational argumentation.[92] And he believes that once persuaded, people will then act on that position.

II. COMMONSENSE REASONING

If this view of the nature of formative contexts is adequate, why has

---

[89] James Boyle suggests that social theory has this effect:

If one takes this general belief in immanent critique and connects it to a supposedly impractical set of ideas such as social theory, a strange thing happens. The more one "does" social theory and reads hard books, the more one comes to believe that it is actually useful and liberating to find out about the philosophical structures behind the richly textured justifications for "the way things are" in every area of social life. Even when this belief is discounted by the inexorable tendency to rationalize the worth of one's own activities, an unmistakable feeling of empowerment remains.

Boyle, *supra* note 7, at 737.

[90] In sketching a grand theory of municipal law, Gerald Frug seems to make the same assumption that the mere presentation of the theory causes its acceptance. Frug, *The City as a Legal Concept*, 93 HARV. L. REV. 1057, 1149-50 (1980); *see* R. Bossert, *supra* note 83, at 16 (Frug's argument assumes its acceptance); *cf.* Sunstein, *supra* note 88, at 1136 ("If nonautonomous preferences of these various sorts were changed through a collective process of discovering and countering the distortions that underlie them, it would be proper to say that freedom was promoted rather than undermined as a result.").

[91] The apparent absence of coercion in the adoption of a new formative context does not continue in its operation. Unger's ideas about rules of capital allocation and about immunity rights both presume some coercive enforcement power in the new society. *See* FALSE NECESSITY at 508-39. Perhaps, such coercion is needed only when humans fall back to the mundane existence within a formative context.

[92] While the foundation of this belief is obscure, I use the term "rationalism" because I think that his view must be based on the idea that there are certain truths about the world that are universal and that these truths can be communicated through rational discourse. *See* Williams, *Rationalism*, in 7 THE ENCYCLOPEDIA OF PHILOSOPHY 69, 69 (P. Edwards ed. 1967) ("the power of a priori reason to grasp substantial truths about the world"). Unger has been said to represent the rationalist strand of the critical legal studies movement. Stick, *Can Nihilism Be Pragmatic?*, 100 HARV. L. REV. 332, 332 n.2, 337 n.17 (1987). Certainly, he is not in the same nihilistic league with Joseph Singer, *The Player and the Cards: Nihilism and Legal Theory*, 94 YALE L.J. 1, 8, 61-62 (1984); *see* Olson, *Nihilism*, in 5 THE ENCYCLOPEDIA OF PHILOSOPHY, *supra*, at 514, 515 ("[T]he term [nihilism] is widely used to denote the doctrine that moral norms or standards cannot be justified by rational argument.").

there not already been a great movement toward empowered democracy or some variation of it?[93] The answer, I believe, is that formative contexts or social structures[94] are far more recalcitrant than Unger would have us think.[95] This is not a quibble with his characterization of the mutability of one or another particular existing formative context. It is instead an argument that his account of the genesis and functioning of formative contexts is unpersuasive.

I agree with Unger that we are all philosophers, but in a very different sense. Unger's microsociological model is descriptively inadequate in that for the most part it ignores the role of everyday routines in social life.[96] For Unger, everyday routine activity is either uninteresting context-preserving activity or highly interesting but rare context-transforming activity. Because of this, Unger overestimates the mutability of formative contexts and misunderstands the sources of social cohesion and change. Assessing the concept of formative contexts using a different microsociological theory—one that is concerned with routine activities—illuminates these problems in a more interesting way, and suggests why Unger's account is less than persuasive.[97]

---

[93] One answer might be that until *Politics*, no philosopher or political theorist has provided the necessary story or vision for this transformation. Of course, although Unger's work makes a contribution to the reformist tradition, he would be the first to admit that it is not entirely novel. In *Passion*, he expressly draws on the Christian tradition's notion that men have fallen or become alienated from the natural state. PASSION at 24-25 (homelessness of man).

[94] I will use Unger's phrase "formative contexts" instead of the more generally employed "social context" or "social structure," in part to avoid the terminological debates and baggage of the latter terms.

[95] Boyle makes a similar point:

What I *am* saying is that it is a mistake to confuse the neat Spinozan lattice of an argument about legitimation with the dense tangle of our actual experience of social life. It is ridiculous to believe that one could disrupt the massively entrenched set of power relations and collective fantasies that "constitutes" repression in our society simply by attacking one of the more formalized and abstract fantasies and claiming that the rest are "dependent" on it. The lines of logical entailment are not the threads that hold together the patchwork of social reality.

Boyle, *supra* note 7, at 772. I am trying to identify the threads that hold the formative context together.

[96] This criticism is not new, nor even new within the critical legal studies movement. *See, e.g.*, Boyle, *supra* note 7, at 773, 775; Gordon, *supra* note 7, at 281; D. Trubek, *supra* note 7, at 37. My criticism presents, I believe, a different angle.

[97] In this analysis, I am drawing on a body of microsociological theory that explains social order by examining its social creation in the routine and everyday interactions between individual members of society. I rely on symbolic interactionism, an offshoot of American Pragmatism, *e.g.*, G. MEAD, MIND, SELF AND SOCIETY FROM THE STANDPOINT OF A SOCIAL BEHAVIORIST (1934); Blumer, *Sociological Implications of the Thought of George Herbert Mead*, 71 AM. J. SOC. 535 (1966); *see* P. ROCK, THE MAKING OF SYMBOLIC INTERACTIONISM (1979) (relation between pragmatism and symbolic interactionism); dramaturgical approaches, *e.g.*, E. GOFFMAN, THE PRESENTATION OF SELF IN EVERYDAY LIFE (1959); social phenomenology, *e.g.*, E. HUSSERL, PHENOMENOLOGY AND THE CRISIS OF PHILOSOPHY (Q. Lauer trans. 1965); A. SCHUTZ, THE PHENOMENOLOGY OF THE SOCIAL WORLD (G. Walsh & F. Lehnert trans. 1972); and ethnomethodology, *e.g.*, H. GARFINKEL, *supra* note 16; A. CICOUREL, COGNITIVE SOCIOLOGY (1972). *See generally* P.

A. Everyday Routine and Formative Contexts

In Unger's world, formative contexts have independent existences: although they are revisable by members of society, they stand apart from and constrain the pure, authentic activity of those individuals. They stand as alien forces that frustrate true and authentic human activity. In contrast, I suggest that formative contexts are not external constraints on individuals in the Durkheimian sense. Rather, they are constantly produced, altered, and maintained by the routine efforts of individual members in society attempting to come to grips with the world as it is presented to them. It is useful[98] to see them as models or theories of the world employed as resources by members of society in negotiating their daily lives—including their economic and political struggles.[99]

1. *Pragmatic Philosophizing.*—On this view, each person is a philosopher,[100] but not in the academic or Ungerian sense. Each is engaged in efforts to spin and employ pragmatic theories of the operation of the world that will help in negotiating the problems and puzzles posed by daily existence. While these theories are quite different in scope from the visionary ideas that Unger and his social actors embrace,[101] they are far more ubiquitous and important in the constitution of society.

This process of coming to grips with the world can be called typification.[102] Individuals approaching practical problems attempt to de-

---

BERGER & T. LUCKMANN, THE SOCIAL CONSTRUCTION OF REALITY (1966) (synthesis of Marxist and social phenomenological approaches to problem of social order).

[98] I am proposing a simplified model of social relations to advance understanding. *See supra* text accompanying notes 1-2. I do not assert that the model provides a comprehensive description of social relations; instead, by postulating that members of society solely seek to understand their world in a pragmatically efficient manner, I hope to generate insights about the idea of a formative context.

My approach is related to but distinguishable from the intellectualist approach in social anthropology. *See, e.g.*, Horton, *African Traditional Thought and Western Science* (pts. 1 & 2), 37 AFRICA 50, 155 (1967). Such an approach attributes to actors a drive to formulate coherent and systematic world views. The social scientist's function is then to find and understand the internal coherence of such world views. *See* C. GEERTZ, THE INTERPRETATION OF CULTURES (1973); P. WINCH, THE IDEA OF A SOCIAL SCIENCE (1958); Winch, *Understanding a Primitive Society*, 1 AM. PHIL. Q. 307 (1964). Unger's approach might be seen as related to that of the anthropological intellectualists.

My view is that social actors theorize only to the extent actually required by the circumstances and do not search for consistency between theorizing episodes unless it is pragmatically required. This may result in individuals holding internally contradictory views and in the prevailing formative context lacking the type of systematicity and coherence that Unger attributes to it. *Cf.* Gellner, *Concepts and Society*, in RATIONALITY 18, 33 (B. Wilson ed. 1970) (critical analysis of aspects of contextual approaches that attribute excessive consistency to use of concepts by actual social actors).

[99] *See* A. GIDDENS, *supra* note 18, at 23 (structure "refers not only to rules implicated in the production and reproduction of social systems but also to resources").

[100] *Cf.* M. WALZER, INTERPRETATION AND SOCIAL CRITICISM 29 (1987) ("[W]e are all interpreters of the morality we share.").

[101] *See infra* notes 127-34 and accompanying text (difference between scientific and commonsense theories).

[102] *See* A. CICOUREL, *Interpretive Procedures and Normative Rules in the Negotiation of Status*

velop routine methods for conceptualizing and handling such problems. They achieve this by characterizing a current experience as an occurrence of a familiar type of experience—that is, by categorizing it as of a specific type and as explainable by reference to a theory about that type.[103] A readily available commonsense theory "has the crucial effect of simplifying experience to manageable proportions. . . . The complexity of reality is drastically reduced by having a small window for viewing it."[104] Order is imposed on what could otherwise be seen as a stochastic series of events.[105]

To take an obvious example, if I am approached on a public street by an individual who appears disheveled and who is babbling incomprehensible sentences, I am likely to categorize that experience as one involving a mentally disturbed person whose condition is explainable by the presence of mental "disease." I may not know precisely what "disease" he has or what his long-term prognosis might be. It is sufficient for my practical purposes that I am able to understand this experience in that way, predict from that understanding this person's short-term behavior, and adjust my behavior accordingly. Although this process of typification is more noticeable in unusual situations,[106] it is essential to everyday life. Routine and habit[107] are the stuff that makes the world turn; without them, we would be forced to think from scratch on each occasion.[108]

---

and Role, in COGNITIVE SOCIOLOGY 11, 35 (1972) (citing A. SCHUTZ, COLLECTED PAPERS II: STUDIES IN SOCIAL THEORY 29-30 (A. Brodersch ed. 1964)) (typifications include "typical human motivations, goals, and action patterns. It also includes knowledge of expressive and interpretive schemes, of objective sign-systems and, in particular, of the vernacular language."); A. SCHUTZ, *supra* note 97, at 81-86 (interpretive schema).

103 Peter Gabel, despite his antagonism toward the reification of experience, may agree that a certain amount of reification is necessary to social life. *See* Gabel, *supra* note 53, at 36 (temporary and conscious use of reification is not "troubling").

104 D. HEISE, UNDERSTANDING EVENTS 8 (1979) (function of definition of situation).

105 *See* P. McHUGH, DEFINING THE SITUATION: THE ORGANIZATION OF MEANING IN SOCIAL INTERACTION 83-92 (1968) (emergence of order from initial definition of situation).

106 Examples of typification have been studied in a number of occupational settings. *See, e.g.*, A. CICOUREL, THE SOCIAL ORGANIZATION OF JUVENILE JUSTICE xviii, 243-91 (1976) (juvenile probation officers rely on commonsense understanding of juvenile delinquency to categorize juvenile behavior and to determine appropriate response); Bittner, *The Police on Skid-Row: A Study of Peace Keeping*, 32 AM. SOC. REV. 699 (1967) (police rely on understanding of setting to categorize events and to determine appropriate response); Cain, *On the Beat: Interactions and Relations in Rural and Urban Police Forces*, in IMAGES OF DEVIANCE 62 (S. Cohen ed. 1971).

107 *Cf.* Moore, *The Rational Basis of Social Institutions*, 23 COLUM. L. REV. 609, 609 (1923) ("A legal institution is the happening over and over again of the same kind of behavior."); A. GIDDENS, *supra* note 18, at 19 (habit is part of routine). Judge Jerome Frank spoke of habitual preconceptions as necessary to stable life. *In re* Linahan, 138 F.2d 650, 651 (2d Cir. 1943) (Frank, J.).

108 As Frank says, "[w]ithout acquired 'slants,' preconceptions, life could not go on." *Linahan*, 138 F.2d at 651.

2. *Formative Contexts as Stocks of Knowledge.*—What makes this effort manageable is that individuals have a reservoir of types and theories available to them for use in daily life. Individuals' resources of this type are their "stocks of knowledge"[109]—that is, their accumulated sets of understandings about the world.[110] These sets of understandings provide each individual with resources to negotiate daily life.

The resources are of several types. First, individuals can rely on their own experiences. A past response that was used in a similar situation is always a likely model for the response now. Second, individuals have available to them a range of described experiences and ideas that are communicated to them by others—in particular by family, friends, and associates. The actual experience of any individual is quite limited, and he or she must rely on the aggregate experience of those close to him or her.

Not only do people draw on their own experience and on the experiences of those close to them, but, more importantly for social theory, they can and do draw on extant theories of different types circulating in their wider social group.[111] For example, common pictures of criminals inform individuals about people so classified.[112] Another example is the commonsense understanding of life in socialist societies. People routinely discuss political questions by relying on understandings about Soviet and eastern European life of which they have neither first-hand nor testimonial evidence.[113]

Of course, people and sociologists can consciously reject received

---

[109] An individual's stock of knowledge is his or her core of accumulated experience. *See* A. SCHUTZ, *supra* note 97, at 77, 80-82.

[110] *Id.* at 183 ("[A]ll experience . . . of contemporaries is predictive in nature. It is formed by means of interpretive judgments involving all my knowledge of the social world.").

[111] "People readily accept definitions of situations provided verbally by others." D. HEISE, *supra* note 104, at 6. "The fact that much of the time—perhaps most of the time—people are operating with situational definitions that have been provided by others implies that all people probably do not give equal attention to problems of defining situations." *Id.* One experiment found that "subjects accepted the experimenter's suggestion that they would experience meaningful psychotherapy via an intercom, and they held to this definition of the situation until overwhelmed by the meaninglessness of random responses from the machine." *Id.* (citing P. McHUGH, *supra* note 105, at 66-67, 109-110).

[112] "[T]he layman's understanding of deviance is based on the more visible types that are classified and presented to him every day. Pressed to explain the *fact* of deviation, he will probably redirect the question by talking about the *type of person* the deviant is thought to be: brutal, immature, irresponsible, vicious, inconsiderate, degenerate." Cohen, *Introduction*, in IMAGES OF DEVIANCE 9, 10 (S. Cohen ed. 1971); *see* H. BECKER, OUTSIDERS: STUDIES IN THE SOCIOLOGY OF DEVIANCE 185 (exp. ed. 1966); D. MATZA, BECOMING DEVIANT 80-81 (1969); McHugh, *A Common-Sense Conception of Deviance*, in DEVIANCE AND RESPECTABILITY 61 (J. Douglas ed. 1969), *reprinted as A Common-Sense Perception of Deviance*, in RECENT SOCIOLOGY No. 2: PATTERNS OF COMMUNICATIVE BEHAVIOR, *supra* note 65, at 152.

[113] The recent miniseries, *Amerika* (ABC television broadcast, Feb. 1987), is a stark example. The effect of the series' message relies on a conception of life under socialism that is shared by a significant segment of the American population.

commonsense pictures of criminals. Certainly, the criminals themselves often do.[114] The point is that many people have no occasion or need to examine the received picture thoroughly. Such reliance on commonsense understanding is essential for most meaningful social interaction to occur. Without it, planning action, making decisions, and even conversation would be impossible.[115]

3. *Merger of the Moral and Empirical in Commonsense Reasoning.*—Commonsense understandings or ideas are often evaluative propositions; pragmatic or commonsense theorizing rarely distinguishes between moral and empirical conclusions in the way more academic discourse does. Moral propositions are treated no differently than empirical propositions; moral prescriptions are considered to be empirical features of the world. Prohibitions such as "do not murder" and "drive only on the right" do not have to be defended by complex moral argumentation. They simply are part of the world, or at least part of the relevant world.[116] Commonsense theorizing provides a natural morality grounded in the way things are thought to be.

Thus, all individuals engaged in routine social activity are guilty, in Unger's sense, of adhering to a faulty naturalistic premise. For most relevant practical purposes in everyday life, individuals do merge the "is" and the "ought," and at least tacitly assume that there is no other way the world could be ordered.[117] As it turns out, the naturalistic premise,

---

114 But David Matza suggests that persons labeled as criminals and deviants by society frequently begin to see themselves as such. D. MATZA, *supra* note 112, at 165-80.

115 Nancy Pennington and Reid Hastie have suggested that in deliberating, jurors construct stories as a method of organizing and evaluating the evidence. The construction of the story depends significantly on jurors' commonsense understandings of the way people behave in given situations. These understandings are the jurors' "world knowledge." Pennington & Hastie, *Evidence Evaluation in Complex Decision Making*, 51 J. PERSONALITY & SOC. PSYCH. 242, 247 (1986); N. Pennington & R. Hastie, A Cognitive Theory of Juror Decision Making: The Story Model 19 (unpublished paper presented at Columbia Legal Theory Workshop, Mar. 2, 1987) (on file with *Northwestern University Law Review*).

116 While the prohibition against murder may be an empirical human universal, the prohibition against driving on the left clearly is not. Individuals are certainly aware that in other countries the convention is reversed. But for everyday activity, the two prohibitions function in similar ways. For all practical purposes, murder and driving on the left are not viable options for the solution of practical problems.

117 Unger's work, in fact, is a more abstract effort to merge the "is" and the "ought." An adequate description of the way the world is put together is believed to suggest ways in which it could be reformed. *Cf.* Boyle, *supra* note 9, at 1071-72 (*Passion* is "rebellion against hegemony of fact/value dichotomy"). Unger's effort is not unique. Much of nineteenth-century social theory—whether the positivism of Auguste Comte or Karl Marx's theory of history—described as fact an evolutionary process that governs society and that dictates a more desirable state of affairs. Much legal scholarship, I believe, also shares this general trait: studies of the existing are often believed to ground prescriptive visions. *See* D. Van Zandt, The New Legal Realism: The Empirical and the Moral in Legal Scholarship (unpublished manuscript) (on file with *Northwestern University Law Review*), *printed in abbreviated and edited form in* Van Zandt, *The New Legal Realism*, YALE L. REP., Spring 1987, at 2.

in addition to being an intellectual sin of certain pre-Enlightenment thinkers, is also a consistent tendency of all but the most reflective and Humean individuals.

This prescriptive feature of the process suggests that the particular stock of knowledge available to individuals not only aids them in negotiating daily life, but also directs their activity along defined courses. Stocks of knowledge present a necessarily limited range of theories and types for understanding the world and planning activities.[118] In this respect, stocks of knowledge are formative contexts in Unger's sense: they close off and make unavailable certain options.[119] To a certain extent, they do constrain individual activity.

But that is not a complete understanding of formative contexts. Formative contexts more accurately can be seen as the general stocks of knowledge available to all individuals in the social group under observation. Formative contexts are the aggregate products of individuals' pragmatic theorizing in managing their daily lives. They emerge from the flux of social interaction and activity. They are a resource available to individuals in the social group that facilitate the negotiation of everyday activity

4. *Evidence and Validity.*—Individuals do not, however, accept the validity of formative contexts or the commonsense understandings that constitute them uncritically. The constituents of formative contexts or stocks of knowledge are routinely and repeatedly tested pragmatically by experience. Every time an idea or understanding enables a person to make sense of a situation or to accomplish a goal, it is a piece of evidence of its validity. Although these tests are not controlled experiments,[120] as with any scientific theory, the more problems the formative context solves, the firmer is the individual's acceptance of it.[121]

---

[118] A common metaphor to explain this idea is that of a tool: formative contexts limit an individual's action in the same way that a gardener's available tools limit his or her options. For example, a garden hoe is only useful for chopping clumps of dirt and for some rather gross scratching. When the hoe is not needed, the gardener switches to another tool. In the same way, individuals can switch among elements of the formative context.

[119] Unger discusses the limiting case of "social closure" in which a formative context makes society invulnerable to struggles over the basic terms of existence because of the oligarchy effect (some groups have privileged access to power and to material supplies), the identity effect (individuals cannot distinguish their self interest from that of the group), and the survival effect (the practical arrangements of society determine the terms on which elementary needs can be met). SOCIAL THEORY at 49-52. "In such a circumstance people lack any ready way to imagine transformation." *Id.* at 41.

[120] Anecdotal evidence plays a major role in people's understandings of their society. The most obvious examples are the use of oral stories, tales, and myths. Individuals routinely accept as highly probative evidence that would constitute hearsay. McCORMICK ON EVIDENCE § 245, at 728 (E. Cleary 3d ed. 1984) (courts frequently admit hearsay evidence because of its reliability).

[121] No justification or validation can ever be absolute. *See* Peller, *The Metaphysics of American Law*, 73 CALIF. L. REV. 1152, 1261 (1985) (cannot justify set of categories through which we inter-

This pragmatic verification does suffer from a confirmatory bias. Individuals prefer to fit a new bit of experience into their preexisting theories of the world.[122] A rule of economy of philosophizing lies behind this bias: individuals engage in only as much novel theorizing as is needed to bring the new experience under a familiar category.[123] Individuals react rationally to the constraints of their situation.[124] Because the purpose of the theorizing or typification process is to provide theories and methods for negotiating life, efficiency considerations dictate that any proof be only to a reasonably useful level of certainty. Thus, individuals seek to validate their commonsense ideas to the extent that they will be accurate for all foreseeable practical purposes.[125] If the new experience does not fit neatly, individuals will engage in complex elaborations before they will relinquish their theory.[126]

B. Commonsense Versus Scientific Theories

Unger attributes to formative contexts the same high degree of co-

---

pret legal or social world); Yablon, *supra* note 14, at 633 (Kripkean indeterminacy is idea that "no particular action can ever be justified as following or not following the rule"). Commonsense understandings are similar to Michael Walzer's moral prohibitions that are not "discovered or invented but rather . . . [emerge from] the work of many years, of trial and error, of failed, partial, and insecure understandings." M. WALZER *supra* note 100, at 24.

122 *See* D. HEISE, *supra* note 104, at 8 ("People have a strong disposition to retain a definition once it has been adopted."); Snyder, *When Belief Creates Reality*, 18 ADVANCES IN EXP. SOC. PSYCH. 247, 248 (1984) (attribution theory); *id.* at 257-61 (people act in ways that confirm their preconceptions of others by inducing confirmatory behavior in others). Peter McHugh found that his subjects expended cognitive effort to bolster their current definition of the situation unless that definition became completely untenable. P. MCHUGH, *supra* note 105, at 108.

123 This process bears some similarity to the psychological method of problem solving called "satisficing." *See* Simon, *A Behavioral Model of Rational Choice*, 69 Q.J. ECON. 99 (1955).

124 Rationality here is given Max Weber's meaning of means-ends rationality. Given a specified level of information, members act rationally to achieve pregiven goals when they choose the means that minimize the costs or efforts expended in the action. 1 M. WEBER, *supra* note 18, at 5 (*zweckrational*). Of course, the available information may be inaccurate or inadequate when viewed from a more comprehensive perspective. Moreover, the information set includes those understandings of the way the world works which are unexamined in the particular episode of commonsense reasoning at issue. These caveats gut the concept of rationality of much of its substantive content. *Cf.* J. ELSTER, SOUR GRAPES 10 (1983) (thin rationality is "nothing but consistent preferences and [anticipation of] consistent plans"). By fiddling with the information set available to the social actor, the observer can conclude that any action is rational or irrational. *See supra* note 98.

125 From a different and more comprehensive perspective, these ideas may not be accurate. They are simplifying devices that may lead to systematic errors in perception and action. *See* Tversky & Kahneman, *Judgment Under Uncertainty: Heuristics and Biases*, in JUDGMENT UNDER UNCERTAINTY: HEURISTICS AND BIASES 3 (D. Kahneman, P. Slovic & A. Tversky eds. 1982), *reprinted from* 185 SCIENCE 1124 (1974).

126 P. MCHUGH, *supra* note 105, at 92-111 (attempts to bolster and elaborate current view before surrendering); *cf.* T. KUHN, THE STRUCTURE OF SCIENTIFIC REVOLUTIONS 35-42 (1962) (normal science is period of puzzle-solving or period of attempts to fit experimental results into currently prevailing paradigm).

herence[127] that philosophers and scientists attempt to achieve in their theorizing. His approach assumes that individuals comprehend the prevailing formative context at a level of abstraction similar to his own. His social theory is designed to break down and replace the current formative context with his preferred formative context of empowered democracy. One systematic theory is to replace another through moral persuasion.

If the above sketch of a microsociological theory is persuasive, however, it suggests that individuals do not see themselves as confronted by a constraining and all-inclusive formative context. Nor do they strive for or believe that they operate with a systematic, coherent theory of the world that interprets and guides all activities.[128] The commonsense understandings or theories that individuals formulate and use differ in several respects[129] from more philosophical and scientific theories about the world.[130]

First, the orientation of individuals in generating commonsense understandings is vastly different. Whereas the individual acting in the world theorizes for the purpose of solving a practical problem, the philosopher-scientist may be seeking a broader perspective. He or she is not attempting to manipulate the environment to obtain a particular result, but is instead attempting to understand how that environment works.

Even when the philosopher-scientist appears to be engaged in minute problem solving, his or her orientation is still different. In such cases, he or she seeks to fill in a particular gap or to test a particular result of a more general theory that attempts to explain a whole set of phenom-

---

[127] Unger's criticism of deep-logic theories is that they assume that a formative context is indivisible; that is, that each element is necessary to the identity of the whole. *See* SOCIAL THEORY at 90-91. Although he eschews that idea, he still maintains that formative contexts have a systematic coherence.

[128] I do not attribute to Unger the assertion that individuals have this level of coherence and systematicity in their everyday thought. The point of my discussion is that theories, highly abstracted from everyday routines, have less ability to alter social arrangements than Unger implies they do.

[129] The differences between commonsense and philosophic-scientific theories that I identify in this section are matters of degree rather than quality. *See* Schutz, *Common-Sense and Scientific Interpretation of Human Action*, 14 PHIL. & PHENOMENOLOGICAL RES. 1, 33-34 (1953); Garfinkel, *The Rational Properties of Scientific and Common Sense Activities*, 5 BEHAV. SCI. 72, 74-75 (1960), *reprinted in* H. GARFINKEL, *supra* note 16, at 267-68. At root, attempts by individuals engaged in practical activities and by philosophers and scientists to understand the world are similar and differ only in the interests being pursued. *See* J. HABERMAS, KNOWLEDGE AND HUMAN INTERESTS 196 (1971) (knowledge-constitutive interests).

[130] Bruce Ackerman's descriptions of both the Ordinary Observer and the Scientific Policymaker fall on the philosophical-scientific side of my distinction. Both attempt to theorize about the world in a relatively abstract, general, and consistent manner—albeit in different ways. The Scientific Policymaker develops his Comprehensive View of the world as a basis for normative prescription, *see* B. ACKERMAN, *supra* note 85, at 29; the Ordinary Observer seeks to identify the dominant institutions to provide a source for normative prescriptions, *see id.* at 96. Ackerman's concern is with two principled approaches to the resolution of legal issues; my concern in this section is with the difference between commonsense and more abstract philosophical-scientific theories.

ena.[131]   By contrast, the pragmatically oriented individual seeks to master a particular practical problem and is not concerned with how the solution to that problem fits into a more general theory. "To master such theory as we have is hard professional work—and unless one intends to become a professional economist [or other type of professional theorist], the practical utility of the training will be dwarfed by its very considerable costs in terms of time, money, and lost opportunity."[132]

A second distinction related to the first is that the philosopher-scientist wishes to achieve a relatively high degree of systematicity and consistency among the different elements of his or her theoretical structure. Systematicity assures him or her that others can understand how the results fit the theory. The philosopher-scientist also wants others to be able to replicate his or her results. Because of the ordinary individual's interest in pragmatic results, however, consistency and systematicity across time and events are not as relevant. Although everyone may strive for some measure of consistency,[133] the orientation toward particular issues and problems will often trump concerns for consistency.

Finally, a philosophical or scientific theory is based on a fuller information set than that employed by individuals facing practical problems. Because of the difference in orientation, the philosopher-scientist seeks out information that pragmatically oriented individuals might forego because it would not marginally improve their decisionmaking process. There is still information selection in philosophical and scientific theorizing, but because of differences in purpose the efficient level of information gathering is higher. By contrast, the individual engaged in the type of theorizing I am describing sets out to acquire only the information that is required to solve the problem at hand.[134]

---

131 *See* T. KUHN, *supra* note 126, at 35-42.

132 B. ACKERMAN, *supra* note 85, at 91.

133 L. FESTINGER, A THEORY OF COGNITIVE DISSONANCE 18 (1957) (drive assumed in cognitive dissonance theory). Festinger's major empirical application of the theory of cognitive dissonance examined situations in which inconsistencies were brought unavoidably to the attention of the individual. When the flying saucers did not land with people from another sphere, the belief that they would was sorely tested. L. FESTINGER, H. RIECKEN & S. SCHACHTER, WHEN PROPHECY FAILS (1956). Thus, only the relevant inconsistencies were subjected to the hypothesized drive for cognitive consistency.

134 I have treated the differences between commonsense and philosophical-scientific theorizing as if they formed a sharp dichotomy. In doing so, I have been using a simplifying model for the purposes of exposition. The two types of reasoning do not differ in any strong qualitative fashion. In fact, a major theme in the ethnomethodological tradition is that social scientific ideas are merely elaborated commonsense theories, *see* H. GARFINKEL, *Common Sense Knowledge of Social Structures: The Documentary Method of Interpretation in Lay and Professional Fact Finding*, in STUDIES IN ETHNOMETHODOLOGY, *supra* note 16, at 76, 100-02, and that each individual in society is a practicing—if untrained—sociologist; *see* A. CICOUREL, *supra* note 106, at 331-36; H. GARFINKEL, *What is Ethnomethodology?* in STUDIES IN ETHNOMETHODOLOGY, *supra* note 16, at 24-31 (practical sociological reasoning); Garfinkel & Sacks, *On the Formal Structures of Practical Actions*, in THEORETICAL SOCIOLOGY 337 (J. McKinney & E. Tiryakian eds. 1970) (formulation of accounts by social actors).

The point of this discussion is that individuals rarely deal with a formative context in the way a social theorist does. They employ the discrete commonsense theories and ideas that constitute it; they develop elaborations and applications of those ideas. On occasion, they do step back from their everyday activity and attempt to formulate a story about the formative context as a whole, but that is uncommon and of not much import for everyday practice.

C. Resistance to Change

To this point, it might appear that the microsociological view I am pursuing demonstrates that formative contexts are actually more malleable and less resistant to change than suggested by Unger's theory. Because they are not external to individuals, but are constant and routine products of individuals' activities, they should be revisable at will. This conclusion, however, ignores the roots of formative contexts in routine life.

Current social arrangements are not social structures that have been pressed on an unwilling populace that is waiting to be liberated. More importantly, they are not the product of some collective faulty reasoning that the haves have been able to impose on the have nots. Instead, they are the product of complex social processes in which individuals have tried to deal with and understand their world as individuals and as a group.[135] As such, they have a plausibility and familiarity based on the empirical experiences of individuals. Formative contexts are not external or alien to individuals; indeed, it is precisely because formative contexts are individuals' own products whose pragmatic utility is constantly reaffirmed through daily use that they take on a correctness or plausibility that is difficult to challenge.

To the extent that current formative contexts are the products of routine commonsense theorizing and activity, simple rational argumenta-

---

[135] This is not to say that no coercion is involved. Surely, there have been many societies in which coercion is the important cement, although I think there are far fewer in which it is the primary cement. Except on rare occasions, the myth of the foreign liberator riding into the village of happy, adoring villagers released from their chains is just that—a myth. Unless the oppression has been reasonably short in duration, it is likely that people in the village will have accommodated to their oppressors in ways that the liberators will disturb.

Nor is it to say that inequality does not exist. Inequality is rampant in all societies. In most cases, it is regarded as the "natural order": commonsense understandings of the world often include the idea of disparate allocations of resources and rights. *See* A. RYAN, PROPERTY AND POLITICAL THEORY 179-80 (1984) (commonsense theory that mere luck is the cause of disparate allocations). Even when these understandings tend to disfavor inequalities, individuals may prefer them to the perceived—correctly or incorrectly—alternatives of instability or violence. This, of course, says nothing about the ultimate desirability or justifiability of inequality. *See* R. NOZICK, ANARCHY, STATE, AND UTOPIA 232-75 (1974); J. ROUSSEAU, DISCOURSE ON THE ORIGIN AND FOUNDATIONS OF INEQUALITY AMONG MEN 157, 160 (R. Masters & J. Masters trans. 1964) (Amsterdam 1755).

tion will be unavailing to change them.[136] Grandiose theories of empowered democracy will be largely unconvincing to individuals because they
do not address the practical problems of daily life in any way more satisfactory than the current ideas in use. Moreover, they are at a level of
abstraction that is often foreign to the person-in-the-street. Appeals to
abstracted reason are inadequate because they are not located or contex-
tualized in any meaningful way. They cannot develop the empirical support that commonsense ideas enjoy from everyday practical activities.[137]

This problem affects many aspects of Unger's program for
change.[138] To take one element of *Politics* as an example, Unger argues
that the idea of consolidated property rights should be dislodged from
the current structure of formative contexts. Consolidated property rights
take all claims to particular divisible portions of social capital or wealth
and assign them to one person.[139] Unger argues that consolidated property rights must give way to a rotating capital fund, which will break up
the control of capital into several tiers of capital takers and capital givers.[140] Pursuant to such a fund, the aggregate social capital will be

---

136 *Cf.* Boyle, *supra* note 7, at 772 ("It is ridiculous to believe that one could disrupt the massively
entrenched set of power relations and collective fantasies that 'constitute' repression in our society
simply by attacking one of the more formalized and abstract fantasies and claiming that the rest are
'dependent' on it.").

137 A natural experiment that provides a partial test of this proposition is provided by the institution of electoral initiatives. In almost half the states, members of the public can place legislative
proposals on the ballot. Allen, *The National Initiative Proposal: A Preliminary Analysis*, 58 NEB. L.
REV. 965, 1007 (1979). While numerous initiatives have been proposed and argued for, often with
the backing of substantial financial resources, Ronald Allen found that radical changes were rare and
the "frivolous or ill-considered measures [were not] enacted with regularity." *Id.* at 1014, 1021,
1030. Successful initiatives usually are the product of long-simmering movements for political reform rather than of new and persuasive argumentation for a novel idea. "[U]sually the voter seems,
quite sensibly, to resolve any doubts he has on a particular measure against it." *Id.* at 1036.

138 FALSE NECESSITY at 395–570.

139 *Id.* at 489–90. Consolidated property rights are the central defining feature of the current
economic system and its historically specific definition of the market. They are:

a more or less absolute entitlement to a divisible portion of social capital—more or less absolute
both in the discretionary use and in the chain of voluntary transfers by successive property
owners. Once this initial identification has been established, the market economy is often further assumed to imply a particular style of industrial organization: the style that puts standard-
ized mass production in the mainstream of industry and flexible production in its vanguard.

Id. at 481.

140 In Unger's scheme, there will be a central capital fund or "social investment fund" that is
"under the control of the central executive and representative bodies of empowered democracy. . . .
[I]ts single most important task is to draw the limits of variation within which the competing investment funds must operate." *Id.* at 493. The investment funds are the second tier and are both capital
givers and capital takers. *Id.* at 492. They "hold capital from the social fund and give it out to the
primary capital takers, who represent the third tier of the economic system." *Id.* The investment
funds specialize in a sector of the economy or a particular type of investment and are "semi-independent bodies, much like contemporary central banks or even philanthropic foundations in contemporary Western societies, with their technical personnel chosen by a combination of appointment
from above and election from the sectors in which they operate." *Id.* at 495.

allocated, through democratic decisions,[141] to those entrepreneurs[142] operating through semi-independent investment funds[143] who will use it best for a limited period of time.[144]

Although the proposal to replace consolidated property rights with rotating capital funds may make some sense,[145] Unger never explains how the proposal is to be implemented. If he were writing on a tabula rasa, his ideas would certainly be a possible way to structure an economic system. Unfortunately, we rarely have that opportunity.[146]

---

[141] The central democratic institutions exercise their ultimate control over the forms and rates of economic accumulation and income distribution by establishing these funds or by closing them out, by assigning them new infusions of capital or by taking capital away from them, by charging them interest (whose payment represents the major source of governmental finance), and, most importantly, by setting the outer limits of variation in the terms on which the competing investment funds may allocate capital to the ultimate capital takers.

Id. at 491-92. Capital may be transferred between investment funds through market transactions: "[W]ithin certain gross limits, the primary capital takers can buy one another's resources by offering to pay the capital-auctioning fund more for the employment of these resources than their current users." *Id.* at 495. Or, capital may be transferred between investment funds on a rotation system. *Id.* at 496.

[142] Unger speaks of "ultimate capital takers," who are "teams of workers, technicians, and entrepreneurs, who make temporary and conditional claims upon divisible portions of this social capital fund." *Id.* at 491.

[143] "The central capital fund does not lend money out directly to the primary capital users. Instead, it allocates resources to a variety of semi-independent investment funds. Each investment fund specializes in a sector of the economy and in a type of investment." *Id.*

[144] *Id.* at 491-92.

[145] Unger never confronts some of the basic problems involved in a system of collective control over resources. Chief among these is how to ensure that the central capital fund or any decisionmaker up or down the line is acting with society's best interests at heart rather than his own. Buchanan, *Rent Seeking and Profit Seeking*, in TOWARD A THEORY OF THE RENT-SEEKING SOCIETY 3, 3-4, 9 (J. Buchanan, R. Tollison & G. Tullock eds. 1981) ("As institutions have moved away from ordered markets toward the near chaos of direct political allocation, rent seeking has emerged as a significant social phenomenon. . . . Rent . . . is an allocatively unnecessary payment not required to attract the resources to the particular employment. . . . [A]ttempts will be made to capture these rents, and resources used up in such attempts will reflect social waste.").

A second problem has to do with the ability of managers of investment funds to make allocatively adequate decisions. *Cf.* A. RYAN, *supra* note 135, at 172 (central problem not addressed by Marx when he describes abolition of private property is "how will decisions [about resources] be taken?"). One of the merits of a pure private property system is that we protect almost absolutely an individual's decision about the use of property we have assigned to him and force him to bear the costs associated with that use. Thus, if the use of the property turns out to be less than optimal, the property owner has only himself to blame. *See* Demsetz, *Toward a Theory of Property Rights*, 57 AM. ECON. REV. 347, 350 (Pap. & Proc. 1967) (private property rights can force holder to consider costs of action). Unger's system involves decisionmakers who are neither actively engaged in the productive activity nor directly accountable for allocation errors.

Finally, the complexity of Unger's system suggests that the transactions costs in deciding, allocating, and monitoring the use of the capital might eat up the entire new value created by the capital. Unger seems oblivious to the fact that democratic deliberation takes both time and money. Simply the opportunity costs of the deliberators' time are enormous. None of these problems are fatal to a collective system of capital allocation. My point is that they need to be addressed by any proposal as detailed as Unger's.

[146] *Cf.* Epstein, *Possession as the Root of Title*, 13 GA. L. REV. 1221, 1241 (1979) ("The common

The idea of consolidated property rights is thoroughly ingrained in individuals' ideas of the structure of society. The commonsense conception of property as absolute ownership of things is rooted in normal ways of thinking and acting with respect to things. Law professors teaching first-year property courses spend a not insubstantial number of hours convincing their students that property is not a Blackstonian absolute right to a thing,[147] but is only a bundle of socially defined rights vis-á-vis other members of society.[148] Even the Supreme Court occasionally forgets this lesson.[149]

Although minor unbundling has always existed and continues to exist,[150] Unger's frontal assault on the idea of consolidated property rights is unlikely to succeed on the basis of rational persuasion alone. People routinely think of and treat material goods, whether personal articles, real estate, or capital, as owned by them.[151] This conclusion is not merely abstract theory, but is bolstered and evidenced in everyday activities. Individuals in routine activity treat things as subject to the absolute control of particular persons, and such treatment is consistently validated by the reactions of others and the pragmatic usefulness of the treatment.[152]

---

law courts, which always began in medias res and which always announced principles that governed particular disputes, never had the luxury of philosophical purity in some original position."). Epstein seems to treat this argument as lending normative support to his position. My use of the argument is empirical: it helps explain resistance to social change.

147 2 W. BLACKSTONE, COMMENTARIES ON THE LAWS OF ENGLAND *2 (right of property is "that sole and despotic dominion which one man claims and exercises over the external things of the world, in total exclusion of the right of any other individual in the universe.").

148 B. ACKERMAN, *supra* note 85, at 26; Grey, *The Disintegration of Property*, in NOMOS XXII: PROPERTY 69 (J. Pennock & J. Chapman eds. 1980).

149 *See* Webb's Fabulous Pharmacies, Inc. v. Beckwith, 449 U.S. 155, 162-63 (1980) (unanimous decision) (interest on principal is in its essence property and cannot be taken under any circumstances without just compensation).

150 Grey, *supra* note 148, at 69-71; *see* Hohfeld, *Some Fundamental Legal Conceptions as Applied to Judicial Reasoning*, 23 YALE L.J. 16 (1913) (typology of basic jural relations). The study of private property law is at its core a study of the permitted and prohibited ways of dividing and transferring separate rights in land.

151 *See* Holmes, *The Path of the Law*, 10 HARV. L. REV. 457, 477 (1897):
> It is in the nature of man's mind. A thing which you have enjoyed and used as your own for a long time, whether property or an opinion, takes root in your being and cannot be torn away without your resenting the act and trying to defend yourself, however you came by it.

Although Holmes was speaking in the context of the adverse possession of a particular thing, the argument is generalizable to the whole group of things currently classified as property. People have developed a reliance interest in a set of ways of defining and treating entitlements. *Cf.* Epstein, *supra* note 146, at 1242 (practical reason for not questioning property rights acquired in past by first occupation is reliance on that system of entitlement definition for extended period of time).

152 The emergence of the concept of absolute property rights under certain environmental conditions might be explained through evolutionary game theory ideas. *See* Axelrod & Hamilton, *The Evolution of Cooperation*, 211 SCIENCE 1390 (1981); Hirshleifer, *Evolutionary Models in Economics and Law: Cooperation Versus Conflict Strategies*, 4 RES. L. & ECON. 1 (1982). The iterated actions and reactions of social actors to each other might tend in evolutionary fashion toward the institution of absolute property rights as the equilibrium. As with any evolutionary theory, however, a change

Unger's own Brazil is at present experiencing a difficult situation in which individual citizens are in effect being asked indirectly to transform their consolidated property rights into a type of politically controlled entitlements allocation. Recent government policies, in particular a price freeze announced late last year,[153] have increased demand for goods far beyond Brazil's ability to supply such goods. One result has been a rapid rise in a previously arrested inflation rate. The practical effect of policy-induced rampant inflation is to convert consolidated property rights in capital or wealth held by Brazilians into wealth over which the central bank and government maintains control.

Many Brazilians of substance have been unwilling to participate in this transformation of their consolidated property rights into a version of a "rotating capital fund," subject to allocation through government monetary policy. Instead, they have converted their wealth into a form—United States dollars or Swiss francs in foreign accounts—that is not subject to central political control: the traditional problem of capital flight.[154] If the government desires to continue its domestic policy, no amount of talk will keep capital flight from occurring; only strict exchange and capital flow regulations backed with the coercive power of the state will do the trick. My argument is not that the change to a rotating capital fund is unwise or that it cannot occur. Rather, I am arguing that such a change is extremely unlikely to occur through the rational persuasion of Brazilian capital owners, and may require the use of coercion. In fact, exchange and capital flow regulations have been regular responses to capital flight in developing countries.[155]

Another current example starkly illustrates the same general point. It is easy but unavailing to argue with South African adherents of apartheid about the evils of that system. Painting a picture of a new world—the step to which might even be Pareto-superior, benefitting black and white alike—does not persuade. This is because the practical experience of the typical apartheid adherent is inconsistent with the new picture. That practical experience has been built up through years of commonsense theorizing and action based on those theories, and has been bolstered by economic self-interest as well.[156]

Apartheid adherents' theories regarding the superiority of whites

---

in the environment initiates movement away from the prior equilibrium. So, as land became scarcer and new uses were invented, the evolutionary equilibrium—at least for real estate developers and property lawyers—was altered toward the bundle of rights conception of property rights.

[153] N.Y. Times, Feb. 16, 1987, at 19, 24, col. 1.

[154] *Id.* at 19, col. 3 (with rise in inflation, government considering strengthening of exchange and currency controls to restrict capital flight).

[155] R. Edwards, International Monetary Collaboration 449 (1985) (capital controls used "to prevent residents from transferring their savings").

[156] At least in the short-term, discrimination by employers can secure higher monetary profits, Donohue, *Is Title VII Efficient?*, 134 U. Pa. L. Rev. 1411, 1419 (1986), and if the employer is personally indifferent to employing blacks, his total profits—psychic plus monetary—will be signifi-

and their morally justified place in South African society obviously seem (to them) better supported by their practical experience than a picture of a mixed-race society.[157] Moreover, social-psychological factors may cause some blacks to behave in ways that confirm the whites' stereotypical views of them.[158] When added to more recent, ad hoc theories about the communist threat and the inevitable economic collapse that will follow the introduction of black rule, these theories become still more powerful. They will almost certainly be adhered to until either coercion or a sufficient threat of coercion can dislodge them.

Of more direct relevance to Unger's enterprise is the fact that commonsense understandings of perceived economic failures in planned economies—particularly socialist economies—also reflect a resistance to change in formative structures. Two theories are generally available in the current formative context to interpret this perception of failure; both assert and depend on a belief in uniform, immutable human nature. First, socialist economies fail, it is thought, because of the moral inferiority of a centrally planned economy, which removes from individuals the freedom they enjoy in Western economies.[159] The second, and less antagonistic, view is that while a socialized economy may be a meritorious moral goal, it can never be achieved because man is universally self-interested.[160] Such conceptions of human nature are particularly resistant to change.[161]

Not only will these ideas encourage resistance to socializing the

---

cantly higher. Gary Becker argues, however, that in the long-term discrimination is inefficient. G. BECKER, THE ECONOMICS OF DISCRIMINATION 39-54 (2d ed. 1971).

157 Paul Gewirtz, in explaining why freedom of choice was not an appropriate rule in the desegregation decisions, refers to distorted attitudes on the part of both blacks and whites caused by "[a] long regime of de jure segregation [that] may skew attitudes, tastes, and perceptions of those exercising choice, and thereby inhibit or channel their choices even though they are now formally free to go to any school." Gewirtz, *Choice in the Transition: School Desegregation and the Corrective Ideal*, 86 COLUM. L. REV. 728, 745 (1986).

158 Snyder, *supra* note 122, at 296 ("As long as people have faith in their stereotypes, they may treat other people in ways that actually elicit from them behaviors that support those stereotypes."); Snyder, Tanke & Berscheid, *Social Perception and Interpersonal Behavior: On the Self-Fulfilling Nature of Social Stereotypes*, in ATTRACTION: WHY PEOPLE LIKE EACH OTHER 391 (1984). Cass Sunstein refers to this as adaptive preferences and uses Jon Elster's idea of sour grapes, J. ELSTER, *supra* note 124, at 109-40, to explain the "acceptance of traditional forms of discrimination by its victims, in the context of gender, class, and even race. Acceptance of traditional distinctions tends to reduce cognitive dissonance." Sunstein, *supra* note 88, at 1147.

159 *See* Sunstein, *supra* note 88, at 1131-32 (objection from liberty to interference with private preferences: "the government ought not, at least as a general rule, to be in the business of evaluating whether a person's choice will serve his or her interests, or even whether the choice is objectionable, except when the choice causes harm to others").

160 *See id.* (objection from futility to interference with private preferences: "[I]nterferences with private preferences will be ineffectual, for those preferences will manifest themselves in responses to regulation that will counteract its intended effects.").

161 A. SCHUTZ, *supra* note 97, at 184-85 (ideal types used in daily life are divorced from flow of intersubjectivity).

economy, but they may also explain problems in existing planned economies. It may be that to the extent socialist economies have failed, it is
because these pictures of human nature are so thoroughly embedded in
the commonsense conceptions of the possibility of society held by citizens of the socialist countries themselves. While the Russian Revolution
sought to create the new socialist man, it was insufficiently aware of the
strength of individuals' commitment to the old view of human nature.
Given Unger's lack of discussion of these issues, he may be repeating the
same mistake.

D.   *Sources of Social Change*

I am not suggesting that formative contexts cannot or do not
change. Clearly, they do and they do reasonably often. Nor am I claiming that the conception of formative contexts for which Unger presses is
necessarily undesirable or pernicious. Unger is right to try to understand
the processes of social change and to direct them toward morally prefera-
ble states.

My point is that such change rarely occurs from consciousness-raising or from appeals of rational moral persuasion such as Unger's.[162]
This is because the individual's sense of social order created through the
above described processes is a grounded "rational" sense. People do not
accept the current formative context because it is an alien structure
forced upon them, or because they reason incorrectly in some absolute
sense—that is, because they suffer from some "false consciousness."[163]
They accept it because for most practical purposes it is pragmatically
validated for them: it works for most problems they confront in every-

---

[162] This is a controversial assertion because it implies that the great moral and political thinkers
such as Hobbes, Locke, Rousseau, Kant, Bentham, Hegel, and Marx have had less impact on the
course of social change than we commonly surmise. Certainly, a claim that they have had no effect
would be naive (the Russian Revolution expressly acknowledged its Marxist roots). Such thinkers
do provide arsenals of ideas and arguments for the agents of social change. But the effect of such
ideas on social change are not direct and not supremely powerful, or so I argue.

[163] Although Unger's theory is not expressly one of false consciousness, the concept that ideas
can cause social change at least shares the structure of false consciousness arguments. Gabel's analysis of the formative context of capitalism certainly asserts that society's members deceive themselves
with respect to their true condition. Gabel, *supra* note 53, at 28-29; *cf.* J. SARTRE, BEING AND
NOTHINGNESS 86-116 (H. Barnes trans. 1966) (discussion of bad faith or self-deception).

  Sunstein, at points, seems to make the argument that preferences change when people realize
through rational deliberation that their initial preferences were unfounded.

  [S]ome preferences are objectionable or the product of distorting circumstances, principally in
  the form of relations of power. Such distortions can, it is thought, be revealed as such through
  deliberation and debate. . . . A political process that subjects private choices to critical scrutiny
  will in this sense produce better laws than a process that takes them as exogenous.

Sunstein, *supra* note 88, at 1154. His discussion of the *Lochner* period illustrates this idea of correction in perception. Interestingly, he can point to no deliberative dialogue that marked the change
brought about by West Coast Hotel Co. v. Parrish, 300 U.S. 379 (1937). Perhaps the coercion of the
Roosevelt court-packing threat or the addition of another Roosevelt nominee was the key to the
Supreme Court's change of world views.

day life.[164]

Social change does occur, however, when the formative contexts, or at least specific portions of them, are no longer adequate for use in accomplishing practical tasks. An obvious source of this inadequacy is the introduction of some factors exogenous to the existing system. Chief among these factors is external coercion. Throughout human history, military and other types of coercion have been used to alter existing formative contexts and impose new ones on societies. In this same category of social change are other factors such as changes in technology, migration of cultures, and events of nature. "News"—the occurrence of random events that members of society could not predict in advance given the available information—is always a factor in the alteration of formative contexts.[165] Individuals must adapt to the exogenous shocks to their world.[166]

Change also can be generated internally, but not in the way that Unger would have it.[167] Endogenous change in formative contexts results from the fact that the commonsense theories that individuals generate and employ are not systematic, and are not necessarily consistent with each other or consistent across discrete areas of practical activity. Faced with new experiences, individuals draw upon and adapt theories already extant in their stock of knowledge or formative context. While most adaptations are reasonably consistent with prior social arrangements,[168] lines are often fudged. Formative contexts may provide a model for coping with a problem, but they are also affected by each application.[169] Moreover, because an individual's orientation is normally practical rather than theoretical, adapting a commonsense theory so that it is useful in a particular situation does not cause major concern.

Although this description of endogenous factors is analogous to the analysis of paradigm shifts offered by Thomas Kuhn,[170] the last feature

---

[164] These are broad generalizations that, again, are part of a simplified model that attempts to shed light on social relations. Surely there are individuals whose compliance has only a coercive source.

[165] The theory of rational expectations has been developed in both microeconomics and macroeconomics. *See, e.g.,* C. ATTFIELD, D. DEMERY & N. DUCK, RATIONAL EXPECTATIONS IN MACROECONOMICS 15-21 (1985). The concept of "news," meaning unpredictable shocks or surprises, forms the basis for the null hypothesis in attempts to predict the movement of flexible exchange rates, a research area almost completely dominated by rational expectations theory. M. MELVIN, INTERNATIONAL MONEY AND FINANCE 133 (1985); Frenkel, *Flexible Exchange Rates, Prices, and the Role of "News": Lessons from the 1970s,* 89 J. POL. ECON. 665 (1981).

[166] *See* W. OGBURN, SOCIAL CHANGE 200-13 (1922) (hypothesis, of cultural lag: culture sphere adjusts to periodic and unpredicted shocks in the material sphere).

[167] Unger has stated that legal doctrine can change through internal development when criticism brings to light conflicting ideals already embodied in the doctrine. *The Critical Legal Studies Movement* at 579-80.

[168] *See* D. HEISE, *supra* note 104, at 8.

[169] *See* A. GIDDENS, *supra* note 18, at 25-28 (duality of structure).

[170] T. KUHN, *supra* note 126, at 52-65 (role of anomaly in scientific discovery).

underscores a difference. Scientists are very concerned about maintaining the internal coherence and broad applicability of scientific paradigms. Adaptations of the paradigm raise problems immediately, particularly if they involve drastic reformulations. The need to stretch the paradigm is an early warning sign of the future need for a shift.[171]

Formative contexts, however, have a great deal more slack or stretching room because individuals are far less concerned with their overall coherence and systematicity. What counts is their pragmatic employability. To the extent that formative contexts work in practice, people have little reason to revise them except for minor tinkering. Of course, at times existing formative contexts begin to fail as resources for action, very often due to changes exogenous to a particular group of individuals. In such situations, alterations or even wholesale substitutions must be made. The point is, however, that social change is driven by changes in the relative usability of formative contexts, not by the presentation of new total ideologies, no matter how attractive they might be.

III. LAW AND COMMONSENSE REASONING

Politics speaks little of the general nature of law and legal rules. The subject of law, however, has certainly been the testing ground for previous versions of the thesis of *Politics*.[172] From his prior work as well as from *Politics*, Unger's idea of the role of law is clear: law presents to individuals as normatively valid a picture of particular forms of human association—in the terminology of *Politics*, a formative context.[173] "Each type of legal right represents, even in its most formal aspects, the incomplete but significant picture of a certain model of human association."[174] An important argument of *Politics* is that a system of consolidated property rights presents a particular vision of the nature of

---

[171] *Id.* at 77-90.

[172] *See, e.g.,* LAW AND MODERN SOCIETY; *The Critical Legal Studies Movement.* The criticisms of objectivism and of formalism expressed in his writing on law are not dissimilar to the criticisms of the naturalistic premise in *Politics.* According to Unger, these negative criticisms seem to present the lawyer with "the general choice: either resign yourself to some established version of social order, or face the war of all against all." *The Critical Legal Studies Movement* at 577. His project for some time has been to transcend this dilemma with a constructive social theory. *Id.* at 588.

[173] "The starting point of our argument is the idea that every branch of doctrine must rely tacitly if not explicitly upon some picture of the forms of human association that are right and realistic in the areas of social life with which it deals." *Id.* at 570.

The system of rights was meant to exhibit on its surface the gross structure of society . . . . Perhaps the most important shift in the history of modern legal thought has been the one that led from this conception to the idea that the constitution and the law should describe the basic possible dealings among people, as property owners and as citizens, without regard to the place individuals occupy within the social order. . . . The critical legal studies movement has committed itself to another change in the conception of the relation of law to society, potentially equal in scope and importance to the shift I have just recalled.

Id. at 585.

[174] FALSE NECESSITY at 513.

democracy and the market in modern society.[175] Law both expresses and enforces the model of human association at the heart of the formative context.

Law also, however, plays a key part in the implementation of Unger's programmatic ideas. Once the system of consolidated property rights is removed, a new system of legal rights must be established both to further and to protect empowered democracy. This system of new legal rights is to be the guardian of negative capability.[176] Law takes on a liberating function: "[l]aw and constitution are now to be seen as . . . the denial rather than the reaffirmation of the plan of social division and hierarchy."[177] The new legal system will create new legal rights that will establish the security of individuals "in ways that minimize both the immunity of institutional arrangements to challenge and conflict and the ease with which some individuals can reduce others to dependence."[178]

The law functions differently in these two cases only because it expresses and reinforces different underlying models of human association. The legal system at whose center consolidated property rights reside is

---

[175] *Id.* at 480-93.

[176] "The ideal aim of the system of rights, taken as a whole and in each of its branches, is to serve as a counterprogram to the maintenance or reemergence of any scheme of division and hierarchy that can become effectively insulated against the ordinarily available forms of challenge." *The Critical Legal Studies Movement* at 585. Unger identifies two "generative principles of a reconstructed system of rights": first, "the security of the individual should be established in ways that minimize both the immunity of institutional arrangements to challenge and conflict and the ease with which some individuals can reduce others to dependence," FALSE NECESSITY at 513; and second, the new legal rights should "suit the obligations of interdependence that characterize communal life," *id.* at 517. Any new rights should provide security to the individual while preventing the petrification of formative contexts, and should foster mutual dependence and vulnerability among individuals.

[177] *The Critical Legal Studies Movement* at 585.

[178] FALSE NECESSITY at 513. The most important of these rights are the market, immunity, solidarity, and destabilizing rights. Market rights are "the rights employed for economic exchange in the trading sector of the society." *Id.* at 520. Immunity rights are rights that "protect the individual against oppression by concentrations of public or private power, against exclusion from the important collective decisions that influence his life, and against the extremes of economic and cultural deprivation." *Id.* at 524. Destabilization rights are the rights that "protect the citizen's interest in breaking open the large-scale organizations or the extended areas of social practice that remain closed to the destabilizing effects of ordinary conflict." *Id.* at 530. They "attempt to deny protection against destabilizing conflict to either institutions or noninstitutional arrangements whenever this immunity to conflict seems to generate stable ties or domination and dependence." *Id.* at 531. Solidarity rights "give legal form to social relations of reliance and trust." *Id.* at 535. They attempt to create "a zone of heightened mutual vulnerability," *id.* at 536, and provide for "the legal protection of claims to abide by implicit obligations to take other people's situations and expectations into account," *id.* at 537. Unger's descriptions of the latter two rights seem to depict general principles, rather than what are commonly understood to be rights. They are at a level of generality that provides little if any information to a judge or actor who is subject to them. They certainly lack clarity in application, which is an important functional characteristic of a right or legal rule; clarity keeps the expenditure of resources to a minimum. Merrill, *Trespass, Nuisance, and the Costs of Determining Property Rights*, 14 J. LEG. STUD. 13, 23-24 (1985) (lack of clear entitlement leads to expenditures in entitlement determination); Rose, *Possession as the Origin of Property*, 52 U. CHI. L. REV. 73, 76 (1985) (requirement of clear act of possession avoids confusion and resource waste).

based, according to Unger, on a reified concept of market relations. By contrast, the new system of legal rights in an empowered democracy reflects a more open-ended type of formative context. In both cases, however, the functioning of legal rules is the same: they are in the now familiar form of constraints on otherwise free individual activity. They are coercive and external to the individual.

Unger's view of law is merely a recapitulation of his more general view of formative contexts, and the problems that stalk his idea of formative context are also present here. Law is external to and coercive of the individual in any particular formative context; it expresses the generally shared model of human association underlying that formative context. Describing law as merely the expression of human association tells us little and ignores the way law operates in actual society. Unger's desiccated view of law, if accepted, would cause legal scholars to despair of having anything of value to say. The role of law in social change for him is in effect minimal; moreover, his view cannot explain the phenomenon of the relative allegiance of the citizenry to law and differences in the levels of that allegiance. Again, the microsociological theory that animates Unger's views causes him to provide an unpersuasive account of law.

A.   Legal Consciousness

This is particularly true of the idea of legal consciousness that Unger shares[179] with a number of the scholars in the critical legal studies movement.[180] Of course, attempts to characterize a particular period of legal thinking on a discrete subject can be valuable contributions to our understanding of law and social relations affected by law. Many scholars both within[181] and without[182] the critical legal studies movement have provided interesting and relevant accounts of the ideas that judges, legal practitioners, and citizens hold about specific subject matters. Members of social groups and organizations do tend to adhere to similar views of the world and of proper action in that world. Karl Llewellyn's famous study of the warranty of quality[183] is an illuminating analysis of the ideas

---

[179] *The Critical Legal Studies Movement; see* KNOWLEDGE AND POLITICS (attempt to reveal deep structure of liberal legal consciousness).

[180] There are as many versions of legal consciousness as there are scholars who employ the term. Kennedy, *Form and Substance in Private Law Adjudication,* 89 HARV. L. REV. 1685, 1725-40 (1976); Kennedy, *Toward an Historical Understanding of Legal Consciousness: The Case of Classical Legal Thought in America, 1850-1940,* 3 RES. L. & SOC. 3, 23 (1980) (hereinafter Kennedy, *Legal Consciousness*); Note, *supra* note 7, at 1677-78, 1679.

[181] *See, e.g.,* Klare, *Judicial Deradicalization of the Wagner Act and the Origins of Modern Legal Consciousness, 1937-1941,* 62 MINN. L. REV. 265, 275-80 (1978); Stone, *The Post-War Paradigm in American Labor Law,* 90 YALE L.J. 1509, 1515 (1981).

[182] *See, e.g.,* ACKERMAN, *supra* note 85; Grey, *supra* note 148; Llewellyn, *On Warranty of Quality, and Society* (pts. 1 & 2), 36 COLUM. L. REV. 699 (1936), 37 COLUM. L. REV. 341 (1937).

[183] Llewellyn, *supra* note 182.

of the market and other factors that influenced New York and other judges around the turn of the century. That study of legal consciousness was pitched at a level that yielded results.

As Unger and others sometimes employ it, however, the idea of legal consciousness attributes an implausible degree of coherence and systematicity to the ideas that individuals in a specific historical period carry in their heads. Legal consciousness[184] is portrayed by some as an omnipresent and seemingly systematic set of ideas that reside in the current formative context. Individuals in the legal system are so dominated by this set of ideas that their decisions and actions are unconsciously driven by the legal consciousness. According to Unger, the value of the critical legal studies movement has been to expose the flaws in current unified liberal legal consciousness.[185]

The notion of formative contexts as stocks of knowledge suggests that legal consciousness is not as monolithic, systematic, or coercive as Unger and others suggest. To the extent that they claim that individuals or even individual lawyers and judges actually carry around in their heads a complex and systematic set of legal ideas that determine results,[186] their view is implausible. Legal doctrine and some sort of legal consciousness do exist, but they are the products of attempts by legal professionals—judges, lawyers, and academics—to produce a coherent, normative picture of the world that can be used to generate unique and persuasive results in individual cases.[187] They are pragmatically ori-

---

184 Kennedy defines consciousness and legal consciousness:

Consciousness refers to the total contents of a mind, including images of the external world, images of the self, of emotions, goals and values, and theories about the world and self. I use the term only in this vague, all-inclusive sense. It defines the universe within which are situated the more sharply-delineated concepts that are the vehicles for analysis.

Legal Consciousness is an only slightly more defined notion. It refers to the particular form of consciousness that characterizes the legal profession as a social group, at a particular moment. The main peculiarity of this consciousness is that it contains a vast number of legal rules, arguments, and theories, a great deal of information about the institutional workings of the legal process, and the constellation of ideals and goals current in the profession at a given moment.

Kennedy, *Legal Consciousness, supra* note 180, at 23.

185 This has been accomplished through criticism of "objectivism" and "formalism" in traditional legal analysis. *The Critical Legal Studies Movement* at 567-76. Critical legal studies scholars claim to have gone beyond the skepticism of the legal realists by demonstrating that liberal legal consciousness rests on untenable visions of human association or untenable social theories. *See* Tushnet, *Post-Realist Legal Scholarship*, 1980 WIS. L. REV. 1383, 1384-86, 1395-99.

186 Peter Gabel's phenomenology of judging seems to suggest this.

[W]e can say that the first movement of the judge's consciousness is the apprehension of the entire social field as a synthetic activity that moves like a thing; or, in other words, he has a sense of the whole culture all at once that he passivizes into the movement of a quasi-object, such that each discrete situation of facts reveals itself to his mind against the background of the total "factual" context from which the law has emerged. . . . This sense of the normal movement of the total "factual" context, without which it would be impossible to apply the law to any discrete situation, has been interiorized by the judge during the course of his conditioning.

Gabel, *supra* note 53, at 31.

187 This, according to Bruce Ackerman, is the role of the legal analyst who is an Ordinary Observer: "By definition, an [Ordinary] Observer is not content to isolate one or another pattern of

ented.[188] The systematic liberal ideology that some critical legal studies movement scholars identify as the prevailing legal consciousness just is not as systematic and monolithic as is claimed.[189]

The actual production of the more systematic and comprehensive theories of law is controlled by a narrower segment of the population— law professors. Their work is conducted during periods of reflection far from the everyday functioning of the legal system. They are products of an intellectual process[190] directed towards the development of comprehensive or scientific theories of the phenomenon of law as a whole.[191] Much critical legal studies' criticism of legal consciousness seems to be criticism directed by one philosophical-scientific theory at another. Although specific characterizations of sets of legal ideas at play in particular areas of the law can be enormously helpful, the concept of an abstract liberal legal consciousness is not particularly useful in the analysis of the actual course of practical legal activity in society. The criticism is at a plane of abstraction far above the commonsense ideas and theories employed by individuals in everyday life, or even by lawyers in practice.

B. Law and Commonsense

Viewing formative contexts as stocks of knowledge available for commonsense reasoning also suggests a more varied and dynamic relation between law and the individual. Law and legal rules always operate against a background of commonsense understandings about the world that constitutes the formative context as a stock of knowledge. Law is

---

institutionalized expectation; he is searching instead for the single pattern of practice that may be called *the* dominant one in a given social system." B. ACKERMAN, *supra* note 85, at 95.

[188] At least since the legal realists, any other view of legal consciousness is implausible. Even prior to the realists' analysis, however, it is extremely unlikely that any participants in the legal system were unconsciously driven by a monolithic legal consciousness of the type Unger describes. Langdellian orthodox legal theory was probably viewed by most practitioners with bemusement; it was criticized by scholars. *See, e.g.,* Dewey, *Logical Method and Law,* 10 CORNELL L.Q. 17, 19 (1924); Holmes, *supra* note 151, at 457.

[189] I do not deny that there are assumptions about the world that are socially shared and that rarely enter into individuals' discursive consciousness. *See* A. GIDDENS, *supra* note 18, at 42-45. However, these are the ideas that form the stock of knowledge that have been built up and that individuals draw on as a resource. They are not a preexisting system imposed from without.

[190] Anthony Giddens distinguishes between practical and discursive consciousness in a way relevant to my point. Practical consciousness is the "reflexive monitoring of conduct by human agents" engaged in pragmatic activity. *Id.* at 44. Discursive consciousness is the ability of an individual "to give a coherent account of one's activities and the reasons for them." *Id.* at 45. Clearly, opinion writing is also a product of discursive consciousness.

[191] The Langdellian model of legal doctrine is the most obvious example. It described law as an independent science in which a set of interrelated and systematic general principles were to be discovered by examination of prior case law. *See* Grey, *Langdell's Orthodoxy,* 45 U. PITT. L. REV. 1, 11 (1983). It, however, is not the only example. Policy science, Lasswell & McDougall, *Legal Education and Public Policy: Professional Training in the Public Interest,* 52 YALE L.J. 203 (1943), law and economics, R. POSNER, ECONOMIC ANALYSIS OF LAW (3d ed. 1986), and critical legal studies are all efforts seeking organizing principles and explanations.

both a product of and a resource for the process of commonsense reasoning of individuals in society. It forms part of their stocks of knowledge, it provides a set of devices for the negotiation of problems in the world, and it can be employed to impose change on others. My remaining remarks are directed at suggesting the complexity of the relationship between law and commonsense reasoning.

1. *Law as a Product of Commonsense Reasoning.*—Law can be seen as an expression or product of commonsense reasoning. Legal rules, of course, are produced in our society by the activity of specific subgroups. Most individuals do confront the law as something not created by them. Judges, administrators, and legislators are each in the business of promulgating rules and declaring what the law is. Although legal rules can be seen as an expression of the sovereign will, as suggested by the positivists,[192] or as the idiosyncratic whims of judges, as some legal realists seem to assert,[193] it is also possible that legal rules are formulations derived from the decisionmaker's commonsense theories of the world.[194] This is true regardless of whether one believes that the legislative product is the result of the activity of self-interested utility maximizers[195] or of more republican-minded public servants.[196]

2. *Commonsense Roots of Legal Rules.*—A legislator's or judge's choice of a legal rule reflects an estimation that the rule is consistent with his or her view of the world. For example, a legislator's evaluation of the potential effectiveness of a new sanction will be based in large part on his or her own understanding of what motivates individual behavior. Although legislators occasionally do call for and claim to rely on "scientific studies" of social problems, the promulgation of most legal rules is based on commonsense judgments about the world. Moreover, those

---

192 J. AUSTIN, THE PROVINCE OF JURISPRUDENCE DETERMINED (rev. ed. 1970) (London 1861-63); *see* H. HART, THE CONCEPT OF LAW 18-25 (1961).

193 J. FRANK, LAW AND THE MODERN MIND 160-61 (rev. ed. 1970).

194 Karl Llewellyn effectively demonstrated that judges faced with cases on the warranty of quality relied on their understanding of the nature of the market. Llewellyn (pt. 1), *supra* note 182, at 723 ("court's background picture of transactions 'of *this* type' "); *cf.* Kelman, *Interpretive Construction in the Substantive Criminal Law*, 33 STAN. L. REV. 591, 671-72 (1981) ("dominant legal thought is nothing *but* some more or less plausible common-wisdom banalities, superficialities and generalities"); Gabel, *supra* note 53, at 39 (law is conceptual representation of normal functioning of capitalist system).

195 Easterbrook, *The Supreme Court, 1983 Term—Foreword: The Court and the Economic System*, 98 HARV. L. REV. 4, 15 (1984) (laws designed to serve private, not public, interests); McChesney, *Rent Extraction and Rent Creation in the Economic Theory of Regulation*, 16 J. LEGAL STUD. 101, 102-03 (1987) (legislators as well as their constituents are rent-seekers).

196 Sunstein, *Interest Groups in American Public Law*, 38 STAN. L. REV. 29, 31 (1985) (republican legislators can "escape private interests and engage in pursuit of public good"); *see* Macey, *Promoting Public-Regarding Legislation Through Statutory Interpretation: An Interest Group Model*, 86 COLUM. L. REV. 223, 250-54 (1986) (practice of statutory interpretation in which judge seeks public goal has effect of reducing effectiveness of private interest legislation).

judgments often frame the problem itself. As a practical matter, legislators and judges must deal with presented issues immediately and do not have the luxury of waiting for systematic studies.

Reliance on commonsense ideas about the world goes beyond judgments about the means-ends rationality of possible legislation. Legislators also rely on commonsense judgments about what is best for society—judgments about the ends of legislation—judgments that at root are moral judgments. Thus, prohibitions on drug use and prostitution are based at times on commonsense conclusions about the likely consequences of these activities that supposedly demonstrate their inherent wrongness. Such prohibitions are not bald assertions of moral positions, but are seen by legislators and judges to be well-founded, "valid" notions of the proper way for the world to be regulated.

An example that crops up frequently in judicial opinions in contract and property cases is the use of the commonsense idea of "bargaining power." A wide variety of rules are justified as attempts to rectify situations of alleged unequal bargaining power.[197] There is a shared commonsense judgment that unequal bargaining power often exists and must be accounted for. Bargaining power may be a useful concept for any number of reasons,[198] but its theoretical underpinnings are neither mentioned nor, most likely, understood.

3. *The Commonsense Roots of the Acceptance of the Law.*—The acceptance of legal rules by individuals is widespread. Although certain rules do not muster a general consensus and therefore cause much debate,[199] most legal rules enjoy almost unanimous support or at least indifference. This is in large part a function of the fact that the commonsense theories that legislators and judges employ in promulgating the rules are essentially uncontested (in the practical sense of that term[200]) in society at large. In fact, legislators and judges count on this uncontestedness to assure the workability of the rules they promulgate. This uncontestability derives not from the coercive nature of a formative context or from the ignorance of the populace, but from the often demonstrated

---

[197] In property law, bargaining power crops up frequently in landlord-tenant law. *See, e.g.*, Green v. Superior Court, 10 Cal. 3d 616, 625 n.9, 517 P.2d 1168, 1173 n.9, 111 Cal. Rptr. 704, 711 n.9 (1974); R. POSNER, *supra* note 191, § 4.7, at 101-05.

[198] Bargaining power may have any of a number of substantive meanings. It may express a social decision about the allocation of entitlements and the distribution of wealth. Or it may be a response to situations that society believes are consistently characterized by irrational bargaining by one class of parties. Finally, it may refer narrowly to situations in which competition is limited.

[199] Obvious examples include the death penalty, legalized abortion, and prohibition of marijuana use.

[200] Of course, many rules rely on theories that can be and are contested theoretically. A rule is in the practical sense uncontested when individuals in the course of their everyday activities do not view it as problematic.

utility in daily life of these commonsense theories about the world and the legal rules they support.

When a legal rule does deviate from commonsense understandings, it fails to gain support. The legal rule may simply lie dormant,[201] or reform movements may arise to redress the perceived divergence between the rules and the reformists' understandings of the world.[202] Jury nullification is an obvious instance in which a deviation of legal rules from commonsense understanding results in nonacceptance of the legal rules. Reacting to a situation in which they thought that judicial decisions were lagging behind social practice, Roscoe Pound and certain legal realists argued that law should be corrected to conform with commonsense understandings and ways of conducting affairs.[203]

4. *Functions of Law.*—If law relies on these collectively shared commonsense judgments about the world that constitute the formative context, then why do we have legal rules at all? If law is only a formulation or expression of these commonsense ideas that everyone should accept, then the coercive force of law would seem to be superfluous. Individuals, however, see the need for legal rules in two areas: to deter faulty judgments about the proper course of action and to provide resources for the negotiation of practical problems.

---

[201] Legal rules that deviate from common understandings may not be employed if the costs of ignoring them are not high. Robert Ellickson's study of Shasta County found that the formal legal rules regarding liability for straying cattle were largely irrelevant to the loss allocation practices of county residents. Ellickson, *Of Coase and Cattle: Dispute Resolution Among Neighbors in Shasta County*, 38 STAN. L. REV. 623, 672-73 (1986).

[202] *See* J. GARFIELD, SYMBOLIC CRUSADE (2d ed. 1986) (temperance movement); H. BECKER, *Moral Entrepreneurs*, in OUTSIDERS 147, 162 (1973) ("Rules are not made automatically. Even though a practice may be harmful in an objective sense to the group in which it occurs, the harm needs to be discussed and pointed out.").

Reform movements can be seen as collective attempts to produce legal rules or entitlements and are governed by the production function for the creation of rules or entitlements. When the aggregate benefits to be derived from a change or new entitlement exceeds the costs of creating and enforcing that new entitlement, then the reform movement will arise and succeed. *See* Anderson & Hill, *The Evolution of Property Rights: A Study of the American West*, 18 J.L. & ECON. 163, 165 (1975) (as with any productive activity, amount of investment in establishing and protecting property rights depends on marginal benefits and costs to investors of allocating resources). Even if a legal rule is out of step with commonsense understandings, there will be no change if the marginal benefits of investing in a change do not exceed the marginal cost.

This may explain Ellickson's Shasta County finding. *See supra* note 201. There, county residents saw nothing to gain from altering the legal rule because the benefits of the alteration would not exceed the costs of the alteration, particularly since they had in operation a satisfactorily functioning loss-allocation mechanism.

[203] Pound, *The Need for Sociological Jurisprudence*, 19 GREEN BAG 607, 608 (1907); *see also* Douglas & Marshall, *A Factual Study of Bankruptcy Administration and Some Suggestions*, 32 COLUM. L. REV. 25 (1932). The Uniform Commercial Code is probably the most ambitious example of this type of reform; the leader of the reform was Karl Llewellyn. *See* W. TWINING, KARL LLEWELLYN AND THE REALIST MOVEMENT 313-21 (1973).

a. Deterring Mistaken Judgment.—First, although individuals' commonsense judgments about the world seem obvious and natural to them, they are keenly aware that not everyone shares those views and that some might act to take advantage of another's compliance. Thus, legal rules backed by the coercive power of the state are necessary to catch or deter the socially incompetent.[204] The "socially incompetent,"[205] it is thought, are those who are unable or unwilling to accept the ideas about the world shared by substantial numbers of individuals.

In addition, individuals also believe that some people belong to subcultures whose understanding of the world departs in important relevant respects from their own. Members of these subcultures may take actions inconsistent with more widely shared notions, thereby undermining the formative context and causing disputes. For example, most people's initial reaction to "free riders"—those who exploit others' compliance to their own personal advantage—is that the free riders are morally wrong and that their judgment is somehow flawed. Legal sanctions, people believe, correct "incorrect" free rider and subcultural judgments by increasing the costs of noncompliance and thus making clear the correctness of the generally shared commonsense idea.

Related to this is the fact that individuals also see coercive legal rules as a way to bind themselves against performing acts inconsistent with their general view of the world.[206] Although an individual may agree that the commonsense judgment expressed by a legal rule is correct, he or she realizes that situations arise in the course of daily life in which there is the potential for faulty judgment or the temptation to deviate from the general judgment. Legal rules backed by sanctions assure an individual that he or she will be less likely to deviate from the preferred view of the world. Again, the coercive legal rule makes the original commonsense judgment more convincing by depreciating the alternative.

b. Resources for the Negotiation of Practical Problems.—Legal rules also provide individuals with resources for going about their daily activity and negotiating practical problems. First, they provide information believed to be reliable about the likely reaction of others. An individual can expect that his counterpart in any transaction will adjust his

---

[204] The economic view of the criminal law as deterring attempts to bypass the market is a formalized version of this commonsense theory. Posner, *An Economic Theory of the Criminal Law*, 85 COLUM. L. REV. 1193, 1195 (1985); Calabresi & Melamed, *Property Rules, Liability Rules, and Inalienability: One View of the Cathedral*, 85 HARV. L. REV. 1089, 1126 (1972); see Klevorick, *On the Economic Theory of Crime*, in NOMOS XXVII: CRIMINAL JUSTICE 289 (J. Pennock & J. Chapman eds. 1985).

[205] My use of the conclusions "socially incompetent," "incorrect," and "inaccurate" does not represent my judgments, but descriptions of judgments that individuals do make. "Competence" and "correctness" are qualities that depend entirely on the benchmarks used.

[206] J. ELSTER, ULYSSES AND THE SIRENS 37 (rev. ed. 1984); Sunstein, *supra* note 88, at 1140.

behavior so that it conforms to legal rules. This, of course, derives from the fact that legal rules are often based on commonsense ideas about the world. A commonsense theory about a particular transaction enables someone holding the theory to predict the behavior of others. If that theory is backed by a legal rule, the predictive value of the theory is enhanced.

Not only do legal rules provide information about daily life interactions, but they also provide a structure or framework that facilitates transactions.[207] Contract law, domestic relations law, and securities laws concerning corporate tender offers all set the background against which parties to such transactions can interact.[208] Such rules reduce the costs of transacting by permitting parties to agree on certain allocations without discussion. Again, this function is successful only to the extent that the legal framework is consistent with commonly shared understandings of the way in which such transactions should occur.

C. Law, Social Change, and Coercion

To this point, I have stressed ways in which law and legal rules rest on commonsense understandings of the world. However, as Unger suggests, law also plays a role in changing formative contexts. In some cases, law is an attempt to alter commonsense ideas of the world in specific areas. Law can be in tension with commonsense theories about the world; it can be an attempt by the legislature or the courts to alter such theories. In this form, law is an ideology imposed from without that seeks to raise the costs of nonadherence so that individuals will alter their pictures of the world and comply.

A common arena for this function is in the actual coercion of one subgroup of society by another. A standard pattern is the imposition of an alien ideology by one geographic group on another. The Civil Rights Act of 1964[209] was such an attempt and a reasonably successful one: it imposed a new idea of race relations on a recalcitrant population.[210] Law in this vein does not seek to persuade, but to coerce. Thus "free choice" was not a viable method of instituting school desegregation in the South,

---

[207] Stewart Macauley has demonstrated how the legal framework of contract law is a resource that business people can call on in governing their commercial interactions, but a resource rarely used. Macauley, *Non-contractual Relations in Business: A Preliminary Study*, 28 AM. SOC. REV. 55 (1963). Egon Bittner's study of peacekeeping also illustrates this function of legal rules as a resource. Bittner, *supra* note 106, at 710.

[208] *See* Mnookin & Kornhauser, *Bargaining in the Shadow of the Law: The Case of Divorce*, 88 YALE L.J. 950, 959-77 (1979). This is not to say that the particular institutional structure established by a set of legal rules is necessarily the best.

[209] Pub. L. No. 88-352, 78 Stat. 241 (codified as amended at 42 U.S.C. §§ 2000a to 2000h-6 (1982 & Supp. IV 1986)).

[210] *See* Sunstein, *supra* note 88, at 1153-54 (laws prohibiting race and gender discrimination based on idea that preference for discrimination is product of distorted preference formation); Donohue, *supra* note 156, at 1411 (critics of Title VII view it as legislative effort to shape private preferences).

and the law performed a coercive function in mandating desegregation.[211]

In other cases, law is designed to "correct" "inaccurate" commonsense ideas held by some segments of the population.[212] Laws such as pollution and helmet statutes, often justified as efforts to force individuals to internalize the externalities of certain activities, are attempts to cause individuals to alter their sense of the proper way to behave. By forcing individuals to adopt new ideas of the world or to incorporate new information into their decisionmaking, such laws attempt to change the institutional structure of society. They affect each individual's decisionmaking process by altering the starting positions and available means.

Of course, it may be that coercive laws of this sort never succeed in altering individuals' commonsense theories of the world, but instead are effective simply because they make noncompliance unacceptably costly. The line between mere incentives and coercive alterations of commonsense theories of the world is not clear cut. For example, tax law changes seem to be an area in which only behavior is highly responsive to changes in the law. On the other hand, the civil rights laws have apparently helped to change a whole population's view on proper race relations, even though resistance remains. Although sudden nonenforcement of antidiscrimination laws might result in a small increase in discrimination, the effect would not be as radical as the change in investment habits that would result from a repeal of the federal tax exemption for interest on state-issued obligations.

IV. CONCLUSION

These insights about law are not particularly new. Many of the legal realists were deeply concerned with the interaction of law and commonsense ideas.[213] Karl Llewellyn was probably the most explicit and persistent.[214] Underhill Moore's studies examined the interaction of law, behavior, and postulated commonsense explanations of adaptation to law.[215] This tradition saw law's effectiveness as in part dependent on commonsense understandings of the world, and on the established rou-

---

[211] Gewirtz, *supra* note 157, at 741-49.

[212] Sunstein assumes that there is a correct rational analysis that is facilitated by legal regulation. *See* Sunstein, *supra* note 88, at 1154-57.

[213] *See supra* note 194.

[214] Llewellyn, *A Realistic Jurisprudence—The Next Step*, 30 COLUM. L. REV. 431, 462-63 (1930) (realistic jurisprudence must be concerned with "folk-law-in-action" and with what lay people believe law should be); Llewellyn (pt. 1), *supra* note 182, at 723 ("court's background picture of transactions 'of *this* type' ").

[215] Moore, *Rational Basis of Legal Institutions*, 23 COLUM. L. REV. 609 (1923) (habitual belief and behavior constitute institutions); Moore & Hope, *An Institutional Approach to the Law of Commercial Banking*, 38 YALE L.J. 703, 705 (1929) (prediction of judicial decisions from standard practice in banking community); Moore & Callahan, *Law and Learning Theory: A Study in Legal*

tines of everyday practical activity. The realist tradition, however, is often forgotten even by those who locate their legacy in it.

My suggestion is that Unger's notion of formative contexts ignores these insights to the detriment of the plausibility of his theory. I agree with him that social change and transformation are very often desirable, and I may even agree with some of his suggestions. But social change, as one notably successful revolutionary theorist realized,[216] never springs full-blown from a comprehensive theory. Nor does it come at the end of a deliberative conversation, no matter how arduous and authentic. The new world, if it is to come, must come from changes in the way people view and understand their everyday practical activity. And such changes are unlikely without a bit of force.[217]

Control, 53 YALE L.J. 1, 61 (1943) (development of commonsense theories to explain alteration in parking and traffic behavior caused by changes in regulations).

[216] V. LENIN, WHAT IS TO BE DONE 212-20 (1973) (first published in Russian in 1902) (immediate calls for spontaneous "attack" to be rejected in favor of "an organization of revolutionaries").

[217] Lenin believed that the suppression of internal dissent was essential if the revolution was ever to succeed. *See id.* at 173 ("[Members of revolutionary organizations] have not the time to think about toy forms of democracy . . . , but they have a lively sense of their *responsibility*, knowing as they do from experience that an organization of real revolutionaries will stop at nothing to rid itself of an undesirable member."); V. LENIN, THE STATE AND REVOLUTION 107 (1973) (first published in Russian in 1917) ("[D]uring the *transition* from capitalism to Communism suppression is *still* necessary; but it is now the suppression of the exploiting minority by the exploited majority. A special apparatus, a special machine for suppression, the 'state,' is *still* necessary, but this is now a transitional state.").

PSYCHIATRY AS SCIENTIFIC HUMANISM: A PROGRAM INSPIRED BY ROBERTO UNGER'S *PASSION*

J. Allan Hobson,

I. INTRODUCTION

A funny thing happened on the way to *Politics*: feeling the need for nothing less than a new theory of the human personality, Roberto Mangabeira Unger wrote a book called *Passion*. This glorious aside—some 300 pages in length—is full of the great essayist's wisdom and grace. I read it with a paradoxical combination of admiration and frustration.

The wide-ranging discourse of *Passion* culminates in a detailed and trenchant critique of contemporary psychiatry. *Passion*'s concluding chapter, "A Program for Late Twentieth-Century Psychiatry," was presented as an invited address to the American Psychiatric Association in 1980 and published in the *American Journal of Psychiatry* in 1982.[1] Unger's Program was brought to my attention in 1984 by my colleagues in the New Psychiatry Seminar, a quasirevolutionary group of Young Turks that was wrestling with the same issues Unger had so skillfully pinioned.

In his Program, Unger promised that his *Passion* would provide a sketch for a new individual psychology that might at once replace the failing constructs of psychiatry (psychoanalysis) and serve as a building block for the social assumptions of *Politics*.

In this Essay, I hope to convey some of my own critical doubts about the validity and utility of this hybrid agenda and voice some fears that Unger's vision of reality and his rhetorical style aroused. I also offer here some ideas, which were inspired by my reading of *Passion*, for the remaking of psychiatry.

To sum up my position at the outset, I believe that Unger's overall analysis of the current problems of psychiatry is correct: Psychoanalysis *is* out of gas, and biological psychiatry *is not yet* up to speed. As a field in crisis, psychiatry is ripe for change. Into the breach walks Unger with his *Passion*. As a means of filling the gap between psychiatry's decadent

---

[1] *See Late Twentieth-Century Psychiatry.*

psychology and its immature biology, I find Unger's theory of personality both irresistibly compelling and hopelessly inadequate. In praising Unger's direct and lucid style, his freedom from technical jargon, his skepticism about psychiatric pseudoscience, I support *Passion*'s endorsement of a dynamic model of human possibilities. By enumerating *Passion*'s scientific inadequacies, I hope to fill a few of the gaps, or at least to outline, more specifically than Unger has done, a programmatic approach to filling them. Thus, I hope to remain both friend and ally to Unger in what I take to be a joint intellectual endeavor.

I begin in part II with a critical overview of the psychological theory in *Passion*. I show why I believe that Unger's theory, while substantially true and eloquently espoused, is not likely to be effective as a humanistic exhortation to professional psychologists, and why I believe it to be categorically inadequate as a scientific base for the study of behavior.

In part III, I present my own view of the intellectual agenda that confronts a New Psychiatry. I develop a much more positive and optimistic appraisal of the prospects of biology than Unger adopts. I also show that many of the psychological assumptions of *Passion* may be evaluated by comparison with already existing biological data. Some are flatly wrong; many others are questionable; and all are in need of quantitative measurement. Only in this way can Unger's psychology advance from a set of slogans to testable hypotheses.

Turning to the need for a new psychology, I articulate in part IV my own Credo for a scientific humanism that attempts to integrate the broadly humanistic spirit of Unger's approach with the operationalism of modern science. The goal of this part is to show that bold propositions such as Unger's need to be considered as hypotheses seeking verification rather than as a priori truths, the credibility of which rests upon emotional appeal and vivid articulation.

Feeling as strongly as Unger does about the pressing need for reform, I conclude in part V with a Manifesto for a New Psychiatry, a call to arms should the proposed Agenda and Credo fail to be adopted. I confess that two scenarios are more likely than the one I propose. One is a conservative retrenchment of both psychoanalysis and biological psychiatry resulting in a continuing cold war; the other is a gradual drift toward utilitarianism forced by economic stagnation, and a resulting vitiation of both scientific and humanistic programs.

II. A Critique of Unger's *Passion*

In his "Essay on Personality," Roberto Unger develops a view of man based upon the presumed universality of "our desire to be accepted by one another and to become, through this acceptance, freer to reinvent ourselves."[2] A key assumption is that each individual's identity is con-

---

[2] Passion at vii.

tinuously changed by interaction with others. This tenet runs strongly counter to the deterministic views of Freud and implicitly denies the priority of either heredity or early experience, with their attendant historical fatalism.

Flying in the face of strong clinical and experimental evidence, this denial will immediately dismay many reasonable practitioners and scientists. In this respect, Unger is typical of liberal architects of social change in denying the power of strong biological forces: the genes that color our skin for life; the hormones that change our brain-minds from month to month; and the powerful early experiences that shape those highly conservative interpersonal bonds that mark our social interactions forever.

In advancing a utopian or revolutionary social program, it is not necessary for the humanist to deny the data of Gregor Mendel, John Bowlby,[3] and E.O. Wilson.[4] There is plenty of room for a dynamic environmentalism within the biological tradition that Unger discounts or ignores. In thus castigating Unger for his highhandedness with regard to some of my own intellectual heroes, I join forces with scholarly critics who wish that *Passion* had been better documented and that it had specified and discussed its inspirational sources.[5]

As a natural scientist, I also wish that *Passion* had presented and discussed *evidence*, rather than relying exclusively upon rhetorical argument. I quickly become both weary and wary of rhetoric: weary because its generalizations create a thirst for concrete examples; wary because its uncritical urgency creates a sense of dictatorial oppression.

Unger's *substantive* aim, to "restat[e] . . . the Christian-romantic image of man,"[6] is both appealing—because I *am* a Christian-romantic— and appalling—because I am *also* a Jew, an atheist, a skeptic, and a hardheaded scientist. Surely Unger does not want to exclude these pluralistic parts of modern man from his neo-Christian sect.

I welcome Unger's *methodological* aim—to reconceive the attribution of normative force to conceptions of personality and society. But this task is quite inconceivable without quantification. Not only are his intellectual progenitors unnamed, there are also no numbers to substantiate his pronouncements! Surely Unger does not wish to exclude statisticians from his modernist workshop.

In sum, Unger's scholasticism invokes specters of medieval rationalism that allow too easy a dismissal of his most salient messages. For example, Unger asserts that "there might be nothing to which the idea of

---

[3] *See generally* J. BOWLBY, ATTACHMENT AND LOSS (1979).

[4] *See generally* E.O. WILSON, ON HUMAN NATURE (1982); E.O. WILSON, SOCIOBIOLOGY: THE NEW SYNTHESIS (1975).

[5] *See, e.g.,* Neu, *Looking All Around for Our Real Selves* (Book Review), N.Y. Times, July 8, 1984, at 24.

[6] PASSION at vii.

a fundamental human identity could refer,"[7] and adds that "a common identity . . . could not be reduced to strong but indeterminate biological constraints, nor to precise but trivial cultural traits."[8] Might our common identity not be our brain-mind? With its capabilities of reflection, feeling, and invention, the brain-mind strongly determines our states, the traits of which include the very openness that Unger extols. Our openness is itself determined: we are determined to be free. Unger thus can look to modern neurobiology and to cognitive science for key building blocks of his theory.

As to "precise but trivial cultural traits,"[9] are we, as a set of brain-minds, also not subject to determinate constraints on our collective state of mind? Thus, while it may be true that "all contexts can be broken,"[10] the state-space of all possible social contexts itself may be bounded by the limits of our brain-minds. And those context shifts that do occur also may be subject to strongly probabilistic sequences.

Sociobiology, that *bête noir* of so many liberal intellectuals, must be as useful to an assessment of the degree to which sociocultural forces are derivative of (and reducible to) biology as it is to an estimation of the limits of any utopian state-space. There must be an analogy—in the realm of dialectic—to the laws of competition and survival in field biology. Is it Marxism? No, Unger rejects that dogma as emphatically as he does Freudian determinism. I agree with both these indictments. The New Psychiatry, like the New Politics, must move beyond these limits.

If not Freud, if not Marx, then who is our theoretical guru? Why *not* E.O. Wilson? Do we envisage a kind of Social Darwinism that sees the brain-mind as the analog of the mutant gene? If so, it might be tempting to assume that all we need do is foster mutation—that is, change our minds. But of course most genetic mutations are nonadaptive. Indeed, most mutations probably are useless if they are only harmless oddities. But some mutations lead to disease and some are even lethal. The limits are set by the fit between the organism's new biochemical capability and its environmental realities.

Unger's analysis of the problems of contextuality is offered in place of an answer to these mechanistic questions. He states that the unlimited quality of mutual dependence and jeopardy leads to the "problem of solidarity."[11] According to Unger, an unlimited need (dependency?) and an unlimited danger (vulnerability?) make accomodation to community so difficult.

Why declare that our need is "unlimited"? This hyperbolic adjective implies infinity, and so echoes Freud's concept of "boundless" nar-

---

[7] *Id.* at 3.
[8] *Id.*
[9] *Id.*
[10] *Id.* at 9.
[11] *Id.* at 20.

cissism. How do we know that this need is not narrowly and specifically bounded? For the utopian social theorist—who is going to make practical decisions regarding such social entities as day care centers—it would seem essential to assume that human needs can be specified, measured, and met. By assuming unlimited need, Unger excuses in advance the failure of such practical schemes.

And why should vulnerability likewise be dubbed "unlimited"? Surely there are conditions that reduce, eliminate, or even invert vulnerability. A behaviorist might say that acts which generate positive feedback will reduce anxiety and discomfort. Unger claims that in the interpersonal domain such acts are due to the generosity that naturally springs from empowerment. This paradigm is reducible to a positive reinforcement learning model. So is Unger a Skinnerian? Yes and no. He shares Skinner's naive utopianism, but he does not acknowledge the existence and power of those punitive structures that seem quickly to emerge when visionary schemes like Unger's become real politics. It is not unusual under such circumstances for the newly empowered to eradicate the intelligensia! Like Skinner, Unger is an extreme environmentalist for whom the human head is but a black box to be programmed at will by the benevolent social engineer.

On further contemplating Unger's vulnerability tenet, a modern psychologist might think of the Freudian concept of defense and its revision by neo-Freudians like Elvin Semrad and George Vaillant. As antidotes to vulnerability there are healthy defenses like sublimation and humor, neurotic defenses like hypochondriasis and conversion, and psychotic defenses like denial and projection. According to this scheme, Unger's vision thus would seem to range all the way from the healthy (sublimation) to the unhealthy (denial).

Unger's reading of the modernist account of reality thus strikes me as overly relativistic. Is there really no unconditional context? Are there no absolute physical limits on an organism's real and potential adaptive capability? Or is Unger's social gene *infinitely* creative? If Unger's hyperbole is rhetorical—that is, he doesn't *really* mean *infinitely*—then how do we know where Ungerian rhetoric leaves off and Ungerian naturalism begins? Scientific naturalism, which I espouse, recognizes interactionism, as Unger would like, but attempts to measure its terms (the interactants) and to model its modes (the interactions). This classical approach, which Unger decries as absolutist, leads ultimately to mathematical models and to the recognition of "higher order principles and rules," which Unger's extreme contextualism denies. But as I will point out in my own agenda for a New Psychiatry,[12] it is precisely a principled approach which is most likely to advance the biological program of psychiatry in parallel with advances in its psychology.

---

[12] *See infra* part III.

The world that Unger promotes does not appear either to acknowledge or to respect the absolute limits imposed upon the organism by physical reality. It thus ignores the power of scientific analysis that is such an important part of any accurate representation of the "modernist view of man." Unger is, sad to say, a scientific ostrich.

Consider *Passion*'s conception of our place in nature and examine the syllogism that links its three types of order: constraint, coordination, and emancipation. A problem arises in Unger's choice of the term "emancipation,"[13] with its implied capacity "to *override* the influence of the constraints."[14] At the physical level of the analogy, emancipation is not the right word because the organism is absolutely constrained by both the limits of its genome and the limits of its physical environment. Recognizing these limits still allows for virtually infinite freedom (via recombination), but it does not allow for *transcendence*. I would substitute a more moderate word for emancipation, such as "creativity," "invention," or "experimentation." These processes do not override (transcend) physical reality; they lead to understanding, to control, and even to imitative replication of its creative processes.

In a naturalistic world view, the psychological and social levels of the analogy will be bound by the same constraints. Unger recognizes that these domains—in their complexity—will be less amenable than even biology to reductionist analysis. The failure of the reductionist strategy poses an ever-present danger: the mystical celebration of complexity that is, I fear, religion. Insofar as Unger's neo-Christian-romantic vision endorses mysticism, I reject it.

In the religious world view the mind is not constrained by the body. Although this view cannot be disproved, most modern scientists consider it untenable. No evidence supports it. The social equivalent of this view is a world of human beings living in the bliss of perfectly harmonious love. This view cannot be disproved either, and, because it is in some ways desirable, I am less sure that it is wrong. But I am skeptical of this view because, as Unger points out, material scarcity does exist, and it is likely to increase. This will increase competition for food supplies and— short of the universal adoption of Gandhi-like abstinence—will lead to conflict, of which there is, anyway, no sign of abatement in the world.

I do not say that war is inevitable. Nor do I deny that mental life and social life have *virtually* infinite degrees of innovative freedom. But I am convinced that a natural context for life and for human discourse does exist. In fact, I believe that such a natural context for life is increasingly evident and well known. For me, biology already provides the theoretical and empirical basis of a naturalistic world view that recognizes interactionism and the dynamic interplay of freedom and restraint. Life

---

[13] PASSION at 17.
[14] *Id.* at 19 (emphasis added).

processes are thus *both* boundless (via recombination of materials) and absolutely limited (via material laws). So too are mental and social processes. To foster creativity and growth we do not need to open the door either to spiritualism or to psychosis. While such mental experiments are naturally determined, in the long run they are likely to be lethal cognitive mutants.

III. An Agenda for a New Psychiatry[15]

Unger and I most strongly agree on the priority that psychology should receive in any revisionist agenda for psychiatry. And we further agree that psychology should be reformulated in humanistic terms that recognize both needs and vulnerabilities. But, while I would build such a psychology *up* from my lowly base in biological science, Unger would build it *down* from his lofty perch in sociopolitical theory.

A. Why a New Psychiatry?

The bankruptcy of the old psychology is increasingly evident. Psychoanalysis simply has been unable to maintain credibility as a central, unifying theory for psychiatry. The institutional isolation, the protectionist orientation toward texts, procedures, and rules, and the drift away from biology and toward hermeneutics all contribute to its impending failure.[16]

If it is to succeed, the New Psychiatry must either reconcile psychoanalysis with modern science or create a new general theory to replace psychoanalysis. If this is impossible, we must recognize clearly our inability to do either while defining profitable areas of inquiry that are potentially integral to an emerging synthesis.

At a more practical level, the institutional function of psychoanalysis also must be replaced so that the psychological progress of the New Psychiatry has a university-based forum for its theoreticians and practitioners.[17]

---

[15] This section is a collection of ideas on a wide variety of topics that emerged in discussion with my colleagues in the New Psychiatry Seminar. Participants included Alan Green, Ned Hallowell, Steve Hoffman, Ben Lopez, David Mann, Ed Mikkelsen, John Ratey, Victoria Russell, Jennifer Stevens, and Margaret Warner.

Many of the themes were further developed in dialogue with visiting scholars in the Academic Conference Series that was organized by the seminar. Participants included John Bowlby, Patricia Churchland, Frederick Crews, Adolf Grunbaum, Julian Jaynes, Jerome Kagan, Ivar Lovaas, Morton Reiser, Paul Roazen, and Frank Sulloway.

The motive for this Agenda—and construction of its essential framework and contents— preceded my awareness of Unger's closely related essay, *An Agenda for Late Twentieth-Century Psychiatry*, and the last chapter of *Passion*. I recognize both the similarity and simultaneity of our respective visions as well as the important differences in orientation that distinguish our views.

[16] *See* Hobson, *Psychoanalysis on the Couch*, 1986 Encyclopedia Britannica Med. & Health Ann. 74-91.

[17] *See infra* part V.

The current instability presents the opportunity for sweeping revision of psychoanalytic theory. This revision will require institutional recognition of flux and support for those who seek alternative ideas and approaches. I believe that the university, which originally excluded Freud and psychoanalysis (and later was excluded by him and his institutionalized followers), should play a more open, aggressive, and affirmative leadership role at the post-graduate level, as well as in appropriately revised medical student and resident psychiatry education programs.

The elements of a change toward a New Psychiatry already are visible. Specific critiques recently have emerged that constitute frontal assaults on psychoanalysis. The response to these challenges has been weak and ineffectual.

In the area of historical study we have seen the appearance of Jeffrey Masson's book, *The Assault on Truth: Freud's Suppression of the Seduction Theory*,[18] with its flood of revelations regarding the behavior of past and present psychoanalysts.[19] No amount of *ad hominem* argument can vitiate the impact of Masson's historical thesis; it joins an impressive array of modern empirical studies indicating that what really happened to people in childhood really matters to their psychology and behavior as adults. Modern evidence regarding the traumas of incest and abuse support Masson's claim that Freud's abandonment of the seduction theory was not only politically slick, but scientifically unjustified. This conclusion resonates with the New Psychiatry's emphasis upon ethology, learning theory, and naturalistic studies of behavior. And it argues—from an environmentalist perspective—against Unger's idea that we are absolutely free to reinvent ourselves.

I await with interest the publication of Peter Swale's book on what really happened to Freud's patients after treatment, anticipating—from the preliminary evidence—at least as much distortion in describing outcomes as Freud applied to the elaboration of their premorbid histories. Such distortion is foreshadowed by Paul Roazen in his book, *Brother Animal: The Story of Freud and Tausk*,[20] detailing Freud's treatment of his colleague Victor Tausk.

Frederick Crews indicates that we soon can expect more in the tradition of historical demythification initiated by Frank Sulloway. According to Crews' new thesis, Sulloway stopped far short of the conclusions justified by his data.[21] Sulloway's superb *Freud, Biologist of the Mind*[22] is a major watershed in Freud scholarship. As the first study by a profes-

---

[18] J. MASSON, THE ASSAULT ON TRUTH: FREUD'S SUPPRESSION OF THE SEDUCTION THEORY (1984).

[19] This story had already been broadcast by Janet Malcolm in her articles, *Annals of Scholarship: Trouble in the Archives* (pts. 1 & 2), NEW YORKER, Dec. 5, 1983, at 59; Dec. 12, 1983, at 60.

[20] P. ROAZEN, BROTHER ANIMAL: THE STORY OF FREUD AND TAUSK (1969).

[21] *See* F. CREWS, *Beyond Sulloway's Freud: Psychoanalysis Minus the Myth of the Hero*, in SKEPTICAL ENGAGEMENTS 88-111 (1986).

sional historian, and the first by a non-Freudian, it provides startling data about Freud's intellectual development and his strategic style.

In the area of philosophy of science, the publication of *The Foundations of Psychoanalysis: A Philosophical Critique*[23] by the professional philosopher of science, Adolf Grunbaum, is another landmark work.

While there have been many previous potshots at the logic and use of evidence in Freud's theorizing, Grunbaum's book constitutes a sustained and thoroughgoing attack on the details of Freud's arguments. It is in the spirit of Michael Sherwood's equally devastating (but largely overlooked) philosophical critique of the influential neo-Freudian Wilfred Bion.[24] But Grunbaum critiques Freud himself, and no fundamental aspect of psychoanalytic theory goes unchallenged.

Grunbaum ridicules the hermeneutic conception in today's psychoanalytic vanguard as muddled, scientifically untutored, and decadent. He prefers the real Freud. Grunbaum rejects Karl Popper as superficially schooled; Grunbaum further skewers Jürgen Habermas, Paul Ricoeur, and George Klein; he then attacks the psychoanalytic clinical method of investigation as, for the most part, hopelessly unscientific. Grunbaum also shows the theory of repression to be epistemically anemic in its formulation of the psychogenesis of neuroses, slips, and dreams. All three phenomena either are not adequately explained by psychoanalytic theory or have more plausible and verifiable alternative explanations, or both. As a *coup de grâce*, Grunbaum's logical razor slashes the central method of free association as incapable of establishing causal connections or yielding probative evidence for the theory's cardinal hypotheses.

A third element of the movement toward a New Psychiatry is the growth of neurobiology and ethology.[25] The fundamental knowledge base relating to the nervous system—which Freud repeatedly recognized as the ultimate and most highly privileged level of causal explanation—is increasing exponentially.[26]

Since it is generally recognized (even by the devout apostles Ernst Kris and James Strachey) that psychoanalysis derives from neurobiological concepts, we need to update almost every one of Freud's basic as-

---

[22] F. Sulloway, Freud, Biologist of the Mind: Beyond the Psychoanalytic Legend (1979).

[23] A. Grunbaum, The Foundations of Psychoanalysis: A Philosophical Critique (1984).

[24] *See* M. Sherwood, The Logic of Explanation in Psychoanalysis (1969).

[25] Ethology is the naturalistic study of behavior with the goal of determining its biological purposes. See *infra* notes 29-30 for references to ethological writings.

[26] The overall relevance of the growth of neurobiology for a comprehensive psychiatric theory is to be found in S. Freud, *Project for a Scientific Psychology*, in 1 The Standard Edition of the Complete Psychological Works of Sigmund Freud 294-397 (J. Strachey trans. 1966).

sumptions about the brain.[27]

A more focused, alternative approach is to derive a dream theory from what we now know of the neurophysiology of sleep. The resulting "Activation Synthesis" hypothesis explains distinctive dream phenomenology without resort to wish fulfillment, censorship, disguise, protection of sleep, or repression.[28] Since Grunbaum has shown that the psychoanalytic dream theory also is not supported by Freud's own data, one can conservatively claim that a new theory is at least worthy of serious consideration, and that its development (from nonpsychoanalytic data) may constitute a more general model of the way that revision and the construction of any new psychological theory may proceed. This no doubt will be contested by those psychoanalysts who believe that the only valid data is that which they collect in the analytic setting.

The growth of ethology also is especially interesting since it deals with the interaction of instinctual drives (fixed action patterns that are based upon innate releasing mechanisms) and their interaction with environmental factors (the ethologists' "releasing stimuli"). Ethology thus follows the fundamental paradigm of dynamic psychology. John Bowlby's attempt to integrate ethological concepts with those of psychoanalysis are good examples of the sort of moderate progressive thinking that generally has been ignored by psychiatrists.[29] But the psychoanalysts don't like Bowlby's scientism. And the scientists don't like his Freudianism! Perhaps a more polemical and direct approach is required to attract attention to this important area. It is remarkable, for example, how little has come of attempts to develop animal models of depression, especially since the implication of such work is that it is the separation per se, and not ambivalence about the introjected object, that is pathogenic.

Another unexplored ethological lead is Niko Tinbergen's analysis of childhood autism, replete with its suggestions for an experimental treatment program.[30] To date, no young psychiatrist has grasped the opportunity to create a new area of inquiry by opening up the psychiatry/ethology interface. On the other hand, learning theory has been applied successfully to the treatment of autism by Ivor Lovaas.[31]

Another interesting area is the growth of information theory, linguistics theory, and systems theory. By information theory, I mean the

---

[27] *See* McCarley & Hobson, *The Neurobiological Origins of Psychoanalytic Dream Theory*, 134 AM. J. PSYCHIATRY 1211-21 (1977); *see also* F. SULLOWAY, *supra* note 22.

[28] *See* Hobson & McCarley, *The Brain as a Dream State Generator: An Activation-Synthesis Hypothesis of the Dream Process*, 134 AM. J. PSYCHIATRY 1335-48 (1977).

[29] *See* J. BOWLBY, *supra* note 3; *see also* J. BOWLBY, LOSS: SADNESS AND DEPRESSION (1980); J. BOWLBY, SEPARATION: ANXIETY AND ANGER (1973).

[30] 2 N. TINBERGEN, THE ANIMAL IN ITS WORLD 175-199 (1972).

[31] *See* Lovaas, *Behavioral Treatment and Normal Educational and Intellectual Functioning in Young Autistic Children*, 55 J. CONSULTING & CLINICAL PSYCHOLOGY 3 (1986).

constellation of disciplines that utilize computer technology to simulate the brain-mind. Artificial intelligence and cognitive psychology intersect at a current hot spot of scientific investigation. Douglas Hofstadter's *Godel, Escher, Bach* [32] is loaded with stimulating and often humorous speculation rooted in sound logic and realistic methodology. Some work has been done in the development of computer models of psychopathology and in computer simulation of psychotherapy. If the major mechanism in therapy is the analysis of transference, it should be possible to simulate it perfectly. If, instead, the process is one of identification with, and modeling of, a real person, then simulation will not work.

The ACT-star model of the mind described by John Anderson in *The Architecture of Cognition* [33] provides a program simulating human thought that clinical and basic scientists can manipulate according to their interests. For example, the model should behave differently when it is less "data driven" (as in dreaming) than when it is input responsive (as in waking). Does it? Can dreaming be simulated given a suitable database? New models of cognition also predict and explain most slips as simple systems errors, which some have called "cognitive demons."[34] The appealing parsimony of this alternative explanation—coupled with Grunbaum's critique of the repression hypothesis of slips—provides another example of how emerging, independent, scientific approaches converge.

Another field that beckons to the young investigator is linguistics, which has been bastardized by Jacques Lacan[35] but eloquently developed and explained by Noam Chomsky.[36] Since words are one of the vehicles of thought and communication, it is surprising that no decent psychiatrist has done scientific work at this important interface.

Politics is a final element leading to the change to a New Psychiatry. Third-party payers increasingly insist on evidence of efficacy and efficiency in psychiatric treatment. They include governmental agencies, which must establish priorities for their limited resources. Even that segment of the public that still can pay its own costs is increasingly well-informed and skeptical regarding psychoanalysis and its offshoot schools of psychotherapy.

B.   What Will Be the Character of the New Psychiatry?

As its field boundaries have blurred in the attempt to be all things to all people, psychiatry has become, at worst, a confusion and, at best, a

---

[32] D. Hofstadter, Gödel, Escher, Bach: An Eternal Golden Braid (1979).

[33] J. Anderson, The Architecture of Cognition (1983).

[34] J. Reason & K. Mycielska, Absent Minded? The Psychology of Mental Lapses and Everyday Errors 38-61 (1982).

[35] *E.g.* J. Lacan, The Four Fundamental Concepts of Psychoanalysis (1978).

[36] *See* N. Chomsky, Reflections on Language (1975).

bland smorgasbord of topics. Beyond today's moderate but pallid eclecticism I visualize a more radical and robust integration.

To realize the many tasks of its integrative agenda, the New Psychiatry needs to abandon its quest for magical leadership. John Ratey predicts that nothing less than the "Cannonization of William James" is necessary for the creation of a new synthesis.[37] But we search the horizon in vain for the synthetic intelligence of either a William James or a Walter Cannon, taking only faint comfort in the fact that, since our era provided the intellectual climate that nourished both, it may be capable of fostering the growth of their successors. And since it took James fourteen years to write *The Principles of Psychology*[38]—which tied together all that was known in 1890—it would be wise to begin writing today with the fateful publication date of the year 2000 in mind! Unger's work has the scope and style that are needed; but James' empiricism and Cannon's experimentalism are not evident in *Passion*. We need those scientific qualities as well as Unger's optimism and enthusiasm.

The New Psychiatry also will be characterized by a reunion with biology that is based upon compatibility. The reunion I envision is a back-to-basics stripping down of psychiatric psychology that should go hand-in-hand with renovation of its dynamics. In this respect, I would go much further than Unger, even if I never could hope to be as eloquent as he. In Unger's view, the New Psychiatry's biological program is too weak to fill the void caused by the impending collapse of psychoanalysis. I agree. But I do not agree that Unger's naturalistic psychology is an adequate replacement of psychoanalysis. His view of psychology is as scientifically limited as his view of biology. As evidence, I note that Unger overlooks cognitive psychology and artificial intelligence as well as ethology. These are the fields upon which psychiatry should rebuild.

The New Psychiatry also will involve the retention and renovation of psychodynamic theory (a new psychoanalysis). What is most exemplary and useful in Unger's psychological approach is its refusal to reduce the human passions (especially love) to the baser derivative elements that may energize, enhance, or be deflected by them (sex, mastery, etc.). Unger's holism is not mere Christian cultism and could inspire the sort of organic and open view of intrapersonal and interpersonal processes that is needed to allow the natural history tradition of biology to speak in the same voice as the analytic tradition in psychology. Were Unger's appealing and rich literary musings on the life of feeling fleshed out with specific examples, the biological ground out of which they arise might even be more clear.

I think, for example, of the relief I experienced when I read Irving

---

[37] Conversation with John Ratey.

[38] W. JAMES, THE PRINCIPLES OF PSYCHOLOGY (1893).

Yalom's *Group Psychotherapy*,[39] which seemed both natural and open, compared with the tension inspired by Wilfred Bion's *Experiences in Groups*,[40] which seemed feigned and categorical. The bridge here could come from further study and emulation of Charles Darwin, who, like Herbert Spencer and William James, was both holist and an analytically acute psychologist.[41] If thinkers like George Vaillant could supplement psychoanalytic jargon with constructs more capable of observational verification,[42] our field could become more than neo-Freudian. Vaillant's natural history approach[43] is a methodological step in the right direction. Prospective, predictive studies using the life-history format are also needed.

The New Psychiatry also will involve the incorporation of learning theory. Learning theory could be integrated more gracefully into our thought if it were seen as less limited than it first appeared on emergence from the pigeon-pecking, black-box paradigm of B.F. Skinner, and less stereotyped than the dog-drooling imagery of its neo-Pavlovian practitioners. The organism is designed to learn, and learn it will. The patient will learn from the therapist at every moment of their interaction; this process includes transference, but it will prove to be but a small part of therapeutic learning. How else could one possibly explain that therapists, not therapies, help patients? In fact, when the therapist variable is removed, the only technique that seems to have any specific utility is behavior therapy—that is, the learning theory aspect. It is thus the method of choice in the treatment of the phobias, where it is clearly superior to insight-oriented approaches. Even in the difficult area of childhood autism, a simple reinforcement paradigm can be used to teach the mute patient to speak; with speech, comes relationship, and with relationship, comes emotion. Autism thus is dissolved.[44]

John Ratey's definition of therapy, the empathic mirroring of states,[45] is teaching by doing in the here and now as much as it is teaching by principled reflection upon the past. Each of us says to the other: "Show me how to be. Show me how to become productive, successful, and happy." In this sense, Unger is correct to be charismatic. For some, at least, he will be an effective role model. But it is the worst error of demogogues to believe that exhortation alone is enough. We also need diligent and devoted caretakers. *They* are unlikely to be charismatic.

It is both a relief and a profound disappointment to realize that imi-

---

[39] I. YALOM, THE THEORY AND PRACTICE OF GROUP PSYCHOTHERAPY (1970).

[40] W. BION, EXPERIENCES IN GROUPS (1961).

[41] *See, e.g.*, C. DARWIN, THE EXPRESSION OF THE EMOTIONS IN MAN AND ANIMALS (1979) (1st ed. 1872).

[42] *See, e.g.*, G. VAILLANT, ADAPTION TO LIFE (1977).

[43] *See* G. VAILLANT, THE NATURAL HISTORY OF ALCOHOLISM (1983).

[44] *See supra* note 31 and accompanying text.

[45] Conversation with John Ratey.

tative modeling is what personal growth is really all about. It is a relief because the concept is so simple; we need to concern ourselves more with the promotion, by example, of healthy behavior. It is a disappointment because we are not the technically sophisticated psychic engineers we have taken ourselves to be. Here I agree with Unger's maxim: Mutual acceptance makes us freer to reinvent ourselves. But only within certain limits!

For those therapists who must have technical complexity to maintain self-respect, there is the study of the nervous system (behavioral neurobiology), the development of realistic mechanical models of the mind (artificial intelligence), and the design of a new dynamics of identification consonant with simple learning principles (interactive plasticity).

The New Psychiatry also will be characterized by the incorporation of ethology. An area of particular promise, linking interactive plasticity to ethology, is an ethologically oriented developmental psychology. As T.B. Brazelton has shown,[46] clinically relevant integrations abound as Bowlby's attachment concept is examined in field studies. This work continues the work begun by Dorothy Burlingham and Anna Freud, and continued at Yale University as the Psychoanalytic Study of the Child, but it sheds the bias of that faulty theoretical framework.

The New Psychiatry also will break with narrow determinism of classical psychoanalytic thought by recognizing and working to enhance creativity. As derivatives of the limited, late nineteenth-century picture of the nervous system as reflexive, which has been carried forward in Freud's metapsychology, the mental models we use are overly committed to a closed-loop paradigm, of which the repetition compulsion is the epitome. Here I strongly agree with Unger's emphasis upon openness and our freedom to reinvent ourselves. We now know that the brain-mind is not adequately described as a reflexive system. Rather, it is an open-loop system capable of producing its own energy and its own information. This recognition demands that we address our innate creative capability more positively. Change can occur by adding new repertoires and does not necessarily or primarily involve the eradication of old ones.

It is at least ennobling so to change our view from the psychopathologically oriented position, derived from psychoanalysis, that constituted the early twentieth century "modernist" vision of man. Ironically, the now intellectually conservative psychoanalysis prides itself on a clinical and moral liberalism that its own precepts do not support. Symmetrically, and equally illogically, it fears that the new biology will return psychology to reductionist mechanical models. But the new biology—with its emphasis on plasticity and creativity—is a solid scientific base upon which liberal humanism solidly can stand.

I use the term "naturalistic" to define, centrally, the character of the

---

[46] *See, e.g.,* T.B. BRAZELTON, INFANTS AND MOTHERS (rev. ed. 1983).

New Psychiatry in its approach to descriptions of individual and interactive behavior. Certainly there are echoes of naive romantic traditions in this term: the voices of Rousseau, Voltaire, Blake, Wordsworth, Coleridge, and the rest, who basked in the ruddy, mystical afterglow of the political revolution, still can be heard. But it is not only a simple return to pastoral and spiritual innocence that is in the air. It is, rather, a tough-minded, if tenderhearted, advance to a new state of observational resonance with personal reality that late twentieth century psychiatry can make by redeveloping its naturalistic character.

New descriptions and new classifications now can lead to radically new models of the human brain-mind. The renaissance at hand could compare favorably with that which occurred between the fourteenth and seventeenth centuries and produced the polyglot, multidisciplined genius of Shakespeare, Galileo, Michaelangelo, and da Vinci. All were naturalists who used both science and art to create a graceful and timelessly accurate picture of man. Now, for the first time in human history, we can take a naturalistic look at the organ of creativity itself, the human brain-mind.[47]

C. How Can Scholarly Work Create a New Psychiatry?

In this section, I summarize points already made in earlier sections and develop a few themes in detail to show promising directions to specific items in the revisionist agenda.

A first priority must be historical and critical revision of psychoanalytic theory. The revision and critique of Freud's *Project*[48] should be extended. The revision will include scrapping the metapsychology (already conceded by all but the diehards) and will proceed to the topographic and dynamic aspects of theory. For example, the March 1985 Gifford Conference in St. Andrews, Scotland, was a concatenation of historical, neurobiological, and philosophical criticism.[49] Hopefully, those that are still within the citadel will hear the clamor outside and decide against merely letting them (us) eat cake.

Scholarly work also must strive toward further demythification. Like the cult of personality, the self-styling of genius is hazardous. Those who live by polemics often die by polemics. I hope this will not be Unger's fate; his rationalistic approach makes me fear for him. When public relations go sour, credibility fades fast. The images of Freud-as-scientist, Freud-as-therapist, and even Freud-as-person all are tarnished by recent revelations. To flourish, a scientific field needs strong, simple

---

[47] Patricia Churchland is one of a new breed of materialist philosophers who articulate a unified science of brain and mind. Noting the parallel growth of cognitive and neural science, she envisages a convergence of these disciplines that has momentous import for psychiatry. P. CHURCHLAND, NEUROPHILOSOPHY: TOWARD A UNIFIED SCIENCE OF THE MIND-BRAIN (1986).

[48] *See* S. FREUD, *supra* note 26.

[49] *See* F. CREWS, SKEPTICAL ENGAGEMENTS (1986).

methods, verifiable data, and strongly predictive models. As psychologists, we psychiatrists still do not have one. We have borrowed heavily from basic science, but, as Unger points out, we have yet to forge a general psychology that will both appeal (as psychoanalysis has done) and endure (as it has not).

Scholarly work must be characterized by a radical stripping down to basics. "Unlearning" goes along with demythification. We must cast off—and even root out—those received ideas that hinder progress. All behavior can be ascribed too easily to post hoc motives. For example, my own criticism of the field can be understood by resort to a post hoc, *ad hominem* analysis of my personal history. But this says nothing about the truth of the arguments I advance. It only establishes an interesting, but ultimately irrelevant, aspect of its context. Here, I accept the scientific assumptions of physical truth describable by mathematical means, which Unger's relativism denies.

In interviewing patients, writing up cases, and formulating theories, we must cultivate that sense of wonder that Lewis Thomas calls "bewilderment."[50] The psychoanalytic "retrospectoscope" works so well as to be suspect. Using it, one may find what one is looking for via suggestion: that on-line data fabrication is a serious problem is suggested by the scientific evidence regarding the natural history of human memory, on the one hand, and the scientific evidence for distortion in hypnotic amnesia, on the other. Let us abandon as hopeless the ideal of "free" association while retaining its level of focus: on feelings, associative thought processes, and adaptation.

The new psychodynamics will center on a radically modern view of the so-called unconscious mind. To begin anew it would be better to call it the non-conscious mind. Psychobiology can now use neurobiology as it develops its psychodynamics. The interface between cognitive psychology (*à la* Anderson), artificial intelligence (*à la* Hofstadter), and state neurophysiology (as modern sleep scientists practice it) is a node at which an integration synthesis might profitably be crystallized.

In the area of basic research, the barriers between ethology, neurobiology, and learning theory have been collapsing for some time. Their coalescence soon will constitute a major new discipline, behavioral biology, which could provide a substantial, scientific base for the New Psychiatry. Desperately needed to round out this picture is a truly naturalistic psychology. In this respect Unger's *Passion* is a step in the right direction, but it needs translation from the rhetorical to the operational level.

In the area of clinical research, scholarly work must proceed toward further development of the state concept, both to account for the unity of the brain-mind and to support a psychophysiological concept of mad-

---

[50] L. THOMAS, THE LIVES OF A CELL: NOTES OF A BIOLOGY WATCHER (1975).

ness. If there is but one mind, complex but unified, and if that one mind normally undergoes a dynamic succession of changes in state, then it seems possible Unger is correct when he asserts there is but one genus of mental illness, if that genus is viewed as a set of potentially infinite alterations in brain-mind state.

This radical thesis—composed of the new state psychophysiology and the new cognitive psychology—makes a mockery of both faculty psychology's endless subdivision of the normal mind and the new descriptive psychiatry's increasingly complex classification schemes. What a relief: one mind, one mental illness. Slightly changing one of many operating properties of the brain-mind can move the system to a new point in the state-space.

Each diagnosis thus might become a set of quantitative coordinates in a state-space. The question is not, "Is this person a schizophrenic?"; we already know enough to modify that sort of reification. We could change the question to, "Does this person have schizophrenia?"; but even that expression is too limiting. The question really is, "How schizophrenic is this, or any other, person, including you and me?" In other words, a vectorial dimension in the state-space is one's degree of relatedness versus separateness from others. Another dimension, in the perceptual domain, is the degree of hallucinoid (internally generated information) versus data-driven (externally generated) information. Still another is mood: "How good does the person feel?"; or, "How energetic/lethargic is the person?"

Such an approach would reconcile the antidiagnostic resistance of those clinicians who already recognize the multidimensionality of brain-mind states (and who tend to be antiscientific-psychoanalytic) with the progressively quantitative impulses of the proto-scientific contingent (who tend to be monistic reductionists). At the same time, it would both rid the field of its constant embarrassment regarding the unreliability of its diagnostic efforts and allow psychiatry to take a stronger position with respect to the richness of its subject. The human personality is not a monotonic function, like blood pressure. In other words, psychiatry could properly and precisely define its scientific "specialness" without the antiscientific special pleading that is so common in modern psychoanalytic circles.

A corollary of this naturalistic approach to diagnosis is to regard psychosis itself as a systems error, understandable in terms of the normal functioning of its autocreative, disoriented "mad" mode so clearly seen in our nocturnal dreaming.[51] We are thus never far from madness, and our proximity is both physiologic and pharmacologic. This concept explains the so-called functional psychosis without recourse to the dubious con-

---

[51] *See* J.A. Hobson, The Marriage of Mind and Brain (1984 Semrad Lecture) (unpublished manuscript available from the author on request).

cept of "defense." But because the state approach is more general, it has no difficulty accommodating the notion of defense in its psychology.

An attractive feature of the state model just sketched is its application to current concepts in psychopharmacology, where it also can relieve the conceptual strain of the multiple category approach to diagnosis. Because one's mental health and disease are but a cluster of factors in a state-space, and because that state-space has specific reference to a complex but unified brain-mind, the introduction of single, significant molecules (affecting neurohormones or neurotransmitters) will affect the state of the whole system.

Instead of speaking of antipsychotic, antidepressive, or anxiolytic agents (and recognizing that psychosis, depression, and anxiety are inseparable—though distinct—dimensions of a single system), one would measure a drug's action in terms of its capacity to change the multidimensional state-space of the brain-mind. Since drugs act peripherally as well as centrally, we must acknowledge the integral nature of the whole body and its signals in our ultimate conception of the state-space.

Agreeing with Unger's indictment of psychiatry's disease model approach to diagnosis and treatment, I note the strong evidence that whether a patient is called schizophrenic or manic-depressive depends upon the availability of treatments supposed to be specific for one condition or the other. Thus the introduction of the phenothiazine drugs in the 1950s was followed by a fourfold increase in schizophrenia diagnoses. Correspondingly fewer patients were diagnosed manic-depressive. Wanting to be helpful, psychiatrists simply were moving patients from one diagnostic category to another. When lithium later was introduced for the treatment of mania, the well-meaning doctors moved patients back out of the schizophrenia category. This shows the robust effects of context upon medical decisionmaking.

Just as the schizophrenic/manic-depressive distinction could be seen as a false diagnostic dilemma, the phenothiazine/lithium treatment conflict also would vanish if we were to adopt Unger's unitary approach to diagnosis and treatment. To oversimplify for heuristic impact, any psychotropic drug might work by simply stabilizing oscillations within the state-space. Or, still more paradoxically, one could understand how we control hallucinating perceptual systems by clamping the motor pattern generators (with phenothiazines).

Since the emerging picture of the brain-mind is open-loop and plastic, learning is a given. The investigation of the cellular basis of classical learning paradigms, in the work of E. Kandel, B. Libet, R. Thompson, and others, already has dissolved one artificial barrier between "psychology" and neurobiology. We can expect the same process to occur at more complex levels.[52]

There is no conceptual difference between the models of psychosis and neurosis to which the new state concept gives rise. The distinction is simple: it is the part of the state-space that is affected. And even this may be more a matter of degree than of kind. For example, when does a fantasy become a delusion? When one believes it? When one says one believes it? When someone else does not believe it? Or when we ourselves do not disbelieve it? Minor perturbations of the system (neuroses) may be more context-sensitive than major ones (psychoses). Thus, programming errors (as contrasted with system design errors) may underlie these coarse clinical distinctions. Reprogramming (psychotherapy) can help in either case, but will be more effective in neurosis because of differences in both severity and mode of mediation.

The relearning model is also a simple one: (1) create an atmosphere such that modeling of the healthy aspects of the therapist's behavior can occur; (2) recognize the ideal of therapeutic neutrality to be illusory, but avoid exploitation or manipulation of patients; and (3) give up the alienating power of aloofness in the interest of empowerment of the other person. (This sounds like Unger, doesn't it?)

In summary, Unger is correct in his assessment of the profound problems of psychiatry and in calling for radical revisions of theory and practice. But to make his critique practical and his prescriptions useful, more specific attention must be paid to scientific realities in the rapidly evolving fields of neurobiology and psychology. Between Unger's lofty position as social critic of psychiatry and the empirical details of day-to-day psychiatric science is a large and fertile field for theory development.

IV. CREDO FOR A NEW PSYCHIATRY: SCIENTIFIC HUMANISM

Having made suggestions regarding the New Psychiatry's intellectual Agenda, I now turn to the most appropriate conceptual and effective attitudes for the architects of change. This part outlines psychiatry's most elementary assumptions and attitudes, and presents them in a most concise and epigrammatic language in the hope of creating an intellectual and attitudinal basis for consensus.

While many of the particular points made in the Agenda are controversial, debatable, and even polemical, I try here to step back to an article-of-faith level, to create a kind of Credo. This is followed in part V by an equally preliminary guide to action, the Manifesto.

A. The Basic Principles of Scientific Humanism

- The human species is the highest known life form.

---

[52] Flicker, McCarley & Hobson, *Aminergic Neurons: State Control and Plasticity in Three Model Systems*, 1 CELLULAR & MOLECULAR NEUROBIOLOGY 123-66 (1981).

- The most distinctive and qualitatively unique aspects of human life are functions of the brain.

- The human brain is the highest known organ form.

- The human mind is the highest known functional state of matter.

- Among the distinctive attributes of the brain-mind, three are particularly remarkable:

Thought: analytic and creative

Feeling: emotional and empathic

Communication: gestural and linguistic

(There is good evidence that the first property of each of the three pairs is shared by other animals, while the second appears to be more uniquely human.)

- Knowledge regarding these matters is still primitive despite roughly 2500 years of systematic inquiry.

B. The Relationship of Psychiatry to Scientific Humanism

- All human activities take place within a context of feeling.

- No human knowledge is transcendent of meaning and value, both of which are related to the context of feeling.

- Human individuals and human societies function well if and only if a balance between thinking, feeling, and communicating is maintained.

- Psychiatry is that branch of natural science and philosophy that concerns itself most directly with human thinking, feeling, and communicating—and with the balance between them.

- Psychiatry can rightly aspire to a high place among the natural sciences.

- Since the expectations of its clients and the claims of its practitioners are vastly disproportionate to psychiatry's competence, the field should both be more modest and reorient the direction and priorities of its ambition.

C. The Challenge to Psychiatry of Scientific Humanism

- Psychiatry is correct to insist upon the whole person as the most meaningful frame of reference for the results of its own investigations. Psychiatry thus must be at once humanistic and scientific.

- Psychiatry should adopt more generally humanistic principles as operating hypotheses. Because of its humanistic impulses and obligations, and because of its scientific orientation, psychiatry at the same time should use more critical modes of thought in evaluating the theoretical adequacy of its hypotheses and should develop more scientific methods of testing their empirical validity.

- The scientific revolutions in neurobiology, computer science, and molecular biology present opportunities for psychiatry that are unparalleled in the past 2500 years of human inquiry. The door is open to both revolution and renaissance. It is both the promise and the threat of these powerful techniques that prompt philosophical reflection.

- Reflection suggests that a secure, useful, and acceptable framework for this endeavor is scientific humanism.

D.   *The Relationship of Scientific Humanism to Other Philosophies*

- Scientific humanism regards man as the product of evolution but takes no position regarding either cosmological first causes or ultimate purposes.

- Because it is open at both ends, scientific humanism can stand alone, or it can be inserted within any world view that accepts its internal premises and principles.

- By defining mental health in functional terms, scientific humanism opens the door to a variety of "treatment" interventions. If they can be empirically demonstrated to promote healthy functioning, such interventions may include those that can be neither scientifically explained nor theoretically justified.

V.   A MANIFESTO FOR A NEW PSYCHIATRY AND A PLAN OF ACTION

This preliminary set of conclusions and its related "plan of action," like the Agenda and the Credo, are an early state of thinking about the social, and especially the educational, setting of psychiatry. They are intended to serve only as seeds for new concepts of institutional reform. In this sense, my essay ends on a note as vague and promissory as the Unger program I have criticized. My only defense is the outstanding success of scientific reductionism in solving other, no less human, problems.

A.   *Assumptions and Goals of the Manifesto*

- Psychiatry remains the most human of the medical specialties, since it deals primarily with human behavior, human thought, and human feeling.

- The theoretical and practical efforts of psychiatry must stay focused at the level of the whole person.

- To progress as a medical science, psychiatry simultaneously must develop at several levels and integrate across those levels.

- Three levels of discourse require development and integration: the biological, the psychological, and the social.

- The strongest level, in a scientific sense, is the biological. Biology thus is properly regarded as a basic science where psychiatry is concerned. But biology can only inform the other levels, not replace them. Biology alone is not enough. Unger correctly assesses the current inadequacy of biology but underestimates its place and its promise in a New Psychiatry.

- Psychology is the second most important science for psychiatry as a medical specialty. But because of its currently disproportional weaknesses, the highest priority must be given to its development. Unger's bold theory of personality—with all of its inadequacies—should be welcomed as a goad to psychiatric theoreticians.

- Of the integrative tasks, that between the biological and the psychological is the most fundamental and the most difficult. At this interface lies the mind-body problem. Unger completely ignores this central issue. A more determined, affirmative, and concerted attack on the mind-body problem should constitute the central intellectual focus of a New Psychiatry. To mount such an attack, difficult choices must be made and deliberate priorities must be established. It is one purpose of the Manifesto to define these choices and priorities.

- The definition of choices and priorities should constitute strong challenges to existing administrative, intellectual, and clinical assumptions. A second goal of the Manifesto is to identify the means of strengthening the challenges within the existing system.

- A final goal of the Manifesto will be to consider more radical means of changing the system should moderate measures fail. The problems of the field have reached the point where revolutionary innovations must be contemplated.

B. Obstacles to Progress—Intellectual

- The mind-body problem remains unsolved. Most people laugh when it is mentioned, considering it to be either a false problem or insoluble. It is neither. It is real, and it is soluble. It should be recognized as the central intellectual issue of psychiatry.

- Biology is a field that is in productive ferment. Molecular biology and neurobiology are among its most active frontiers. These fields have taken little notice of psychiatry (as we have defined it), and psychiatry (as it exists) has taken little notice of them. Both sides, especially psychiatry, need to take responsibility for this mutual neglect. Psychiatry has more to gain from doing so, and psychiatry has more to lose from not doing so.

- Psychology is weakened by its intrinsic methodological handicaps and by the splintering that serves to protect its many special interest subgroups against attack, dissolution, and takeover. Unfortunately, this is particularly true of psychoanalysis, psychiatry's own favorite psychology. The problem of psychoanalysis is so severe and so special that it must be treated separately.[53]

- The few areas of strength in modern psychology are still remote from psychiatric attention.

- *Cognitive psychology* remains the province of university-based aca-

---

[53] *See* Hobson, *supra* note 16.

demic psychologists who carry on the "mental faculty" approach of the nineteenth century. Cognitive psychology is unattractive to psychiatrists because it tends to deny or to ignore feelings.

- *Behavioral psychology* (including ethology, learning theory, and communications, and even the rigorous side of linguistics) has had limited impact because it denies and ignores mental life.

- *Developmental psychology* contains cognitive and behavioral aspects, but it adds the dimension of longitudinal study to each. The concept of "critical period" needs to be incorporated into the "life stage approach" that is now quite popular in psychiatry.

- Psychiatry fools itself when it considers such fields as psychopharmacology and related neuropsychiatric endeavors to be either biological or truly basic. These fields are rarely biological in any fundamental sense. Rather, they apply superficial, medical-model paradigms to psychiatry in a feeble effort to retain dignity in the face of the shoddy psychological thinking and sentimentalism that prevails in other quarters of the field.

- The weakening of tough-mindedness by tenderheartedness complements the still unresolved mind-body problem. The goodness of intent that brings many physicians to psychiatry, combined with the futility of even their most sustained efforts to cure serious mental illness, fosters abstract, logically loose, and literary thinking. Psychiatry thus fools itself again when it considers its psychological theories to be so deep, so advanced, and so complex as to defy scientific test. Unger is as mistaken as other utopian visionaries in failing to state his hypotheses in terms that are compatible with the paradigms of natural science. While rhetoric usually only begets more rhetoric, experimentation can test and thereby alter theory.

C. Obstacles to Progress—Educational

- The popular mind is now thoroughly accustomed to the shoddy thinking of psychiatry. In a permissive society, post hoc reasoning is the order of the day. Since we all are raised in this casual ambiance we find it doubly difficult to escape it. And those who try will find their views unpopular. In a democracy where anything goes, the loosest ideas are the most serviceable, supple, and sought after.

- Secondary and collegiate education hardly touch upon the issues at hand. With the decline of classical education, logic and philosophy are antique. Some students become science whiz kids and pursue physics, chemistry, or perhaps biology. But most are steeped in the rhetoric of "appreciation"—"compare and contrast." Humanities blue books are filled with analogical reasoning. Analytic inquiry takes a back seat. Unger is a classic example of this trend.

- Premedical students take science courses to get into medical school. Scientists teaching in liberal arts schools resent this perfunctory participation and make the obstacle course more difficult and unpleasant. The fun of science—its humanistic aspect, and its importance to human concerns—is hard to discern. Most colleges conform to C.P. Snow's "Two Culture" caricature: Either-Or.[54]

- Medical school is split into abstract basic science—a continuation of the obstacle course approach—and technologically oriented medicine. Neither appeals to the would-be psychiatrist, who is often a fugitive from both science and technology, and who elects psychiatry as a way back to the holistic, soft, poetic atmosphere of liberal studies. Those who can, do science; those who can't go into psychiatry.

- Psychiatric training deepens the split between basic science and technology. The tough-minded are horrified by the laxness of psychological thinking and retreat to the library or laboratory. The tenderhearted see this strategic withdrawl as a lack of capacity to feel. Thus begins the *ad hominem* division of the field. Rare is the tough-minded, tenderhearted mediator that the field needs most. And when he comes forth, he risks dismemberment for his efforts.

- Academic reward for science goes to the superficially biological. When recognition is won for psychological work it rarely is deserved in any real scientific sense. Psychiatric leaders are almost never great scientists and rarely even great clinicians; and, to the extent that they were ever either, they usually cease being so after assuming leadership. There is so much to administer, especially when the line between psychiatry-as-scientific medicine and psychiatry-as-politics becomes blurred. By raising expectations further, Unger's work will not help to sharpen this distinction.

- Post-graduate education in psychiatry offers two paths: the biological and the psychoanalytic. Rarely, if ever, are the two effectively combined. The academic psychiatrist says good-bye to psychology, and the psychoanalyst says goodbye to science.

D. The Plan.

Implementation of the Agenda and adoption of the Credo will be enhanced by and centered in new university-based programs.

1. *Revised Medical Curricula.*—Subject matter will be structured from the bottom up, from behavioral to clinical science. This will require strong commitments of time, especially in the first year of medical school.

It also will require new alignments, new programs, and a reorganization of faculty to bring the existing pieces of psychiatry's scientific base together. For scientific humanism to become a two-way street—rather

---

[54] C. Snow, The Two Cultures and the Scientific Revolution (1959).

than two one-way streets—there must be more effective interpenetration of the ideas in the Agenda and Credo.

In addition to traditional teaching models, the creation of longitudinal seminar structures is essential. These settings will provide intense, prolonged, and repetitive exposure to problems, methods, and role models.[55]

2. *Revised Residency Programs.*—Academic training centers must struggle to protect the psychiatric resident from the intellectual diffusion, physical fatigue, and moral disenchantment that are the fallout of excessive social demands upon a socially overcommitted psychiatry.

This retrenchment must be distinguished from withdrawal from the unequivocally legitimate demands of the public for the humane and devoted care of the severely ill patient. Unger's social concerns are consonant with this obligation.

The maintenance of humane treatment requires the institution of more realistic custodial arrangements. Thus, leaders of academic training centers must be as aggressive in promoting novel modes of care as they are defensive of their fledglings, who must not be viewed only as caretakers. While caretaking is rightly of the highest social priority, it is often an impediment to analytic problem solving in psychiatry.

In their didactic programs, residents should be exposed early to the same set of principles that inform revised medical student curricula. We should inform them clearly and repeatedly that there is no escape from the central tension of the mind-body dilemma and that even the most elegant neurological or psychoanalytical analysis alone is as inadequate as caretaking in solving the central problem of psychiatry.

As in medical school, longitudinal multidisciplinary seminars are the only possible antidote to specialist fragmentations that circumvent the central issues. As yet, we have not experimented with this mode in teaching our residents.

3. *Revised Postgraduate Education.*—University centers must develop alternatives to the current career split between private sector psychotherapy (via the psychoanalytic institutes) and biologically oriented research (via National Institute of Health fellowships).

Such programs should combine attention to primary clinical material (cases) and to treatment processes (psychotherapy and/or psychopharmacology) with fundamental scientific work (theoretical or empirical).

Junior faculty, like residents, must have their time protected for

---

[55] The William James Seminar Program at the Harvard Medical School attempts to play this role. 1 S. DENLINGER & A. HOBSON, ANNALS OF THE WILLIAM JAMES SEMINAR, 1981-1982 (1982); 2 S. DENLINGER & A. HOBSON, ANNALS OF THE WILLIAM JAMES SEMINAR, 1982-1986 (1986); Saver & Denlinger, *Which Doctor Is Not a Witch Doctor?*, 2 ADVANCES 20 (1985).

thought, for writing, and for discussion. Structures to support these activities also must be created. Here, as in undergraduate education, tutorial relationships with mentors and longitudinal seminars with peers must be fostered by encouragement and reward of senior faculty who engage in this important work.

VI. CONCLUSION

Unger's critique of psychiatry is inspiring but inadequate. While I agree with Unger's rejection of psychoanalysis and welcome his alternative emphasis upon passion as the felt tension between our longing for one another and our vulnerability to rejection, I propose that Unger's view of man, and of psychiatry, is biologically uninformed. Unger ignores scientific evidence that ultimately both supports and challenges the fundamental tenets of his social theory.

I have attempted to redress this imbalance by proposing that the reconstruction of psychiatry proceed as scientific humanism. I call my alternative view of man "scientific humanism" to emphasize what I take to be robust biological evidence for both the evolutionary capability of the human brain-mind—which Unger recognizes—and for the physical basis and constraints on that system—which Unger ignores. The Agenda for the New Psychiatry that I have outlined calls for exploration of both the capabilities and limitations of the brain-mind using many of the modern scientific methods that Unger eschews. Because a New Psychiatry ultimately will flourish or not according to new psychiatrists, the implementation of a program of scientific humanism requires fundamental changes in both medical and psychiatric education.

PROGRAMMATIC THOUGHT AND THE CRITIQUE OF THE SOCIAL DISCIPLINES

David M. Trubek

In Politics, Roberto Unger seeks to transform the social disciplines and reorient the relationship between the study of society and the struggle to transform social life. One of the boldest and most controversial claims made in *Politics* is the assertion that programmatic thought must be made an integral and essential aspect of all social inquiry. This assertion challenges the current practices of most social researchers in the modern university.

Much of *Politics* is devoted to the program of "empowered democracy." This program, which includes ideas for a radical revision of individual and collective rights, proposals for reorganizing state and economy, and the sketch of a new constitutional system, has a two-fold significance. First, it demonstrates some of the concrete implications of Unger's broadest ideas about personality and society. Second, it makes a basic methodological point, illustrating Unger's contention that an adequate *theory* of society must include efforts to reimagine social arrangements. By insisting that programmatic thought is not just a by-product or "application" of social knowledge, but an essential element in its production, Unger makes his broadest challenge to current practices of social inquiry and illustrates the deepest roots and most ambitious goals of his project. I believe Unger's call for programmatic thought is one we must heed.

I. THE RADICAL PROJECT

No idea is more important to *Politics* than the concept of a "radical project." Unger wants to remake social thought because the existing disciplines, whether Marxist, postmodern, or positivistic in inspiration, hinder the accomplishment of "radical" aims. But at the same time the existence of a radical project—an actual embodied practice of conflict and struggle in thought and society—helps support the normative position from which existing social practices and disciplines are critiqued and on which the programmatic ideas of *Politics* are developed.

There is some irony in Unger's use of the term *radical project* and a real chance for misunderstanding what he means. Where the uninformed reader might conjure up the vision of this project as a marginal enterprise of visionary agitators, Unger means to evoke fundamental tendencies in modern civilization which, he asserts, embody basic truths about personality and society. From these truths, reflected in the wide range of doctrine and practices which are described as the radical project, Unger both mounts his critique of the social disciplines and develops his program of social reconstruction.

Unger describes the radical project as the continuation of the Christian-Romantic tradition, revised in light of the insights of modernism and classical social theory. His idea of a radical cause draws on a conception of the self which was developed in an earlier study entitled *Passion: An Essay on Personality* (1984). In *Passion,* Unger first makes the claim that we can develop a concept of personality which has normative weight for social theory. He then develops what he calls the "modernist view of the self." In this conception, the personality is "an infinite imprisoned within the finite,"[1] The self always contains capabilities and demands disproportionate to the social and personal circumstances in which it is embedded. Yet only within these constraining contexts—modes of thought and perception, forms of personal attachment, social and political institutions—can we realize ourselves. Finally, although we are dependent upon our contexts, these contexts are always conditional, imperfect, and transformable.

Unger's concept of the self seems to rest on a paradox: There is no self outside of social contexts, but no context exhausts the possibilities of the self. But it is the resolution of this paradox that gives Unger's view of the self normative force for the social disciplines. This resolution comes from his notion of the relative "plasticity" of all social contexts, including discourses, relationships, and institutions. The more a context is plastic, the more easily it can be *revised,* the more it will permit self-realization, given the infinite possibilities and contextual nature of the self. The radical project, as Unger conceives it, involves the search for ever more revisable bodies of knowledge, personal relations, and social institutions, for these will free us *from* bad contexts and free us *for* good relations.

Radicalism then, means the quest for more self-realizing contexts. Unger argues that the radical cause has its roots in Christianity and the Romantic movement, left politics, and modernist literature. While radicals of many stripes have in the past contributed to this idea of human potential, Unger thinks they have failed to carry through on, or integrate, their varied visions.

Politics seeks to bring together disparate aspects of the radical project. Unger highlights the separate leftist and modernist strands within radicalism. Leftists have emphasized political and economic barriers to emancipation: They want to dissolve structures of power

---

[1] Passion at 4.

and hierarchy in economic and political relations. Modernists have focused on the fine grain of private life and the constraints private life places on the development of the self. He wants to draw these strands together: *Politics* offers a social theory adequate for a "unified version of the radical cause."[2]

II. False Necessity

The central volume is called *False Necessity* because that's what is wrong with social thought and thus with radical politics. Unger thinks our modes of understanding the world have failed fully to recognize the plasticity of society and thus the possibilities for transformation. He offers three concepts—*formative contexts, negative capability* and *history without a script*—which embody the theme of liberation from false necessity. Formative contexts are the institutional and imaginative practices that shape a society's routines. Formative contexts are structures—like the modes of production in Marxism—that limit what can be imagined and done. Unger wants us to recognize the importance of such contexts, but also grasp their mutability. No formative context is necessary or inevitable and contexts can be changed in many ways and in many directions. Moreover, not all contexts are equal: Some are more easily revised and thus made more likely to realize human potential. Unger uses the term *negative capability* to measure the degree of revisability, or the absence of entrenched power, in any formative context. To complete the radical project, Unger tells us, we must grasp the mutability of formative contexts and work toward contexts with greater negative capability.

These efforts must be guided by a recognition that there is no reordained path in history. Unger rejects the idea that history has a script, i.e., that the outcome of social struggle is determined by forces the contenders cannot master or restraints they cannot alter. Unger thinks most contemporary social thinkers, from Marxists to positivist social scientists, fail to grasp the mutability of contexts, the possibility of more revisable contexts, the "it could always have been otherwise" nature of historical outcomes. In doing this, the social disciplines have succumbed to false necessity and betrayed the radical project.[3]

III. The Situation of Social Theory

Social Theory: Its Situation and Its Task critiques the social disciplines. Marxism, neo-classical economics, and positivist social science are singled out for detailed analysis. All three have failed fully to

---

[2] Social Theory at 13.
[3] *See Id.* at 117, 223–24.

emancipate themselves from the idea that society has a natural order. All succumb to the vice of false necessity. Another strand of radical thought, called *ultra-theory* and associated with existential radicalism and postmodernism, is dealt with as well. This doctrine is criticized for merely appearing to have freed itself from false necessity, while actually succumbing to the idolatry of existing social structures.

Social Theory critiques all forms of social theory which make the following "deep structure" assumptions: (1) We can draw clear distinctions between the frameworks (formative contexts) of society and the routines these frameworks shape; (2) such frameworks (like the capitalist mode of production) are indivisible and repeatable; and (3) they must succeed each other in a predetermined sequence (e.g., capitalism must follow feudalism). Unger argues that deep structure theory disempowers radical politics. By insisting on indivisibility and sequence, it "disorients political strategy and impoverishes programmatic thought."[4] Committed to false necessity, deep structure theory obscures the relationship between structure and agency, and limits our ability to grasp transformative possibilities. To escape from these limits, Unger insists, we must rework the notion that frameworks shape social routines, removing any determinist implications of the "framework" idea. And we must jettison ideas of indivisibility and sequence altogether.

Politics contains an undisguised polemic against Marxism, which Unger feels is incurably wedded to deep structure and false necessity. While he recognizes anti-necessitarian strands in Marx's own work and appreciates the efforts of latter-day Marxists to loosen deep-structural assumptions, Unger asserts that no amount of revision can cure this doctrine's commitment to indivisibility and necessary sequence. As a result, Marxism reifies structures, fails to grasp transformative possibilities, and cannot generate meaningful programmatic ideas.

Since Unger indicts Marxism for reifying structure and thus paralyzing radical politics, one might expect him to applaud those who want to move away from structure altogether. But he doesn't: *Politics* also includes an attack on the ultra-theorists who are accused of not taking structure seriously enough.[5] Unger is more charitable to ultra-theorists than to the Marxists. Since, like Unger himself, the ultra-theorists recognize that "everything is politics," they are allies in his struggle against necessitarian social thought. But he sees their wholesale rejection of all notions of structure as equally dangerous to the radical cause. Unger thinks the ultra-theorists (he has in mind Michel Foucault and some radical thinkers in the Critical Legal Studies movement) cannot produce the explanatory accounts and programmatic

---

[4] *Id.* at 93.
[5] *See Id.* at 165–69.

ideas he believes are needed for radical politics. Ultra-theory, he suggests, tends toward the existential, modernist heresy that " . . . true freedom consists in the perpetual defiance of all settled structure."[6] As a result, while ultra-theory initially seems liberating, it actually leaves the *status quo* intact.

IV. THE ALTERNATIVE: "CONSTRUCTIVE" SOCIAL THEORY AND THE PROGRAM OF EMPOWERED DEMOCRACY

The critique of the social disciplines is a prelude to the exposition of Unger's own social theory. These are set out in *False Necessity,* which has two missions. First, Unger sets forth an explanatory theory of society, which he labels *super theory* and describes as a "radical alternative to Marxism."[7] Second, he outlines a program for social reconstruction which, he argues, could push the radical project beyond social democracy. Unger sees social democracy as the only real programmatic idea which the radical cause in the West has produced so far: He tells us we can and must do better. *Politics'* explanatory theory is rich in ideas about the current situation in advanced industrial societies, and its program is replete with novel notions for reorganization of state, society, and economy. He offers an account of the current stasis in politics in the West and a parallel sketch of similar processes in the socialist bloc. He sets forth a rather detailed program which provides an alternative both to bureaucratic socialism and laissez-faire captialism, while incorporating attractive features of both. *Politics* argues that no false necessity stands in the way of our realizing such a program.

Looked at from the perspective of current work in the social disciplines, Unger's juxtaposition and close linkage of explanatory and programmatic argument is striking and far from accidental. Rather, the dual commitment to social explanation and the development of relatively detailed ideas for large scale social transformation is an essential part of what he calls *constructive social theory.* By arguing that programmatic thought and social explanation are *inseparable,* Unger presents a clear alternative to most current styles of academic work.

Unger devotes almost half of *False Necessity* to the "program of empowered democracy."[8] He feels this detailed outline for a reform of economy, individual rights, government and the constitution are essential to his project, and he is right for two reasons. First, the juxtaposition of explanation and program gives both parts of his constructive social theory a vitality that either might lack in isolation. Second, the

---

[6] *Id.* at 169.
[7] FALSE NECESSITY at 1.
[8] *Id.* at 341–595.

juxtaposition reflects Unger's most fundamental views about humanity and society. If one accepts the radical project as Unger restates it, one is forced to recognize that programmatic imagination is an essential element of social theory.

Unger's discussion of rights illustrates how the explanatory and programmatic aspect of *Politics* enrich each other. In his analysis of the formative context of the modern West, Unger highlights the current private rights complex of property and contract. In the program of empowered democracy he outlines an alternative concept of rights. The two discussions are closely related. The genealogy of modern private law draws out suppressed values which help form the basis of the new system of rights. The fuller development of a transformed concept of rights makes it easier to see the normative perspective underlying the critique of our existing "private rights" complex.

Unger's account of the role of private rights in the formative context of the West illustrates many of the most basic themes of *Politics*. He wants to show that ideas of absolute property and freedom of contract have played a significant role in Western history, but not the one their most ardent defenders would claim. The defenders of absolute property and unrestricted freedom of contract contend that these institutions are both desirable for the realization of liberty and necessary for economic efficiency. In the conventional account, the emergence and development of these institutions shows functional economic necessity at work, while efforts to preserve them reflects both economic prudence and liberal zeal.

Unger recognizes that the private rights complex plays an important role in maintaining the *status quo* in the West:

> It gives bosses and investment managers the authority to organize labor in the name of accumulated property. It sets the basic terms on which disinvestments can frustrate reform. And it denies would-be reformers a tangible picture of an alternative style of economic organization.[9]

Unger shows how this rights complex plays a hegemonic role in our current formative context. But he wants to demonstrate that this hegemony is not based on true social necessity, pragmatic effectiveness, or moral superiority.

Unger attacks the necessitarian "mythical history" of the rise of the private rights complex. "Liberals and Marxists alike," he says, "view the private-law arrangements and ideas of early modern Europe as necessary points on the continuum that led to current contract or property law, a law that could in turn be seen as an indispensable prop to the market system.[10] His alternative genealogy of the origins of the private rights complex seeks to demonstrate that our current institu-

---

[9] *Id.* at 71.
[10] *Id.* at 197.

tions of property and contract only work because they are linked with other arrangements (like hierarchical power in the workplace) that negate the liberal ideals they seem to encode, and have been preserved only by dint of complex intellectual maneuvers that mask structures of domination and present adventitious and jerry-built arrangements as accommodations to functional necessity.

A key feature of this genealogy is the argument that, in the course of defending the private rights order, apologists for the system have been forced to introduce a series of exceptions and counter doctrines which, taken together, prefigure a radically different form of social organization. "Contract law," he argues, "included deviant elements that pointed toward a private-rights order that gave legal force to relations of reciprocal dependence."[11] He thinks that these deviant tendencies, originally introduced as justificatory moves within conventional legal discourse, would, if more fully developed, form the basis for a radical alternative to existing economic relationships and institutions. In the program of empowered democracy, Unger develops these "deviant" strands, articulating such novel concepts as a right to solidarity, grounded on reliance and trust, a right to destabilization, grounded on the necessity to constantly revise institutional contexts, and a right to immunity, grounded on the individual's need for security as a precondition to participation in transformative politics.[12]

By juxtaposing explanation and program, Unger argues, we can both better understand our situation and identify elements in the present—like the deviant tendencies in contract doctrine— which prefigure the future we aspire to. But *Politics* makes a further, more fundamental claim for the essential unity of programmatic and explanatory thought. The need to imagine the future as we explain the past is grounded in Unger's most basic ideas about the relationship between self and society, and his view of the true nature of transformative work.

Unger stresses two aspects of the self: its unlimited potential and its necessary contextuality. His concept of empowerment rests on the constant struggle to revise contexts which do not foster the full potential of the self. Self-realization does not come about, however, by passive contemplation or solipsistic withdrawal. Rather, we must realize the self through active, usually collective, engagement in the endless task of context revision. Ultimate self-realization (to the extent there is such a thing) requires contexts with greater negative capacity than those we live in today. We can only become ourselves, he argues, to the extent that we are engaged in struggles to create such contexts and come to live in contexts of greater plasticity. Unger wants to free us

---

[11] *Id.* at 207.
[12] *Id.* at 508–37.

from existing relations, not so we can exist as isolated individuals, but so we can exist in better relationships.

The struggle for plasticity, however, occurs in a social situation that is always made and imagined. Imaginative structures—the models of possible and desirable association that we work with—form part of the glue that holds society together, and constitute one of the arenas of struggle for those who espouse the radical cause and accept its ideal of a transformative vocation. One of the main obstacles to this struggle, Unger notes, is the lack of credible alternatives to our present situation. Without these, we remain imprisoned in our existing imaginative structures or discourses. The only way to break this impasse, and to release energy for self-realization and institutional revision, is to devise alternative ideas about social, political, and personal life. *Politics* argues that we can and must do this work, and charges the social disciplines with this essential task of imaginative reinvention. Since history has no script and societies obey no deep logic, we *can* devise alternative futures without fear that they will be irrelevant. Since the only way we can revise the institutions that contain us is first to imagine how they could be otherwise, we *must* engage in programmatic thought or give up on the radical cause altogether.

Thus the argument comes full circle. For with the development of the program of empowered democracy, Unger completes the critique of the social disciplines launched in *Social Theory*. It is not that he disagrees with other people's programs—he thinks they have none. The great failure of all our contemporary social disciplines is not in the detail of their programmatic vision, but in the lack of any such vision. He thinks that all the main currents of modern social thought share the same failing—their inability to grasp the necessity and inevitability of programmatic thought. Marxists wait for the turn of history, positivists accept the current parameters of social life (today's formative context) as inevitable, if not also desirable, ultra-theorists engage in purely negative trashing. Unger calls on all of these thinkers, in the name of the radical project which many of them espouse, to turn toward programmatic thought. And he gives us a rich set of examples of what such thinking should look like.

V. CRITICAL OBSERVATIONS

Politics covers so many topics, from economic, legal, and military history to moral philosophy and political doctrine and programs, and takes so many bold controversial positions, that specialists could spend lifetimes critiquing any part of the argument. It seems to me, however, there are several major themes that require close analysis if we are to accept and develop the call for constructive social theory.

The first of these is the relationship between Unger's concept of the self and his theory. Unger denies that the former is the grounding of the latter; in *Passion* he says, "[W]e cannot hope to deduce views of the self and of society from each other,"[13] and in *Social Theory* he characterizes the relationship between those two aspects of his theory as merely "mutually reinforcing."[14] Yet the argument of *Politics* draws on the Christian Romantic modernist idea of the self to such a degree that the book lacks persuasive force if one rejects this account of personality. This suggests that the ultimate impact of *Politics* depends, in no trivial sense, on Unger's ability to persuade us that his theory of the self is one to which we are prepared to assent. Critics have argued that Unger's conception fails fully to grasp the modernist's recognition of the decentered nature of the self and is insufficiently attentive to communitarian considerations. Moreover, readers of *Passion* may wonder if this book really does more than set forth, as opposed to fully support, the conception argued for. While I think these criticisms can be answered, Unger needs to address them. Hopefully, the promised future volumes of *Politics* will do this.

The second is Unger's stance toward Marxism. *Politics* includes a root and branch condemnation of Marxism: Why does he devote so much energy to an effort to condemn all varieties of Marxism to the dust bin of intellectual history? After all, Unger recognizes that recent efforts to rethink Marxism have softened, if they have not yet completely eroded, this doctrine's commitment to what he calls "deep structure." Further, Unger's social explanations draw heavily on Marxist-inspired work, and his program of empowered democracy includes elements drawn, *inter alia,* from contemporary Eastern Europe experiments. Finally, a large portion of the adherents to the radical cause profess adherence to Marxism, however diluted. Unger might have sought them as allies but he insists that they join him as converts. What explains this position?

Finally, Unger's call for programmatic thought in the social disciplines might have been more effective if he had drawn attention to, and discussed, the work of others who accept this view of social thought. Unger is not the first academic to believe that programmatic thought is an essential element of social theory, and other contemporary writers have developed programs with elements similar to his. More recognition of parallel trends in the social disciplines—including Marxist-inspired work—would have strengthened, not weakened, the arguments of *Politics*. In his analysis of legal history, Unger drew skillfully on deviationist tendencies in law to demonstrate alternative possi-

---

[13] PASSION at 85.
[14] SOCIAL THEORY at 223.

bilities for social life; the same could have been done for a full account of the state of social theory today.

Perhaps this is the ultimate challenge for Unger and for those of us in the social disciplines who accept his views on the necessity for programmatic thought. We all must look more closely at the work that is already being done, and develop those aspects of the programmatic imagination already present in our fields. If *Politics* spurs such an effort, it will help realize Unger's deepest ambition, which is to reunite speculative inquiry, academic research, programmatic thought, and transformative struggle.

RELIGION AND THE MAKING OF SOCIETY

Charles Davis

I. INTRODUCTION

There is no doubt that Unger has identified an insight basic to modern society and to modern social and political theory: society is an artifact. I fully endorse his attempt to consistently work out the implications of that basic insight against the constant temptation of human beings to give unconditional authority to conditional forms, thus concealing from themselves the process of imagining and making society and its institutions. Unger is right in supposing that viewing society as an artifact combines the liberal/leftist aim of freeing society from structures of dependence and domination with the modernist goal of rescuing subjectivity and intersubjectivity from rigid roles. I find no difficulty, then, in responding favorably to Unger's work as a major contribution to our thinking about society. The clarification of our freedom to reimagine and remake the social worlds which we have constructed and in which we live is undoubtedly the way forward from our present situation.

At the same time, coming to the question of society from the study of religion and the philosophy of history, I confront a series of difficulties and objections in embracing the thesis that society is an artifact. In the pages that follow, I will sketch out some of these problems.

Although religion has sometimes fueled revolution, it has historically more often been a factor of social integration. It has secured the social order by declaring that order sacred (or at least of sacred origin), thus giving it what Unger would label a false necessity and a mistaken unconditionality. It is true that, in the Christian West, the frequent conflict of church and state has forged a distinction between the sacred and the secular. Nevertheless, because the Church with its sacred institutions often legitimized and solidified the state and other parts of the social fabric, society was frequently conceived as an affair of divine ordinance rather than a product of human freedom. Unger's argument, then, poses a problem for religion: how can one free social forms from an unnecessary rigidity without denying religion a role in the making of society? Is there no relationship between the authority of the social world and the authority of ultimate reality? Must every attempt to establish a relationship be an illegitimate conferring of unconditional authority upon conditional forms?

I assume that Unger does not want to deny validity to all forms of religious faith. But any religious faith implies privileged beliefs. As a complex of symbols and as a cultural institution, religion claims in some form to provide answers to questions of ultimate meaning, questions about the nature and destiny of human beings. And religion, unlike comprehensive ideologies (such as Marxism), seeks its answers in a transcendent realm, in an appeal to some form of superhuman power. Inevitably, therefore, a religious person will hold that human life—and human society—are founded upon transempirical truths. To the religious, certain principles of faith and morality stand over the whole order of social life, whatever its particular form. All this implies constraints upon human freedom to imagine and make society. Religion sets criteria for judging what human beings do with their social life. It insists that not everything human beings imagine or make is good and worthwhile. It questions whether we are right to regard as valueless everything we have not made ourselves.

That last sentence echoes the comment of Schumacher on the modern economic order. In criticizing the modern tendency to dissipate unrenewable natural resources and to treat irreplaceable capital as though it were income, Schumacher writes: "[W]e are estranged from reality and inclined to treat as valueless everything that we have not made ourselves."[1] His comment illustrates that viewing society as an artifact might be troublesome not only to the religious, but to any perspective that holds society to be more than the sum of its current members.

The Unger thesis, if unqualified, overlooks the ambiguity of modernity. The critique of modernity has been an increasing preoccupation of philosophers and social theorists, especially since the rise of critical theory and the work of the neo-Marxist Frankfurt School. Reason, once hailed as an instrument of liberation, has become (it is argued) a means of entrapping us in an iron cage of unfreedom, pushing us towards a totally administered, bureaucratized society. The theoretical critique of modernity has become linked with a variety of causes promoted by social activists. There is profound dissatisfaction, both theoretical and practical, with the modern project and its presuppositions. A consistent argument that society is an artifact must come to terms with the reaction against modernity on the Right (which seeks a return to authority and tradition), and on the Left (which seeks anarchism and quietism).

To contend that society is an artifact would seem to betray an uncritical acceptance of modernity. To call society an "artifact" is to view the formation of society as a *poiesis* (a making) demanding *techne* (a skill), rather than as a *praxis* requiring *arete* (virtue) as well as skill. Such a view adopts one of the presuppositions of modernity—that all human

---

[1] E.F. SCHUMACHER, SMALL IS BEAUTIFUL: ECONOMICS AS IF PEOPLE MATTERED 15 (1975).

action can be described as a series of techniques, which can be judged by an instrumental rationality in terms of usefulness or success. Human action understood in that way results in a product, but that product may not have been freely chosen by the maker and it may not remain under the maker's control. It may be used for ends the maker does not want or approve.

In contrast, the view that human action is *praxis* emphasizes doing, not making. The doing is intrinsically formed by ends freely chosen by the agent. What results may be virtuous or vicious conduct, with morally good or morally evil consequences for social interaction and the cumulative social situation. As individuals choose and follow norms, they are engaged in a process of communication with others that leads to agreements about the institutionalization of norms in the social order.

We can agree that society is the result of free human action. It is not a structure given from above by a superhuman power nor determined from below by natural necessity. The key issue is how we conceive that human agency in the formation of society. Is it as a *making*, requiring only technical skill and to be judged in terms of efficiency or success? Or is it a matter of *doing* (and hence ultimately of *being*), to be judged by norms embodied and pursued in the conduct that intrinsically constitutes social relationships?

These are the principal difficulties I perceive between religion and the Unger thesis—even assuming a fundamental agreement with and sympathy for the thrust of Unger's work. In the remainder of this essay, I will try to explain how, despite a critical attitude towards modernity and an acceptance of the permanent validity of religious faith, I still see society as a conditional result of human freedom.

II.   RELIGION AND THE PROJECT OF MODERNITY

What is modernity? There have been a variety of answers to that question, though the answers converge in a way that suggests an underlying unity of conception.

Some identify modernity with autonomous self-consciousness. According to this conception, those who are modern have appropriated their own inner freedom, so that they are fundamentally independent of truth-claims, traditions, laws, or norms that cannot be recognized as originating in the inner dynamism of their own consciousness. Modernity's immanence refuses submission to anything that attempts to impose itself upon human consciousness from without in the name of knowledge or of value. Hence for moderns, knowledge must be immanently generated or at least subject to intersubjective verification, not making a purely external claim in the name of tradition or of revelation from on high. As for morality, moderns are self-legislating persons, following moral norms that they themselves have created in a process of reaching agreement with others concerning common needs, interests, and values. The project of modernity, not yet completed, is to release human autonomy from constraints that are in fact self-imposed, but have taken on an illusory force of nature-like necessity.

For other thinkers, modernity chiefly implies a contrast with the culture of traditional societies. From this standpoint, the characteristic feature of modernity is differentiation. Traditional cultures are compact. They form undifferentiated totalities. Within them no clear distinction is made among kinds of value or types of meaning. Modern culture is differentiated because it separates value and meaning. In particular, the cognitive is clearly distinguished from the normative and subjective. Although not all knowledge is scientific, that which is cognitive is often defined as that which can be objectively verified as true. In other words, modernity implies the transition from *mythos* to *logos*, because myth mixes together knowledge, norms, and subjective expression.

Another understanding of modernity is to see it as a process of rationalization—the gradual rise of reason in history. This was Max Weber's approach. However, Weber had a narrow conception of reason and of rationalization. He identified rationality with *Zweckrationalität*, the instrumental rationality of technique and calculation, of organization and administration. For Weber, reason could not determine the norms by which we guide our lives; it could not lead us to higher values. Thus, reason did not, in Weber's view, lead to universal human freedom. Rather, it led to what he called the "iron cage" of bureaucratic rationality from which there was no escape. This problem can be called "the pathology of modernity": rationality stifling rather than expanding freedom, combined with a relativism that denies any rational foundation for moral and spiritual norms and values. Is this the fruit of reason?

Jürgen Habermas argues that the pathology of modernity is not due to rationalization as such, but to the one-sided way in which it has thus far developed.[2] There has been a failure to realize in social institutions all the different dimensions of reason. Habermas distinguishes two different types of action: purposive-rational action and communicative action. Each type of action requires a distinct process of rationalization. Weber's rationalization (the growth of *Zweckrationalität*) corresponds with purposive-rational actions. The rationalization of communicative action—neglected by Weber—is radically different. It means overcoming the forces that systematically distort human communication, hinder social interaction, and produce structures of domination.

Of course, Habermas' critique of Weber and the alternative interpretation of rationality he offers do not alter the fact that modern society is increasingly dominated by instrumental, calculative, bureaucratic ration-

---

2 This is the thesis of his recent major work, J. HABERMAS, THEORIE DES KOMMUNIKATIVEN HANDELNS (1981). Volume I of this two volume work has been translated as THE THEORY OF COMMUNICATIVE ACTION I: REASON AND THE RATIONALIZATION OF SOCIETY (1984).

ality. It is not therefore surprising that some thinkers see a profound incompatibility between religion and modernity. Robert Bellah, the sociologist and religionist, is one of those who finds an incompatibility between modernity and religion. Following Schumacher, he believes that the ideology of the modern West is subsumed under four general concepts: positivism, relativism, reductionism, and evolution.[3] Clearly, if modernity is correctly defined by those "isms," it is indeed incompatible with religion. But it is possible to show that each of those concepts mirrors only a distorted facet of modernity, which, when seen more clearly, is free from the pathology of modernity and compatible with religion.

Positivism, as normally understood, is the view that valid knowledge must be derived from scientific methods. Adherence to this view has produced disastrous consequences. It has led many to deny that human value judgments can have any objectivity, thus implying that our choices of values are purely arbitrary decisions based on subjective emotions. It wrongly excludes the form of knowledge found in the historical-hermeneutic disciplines, where access to the object studied could be attained only through the understanding of meaning (that is, these disciplines can only derive knowledge from the interpretation of texts, taking into account the context and prior judgments of both the authors and the interpreter himself). Positivism has also excluded from knowledge the type of critical reflection that uncovers hidden forms of domination and repression (a potent emancipating knowledge).

However, despite the one-sidedness of positivism, it contains an important insight that, in undistorted form, is compatible with a more benign view of modernity. That insight is the differentiation that has marked off the cognitive realm of meaning from the normative and the expressive cultural realms. Cognition or knowledge is the discovery of what can be verified objectively. It differs from the normative, which consists of meanings not discovered but created by human beings. However, norms are not created out of nothing. They are formed out of the needs, interests, and wants of actual human beings. The normative thus presupposes and builds upon the factual truths about human beings established in the cognitive sphere of culture; but the normative should be distinguished from the cognitive. Human beings come together in society, creating norms and embodying them in institutions through a process of social interaction.

Unger rejects positivist social science on grounds of its narrowness. It limits itself to seeking narrowly framed explanations for narrowly described phenomena, and gives up the search for comprehensive social or historical laws. That critique may be well founded. Nevertheless, as soon as one clearly distinguishes the cognitive from the normative and

---

3 Bellah, *Faith Communities Challenge—and Are Challenged by—the Changing World Order*, in WORLD FAITHS AND THE NEW WORLD ORDER: A MUSLIM-JEWISH-CHRISTIAN SEARCH BEGINS 148-68 (J. Gremillion & W. Ryan eds. 1977).

expressive, one has to recognize that human knowledge is limited and fragmentary, changing and relative. Comprehensive explanations remain largely hypothetical. To say this implies that I am inclined to opt for ultra-theory rather than for super-theory.[4] But the point I want to stress is that positivism, though admittedly in a distorted and exaggerated way, has rightly insisted that knowledge requires the strict observance of criteria to be valid, and thus must be clearly distinguished from the free creation of norms and the expression of subjective attitudes and feelings.

This qualified acceptance of positivism has inescapable application to religion. Religion, as embodied in religious traditions and in the practices of religious communities, includes a large measure of normative expression and does not always claim absolute truth. Religious beliefs that are authoritatively asserted as dogma are primarily community rules and only indirectly make propositional truth-claims. However, insofar as they do claim to embody valid knowledge, religious beliefs are subject to the relativity, mutability, and cultural limitations of all human knowledge. A large part of the struggle between religion and modernity has stemmed from the reluctance of organized religion to recognize this fact. Overcoming the distortions of positivism should allow the religious to acknowledge the measure of truth in the resistance of positivists to religion's claim to a higher knowledge. It should also allow human creativity to imagine and make society free of the false necessity imposed upon social institutions and practices by religion's excessive claims to higher knowledge.

The second of Bellah's "isms" is *relativism*. Relativism views reason as a tool for self-preservation and self-interest. Reason is merely a technical instrument for ordering the basically irrational components of human life into systems of manipulation and control. Such systems necessarily have only a relative truth, determined by their usefulness in dominating a particular situation. The diversity of situations gives rise to a diversity of formal systems for their control, each relatively true.

Here again I want to distinguish the valid insight from its distortion. Pluralism captures the positive elements of relativism. The liberal opts for pluralism. Conservatives tend to oppose pluralism. They insist that there is only one valid account of reality. Truth for them is absolute and exclusive, and they denounce liberals as relativists. It is true that liberals have often made only unsatisfactory attempts to conceive and express the goal of pluralism. Pluralism may very easily slip over into relativism. But in a deeper sense, pluralism goes back to a different concept of reason. Reason is understood as an unrestricted openness to reality. Reason is not a mere instrument of calculation, but a way of participating in reality, and ultimately in the Infinite, the Transcendent. But reason re-

---

4 For Unger's account of the difference between super-theory and ultra-theory, see SOCIAL THEORY at 165-69.

mains finite, a limited participation in the Unlimited. Pluralism in this context is the response of finite intelligence to a reality so rich that it constantly escapes existing categories and calls for the convergence and complementarity of various cultures and modes of experience. Pluralism is the counterpart of finitude. Where pluralism is denied, finitude is forgotten, and faith is corrupted into an idolatrous absolutizing of one of its particular expressions.

From the standpoint of religion, the insistence upon society as an artifact and the rejection of an alleged necessity that would exclude our freedom to remake the institutional order of society is the overcoming of idolatry and superstition. At the same time, one can only regret the use of the concept of "artifact," which is redolent of a calculative or purely formal rationality.

Our third "ism" is *reductionism*, which is defined by Bellah as the belief that all higher manifestations of life are nothing but disguised expressions of class interests, libidinal energies or other lower determinants. Reductionism in that pejorative sense makes of analysis a sort of pathology. Unger's work is the very opposite of reductionistic, because his analysis (particularly his distinction between routine and framework) specifically seeks to counter lower-level determinants and to release human imagination and freedom in the transformation of society. We are not completely governed by the established imaginative and institutional contexts of our societies, says Unger; nor are these contexts entirely determined by general laws (hence Unger's rejection of the deep-structure social theory of Marx). Unger's analysis will tend to quiet religious fears of reductionism. But is the religious claim that man is not the highest authority compatible with such a radical interpretation of social freedom?

Bellah's fourth and last constituent of modern ideology is *evolution*. But evolution, as applied to social phenomena and history, can be interpreted in two fundamentally different ways. Bellah and Schumacher view evolution as a natural and automatic process, determined by such biological factors as competition and the survival of the fittest. This implicitly denies the human ability to revise not only the routine, but also the context of human action. It is incompatible with the anti-naturalistic social theory of Unger. It is also incompatible with religious hope.

But there is a second way of understanding social evolution, which is to see it as the effect of human rationality in history. Reason follows an orderly (or "logical" in the wider sense of that term) sequence in the answering of questions and the solution of problems. The answering of one question opens up a new question; the solving of one problem makes it possible to discern the solution to another related problem. There is nothing automatic about the process. People can ignore, forget, or suppress answers to age-old problems. There can be regress as well as progress in human history. Nevertheless, insofar as rationality governs human action, there is a development or evolution in human knowledge and practice. The evolution is more marked in the sphere of science and technique where moral values are not directly a factor. But even in the sphere of ethics, some development is discernible.

The modern ideology of evolution has a complex relationship to traditional religious belief. It reinforces the Western religious view that history is linear, but clashes with the Eastern conception of cyclical history. It shares with religion a hope in eventual human perfection, but secularizes that hope, denying its transcendent source. In its secular form, it often swings from hope to despair, producing dystopias as well as utopias.

Is, then, modernity compatible or incompatible with religion? The answer is bound to be qualified. Modernity designates a fundamental shift in human culture, which can be roughly circumscribed with key words—freedom, science, rationalization, differentiation. In contrast, traditional culture is tied to such words as authority, perennial truth, reason, compactness. That shift, I contend, has taken place in a one-sided fashion, producing distortion. In their distorted form, represented by positivism, relativism, and a purely calculative rationality, the insights of modernity are incompatible with religious faith. In their authentic form they are not, though their acceptance demands a transformation in the conventional understanding of religion. I now examine that transformation in its relation to the making and the reform of society.

III. OBEDIENCE OR CONSENSUS?

Upon what does the social and political life of human beings rest? What is the foundation of human society? There are undeniably pre-rational factors: blood-relationship; a particular natural environment; the pressure of basic needs for food, shelter, and protection; the continuance of common interests. However, if we are to distinguish human society from the horde, we must acknowledge the intervention of human rational intelligence in articulating common needs and interests, and in further developing and institutionalizing the manifold instances of social interaction. Society thus becomes a project of human intelligence, a work of human reason. We can therefore ask: What is the scope of human creativity in the making of society? What is the rational foundation, the foundation within human reason, upon which society is built?

Society as the product and expression of human rationality can rest upon the empirical sciences, which produce not ultimate truths, but only probable findings. Those sciences deal with facts, not values or norms. Admittedly, fact and value are inextricably intertwined in the social sciences, so that non-trivial judgments of fact always presuppose some prior judgments of value. Nonetheless, scientific methodology is not appropriate for answering questions of value. As noted above, positivists give a purely decisionist or emotivist account of values, denying them any rational foundation. But society as a human, rational enterprise cannot be built upon empirically determined fact alone. The moral norms so essential to society are less concerned with what human beings are than with what they ought to be. To try to draw norms from empirical fact alone is to identify success, however achieved, with moral goodness. Such an approach canonizes the existing order, because there is no basis from which to criticize it. It hands society over to the technocrat, and makes the process of efficient goal-attainment supreme over the public discussion of the goals and values themselves. We have witnessed this process in our own time—an unquestioning devotion to the process of continuous economic expansion—and have seen how it can have disastrous consequences and, indeed, can call the entire project of modernity into question.

For the building of society, we must therefore appeal to a higher order of truth than mere empirical fact. We must ask fundamental questions: What is the human condition? What is the order of the values governing human action? What is the nature of human relationships? What may human beings reasonably expect? Such questions can be tackled only through religious and philosophical argument. Kant summed up his work as a critical philosopher in three questions: What can we know? What ought we to do? What can we hope for? The answer we give to each of those questions will profoundly affect the manner in which we endeavor to transform society. Even so, does that mean a turning back to the dominance of politics by metaphysical or theological systems, and the imposition of a pre-written script upon social and political experience? If we organize society in the light of unchanging truths, shall we not give to social institutions a supremacy they should not have?

Certainly, that was the pre-modern, traditional approach, reinforced by an appeal to religious truth as found in divine revelation. The social order was seen as part of the cosmic order, created by God. Although the fall of man and his sinfulness affected the social order, established institutions generally enjoyed divine providence. Such varied theologians as Augustine, Martin Luther, Robert Bellarmine, and Leo XIII have taught that divine providence sanctions human rulership, so that political authority is invested with sacredness. Though exceptions to the duty of submission have always been allowed (often reluctantly), the usual attitude inculcated through Christianity has been unquestioning obedience to the ruling powers. Behind such an attitude lay the conviction that life in society rested upon universal truths about the human condition, human nature, and human sinfulness. Although rebellion might at times be helpful in rescuing society from a tyrant, no radical remaking of society should follow. Furthermore, the universal truths suggested that only one type of social organization was ideally suited to the human condition.

The modern acceptance of pluralism—in particular, ideological pluralism—and the individual freedom that follows from pluralism has changed all that. How can a society be founded upon pluralism? I find the answer to this question in a statement of Thomas Gilby: "Civilization is formed by men locked together in argument. From this dialogue the community becomes a political community."[5] This process of rational deliberative argument within political associations, John Courtney Murray has commented, is a unique feature of human society.[6]

What is the argument about? According to Murray, it has three major themes: public affairs (matters requiring public decision and action by government); affairs of the commonwealth (matters outside the scope of government but bearing upon the quality of common life, such as education); and the constitutional consensus (matters that give a society its identity and sense of purpose). As Murray notes, the argument does not cease when agreement is reached. On the contrary, argument presupposes a context of agreement. This is so with scientific and philosophical argument, and it is likewise true of political argument. If there is a civilized society, there will be a context of agreement, from which argument can proceed. What is the content of the social agreement? Murray, whose general stance is conservative, sees the agreement as a patrimony of substantive truths, a heritage of rational belief, a structure of basic knowledge. While there is thus an ensemble of agreed affirmations, argument continues because the content of the consensus must be constantly scrutinized and developed in light of ongoing political experience.

We may grant Murray that every civilized society has a patrimony of agreed truths and values that serve as the initial context and starting point of argument. But given the present struggle between liberal pluralists and fundamentalists, between those who welcome and advocate radical changes in our traditional beliefs and those who staunchly insist upon the total validity of established tradition, we should not overstate the extent of our common social ground. Rather, we must identify the minimum level of consensus required to base society on rational argument. I suggest that, at a minimum, we must agree to those truths and values implicit in the acceptance of rational argument as the appropriate basis for political society.

This suggestion directly links the generally conservative Murray to the neo-Marxist Habermas. In his communicative theory of society, Habermas distinguishes two types of human action: purposive-rational action and communicative action.[7] Purposive-rational action is directed at success—that is, the efficient achievement of ends by appropriate means. Communicative action is directed to mutual understanding, lead-

---

5 T. GILBY, BETWEEN COMMUNITY AND SOCIETY (1953), *quoted in* J.C. MURRAY, WE HOLD THESE TRUTHS: CATHOLIC REFLECTIONS ON THE AMERICAN PROPOSITION (1960).

6 *See generally* J.C. MURRAY, *supra* note 5, at 5-24.

7 *See* J. HABERMAS, COMMUNICATION AND THE EVOLUTION OF SOCIETY (1979).

ing to an agreement. Communicative action, as suggested earlier, is essential for an emancipated society. Purposive-rational action alone leads to the "iron cage" of bureaucratic rationality.

All communicative action takes place in the context of consensus, but that consensus may break down. Since consensus requires acceptance of the validity claims raised in communicative action, the consensus breaks down when these validity claims are questioned or rejected by the participants. Consensus must then be restored, Habermas suggests, by moving to "the level of discourse"—that is, to argumentation. Discourse or argumentation is governed by what Habermas calls the "ideal speech situation," an ideal-type or counterfactual hypothesis of a situation where the only force is the force of the better argument, with all other types of coercion or domination being excluded. The ideal speech situation provides both a model and a rational foundation for an emancipated society. It provides a model, because it embodies the essential values of such a society: freedom, equality, and justice. It provides a rational foundation, because these values are implied in the ideal speech situation. Thus, for Habermas as well as Murray, a civilized or emancipated society is an association built upon the permanence of rational argumentation, based on a consensus about the truths and values necessarily implied in rational argumentation itself.

In this conception of a pluralistic society, built upon consensus rather than obedience, what is the function of religion? Here I must distinguish my views from Habermas, for whom religion is obsolete, and from Murray, for whom religion is an orthodoxy, and give my own interpretation of the role of religion in modern society.

It is first necessary to distinguish faith and beliefs. Faith is the fundamental religious response. It is an orientation towards the Transcendent, an unrestricted opening of the mind and heart to Reality as Unlimited, or to the Infinite. It can be described as a basic trust in Reality or as a universal love of Reality. It is not merely relatively transcendent, but absolutely so, inasmuch as it is a thrust beyond every human order of meaning, beyond all the particular forms through which it is mediated in the different religious traditions. As an orientation it has a term, the Transcendent, but no object, because the Transcendent remains unknown. The term of the response of faith is mystery, because we have no proper knowledge of the Transcendent. We cannot grasp the Transcendent as an object; we can merely indicate the Infinite, the Unlimited, through symbols.

The response of religious faith as an awareness of the Transcendent constitutes a fundamental stance on the subject which, like an originating idea, takes possession of the mind and heart and widens the horizon within which the person thinks, judges, decides, and acts. This, in turn, gives rise to a body of religious beliefs. The fundamental stance or originating idea provokes and governs the apprehension and judgment of values. Judgments of value constitute the first type of religious belief. The second type is judgments of fact. Factual beliefs arise as the mind, animated by faith, strives to interpret a profusion of data about the external world and the interior world of consciousness. Both kinds of religious belief—judgments of value and judgments of fact—are thus the product of interpretive reflection by the human mind within the horizon opened up by faith. The function of religious beliefs in shaping society is to form part of the patrimony of truths and values that are debated through politics. Societies begin not with a *tabula rasa*, but with an inherited tradition; religious beliefs are always part of that tradition. Like all human creations, however, religious beliefs are relative, mutable, and limited by culture. To suppose otherwise is to fall into idolatry, making the conditional unconditioned and confusing religious beliefs with religious faith. Religious beliefs are the changing, limited, culturally particular manifestation of religious faith. Therefore, in political argument, religious people must be prepared to see their religious beliefs challenged. They must refrain from using any weapons to advance their beliefs other than the force of the better argument. To act otherwise is to substitute the political argument of civilized society for the brute force of barbarism. The religious, and religious institutions, can only help to complete the project of modernity (that is, releasing the social enterprise from all false necessity) if they advance their beliefs as something other than unchanging and unquestionable. Those beliefs can then enter fruitfully into the political argument.

Does religious faith have a role in this process that is distinct from the role of particular beliefs? Yes; it has the vital role of keeping the argument open. Religious faith may be seen as following a narrow ridge between the two abysses of nihilism and idolatry. Nihilism denies the validity of all truths and values and reduces human life and human society to a contest of unrestrained selfishness and exploitation. Idolatry, in contrast, makes one set of truths and values absolute and seeks to freeze human life and society into conformity with those beliefs. Both nihilism and idolatry refuse the authority of rational political argument; both remain content with a purely calculative rationality. It is a mistake to suppose that human beings easily relinquish their prejudices or readily allow their cherished convictions to be questioned. Political arguments that touch deep-seated truths and values cannot be sustained unless the members of society can transcend their individual selves (and, indeed, transcend humanity itself) to open out to Unlimited Reality with an unlimited response. Religious faith is best viewed not as a set of beliefs, but as an unrestricted openness to Reality. As such, it is a critical foundation for the permanent argument that constitutes political society. Human rationality, when taken beyond the efficient adaptation of means to ends, is a more fragile and elusive achievement than we often realize. Paradoxically, it requires religious faith for its survival.

Religion has historically played both socially integrative and revolutionary roles in society. Both religious belief and religious faith have contributed to each role. First, consider the role of religious beliefs. Some beliefs support submission to the existing institutions of society and strengthen the established order; for example, the belief in God as author of the cosmic and social order. Other beliefs, such as the teaching of the Hebrew prophets on social justice or the Gospel message of concern for the poor and the outcast are revolutionary in their implications. Within the same religious tradition are specific teachings that can be selected to support opposing views. This does not mean that religious beliefs are simply used to bolster pre-existing prejudices. The possibility of diverse interpretation simply shows the need for argument.

The role of religious faith in society is primarily a revolutionary one (though perhaps I should say "transforming" to avoid some of the intellectual baggage that comes with the word "revolutionary"). Religious faith, by pushing us towards the Transcendent, relativizes every existing order. In so far as any existing social order absolutizes itself, religious faith becomes subversive and revolutionary in the usual political sense. The difference between revolution and other kinds of social change is that revolution calls into question the principles of rulership and the legitimacy of the existing social order. Since every social order tends to make itself absolute, it is the constant function of religious faith to remind human beings that even basic principles are subject to revision as human understanding grows. Religious faith protects human creativity from social inertia.

There are two reasons, however, why it is misleading to speak of religious faith as revolutionary in the ordinary, political sense. Revolutionary movements and ideologies often yield to the temptation to absolutize themselves and their cause. But religious faith rejects all absolutism—both that of the existing order and that of particular revolutions. Authentic religious faith resists the fanaticism of both Right and Left, of both revolutionary millenarianism and the ideology of Christendom. There is a utopian element in religious faith (for example, unfailing hope), but unrestricted utopianism is a corruption of faith, forgetting as it does that the term of religious faith is mystery, not a product of human desire.

The second reason why religious faith is not necessarily revolutionary is that "revolution" stresses the overthrow of the old rather than the emergence of the new. But religion is primarily concerned with transformation and only secondarily with destruction. The old is renewed, not annihilated. Even when religion speaks of apocalypse, it is far more concerned with the coming of the new order (for example, the new Jerusalem) than with the destruction of the old.

If some have found these reflections too wide-ranging, I can only plead that they attempt to respond to a very wide-ranging book. I hope, however, that the central thrust of my reply to Unger is clear. He has set out to develop the idea of society as artifact to the hilt. As a religious thinker I find myself in agreement with that aim, in part because it provides a better framework for defining the relation of religion to society than other social theories. But I have one major proviso: Unger's project should be cleansed of a narrow conception of reason (as merely a calculative instrument or tool for efficient manipulation), and should embrace the wider conception articulated by Habermas (which includes reason as a means to communicative action). The narrower conception of reason is unfortunately reflected in the programmatic sentence: "Society is an artifact." I am calling attention to the need to free the project of modernity from the pathology of modernity.

BETWEEN DEWEY AND GRAMSCI: UNGER'S EMANCIPATORY EXPERIMENTALISM

Cornel West

Roberto Unger's distinctive contribution to contemporary social thought is to radically deepen and sharpen John Dewey's notion of social experimentation in light of the crisis of Marxist theory and praxis. Unger's fundamental aim is to free Marxist conceptions of human society-making from evolutionary, deterministic, and economistic encumbrances. He seeks to accomplish this by building upon Deweyan concerns with the plethora of historically specific social arrangements and with the often overlooked politics of personal relations between unique and purposeful individuals. Unger's fascinating effort stakes out new discursive space on the contemporary political and ideological spectrum. This space is neither simply left nor liberal, Marxist nor Lockean, anarchist nor Kantian. Rather, Unger's perspective is both post-Marxist and post-liberal; that is, it consists of an emancipatory experimentalism that promotes permanent social transformation and perennial self-development toward ever increasing democracy and individual freedom.

Yet, in contrast to most significant social thinkers, Unger's viewpoint is motivated by explicit religious concerns—such as kinship with nature as seen in romantic love, or transcendence over nature as manifested in the hope for eternal life. In this way, Unger highlights the radical insufficiency of his emancipatory experimentalism—though it speaks best to penultimate human matters. For Unger, ultimate human concerns are inseparable from, yet not reducible to, the never-ending quest for social transformation and self-development.

In this Essay I shall argue three claims regarding Unger's project. First, I shall suggest that his viewpoint can best be characterized as the most elaborate articulation of a *Third-Wave Left romanticism* now sweeping across significant segments of the First World progressive intelligentsia (or what is left of it!). Second, I will show that this Third-Wave Left romanticism is discursively situated between John Dewey's radical liberal version of socialism and Antonio Gramsci's absolute historicist conception of Marxism. Third, I shall highlight the ways in which this provocative project—though an advance beyond much of contemporary social thought—remains inscribed within a Eurocentric and patriarchal discourse. This discourse not only fails to theoretically consider racial and gender forms of subjugation, but also remains silent on the feminist and anti-racist dimensions of concrete progressive political struggles.

In reading Unger's work, one is most struck by his unabashedly pronounced romanticism. By romanticism, I mean quite simply a preoccupation with Promethean human powers, a recognition of the contingency of the self and society, and an audacious projection of desires and hopes in the form of regulative emancipatory ideals for which one lives and dies. Unger's romanticism is both refreshing and disturbing in these postmodern times of cynicism and negativism: after the unimaginable atrocities of Hitler, Stalin, Tito, Mussolini, and Franco; the often forgotten barbarities committed in Asia, Africa, and Latin America under European and American imperialist auspices; and, during the present period, the rise to power of Khomeini, Pinochet, Moi, and Mengistu in the Third World, bureaucratic henchmen in the Second World, and Reagan, Thatcher, Kohl, and Chirac in the First World.

The ameliorative energies and utopian impulses that inform Unger's work are refreshing in that so many of us now "lack any ready way to imagine transformation."[1] We feel trapped in a world with no realizable oppositional options, no actualizable credible alternatives. This sense of political impotence—"this experience of acquiescence without commitment"[2]—yields three basic forms of politics: sporadic terrorism for impatient, angry, and nihilistic radicals; professional reformism for comfortable, cultivated, and concerned liberals; and evangelical nationalism for frightened, paranoid, and accusatory conservatives. Unger's romantic sense that the future can and should be fundamentally different and better than the present not only leads him to reject these three predominant kinds of politics, but also impels him to answer negatively "[t]he great political question of our day . . . : Is social democracy the best that we can reasonably hope for?"[3] Unger believes we can and must do better.

Yet Unger's Third-Wave Left romanticism is disturbing in that we have witnessed—and are often reminded of—the deleterious consequences and dehumanizing effects of the first two waves of Left romanticism in the modern world. The first wave of Left romanticism—best seen in the American and French Revolutions—unleashed unprecedented human energies and powers, significantly transformed selves and societies, and directed immense human desires and hopes toward the grand moral and credible political ideals of democracy and freedom, equality and fraternity.

Two exemplary figures of this first wave of Left romanticism— Thomas Jefferson and Jean-Jacques Rousseau—would undoubtedly af-

---

[1] SOCIAL THEORY at 41.

[2] *Id.*

[3] *Id.* at 14.

firm the three basic elements of Unger's conception of human activity: namely, the contextual or conditional quality of all human activity, the possibility of breaking through all contexts of practical or conceptual activity, and the need to distinguish between context-preserving (routinized) and context-breaking (transgressive) activities.[4] Furthermore, both Jefferson and Rousseau would agree with Unger's romantic conception of imagination as a human power that conceives of social reality from the vantage point of change and for the purposes of transformation.[5] In this regard, Unger is deeply set within the North Atlantic romantic tradition. Why then should we be disturbed?

Despite the great human advances initiated and promoted by First-Wave Left romanticism, its historical and social embodiments reinforced and reproduced barbaric practices: white supremacist practices associated with African slavery and with imperial conquest over indigenous and Mexican peoples; male supremacist practices inscribed in familial relations, cultural mores, and societal restrictions; and excessive business control and influence over the public interest as seen in low wages, laws against unions, and government support of select business endeavors such as railroads. These noteworthy instances of the underside of First-Wave Left romanticism should be disturbing not because all efforts to change the status quo in a progressive direction are undesirable, but rather because any attempt to valorize a historically specific form of human powers must be cognizant and cautious concerning who will be subjected to those human powers.

The second wave of Left romanticism—following upon the heels of profound disillusionment, disenchantment, and dissatisfaction with the American and French Revolutions—is manifest in the two great prophetic and prefigurative North Atlantic figures: Ralph Waldo Emerson and Karl Marx. Both were obsessed with the problematic of revolution—that is, with specifying and creating conditions for the possibility of transforming context-preserving activities into context-breaking ones. Both had a profound faith in the capacity of human beings to remake themselves and society in more free and democratic ways. And both looked toward science—the new cultural authority on knowledge, reality, and truth—as an indispensable instrument for this remaking and betterment.

A number of Emersonian themes loom large in Unger's work: the centrality of a self's morally laden transformative vocation; the experimentation of the self to achieve self-mastery *and* kinship with nature; and, most importantly, the idea of self-creation and self-authorization.

---

[4] *Id.* at 18-22.

[5] *Id.* at 43.

In fact, the penultimate paragraph of Unger's Volume One reads as if it comes right out of Emerson's *Nature*:

> In their better and saner moments men and women have always wanted to live as the originals they all feel themselves to be, and they have sought practical and passionate attachments that express this truth. As soon as they have understood their social arrangements to be made up and pasted together they have wanted to become the coauthors of these arrangements. Some modern doctrines tell us that we already live in societies in which we can fully satisfy these desires; others urge us to give them up as unrealistic. But the first teaching is hard to believe; the second is hard to practice.[6]

Similarly, Marxist motifs—the centrality of value-laden political struggle; the fundamental transformation of present-day societies *and* of control over nature; and, most pointedly, the notion of human powers reshaping human societies against constraints always already in place—play fundamental roles in Unger's project. Indeed, the last paragraph of Volume One invokes the same metaphors, passions, and aims as Marx's *1844 Manuscripts* and *1848 Manifesto*:

> The constraints of society, echoed, reinforced, and amplified by the illusions of social thought, have often led people to bear the stigma of longing under the mask of worldliness and resignation. An antinecessitarian social theory does not strike down the constraints but it dispels the illusions that prevent us from attacking them. Theoretical insight and prophetic vision have joined ravenous self-interest and heartless conflict to set the fire that is burning in the world, and melting apart the amalgam of faith and superstition, and consuming the power of false necessity.[7]

The second wave of Left romanticism was dominated by Emersonian ideas of America and Marxist conceptions of socialism. From roughly the 1860s to the 1940s, human desires and hopes for democracy and freedom, equality and fraternity around the globe were divided between the legacies of Emerson and Marx. Needless to say, European nation-building and empire-consolidating efforts—the major sources of Second-Wave Right romanticism—violently opposed both the Emersonian and Marxist legacies. Yet by the end of the Second World War, with the defeat of Germany's bid for European and world domination at the hands of Allied forces led by the United States and USSR, the second wave of Left romanticism began to wane. The dominant version of the Marxist legacy—Marxist-Leninism (at the time led by Stalin) was perceived by more and more Left romantics as repressive, repulsive, and retrograde. And the major mode of the Emersonian legacy—Americanism (led then by Truman and Eisenhower) was viewed by many Left romantics as racist, penurious, and hollow.

The third wave of Left romanticism proceeded from a sense of deep

---

[6] *Id.* at 214.
[7] *Id.* at 214-15.

disappointment with Marxist-Leninism and Americanism. Exemplary activist stirrings could be found in the Third World or among people of color in the First World—Gandhi in India, Mariatequi in Peru, Nasser in Egypt, and Martin Luther King, Jr. in the United States. Yet principally owing to the tragic facts of survival, myopic leadership, and limited options, most of Third World romanticism swerved away from the third wave of Left romanticism and into the traps of a regimenting Marxist-Leninism or a rapacious Americanism. The major attempts to sidestep these traps—Chile under Allende, Jamaica under Manley, Nicaragua under the Sandanistas—have encountered formidable, usually insurmountable, obstacles. Needless to say, similar projects in Second World countries—Hungary in 1956, Czechoslovakia in 1968, Poland in 1970—are tragically and brutally crushed.

The two great figures of the third wave of Left romanticism are John Dewey and Antonio Gramsci. Dewey extended and deepened the Jeffersonian and Emersonian viewpoints into the concrete historical and social realities of our century. Similarly, Gramsci sharpened and revised the Rousseauist and Marxist perspectives into these realities. In numerous essays, articles, reviews, and—most importantly—texts (*The Public and its Problems,*[8] *Individualism: Old and New,*[9] *Liberalism and Social Action,*[10] and *Freedom and Culture,*[11] Dewey advanced a powerful interpretation of socialism that built upon yet went beyond liberalism. This interpretation highlights a conception of social experimentation that "goes all the way down";[12] that is, it embraces the idea of fundamental economic, political, cultural, and individual transformation in light of Jeffersonian and Emersonian ideals of accountable power, small scale associations, and individual liberties.

In various fragments, incomplete studies, and political interventions—as in works such as *The Prison Notebooks*[13] and *The Modern Prince*[14]—Gramsci set forth a penetrating version of Marxism that rested upon yet spilled over beyond Leninism. This version focuses on a notion of historical specificity and a conception of hegemony that precludes any deterministic, economistic, or reductionist readings of social phenomena. In this way, Dewey and Gramsci partly set the agenda for any acceptable and viable third wave of Left romanticism in our time.

Unger's provocative project occupies the discursive space between Dewey and Gramsci; it is the most detailed delineation of Third-Wave

---

[8] J. Dewey, The Public and its Problems (1927).

[9] J. Dewey, Individualism: Old and New (1929).

[10] J. Dewey, Liberalism and Social Action (1935).

[11] J. Dewey, Freedom and Culture (1939).

[12] The phrase "all the way down" is my own way of highlighting the radical implications, *i.e.,* democratic socialist ones, of Dewey's social experimentation.

[13] A. Gramsci, The Prison Notebooks (L. Lawner trans. 1973).

[14] A. Gramsci, The Modern Prince and Other Writings (L. Marks trans. 1957).

Left romanticism we have. Unger stands at the intersection of the Jefferson-Emerson-Dewey insights and the Rousseau-Marx-Gramsci formulations. Ironically, as an intellectual with Third World origins and sensibilities (Unger is Brazilian), and First World academic status and orientations (Harvard law professor), Unger is much more conscious of and concerned with his Rousseau-Marx-Gramsci heritage than his Jefferson-Emerson-Dewey sentiments. In fact, his major aim is to provide an alternative radicalism to Marxism—at the levels of method and of political and personal praxis—in light of his Third World experiences and First World training:

> *Politics* is also the product of two very different experiences. One experience is exposure to the rich, polished, critical and self-critical but also downbeat and Alexandrian culture of social and historical thought that now flourishes in the North Atlantic democracies. This social-thought culture suffers from the influence of a climate of opinion in which the most generous citizens hope at best to avert military disasters and to achieve marginal redistributive goals while resigning themselves to established institutional arrangements. The other shaping experience is practical and imaginative engagement in the murky but hopeful politics of Brazil, a country at the forward edge of the third world. There, at the time of writing, at least some people took seriously the idea that basic institutions, practices, and preconceptions might be reconstructed in ways that did not conform to any established model of social organization.
>
> Much in this work can be understood as the consequence of an attempt to enlist the intellectual resources of the North Atlantic world in the service of concerns and commitments more keenly felt elsewhere. In this way I hope to contribute toward the development of an alternative to the vague, unconvinced, and unconvincing Marxism that now serves the advocates of the radical project as their lingua franca. If, however, the arguments of this book stand up, the transformative focus of this theoretical effort has intellectual uses that transcend its immediate origins and motives.[15]

In this sense, Unger privileges Marxist discourse. On the one hand, Marxism's "institutional and structure fetishism"[16]—its tendency to impose historical and social scripts in the name of deep-structure logics of inevitability, inexorability, or inescapability—stands as the major impediment to Unger's radical project. On the other hand, Marxism contains the resources and analytical tools—more so than any other social theory—to resist this tendency and thereby aid and abet Unger's work.

Much of this book represents a polemic against what the text labels deep-structure social analysis. The writings of Marx and his followers provide the most powerful and detailed illustrations of the deep-structure moves. Yet Marx's own writings contain many elements that assist the effort to free ambitious theorizing from deep-structure assumptions. People working in the Marxist tradition have developed the deep-structure ap-

---

15 SOCIAL THEORY at 223-24.
16 *Id.* at 200.

proach. Yet they have also forged some of the most powerful tools with which to build a view of social life more faithful to the antinaturalistic intentions of Marx and other classic social theorists than Marx's original science of history.[17]

Unger associates his project even more closely with a particular group of Marxists (whom he dubs "political Marxists"), though he by no means affirms their efforts to stay within the Marxist explanatory framework. The major figure in this group is Antonio Gramsci. Indeed it can be said with assurance that Gramsci's flexible Marxism, which emphasizes and explores *"the relative autonomy of class situations and class consciousness* from the defining features of a mode of production like capitalism,"[18] serves as the principal springboard for Unger's work. His explicit acknowledgement of his debts to political Marxists such as Gramsci—a rare moment in Unger's self-authorizing texts—bear this out:

> At times the political Marxists have sacrificed the development of their insights to the desire to retain a connection with the central theses of historical materialism. To them these tenets have seemed the only available basis for theoretical generalization and for critical distance from the arrangements and circumstances of the societies they lived in. At other times, the political Marxists have simply given up on theory. . . . They have then paid the price in the loss of ability to convey a sense of sharp institutional alternatives for past, present, and future societies. The constructive theory of *Politics* just keeps going from where the political Marxists leave off. It does so, however, without either renouncing theoretical ambitions or accepting any of the distinctive doctrines of Marx's social theory.[19]

Unger believes it necessary to go beyond Gramsci not because Gramsci is a paradigmatic Marxist "super-theorist" who generates theoretical generalizations and schemas that fail to grasp the complexity of social realities. Rather, the move beyond Gramsci is necessary because Gramsci—despite his Marxism—is an exemplary "ultra-theorist" who attempts to avoid broad explanations and theoretical systems in order to keep track of the multifarious features and aspects of fluid social realities.[20] As an unequivocal super-theorist who tries to avoid the traps of positivism, naive historicism, and deep-structure logics, Unger criticizes ultra-theorists like Gramsci and Foucault for rejecting explanatory or prescriptive theories. In Unger's view, this rejection ultimately disenables effective emancipatory thought and practice. According to Unger, the ultra-theorist sees a deep-structure logic inside *every* theoretical system, confuses explanatory generalizations with epistemic foundationalism, and runs the risk of degenerating into a nominalistic form of conventional social science. In short, the major lesson Unger learns from

---

[17] *Id.* at 216.

[18] *Id.* at 233.

[19] *Id.* at 219 (citation omitted).

[20] *Id.* at 165-69.

Gramsci is to be a more subtle, nuanced, and sensitive super-theorist than Marx by building on elements in Marx and others.

Despite the prominence of certain Deweyan themes in his project, Dewey is virtually absent in Unger's text. Furthermore, Unger's one reference to Dewey is a rather cryptic and misleading statement. After alluding to Foucault and Gramsci as major ultra-theorists, Unger adds:

> Moreover, it would be wrong to associate ultra-theory solely with leftist or modernist intellectuals. Why not, for example, John Dewey (despite the gap between the commitment to institutional experimentalism and the slide into institutional conservatism)?[21]

This passage is perplexing for three reasons. First, is Unger implying that Dewey was neither a leftist nor a modernist intellectual? Second, is Unger drawing a distinction between his social experimentalism and Dewey's institutional experimentalism? Third, how and when did Dewey slide into institutional conservatism? If Unger answers the first question in the affirmative he falls prey to the misinformed stereotypical view of Dewey as a vulgar Americanist. Yet Dewey's sixty-five year political record as a democratic socialist speaks for itself. And no argument is needed as to whether Dewey was a modernist intellectual—when he stands as the major secular intellectual of the twentieth century United States. Furthermore, Unger cannot distinguish his form of experimentalism from that of Dewey unless he remains fixated on Dewey's educational reform movement, neglecting the broader calls for fundamental social change put forward during the years when Dewey focused on progressive education—and especially afterwards (for example, in the late 1920s, 1930s, and 1940s). Finally, the implausible notion that Dewey slid into institutional conservatism holds only if one wrongly views his brand of anti-Stalinism in the 1940s as conservatism—for his critique of American society remained relentless to the end.

I do believe Unger has simply slipped in his brief mention of Dewey. Yet this slippage is significant because Dewey could provide Unger with some enabling insights and tools for his project. These insights and tools will not be comparable to those of Marx—for Dewey was not a social theorist. Yet, as with Gramsci, Dewey's own brand of ultra-theory could chasten and temper Unger's super-theory ambitions.

For example, Unger's attempt to work out an analogical relation between scientific notions of objectivity and social conceptions of personality is prefigured—and rendered more persuasive—in Dewey's linkage of scientific temper (as opposed to scientific method) to democracy as a way of life. The key notions become not so much objectivity—nor even Rorty's ingenious reformulation of objectivity as self-critical solidarity[22]—but, more fundamentally, respect for the other and accountability

---

21 *Id.* at 237.

22 Rorty, *Solidarity or Objectivity?*, in POST-ANALYTIC PHILOSOPHY 3-19 (J. Rajchman & C. West eds. 1985).

as a condition for fallibility.

Similarly, Dewey's brand of ultra-theory does not exclude, down-play, or discourage explanatory generalizations. In fact, Dewey holds that we cannot get by without some form of super-theory—for the same reason Unger invokes—that is, it is necessary for explaining and regulat-ing our practices. Yet Dewey admonishes us to view super-theories as we do any other instruments or weapons we have. We use them when they serve our purposes and satisfy our interests; and we criticize, reject, or discard them when they utterly fail us. The significant difference be-tween Gramsci and Dewey is not that the former accepts Marxist theory and the latter rejects it, but rather that Gramsci tenaciously holds on to Marxist theory even in those areas where it is most problematic, such as politics and culture. Dewey accepts much of the validity of Marxist the-ory; he simply limits its explanatory scope, circumscribes its area of ap-plication, and rejects its imperial monistic and dogmatic versions.

Dewey's radical liberal version of socialism might dampen the fires of Unger's utopian quest; Dewey recognized that authoritarian commu-nisms and liberal capitalist democracies were and are the major *credible* options in the First World and Second World. And social experimenta-tion in the Third World remains hampered by these limits. This is not to say we ought not dream, hope, live, fight, and die for betterment. Yet such romantic longings and yearnings, even when dressed up in sophisti-cated social thought, do not alter the severe constraints of international capital coordination in the West or of the bureaucratic stranglehold in the East. In this sense, Dewey's petty bourgeois radicalism—which is no tradition to trash despite its vast shortcomings—could not but be an in-cessant effort at radical reform in the West, and a beacon light on repres-sion in the East. Similarly, Gramsci's communist party leadership—whose legacy now resides principally in Italy and Sweden—could not but be an audacious attempt at democratization in the East and a beacon light on socially induced misery such as poverty and racism in the West. The fundamental challenge to Unger is whether there is any historical maneuvering possible—any space for his emancipatory experimental-ism—between Dewey and Gramsci, between petty bourgeois radicalism and Marxian socialism.

This query should be approached on two levels: that of highbrow academic production and consumption, and that of popular political or-ganization and mobilization. Both levels have their own kinds of signifi-cance. Humanistic and historical studies in universities, colleges, and some professional schools—though shrinking in the age of hi-tech and computers—still provide one of the few institutional spaces in liberal capitalist democracies in which serious conversation about new ideolo-gies can take place. Indeed, it is no accident that much of the legacy of the New Left from the 1960s now resides in such places. Most of the consumers of Unger's project are these progressive professional-managers who exercise some degree of cultural authority in and from these educational institutions. Their importance—especially as transmitters of elite cultural values and sensibilities—should not be overlooked.

But neither should their influence be overexaggerated. In fact, what they produce and consume of a Left political orientation remains largely within the academy. Despite Unger's admirable efforts to write in a relatively jargon-free language, this will probably be true of his own texts. So his attempt to put forward a Left project between Dewey and Gramsci will more than likely remain the property of the very disillusioned and disenchanted progressives he chastises. Yet to influence the Left sectors of the "downbeat Alexandrian" intellectual culture of our time ought not to be minimized. Nevertheless, Unger wants to do more than this—he wants to make a significant programmatic intervention in the real world of politics.

This brings us to the level of political organization and mobilization. Unlike Dewey and Gramsci, Unger pays little attention to the burning cultural and political issues in the everyday lives of ordinary people—issues such as religious and nationalist (usually xenophobic) revivals, the declining power of trade unions, escalating racial and sexual violence, pervasive drug addiction and alcoholism, breakdowns in the nuclear family, the impact of mass media (TV, radio, and videos), and the exponential increase of suicides and homicides. Unger invokes a politics of personal relations and everyday life, yet he remains rather vague and amorphous regarding its content.

When I claim that Unger's discourse remains inscribed within a Eurocentric and patriarchal framework, I mean that his texts remain relatively silent—at both the conceptual and the practical levels—on precisely those issues that promote and encourage much of the social motion and politicization among the masses. I am suggesting not that Unger write simple pamphlets for the masses, but rather that his fascinating works give more attention to those issues that may serve as the motivating forces for his new brand of Left politics. To read a masterful text of social theory and politics that does not so much as mention—God forbid, grapple with—forms of racial and gender subjugation in our time is inexcusable on political and theoretical grounds.[23] To do so is to remain captive to a grand though flawed Eurocentric and patriarchal heritage. More pointedly, it is to miss much of the new potential for a post-liberal and post-Marxist Left politics. Needless to say, to take seriously issues such as race and gender is far from any guarantee for a credible progressive politics—but to bypass them is to commit the fatal sin of supertheory: to elude the concrete for the sake of systematic coherence and consistency.

---

23 For a preliminary effort in this regard pertaining to race, *see* West, *Race and Social Theory: Towards a Genealogical Materialist Analysis*, in THE YEAR LEFT 74-90 (Sprinker et al. eds. 1987).

In conclusion, Unger's ambitious project warrants our close attention and scrutiny. It is, by far, the most significant attempt to articulate a Third-Wave Left romanticism that builds on the best of the Jefferson-Emerson-Dewey and Rousseau-Marx-Gramsci legacies. Unfortunately, he remains slightly blinded by the theoretical and practical shortsightedness of these grand North Atlantic legacies. Yet Unger would be the first to admit that all prophets are imperfect, and that all emancipatory visions and programs are subject to revision and transformation.

PLASTICITY INTO POWER: TWO CRISES IN THE HISTORY OF FRANCE AND CHINA

J.C. Cleary
Patrice Higonnet

Roberto Unger's massive opus turns on the two interwoven axes of theory and applied history. It is to the latter, and for him the less important of these two dimensions, that we address our remarks. Our limited purpose here is to consider two events in the context of his work. The focus of our concern centers on Unger's urgent perception of the latent plasticity of most historical "arrangements."[1]

I. PLASTICITY IN EARLY MODERN CHINA

The Chinese puzzle for comparative history and social theory is this: Why did the most technologically advanced and bureaucratically organized society of the middle ages, the Chinese Empire, fail to emerge as a great power in the modern world of capitalism and science?

For a long time in the Western world, images of a changeless China, timeless and stagnant, seemed a sufficient answer to this question. Because they lacked an adequate appreciation of the historical diversity and progression of Chinese civilization, Western social theorists overlooked the openness of China's early modern culture and politics, with its potential for development along a different historical path. They saw instead in the abject China of c. 1840-1945 a picture of ageless political and cultural debility, held in place by an ideology with no critical or innovative standpoint.

But if we form a more detailed picture of Chinese developments contemporary with the early modern breakthrough in Europe, we see a society deep in the throes of institutional malaise and of economic and cultural changes. Here was a situation that held the promise, or so it seemed, of many possibilities for new directions in social forms and self-conceptions. In sixteenth- and early seventeenth-century China, the "formative institutional and imaginative assumptions of social life"[2] were widely challenged in both theory and practice. China was in a period of

---

[1] *See* PLASTICITY INTO POWER at 131-34.
[2] *Cf.* SOCIAL THEORY at 411.

relative "plasticity" amidst intensifying social conflict.[3] If we look only at this period itself, without assuming in advance the actual outcome of the struggle, it is evident that Chinese society had before it many potential new paths to increased wealth and power. When we observe how this period of plasticity ended, with power struggles decided in favor of a reinforced backward-looking orthodoxy, we can arrive at a more interesting idea of why China "failed to progress" in a way comparable to the early modern West.

In many important respects, the Chinese case dovetails well with Unger's reflections on history and the mechanisms of social change set forth in *Plasticity into Power*. His account of the political options available to agrarian empires could have been constructed with China specifically in mind. In stressing the key role of collective struggles from below in shaping history, Unger echoes Mao Zedong's celebrated dictum which holds that the struggle of the people has always been the motive force in historical progress. Unger's own account of later imperial China is blurred,[4] no doubt due to the defects in his Western language sources. However, the fundamental link he sees between constraints on collective conflict and the failure of institutional invention is well illustrated in the history of early modern China.

A. Later Ming China: An Age of Plasticity

The age of Machiavelli, of Galileo and Kepler, and of Mazarin and Descartes in Europe was the period of the later Ming dynasty in China. These were for the Celestial Empire years of disconcerting changes. In

---

[3] For primary sources on sixteenth- and early seventeenth-century China, see N. TRIGAULT, THE CHINA THAT WAS: CHINA AS DISCOVERED BY THE JESUITS AT THE CLOSE OF THE SIXTEENTH CENTURY (J. Gallagher trans. 1942); THE GOLDEN LOTUS (C. Edgerton trans. 1972). The work of Frederic Wakeman provides a social-historical account of the Ming-Qing transition in the mid-seventeenth century. *See* F. WAKEMAN, THE GREAT ENTERPRISE: THE MANCHU RECONSTRUCTION OF IMPERIAL ORDER IN SEVENTEENTH-CENTURY CHINA (1985). There are also a number of accounts in Chinese: COLLECTION OF ESSAYS ON THE HISTORY OF SOCIETY AND ECONOMY IN THE MING PERIOD (Zhou Kangxie ed. 1975); FU YILING, MERCHANTS AND MERCHANT CAPITAL IN THE MING AND QING PERIOD (1956); JI WENFU, THE HISTORY OF LATE MING THOUGHT (1944); LIANG FANGZHONG, THE SINGLE WHIP LAW (1936); RONG ZHAOZU, A HISTORY OF MING PERIOD THOUGHT (1962); WANG YANGMING, COMPLETE WRITINGS (1933); Li Shoukong, *A Study of the White Lotus Religion in the Ming Period*, 4 J. CULTURE, HIST. & PHIL. (1952); Liu Yan, *The City People's Movement Under the Impact of the Urban Economy in Late Ming*, in COLLECTION OF ESSAYS ON THE HISTORY OF SOCIETY AND ECONOMY IN THE MING PERIOD (Zhou Kangxie ed. 1975); *see also* WU CHENG'EN, JOURNEY TO THE WEST (1972) (the classic vernacular novel, dating from the sixteenth century, turning a shrewd satirical eye on all customs, religions and human foibles: its stories are still widely known. It was deemed by Taoists and Buddhists to be an esoteric design for the perpetuation of truth in the early modern upheaval); YUNQI ZHUHONG, DHARMA COLLECTION OF THE MASTER OF YUNQI (1897) (a vivid portrayal of sixteenth-century popular religion by a leading Buddhist teacher of the time); ZIBO ZHENKE, COMPLETE RECORD OF ZIBO (1912) (teachings of the leading Zen teacher of the late Ming, who laid down his life protesting against the government).

[4] PLASTICITY INTO POWER at 50-61.

the economy, commercialization spread through the countryside; the landed gentry became deeply involved in commercial transactions, and the peasant producers in some areas depended on the market for their food while working to grow cash crops. With the increasing monetization of the economy, the state and the landlords were time and again able to substitute payments in money for the diverse taxes and rents, payments in kind, and labor services due from the rural masses. Simultaneously, in politics, the later Ming was a time of deepening alienation of the upper class, educated, cultured Chinese from the central state that was supposed to be the focus of their loyalty—and the guardian of their interests. Later Ming culture saw the emergence of a vibrant vernacular language literature into respectability, the proliferation of printed books, and the spread of various movements of popular education and moral uplift. Open challenges to the conventional customs and roles and standards of right and wrong emerged, as well as attacks from all quarters on the governmental institutions of the time. In the writings of the elite, an ominous mood of growing unease with the status quo developed—a feeling that change must come, that society had slipped its moorings and was drifting off toward the unknown. The high art painting of the period portrays a world contorted by inner pressures, its latent design twisted and brought to the surface, yet unable to reach a new equilibrium.

1. *Development from the Early Ming.*—The Ming regime had begun in the later fourteenth century, as Mongol rule over China crumbled in response to widespread millenarian-inspired rebellions from below.[5] Throughout central China, heterodox religious communities who believed in the imminent coming of the Future Buddha and a new age of social justice and harmony staged open armed uprisings in attempts to form their own ruling systems. Throughout the 1350s and 1360s various local statelets warred against each other and against the remnants of the Mongol power system.

The founder of the Ming dynasty emerged from the military leadership of one of the millenarian organizations. However, as military success brought nationwide power within his grasp, it seemed more politic to disavow millenarian expectations and to assume the mantle of protector of social order. Once in power, the Ming regime quickly banned as heterodox the very sort of millenarian White Lotus Buddhism in which it had been rooted, returning instead to the formative institutional and im-

---

[5] For sources on the early and middle Ming period during the fourteenth and fifteenth centuries, see 5 CAI MEIBIAO, COMPREHENSIVE HISTORY OF CHINA (1978); LI GUANGBI, OUTLINE HISTORY OF THE MING DYNASTY (1957); LI JIANNONG, DRAFT HISTORY OF THE ECONOMY OF SONG, YUAN AND MING (1957); YUNQI ZHUHONG, OUTLINE STUDIES OF EMINENT MONKS OF THE IMPERIAL MING (1912); *see also* CHUSHI FANQI, RECORDED SAYINGS (1912) (leading Zen teacher of the period); WU HAN, THE BIOGRAPHY OF ZHU YUANZHANG (n.d.) (the story of his rise from starving orphan-monk to millenarian war-chief to emperor of China and defender of the status quo).

aginative frameworks of traditional Chinese statecraft as practiced in the
last generations of the (Mongol) Yuan dynasty.

These frameworks entailed a comprehensive system of ascribed sta-
tuses, which classified people and assigned obligations accordingly. For
example, soldiers were drawn from a set of hereditary "military families"
who were registered with the government and obligated to furnish men
for the army. A similar system was in effect for the low-level bureaucratic personnel of the local governments. Craftsmen were expected to
hand down their specialties to their sons; they were registered and taxed
in products and services. Buddhist and Taoist monks, nuns, temples,
and shrines were classified by type and required to have government permits. Locally prominent landed families were assigned duties as tax-cap-
tains and village-heads. Responsible for organizing tax collections on
behalf of the state, they made known to the common people the commands of the imperial bureaucracy. Through the mouths of its officials
the government tried to instruct the people in the basic maxims of
orthodoxy.

The early Ming regime did everything in its power to bring to a
close the mid-fourteenth-century period of intense social upheaval. The
early Ming policy ideal was thus the antithesis of plasticity: everyone in
his place, now and forever, all contributing to maintain the status quo.

2. *Destabilizing Forces and the Transition to the Later Ming.*—But
even though the Ming regime wished to freeze the formative frameworks
of society into a stable perpetual system, many forces both within and
beyond China remained outside its control.

Culture was the first field of dissent. Despite its resolve to close the
door on subversive religious beliefs and to sanitize and limit Buddhism
and Taoism politically, the Ming government was never able to erase by
legal fiat long established popular religious organizations and beliefs. Because temples and clergy retained local connections and sponsors, quotas
on the numbers of Buddhist and Taoist temples and clergy were never
enforced widely. Millenarian scriptures were burned, White Lotus inspired groups were discovered and dissolved, but the Ming state failed to
eradicate heterodoxy. White Lotus rebels were still active in the peasant
wars that brought down the Ming regime in the seventeenth century.
Their continued belief in the inevitable downfall of the present order and
a utopia to come under Maitreya the Future Buddha provided an enduring imaginative framework abroad in Ming society.

The imperial state had always had to deal with subversive heterodox
religions, and it was possible to view these travails as an intermittent
problem. "Mainstream" versions of Buddhism, Taoism, and Confucianism which the state had to tolerate posed a more difficult problem. By
the middle of the Ming period, however, these groups began to sprout
new forms with disturbing critical implications for existing imaginative

frameworks. Here was a second field of discontent: the social elite felt increasingly equivocal toward the state, ideally the focus of their loyalties and the protector of their interests and culture. Confucian gentlemen began to doubt that they could maintain their personal integrity if they entered state service. Some opted out and avoided politics; some took the risk of advocating reform and criticizing the status quo. Inspired by Buddhist and Confucian ideals of moral leadership, some members of the educated elite worked as popular teachers, moving outside the channels of the status quo to bring the lessons of the classics to the masses.

It matters critically here that the bureaucratic state was the key formative institutional framework in old China, drawing into its service as officials educated men of propertied families from throughout the country. The gap in this respect between expectation and reality was another source of deep disorder.

As is well known, an official career was the focus of ambition for the elite men, because it provided the best route to family honor, wealth, power, and fame. The goal of elite education was preparing sons to pass the examinations that led to official rank; the curriculum was designed to produce gentlemen generalists solidly grounded in orthodox political and moral thought.

Orthodoxy from the later Yuan dynasty through the Ming and Qing stressed an absolute ontological basis for the system of roles and values for cultured gentlemen codified in Confucianism. The formative frameworks of orthodox society were hypostatized—projected as inherent parts of the true pattern of reality. Moral self-cultivation guided by the classics would prepare the gentleman to fulfill his proper role as the natural leader of local society and a loyal minister to the monarch. Though only a few thousand men in each generation would win examination success and serve as officials, it was nonetheless true that a whole class of families had sufficient wealth or culture or both to treat officials as respected peers and to aspire to official careers for their sons. By rights and self-conception, the Chinese state should have been their state.

The officials served the state as its representatives in the localities (roughly a thousand districts called *xian*) and staffed its central ministries in the capitals. Local officials were shifted through a series of postings away from their home areas. They were expected to get along with local high society, keep the peace, and enforce tax and service quotas. The entente between central state and local society was expressed in fixed tax quotas set in the early Ming and retained unchanged thereafter, almost sacrosanct. The local officials and the propertied elite of the area were responsible for enforcing the quotas, but were left the power to apportion payments as they saw fit on the local scene, and to keep a share of tax revenues for themselves.

Ideal in its principle, this bureaucracy often failed in practice. In local society the face of the government was not so much the centrally appointed officials, who were lofty and faraway figures (except to local high society), but rather the petty functionaries employed at the government offices who carried out the dirty work. Chinese records abound with vilification of the *xu-li*, the petty functionaries, often hereditary occupants of the role. Armed with the power of the law, these functionaries were feared and loathed as petty tyrants and grafters who extorted money and services and deference from the commoners. Their unscrupulous greed was proverbial. Principled Confucian officials often lamented that despite their best intentions, the entrenched corruption of the petty functionaries made it impossible to put into effect a truly moral administration. In the immensely popular sixteenth-century vernacular novel *Tales of the Water Margin* (*Shui Hu Zhuan*), the heroes are indomitable common men pitted against evil officials and their henchmen: the novel suggests that the commoners saw the government as capricious, oppressive, and unjust. In peasant uprisings, and in particular in the great revolt in North China that toppled the Ming dynasty, the functionaries and officials were special targets of the rebels' violent wrath.

Officials confronted the peasant masses, and in a more modest register, the state as well. Bureaucrats were not the only force within the apparatus of the state. In the central state itself, the officials worked with the emperor and the executive organs of the imperial household. The Ming regime was distinctive among variants of the Chinese imperial state because of the initial antipathy between the central power and its "natural allies," the cultured propertied gentlemen. The Ming founder, a plebeian-born war-chief distrustful of educated gentlemen, contrived to place the six traditional departments (Finance, Works, War, Ritual, Punishments, Appointments) directly under the Emperor. This eliminated the Prime Minister's office, which in the past had been staffed by men of the bureaucracy in charge of day-to-day executive direction.

As time wore on and the heirs to the Ming throne became preoccupied with interests outside of politics, the power of the throne was wielded by a series of Grand Secretaries who presided over Privy Councils. The Secretaries received powerful assistance from organizations "within the palace" whose personnel, often eunuchs, functioned as investigators, ad hoc project managers, and political police. From the middle of the Ming on, the officials and members of their class often viewed the ruling directorate as guilty of unprincipled factionalism, or worse, of surrendering real power to eunuchs and their cliques.

The role of these eunuchs and the traditional image of that role need to be emphasized. The figure of the evil eunuch in high places was popular in traditional official Chinese histories. The eunuch was portrayed as cruel, cunning, uncultured, an avaricious nouveau riche, morally depraved, politically dangerous—the master villain, the source of wrong policy, the misleader of emperors. To the Confucian-minded writers of official Chinese history, the eunuch in power was the archetypical anti-man, the representative of the central power against the interests of the social elite. Confucianism was a political philosophy of local elites looking in to a center; they owed the center loyalty, but the center in turn was to abide by certain norms and do nothing against the elites' local power and position. Cultured gentlemen had the supreme duty of monitoring and criticizing the conduct of the ruler and his government in light of Confucian norms of government. The central power could rule well only by drawing the talented and virtuous from among the educated elite into its service.

The much-resented eunuch was the negation of this peaceful vision. He was the man who had no existence except as tool of the state, no normal family life, no culture, and no breeding. He was a man with no independent moral standpoint, no loyalties in civil society. Ming history is replete with stories of evil eunuchs holding effete emperors under their spell and wielding independent power through their own cliques. Special scorn was reserved for those officials who made their careers as collaborators with eunuchs. Confucian historiography treats high eunuchs with disdain and horror; they personify the central power gone out of control from the standpoint of the cultured, propertied elite.

The figure of the eunuch within this framework of the Confucian political imagination exemplifies one of the general structural themes of Chinese history critical to our understanding of historical plasticity: attempts to strengthen the power of the center and to increase its share of the surplus were greeted with dread and condemnation by the social elite. Proponents of reforms to strengthen the center were castigated as "Legalists," that is, spiritual heirs of the cruel and ruthless anti-elitist policies of Qin Shi Huangdi (First Emperor of the Qin dynasty and original unifier of China in the third century B.C.) and his advisers.

These various issues (commercialism, cultural schism, taxes, and the symbolic role of eunuchs) were still in contest during later Ming times.[6] In the late sixteenth century the Ming government attempted to increase its revenues to meet rising military expenses. The infamous (to the Confucians) Zhang Juzheng, Grand Secretary and "traitor to his class," attempted to increase central government revenues through stricter application of the land tax rates. Zhang used his executive powers to harass the private Confucian academies that were focal points of opposition to his policies. But in the end, local landed society and its representatives within officialdom checkmated Zhang and after his demise ousted his followers from positions of influence. When the Japanese invasion of Korea in the 1590s led to more military expenses for the Ming, the regime resorted to ad hoc levies on various enterprises and resources. Special eunuch commissioners dispatched from the center used full coercive power to enforce the levies, despite great local resentment. With the rise

---

[6] *See* sources cited *supra* note 3.

of the Manchus in the 1620s, military pressures increased, but the Ming regime never found a way to obtain more of the wealth of society without exacerbating inequality and bringing the people's discontent with their precarious livelihood to the boiling point.

During the last century of Ming rule, c. 1540-1640, tension and dissonance increased in the intertwined institutional and imaginative formative structures which linked the Ming state to the rest of society. Throughout Chinese society, economic structures shifted. Many payments previously made in labor and in kind were commuted to money payments. More people depended on the market economy; more people traveled in search of work. More towns became major trade centers and more of the countryside was devoted to specialized production for market. Middlemen proliferated not only in commerce but also in rent-collection and in crafts-production. Urban mercantile culture became rich and self-conscious enough to support a bountiful literature of vernacular stories with characters who were commoners, often merchants; the business of printing and selling books boomed. By the late sixteenth century, silver was flowing in from the European dominions in the New World and European merchants were established in East Asian waters.

The institutional framework and policy outlook of the Ming state often conflicted directly with emerging trends in the society's economic life. Officialdom was open to men of merchant class backgrounds, but only when they had proven themselves converts to the traditional agrarian bureaucratic outlook of the state. The officials were always wary of large concentrations of workers, whether in workshops or mines; they might be strong and wild fellows difficult to control in such numbers. The state's use of monopolies and licenses to garner part of the profits in the salt, tea, and liquor trades gave rise to elaborate counter-organizations of smugglers.

For much of the sixteenth and seventeenth centuries the Chinese state, at odds with peasants, bureaucrats, and Confucians, was also at war with dynamic mercantile elements of its own coastal populations, futilely trying to enforce a ban on private overseas trade, and prosecuting as pirates those Chinese who engaged in it. Special government commissioners sent to enforce the maritime prohibition had to proceed cautiously and deliberately, gradually building up bases and forces, and using threats and bribes to split up the "pirate" alliances. The imaginative framework of the central state policy makers was blind to potential enrichment from overseas traders; it saw only the threat of political subversion by overmighty Chinese merchants using foreign contacts. So it happened that just as the European merchant-adventurers were arriving offshore, the Chinese state placed itself mortally at odds with its own most powerfully organized seafaring entrepreneurs. If all of pre-modern history was a race to power in the international world that has developed since early modern times, this was a major strategic blunder by the Chinese authorities, a major failure of imaginative vision, a major failure of institutional invention in the face of entrenched privilege.

3. *Contending Currents and Plasticity in the Late Ming.*—The existence of other possibilities in Chinese history, the openness and potential for new directions, is most apparent in the avant-garde high culture of the later Ming period, and in the associated trends in popular education and broadened culture characteristic of the time. Here we can see attempts to construct new formative frameworks to replace the moribund and corrupt imaginative and institutional structures of the status quo. The late Ming educated avant-garde argued not only that the institutional and imaginative structures of the status quo were out of touch with current reality, but that they went against the true intent of the ancient sages, which moderns must *reinvent to be worthy of.* Their mood was one of deep frustration with the status quo, in some cases giving way to a kind of frantic despair. Nevertheless, their basic theoretical viewpoint was in principle optimistic, recognizing everyone's inherent capacity to return to the Way of the Sages and to create institutions appropriate for a truly civilized society.

Confucianism in the later Ming period shifted its emphases under the influence of Wang Yangming (d. 1527) and his followers. Accused of yielding to Zen Buddhist influence, this stream of Confucianism maintained that all people possess an innate moral intelligence, even a potential for sagehood, which they can and must cultivate. This innate moral faculty, properly developed, can serve people in all stations of life as a sure guide to action through all shifting circumstances. Adhering to their belief that knowledge and action must be united, many Confucians of this stripe created careers as popular educators, preaching to assemblies and founding study associations. Because they appealed to the people directly in the name of the classic values, such Confucians often aroused the ire and opposition of local elites and officialdom, whom they accused of having lost the Way of the Sages. These Confucians emphasized the absolute necessity of social solidarity. At stake here was the desire to restore "village compacts" in which local people from all walks of life in a given locality explicitly affirmed the duties and mutual obligations of their social stations.

Despite their impact on Confucian thought and action, the followers of Wang Yangming in the late sixteenth and early seventeenth centuries had little influence on national state policy. But another faction in late Ming Confucianism which labeled itself the "Pure Stream" did directly challenge the status quo within the bureaucracy, and tried to rally a return to purist values among the official class. During the last two generations of the Ming period, they became a persistent and organized critical force which used the lofty ideals of the Confucian sages to call into question the routine practices of the time. The "Pure Stream" had a wide following among propertied men, especially in the economically most developed parts of China, and was linked with influential private academies that trained young literati and sponsored great public lectures on morality and politics. This was a deliberate attempt to shape elite public opinion. The "Pure Stream" took the ruling authorities to task for their corruption and immorality and lack of positive policy, for deviating from the Way of the Sages, and for bringing calamity on society. To their enemies, the "Pure Stream" were self-righteous factionalists lacking the capacity for compromise so necessary in bureaucratic life. When the "Pure Stream" got their brief chance at power in the 1620s, their attempts to clean up the bureacracy touched off a ferocious counterattack and eventual counter-purge, intensifying the severe factionalism that hampered the Ming regime as it faced its final crises.

Another trend of social criticism in late Ming elite culture appalled both the "Pure Stream" and the business-as-usual bureaucrats. Scoffed at by its opponents as "Crazy Zen," this stream of thought was propagated by Confucian-educated gentlemen who rejected root and branch the social norms and personal roles current in late Ming society. They questioned and rejected even sacrosanct values such as male supremacy and the patriarchal imperial state. Their most brilliant and famous spokesman, Li Zhi, wrote works with titles like *A Book to be Burned* and *A Book to be Hidden Away.* He attracted much acclaim and avant-garde elite patronage, but also increasingly bitter opposition from official society. Deeply versed in the classics and histories, Li Zhi delighted in presenting novel interpretations of classic historical exemplars, using them to support his own iconoclastic views. He complained that the imperial state was a big thief, and recommended that the government promote instead of dampen the energies of the commercial classes.

Li Zhi had a strong historical sense that times had changed. He challenged his elite contemporaries, arguing that blind allegiance to past norms was stupid and wrong. To be worthy followers of the ancient sages, he maintained, we must do as they did: independently invent forms of social life that fit our times and our true selves. Li Zhi was branded a heretic, and eventually hounded to suicide, but he exerted a wide influence in elite society. Indeed, it is an indication of potential plasticity in late Ming society that such opinions could become explicit and much debated among the elite.

In common with many of the late sixteenth- and early seventeenth-century Confucian activists, and despite mounting political pressures and the turmoils of his inner life, Li Zhi adopted the optimistic view of the Wang Yangming school (also basic in Buddhism) in his philosophy of human nature. This view holds that our true identity is to be good: every individual has the innate potential for accurate perception and correct action. The problem becomes how to recover this pristine capacity for true moral judgment when it has been screened out by misguided or corrupt customs, social patterns, and conditioned desires.

This program for personal realization was adopted by many in the social elite (and also by many below) during the late Ming. It calls for Zen-style meditation plus worldly action which applies correct values, so that meditation and action clarify each other. Thus the first step in political action is popular education: if people could just heed their innate mind, they would make the correct moral choices. Then they would pick customs and institutions—"formative frameworks"—that correspond to their true nature, the cosmic pattern, and the trend of the times; this would recreate social and political harmony. Meanwhile the cultured man who truly honors the Way of the Sages must work to educate the people, to encourage them to return to their true mind, and to follow the lessons of the Sages. Late Ming Confucianism produced many elite men who made this their career. They worked, as we would say, to create awareness of new possibilities among various classes of people—not only the social elite, but also the commoners who had enough time for reflection. They advocated *spontaneity* and *innovation* as the distillation of the wisdom of the classics.

This type of intellectual ferment was heightened during the late Ming, as it had been earlier, by the influence of Zen Buddhism on the cultured elite. Zen contained teachings on the relativity of judgments and perceptions, and warnings against conditioned opinions and conventional views. Zen and certain forms of Taoism offered techniques for reintegration of the personality beyond the confines of the conventional world. Though few pursued such studies to their ultimate depths, Zen exerted a perennial attraction through its provocative sayings and the air of freedom around its practitioners. Its critics blamed Zen for the antinomian current and taste for innovation which ran through late Ming elite culture.

Other streams of Confucianism rejected Buddhism and Taoism completely. Some stressed the shared intent of the "Three Teachings." By the sixteenth century "Harmonizing the Three Teachings into One" was a common attitude; the so-called "morality ledgers" prevalent in the later Ming illustrate this vividly. People used books and booklets published in various price ranges to keep track of their good and bad deeds, quantify their merits and demerits, and thus keep a moral balance sheet on their lives. The ledgers invoked Confucian, Buddhist, and Taoist sets of values side by side to define and rate the seriousness of good and bad deeds. Though religious skeptics and cynics abounded in the late Ming period, as the vernacular novels show, one does find a widely shared belief, high and low, in karmic retribution for wrongdoing, which would befall oneself or one's family and descendants. Evil excess was known to damage one's vital energy, and destroy one's health and peace of mind.

It was as if Buddhism, Confucianism, and Taoism had joined forces in an attempt to deter greed and violence and folly.

No one can examine the contending currents in late Ming elite and popular culture and remain unimpressed by the sense of flux, of uncertainty and unease and rising contention, of reaching out for new answers. The sheer diversity and fecundity of the period is especially striking. Ming era Confucianism fostered lively social criticism, holding the status quo up to a lofty standard of solidarity and sagely creativity. Buddhism and Taoism perpetuated their inner traditions of transcending common sense reality, and spawned a myriad of outer worldly forms—some practicing acquiescence and soothing anxieties, some joining with Confucianism to promote ordinary social morality, some organizing counter communities as seeds of the utopia to come, some promoting transcendence in this lifetime.

This surely constituted a moment of *plasticity* in China's social history, a moment when new possibilities and newly imagined roads to alternative futures were open—a time when embryonic forms of new formative imaginative and institutional structures were abroad in society. During this period, moreover, numbers of committed people with a "transformative vocation" worked conscientiously at all levels to introduce change. Such are the golden moments of historical possibility, according to Unger's vision.

Yet no breakthrough to new forms of thought and society happened in sixteenth- and seventeenth-century China. China went on from its early modern moment of plasticity to become a prototypical case of "oriental stagnation," enduring nineteenth-century purgatory as a downtrodden semicolony.

B. The Late Ming Failure

What went wrong? What led Ming/Qing China to its later institutional ossification and military weakness? What decided the fate of the many contending interpretations and imaginative frameworks? What was the role of contests between entrenched privilege and collective struggle? From countless European examples we are all too familiar with the major impact that "pressure from below" can have on struggles among the social elite to adjust their differences and come to new formative arrangements and distributions of power. This was also the norm of Chinese history in this epoch. Imminent threat from below acted as a bracing tonic for factious elites, impelling disparate elite parties to somehow stand together against the common threat.

The generations of Chinese intellectuals who lived through the fall of the Ming and the ensuing age of stability in the eighteenth century had their own answer to these questions. They looked back with horrified condemnation on Ming intellectual trends, and repudiated the Ming innovative spirit as reckless and doomed to fail. They blamed the cultured elite of the late Ming for abandoning all standards of conduct: moral failure led to political failure. They also faulted Ming Confucians for their unwarranted, Buddhist-influenced interpretations of the words of the Confucian Sages. In sum, the very plasticity of the later Ming era was condemned as a terrible aberration and an invitation to disaster.

As modern observers looking on from afar, we can discern some broad outlines. As contemporaries often lamented, the political situation in China went from bad to worse throughout the later Ming period. The rift between the central executive "within the palace" and the official class widened and began to disrupt the state apparatus. A number of emperors forsook state affairs for personal extravagance and outlandish religious pursuits. The real power-holders, whether high eunuchs or cliques of officials, commanded no real allegiance among the political class. Very moral, or simply prudent, people of substance began to shun government service. Would-be reformers warned of the progressive breakdown of social solidarity, the rising hatred and tension between rich and poor.

Telling evidence of class antagonism is provided in the *Wu Bei Zhi (Treatise on Military Preparedness)*, a compendium of military technique and theory from 1628 in the historical-encyclopedia style typical of the Ming. This vast book describes the state of the art of warfare and quotes liberally from the great classics of Chinese military thought on all topics, including strategy and tactics, troop training, logistics and supply, command and communication structures, and techniques for determining lucky and unlucky days. This was a tradition that placed primary emphasis on the political and psychological aspects of war and of organizing the people. Its basic premise was that a nation can only be strong militarily if it is morally united within, with strong solidarity and mutual loyalty between the leaders and the led.

In striking contrast, the writings from the Ming period itself that are included in *Wu Bei Zhi* now made it evident that the primary enemy to the strategists were Chinese peasant rebels; hence the emphasis on the defense of walled towns—on organizing patrols throughout the surrounding countryside to watch for raiding bands, registering reliable elements in the population so that they could be enlisted in defensive efforts, working with wholesalers to procure goods and keep prices steady, and organizing advance plans for bringing all supplies and stores of wealth quickly inside the town walls in order to withstand rebel attack. According to this account, local officials should cooperate with military specialists on their staffs and with the propertied people in their areas to organize the population for defense against the "robbers," the peasant rebels. Here was a view that ran counter to what Chinese political theory saw as a picture of good order; according to the military classics, a state on guard against its own people cannot be militarily strong.

Necessity gave practical embodiment to this divisive strategy. The emergence of well-armed enemies from beyond the frontier—the Oirat Mongols, the Japanese in Korea, the Manchus in the northeast, the Europeans by sea—now made it urgent that Ming China make the institutional changes necessary to add to its "national strength." Increasing military expenses after the 1550s put growing pressure on the existing formative institutional structures of state finance, which were a patchwork of local variations all geared to fixed tax quotas and inefficient collection methods. The drain of war on society was felt more acutely in North China, which was poorer in natural endowments than the South and more directly linked to the most militarized frontier.

The upper levels of Ming society were thus constrained in their efforts to solve their inner ideological and factional struggles—by rising pressure from below, by the mounting tide of rent resistance and even armed outbreaks, and by increased threat from abroad. Even gentlemen infatuated with antinomian subjectivism and spontaneity, who despised the hypocrisy of Confucianism in official society, might need the ultimate backing of the state's force to guarantee their income from their tenants. The defenders of orthodoxy argued that the "every man a sage" faith of "Crazy Zen" might have disturbing and subversive political implications, if taken up by ignorant commoners claiming the right to interpret morality and duty however they saw fit. Many propertied men saw danger in allowing zealous Confucian activists to appeal directly to the authority of the Sages when talking to the people, over the head of the moral leadership claims of the local elite. From here it was a short step, they feared, to totally unorthodox "monks of the people" spreading wild ideas of a new age to come, "deluding the masses with the Left Path,"[7] organizing secret millenarian cults with subversive plans. Thus, the increased plasticity of late Ming times, the rise of openly contending ideological currents, was anything but a welcome development from the point of view of the entrenched elite. A precarious feeling pervaded the "political class." As many rallied to particular viewpoints, and as partisanship intensified, the field of contending imaginative structures might narrow. True, the pressure of the fight and the need to keep disparate allies together might also promote plasticity in institutional arrangements. But it was also true that at a given point down a particular path, new formative structures might not have the time to jell from within before shocks from outside imposed another order.

In early modern China, a tension of this kind was resolved when the period of unusual plasticity that had existed for a century came to its conclusion in the 1640s. Still riven internally and estranged from its natural allies, the Ming government lost control over wide sections of North

---

[7] The phrase "deluding the masses with the Left Path" is a standard phrase in official sources from the Song period onward: for example, it is found in the Ming Law Code. All heretical and subversive religious groups and teachings were grouped under the term "the Left Path," and were forbidden by law.

and Central China to leagues of peasant rebels. Government forces holding out in scattered centers lost their overall cohesion, and the state began to break apart. In 1643, after more than a decade of war shifting across the North China plain, the rebels captured the northern capital. They took vengeance with executions and expropriations against the official class there. Ming military commanders in the northeast made a pact with the Manchu leaders, and invited their forces into China to help defeat the rebels. The Manchus not only drove the rebels back, but stayed on to rule the country, courting the Chinese elite with promises of restoration of lands lost in the rebellion.

At first the Manchus employed a ruling system based upon their military structure of hereditary banner armies; they used their own ethnically mixed bannermen as garrison soldiers and administrative officials.[8] Gradually the traditional Chinese bureaucratic structure reemerged and gained authority alongside the banners. As the conquest organizations atrophied, the bureaucracy regained its old prominence. After three generations of state-building, and a generation as masters in China, the Manchu Qing dynasty became patrons of Chinese culture in the traditional imperial manner. But under the new masters, gentlemen of culture were well advised to steer clear of discussions of politics and recent history, except to condemn the Ming for moral failure. Qing Confucians turned to textual philology to correct earlier misinterpretations of the classics on the part of Song and Ming Confucians; the Qing blamed these misunderstandings on Zen Buddhist influences. The flamboyance, spontaneity, and unbridled subjectivism of late Ming imaginative culture were abandoned, along with its mood of openness and uncertainty. Now polite opinion knew where the straight and narrow lay.

With the moment of plasticity gone, with the old pattern of formative structures reinforced by a superimposed conquest state, with imagination driven underground, the Qing Empire grew to formidable proportions and enviable stability while society in Europe went from Reformation to Enlightenment. Not until the mid-nineteenth century did "runaway social warfare" within China, intensified by economic invasion from overseas, create a new moment of plasticity in which high Qing certainties crumbled and new imaginative and institutional structures emerged over decades of struggle.

C. The Chinese Case and Unger's Theory

When we reflect on the great plasticity of the later Ming period and the reinforced rigidity of the Qing period that followed it, we are left with

---

8 The Manchu "state" began as a military organization: the sworn followers of the Manchu leaders organized into units called "banners." As the organization expanded with success, new banners were organized, so that there came to be not only Manchu banners but also banners composed of Mongols and other peoples as well as banners of Chinese loyal to the Manchus. The banners provided the military might and executive personnel of the Manchu state in the seventeenth century.

a less optimistic feeling about the directionality of history than Unger wishes to create in *Plasticity into Power*. We note the tenacity of formative contexts, the way they can be reestablished after long decades when they falter in the face of widespread challenge. We feel the great inertia of routine, the deeply rooted habit-energy behind the institutional and imaginative patterns of the status quo. The social struggle in China highlights vividly for us both the role of a balance of forces and an element of sheer contingency in determining why certain formative contexts prevailed and others did not.

It is easy to imagine other routes that China might have taken from the sixteenth century onward. The secession of the most economically advanced areas in the southeast from the central state—in the manner of the revolt of the Netherlands from the Hapsburg empire—would have provided a potential locus for the development of novel social patterns and structures. A new concept of the state that allowed private commercial interests legitimacy might have emerged within this territorial base area, and congealed into a new formative structure. If the Manchu state across the border had not been at a peak of military power, tight organization, and skillful leadership through the 1620s, 30s, and 40s, the great peasant revolts in North China that brought down the Ming regime would have had more time to develop and solidify new institutional patterns. If the Western Europeans had not, in their own period of early modern plasticity, undertaken a global search for profit, the network of Chinese merchant communities firmly established throughout Southeast Asia and the South Seas—and influential at royal courts throughout the region—might have eventually, with the backing of a more mercantilist oriented Chinese state, jelled into a Chinese commercial-colonial sphere.

Examining such alternative possibilities, what was and what might have been, we are necessarily struck by the importance of the relative timing of developments in different cultural worlds, and by the resulting series of impacts and foreclosures. The late Ming sprouts of capitalism in China were scorched not only by endogenous factors; in a China "left to itself" and "given time" the embryonic forms of new imaginative and institutional patterns might have matured to reshape the society. But what revolution—or even mild reform—has ever been "left to itself" or "given time"? Such plasticity as emerges comes about under duress and unwittingly, not only because of the opposition of vested interests, but also because the lifelong habits of whole populations resist change. Even when interrupted by catastrophe, the old ways are most often re-created later by the survivors and persist, in forms that only gradually slide toward qualitative change.

This observation does not deny or minimize the role of struggle in the forward progress of human affairs. In the history of early modern China, much explicit evidence shows quite well that the bitter revolt of the peasants at the end of the Ming dynasty did induce the ruling landowners (restored by the Qing regime) to liberalize the terms of servitude of the cultivators of the soil. Revolt also increased landowners' awareness of their responsibilities for maintaining social solidarity and for moderating excessive exactions from the direct producers. In the Maoist interpretation of Chinese history, even the losing struggles of the broad masses played a positive role, because they forced the ruling stratum to allow for more freedom and thus let society advance. This conception accords well with the account of historical progress Unger seeks to build.

But Unger's vision—runaway social struggle leading to periods of plasticity that enable fundamental, progressive revisions of the formative imaginative and institutional contexts—could equally well be judged from another quintessential Chinese point of view, usually called "Taoist." This raises a tactical consideration valuable to rebels and progressives in all historical moments: namely, that extremism tends to evoke a corresponding opposition. Acute polarization can lead to wild shifts "backwards" as well as "forwards." Strategically, plasticity will lead to progressive syntheses only when those with "transformative vocation" are well aware of the exact dimensions of the resistance they are likely to provoke, and temper their public program with this in mind. They would have to consider the deep-seated habits of deference and patterns of perception inculcated into all strata of society under the "old order," and carefully design programs of belief and action that bring the various segments of the population gradually, despite themselves, to new levels. To hit the mark, self-conscious social revolutionaries would thus have to know how to adjust their aim, and renounce their personal biases, bearing in mind how routine conceptions and habitual action patterns will deflect the proclaimed purposes of programs of reform and change. This is a very subtle science, far from the realm of pseudo-objectivity, strident self-righteousness, and blinkered partisanship more familiar to us under the name "political commitment."

D. *Comparing China and France*

Can we meaningfully compare the moments of plasticity embodied by Revolutionary France and Late Ming China to speculate further on Unger's view of historical progress? Any such comparison is made difficult by the obvious disparity in the historical discourse that addresses these two key periods. The gap is both quantitative and qualitative. A classic event in European history and hence in modern world history, the French Revolution has been studied in exhaustive detail from many angles. Whole libraries have been written to chronicle the sequence of events, to gauge the motivations and policies of major actors, to unravel particular junctures, and to assess overall meaning. The case of early Modern China is entirely different. Even the basic facts of the period are barely known to the Western historians, much less the detailed sequences and nuances of interpretation given to them. In the Far East itself historiography on the subject has been in the grip of restrictive ideological preconceptions that reduce historical judgments to pre-ordained cliches.

Nevertheless, some lessons about plasticity and formative contexts emerge from a comparison of revolutionary France and China. In French history, we have the contrast between the feeling of total openness and plasticity in the early revolutionary years, and the external Tocquevillean observation that a substantial continuity in formative contexts links the Ancien Régime through the revolution to the nineteenth century and beyond. Profound social change and the progressive empowerment of the nation were thwarted somehow from within. Likewise, attempts in China at a new ruling system and a reordering of society—such as the Taiping Heavenly Kingdom in the nineteenth century and the Communists in the twentieth—have clearly borrowed much from the preexisting stock of images of authority and patterns of deference, to the detriment of revolutionary ambitions.

It does not seem too bold to suggest that the juxtaposed study of China and France and their possibilities for social change can lead us to reflect usefully on some of the basic issues involved in Unger's approach to history. Both French and Chinese history offer concrete examples of people in past ages trying to remake the formative structures of social life. In the West we sigh with admiration at the optimism and hard-won faith in rationality of the European Enlightenment, at its confidence that the world could be measured and remade. Its later day descendants, shriveled by the historical failures of our century, have shrunk away from the *philosophes'* vision of empowered freedom. But their lucid social thought stands as a monument. It still offers revolutionary lessons for us today. Likewise in the China of our own times, whether mainland or overseas, the uncompromising individualism and bold freethinking of sixteenth-century ancestors still stands out as shocking and iconoclastic to all but a few.

The compared histories of the two nations also show that the formative contexts of historical experience must be located in everyday life, which includes routine activities and attitudes that mutually reinforce each other and give shape to a status quo. Unger's "modern Western" view of this issue has analogues in Chinese Buddhism or Taoism. Under stress, these everyday arrangements may be challenged or set aside, but customary attitudes and self-definitions linger, ready to recreate a semblance of times gone by once the crisis has abated.

The history of these two ancient nation states reveals finally that to advance the process of "transformative vocation" to a new level, radicals must transcend the partisan mentality and self-righteous focus that have blinded the strategists of so many innovative political movements and engendered results contradictory to original goals. Radicals must see through to what holds the formative contexts in place, so as to patiently undo these bonds. At stake are the arenas of social and political action which play directly on the structural gaps that weaken the prevailing formative contexts. It is their task to keep motivations intact and to adjust their tactics without relying on simplistic systems of belief. Given the mentality of the leadership and the fighting forces of great movements of social change and revolution in the past, this in itself would be a change of some magnitude.

II. PLASTICITY IN REVOLUTIONARY FRANCE

The stunted evolution of Chinese society in the sixteenth and seventeenth centuries is the central cultural and political puzzle of Asian history. The inability of the French Revolution to conciliate individual liberty and social equality is, in terms of its importance for world history, the political analogue in Europe of "non-capitalism" in the history of the Far East.

In his Prelude, Wordsworth, who was in France in the early 1790s, wrote:

Bliss was it in that dawn to be alive,
But to be young was very Heaven![9]

Seldom before—if ever—had the sense of opening, which is so important to Unger's *Weltanschauung*, been so strongly felt. Unlike Americans, who took some time in the mid 1770s to understand their Revolution as a world historical event, but very much like the Chinese, who took it for granted that the fate of their Empire in the sixteenth century had inherent universal value, the French immediately assumed that they had, with the fall of the Bastille, turned over a new page in the history of mankind. This apprehension was rationalized and made explicit in the works of contemporary German idealist philosophers, Fichte and Hegel especially.[10] Indeed, it was not enough for the French to have opened a new path for the future. After 1789, many of them felt it necessary to rewrite the past as well, so that it might fit their rejuvenated vision of human nature. In 1790, the Jacobin playwright and politician Fabre d'Eglantine, later to become the author of the Revolutionary calendar as well as a victim in 1794 of the Committee of Public Safety, staged his *Philinte*, a rewrite of the *Misanthrope*, a new text whose aim it was to correct Molière's ironic satire of unbending virtue. Nor was this an isolated instance. In that same year, Collot d'Herbois, another Jacobin writer who would later be a key member of the Committee of Public Safety, presented a play entitled *Socrates* that ended with the gathering of a mob intent on releasing the condemned philosopher. The Jacobins were not content to transform French society as it had become, or even Europe as kings and priests had made it. They wished also to reinterpret

---

9 Wordsworth, *Prelude*, BOOK XI, lines 108-09.
10 G. HEGEL, PHILOSOPHY OF HISTORY (J. Sibree trans. 1944); J. FICHTE, BEITRAG ZUR BERCHTIGUNG DER URTEILE DES PUBLIKUMS ÜBER DIE FRANZÖSISCHE REVOLUTION (1793).

history and literature, and to change the configuration of space and time, at least in France, by renaming places and institutionalizing Fabre's new anti-Christian calendar. Their sense of social plasticity was unrivaled, and it is against that standard that we gauge the disappointments of 1794-99.

Historical hindsight forces us to set the history of the French Revolution in a different, more modest, and far more pessimistic register. We do still see the fall of the Ancien Régime as an exceptional moment of sociological opening in the history of Europe, but we also sense that it may have been the sequel, as Tocqueville thought, of some determining and illiberal incidents in the history of France. Contemporary historians of the Revolution often lean to a hypothesis of inherent decay. For the followers of François Furet,[11] the Terror of 1793-94 was embedded in the events of 1789, just as we apprehend also that Robespierre's tyrannical reign of virtue foreshadows the unrelenting totalitarian closures on our own century.

A. The French Revolution

With the Night of the 4th of August and Le Chapelier law of June 1791 (which Marx rightly understood to be the critical legislation of the entire period), that is to say, with the dissolution of the guilds, estates, provinces, and *corps* of every kind, the French Revolution stood at the threshold separating the organicist, corporatist *Gemeinschaft* of "traditional" Europe, and the socially individualistic and politically parliamentary forms of "modern" systems. Here was the moment when a society of individuals replaced in the legal order an expiring and corporate traditionalism as the organizing principle of social life. 1789 is one of those rare moments in history when the void left by the decomposition of older social structures has—seemingly at least—not yet been filled by new, possibly liberating but possibly constraining, institutional structures,[12] and in some deep sense, Frenchmen were right to think that their society had become uniquely plastic, that they might rebuild it in unprecedented fashion.

In no small measure, contemporaries also had reason to see the political opening of 1789 as the belated fruition of numerous profound and antecedent economic and technological innovations. The century that preceded the French Revolution presents to us many of the ingredients which Unger has characterized as material grounds for an optimistic appraisal of radical and empowering politics.[13] Culturally, technologically, and economically, the eighteenth century was a period of unprece-

---

[11] F. FURET, PENSER LA RÉVOLUTION FRANÇAISE (1978).

[12] For an elaboration of this view, see P. HIGONNET, SISTER REPUBLICS: THE ORIGINS OF FRENCH AND AMERICAN REPUBLICANISM (forthcoming).

[13] For a general discussion of this mood, see R. PALMER, THE AGE OF DEMOCRATIC REVOLUTION: A POLITICAL HISTORY OF EUROPE AND AMERICA 1760-1800 (1964).

dented growth for France. Rates of literacy and readership rose significantly. Though French agriculture remained essentially untransformed, mass starvation became a thing of the past; the last great famine took place in 1709. With varying degrees of success, a more sizable peasantry did manage to feed a growing urban sector. France's overall population rose by more than a quarter in the century before 1789. Diderot's *Encyclopédie* speaks also to the technological wizardry of the age, just as Buffon's taxonomy and Cook's or La Pérousse's voyages do to a spirit of inquiry—and to the Enlightenment's confidence in its ability to make of the cosmos a finite, *lisible*, and therefore improvable entity.

In line again with Unger's overall argument, the weakening in eighteenth-century France of corporate solidarities, deployed as it was by technological and economic change, also brought into the public sphere collective forces that had before been passive or even mute. In many parts of France, peasants more or less ceased to pay feudal dues. One can point also to the new consciousness of propertiless laborers in modern urban centers like Lyon where strikes took on a new, more modern face. (The French word for strike, *grève*, was coined in 1785.) So did the workers' perception of their propertied employers, who like them were members of a *corps*, but unlike them were wielders of economic power. A new enlightened and propertied elite drawn from both the aristocracy and the "rising middle class" appeared on the ruins of the older estates, remolding French social structure. This subject has been the object of raging debate, but by now revisionist historians have mounted a good case to show that adherence to new cultural forms had by 1789 produced a new class of enlightened landlords and officials—some of them nobles, some of them not. In this new arrangement, the older conflict of nobles and bourgeois lost much of its relevance. Obviously, this social reordering offered the possibility for institutional reconstruction which is for Unger a critical aspect of synthetic moments of historical change.

The collapse in 1787-89 of the Ancien Régime as a political system dramatized these patterns of material or social change and of public empowerment. Nearly half a century ago, Georges Lefebvre familiarized the idea of a multiple Revolution, where the fall of the monarchy in the summer of 1789 had as its immediate cause the conjunction of very different political movements.[14] These movements, placed end to end, encompassed the whole French nation: a revolt of the aristocracy against the intransigence of the Parlements; a revolution of the new Enlightened elite in the Estates General; a revolt of the peasants against the "Grande Peur"; and a revolt of the urban poor in Paris and many other cities as well.

Recent work on the Revolution has likewise heightened our understanding of the involvement of new broad categories of people in the

---

[14] *See* G. LEFEBVRE, THE COMING OF THE FRENCH REVOLUTION (1957).

political process during the Great Revolution itself. The mobilization of the nation in 1789 proved to be a durable phenomenon. The new historiographic emphasis on the power of cultural forms as a tool of political mobilization is of great relevance here; for Mona Ozouf,[15] Judith Schlanger,[16] and Lynn Hunt,[17] for example, the salient aspect of Revolutionary politics is its reliance on imagery and symbolism as means of communication. Through these symbols, everywhere present, spontaneously developed and often imposed by the Jacobin clubs or the Revolutionary state, the mass of the population was for the first time in French history truly involved in politics. The rhetoric of Jacobinism, rather than its social foundation (as in the classic work of Brinton), is now a central concern for historians. That shift of method enables us to grasp, as was not possible before, how widespread and empowering the political effect of the French Revolution was.

B.   The Failure of the Revolution

But why then did the French Revolution fail? What went wrong? Why did the Revolution, Saturn-like, devour its children and debouch on a military dictatorship whose first purpose was to suspend politics? Why did the political struggle of the French nation in 1789 not definitively and fundamentally revise that society's formative and imaginative social and cultural contexts? Why did France's moment of political plasticity, like the opening of Chinese society a century and a half before, have as its most obvious consequence the institutional ossification of the state as the shield of social retrenchment?

The explanation—or, more realistically and modestly, another explanation—of that failure, whose explanation has mobilized the energies of historians for nearly two centuries, starts from two statements, the first on the assertion of possessive individualist values in 1789-91, the second on the nature of Jacobinism in 1792-94.

1.   *1789-1791.*—It is common to speak of a terroristic *dérapage* in 1793-94, in which the revolution slid away from a liberal assertion of the natural rights of man, and toward a proto-totalitarian assertion of a communitarian and determining reign of virtue. However this was actually the second *dérapage* of the Revolution, the first being the radical individuation of French social and economic forms that took place between the calling together of the Estates General in May 1789 (or even before) and the immediate sequels of the king's flight to Varennes in June 1791.

In 1787-89, during the introductory moments of this individuating *dérapage*, the task of the Enlightened and propertied elite was to destroy

---

[15] M. OZOUF, LA FÊTE RÉVOLUTIONNAIRE, 1789-1799 (1976).

[16] J. SCHLANGER, L'ENJEU ET LE DÉBAT (1979).

[17] L. HUNT, POLITICS, CULTURE, AND CLASS IN THE FRENCH REVOLUTION (1984).

the Ancien Régime, or rather, to abandon it to its fate. Unable to pay its way, unable to rely on corporate groups that its bureaucratic practice had itself done much to destroy, unable to enforce its absolutist will on reticent Parlements that had become the spokesmen of aristocratic resistance, the French Ancien Régime suddenly collapsed.

The convocation of the Estates General marks the true beginning of liberal empowerment and general social upheaval. In August 1789, the deputies of the Third Estate, together with their allies in the liberal wings of the clergy and the aristocracy, proclaimed the rights of man. More practically, they also wiped out the bloodless remains of the corporatist body social: provinces were wiped out, as were guilds, feudalism, the judicial system, charitable institutions, and in some measure the Church itself. In 1792, divorce was not only legalized, but made readily accessible. The rights of the family were lessened, and the rights of those individuals which comprised the family increased. The symbol of this first and liberal *dérapage* is the celebrated Le Chapelier law of 1791.[18]

Not surprisingly, this extreme and unprecedented individuation of social forms, so extreme as to be unique in world history, aroused fierce hostility, first on the traditional right, but soon on the left as well.[19] The neo-corporate opposition of clerical "obscurantists" in 1790-91 is one side of a coin on which were also impressed, after 1792, the equally anti-individualist communitarian claims of the Parisian *sans-culotterie* and of their Montagnard allies. In late 1791-92, the liberal, parliamentary, and individuating arrangement gradually decomposed. On August 10, 1792, the *sans-culottes*, abetted by the more radical wing of the bourgeois party, overthrew the king, who had tried to flee to Varennes the year before. In the ensuing months, a now radical Revolution was further radicalized by war and run-away inflation.

Our central focus in these pages will be to consider the causes of this first revolutionary and liberal *dérapage* or failure of 1789-91.[20] It is in that setting that we can best gauge for the history of France (and perhaps of Europe) the relevance of Unger's theoretical vision of empowerment and social change to applied history. Sadly, as will be shown, a sound argument can be mounted to show that here, as in the case of late Ming China, empowerment was to a large extent illusory because the very factors which brought down the Ancien Régime had embedded within them the cause of subsequent disappointment. But before turning to that question, it will be useful to deal briefly with the problem of Jacobinism, that is to say, with the nature of the next and communitarian phase or *dérapage* of the revolution.

---

18 *See supra* section II A (noting that Marx correctly saw the Le Chapelier law as the pivotal legislative act of the French Revolution).

19 Indeed, the terms left and right were coined in Paris at this time.

20 For a description of this first *dérapage*, see P. HIGONNET, *supra* note 12, ch. 6.

2. *1792-1794.*—This second phase ran from the failure of liberal, constitutional monarchy in 1791-92 through the fall of Robespierre in July 1794.[21]

For classic center-left historians of the Revolution like Aulard,[22] the problem of jacobinical excess is not as critical as might at first appear. This extraordinarily sophisticated and developed scholarly corpus explains the leftward drift of French politics essentially through reference to contemporary events, such as the war, economics, paper currency, food shortage, the natural savagery of the people, institutional disorganization, and counterrevolution. Much is to be said for an explanation focusing upon these types of factors, whose analogues in Chinese history are numerous and obvious.

For the classical Marxists, whose point of view few historians would defend today, the dictatorship of the Montagne is more interesting, but again, readily explicable. In 1789, one readily identifiable class (the bourgeoisie) displaced another readily identifiable class (the aristocracy), and then reshaped both state and society to suit its individualistic ends. The French Revolution of 1789 cleared the decks of history for the growth of nineteenth-century capitalism. The appearance of yet a third class or proto-class—the *sans-culottes*—owes to the unexpected difficulty that the bourgeoisie encountered in trying to extirpate feudalism entirely. The Terror is a plebeian way of completing the overthrow of the Ancien Régime. 1794 is not the negation but the completion of 1789. During the Terror, the bourgeoisie used the people to carry through its own historical mission, namely the destruction of "feudal modes of production." But, of course, in this closely choreographed ballet, the people were allowed to act only within narrow and well-surveyed limits. The inability of the populist *enragés* to create in 1793-94 a self-sustaining *sans-culotte*, or Parisian popular movement; the defeat of the counterrevolutionary Vendéean peasants at the same time; and the countervailing collapse of the politically exhausted but basically triumphant bourgeoisie when Napoleon rose to power, all are in some sense foreordained. The politics of the French Revolution are in some sense of limited interest because they do no more than actualize a set of latently present relationships of social power.

Recent revisionist work on Jacobinism, however, has presented it in a less favorable light.[23] Jacobinism here is not perceived as a weapon of social change, even of a predetermined and close-ended kind. It is seen instead as a mask for the bourgeoisie's social and ideological impotence during the second phase of the Revolution, from 1792 to 1794.

In this view, the first premise of Jacobinism centers on the "trans-

---

[21] For a description of the second *dérapage*, see F. FURET, *supra* note 11.

[22] A. AULARD, HISTOIRE POLITIQUE DE LA RÉVOLUTION FRANÇAISE (1901).

[23] For examples of recent revisionist work on Jacobinism, see F. FURET, *supra* note 11; M. OZOUF, *supra* note 15; *see also* Higonnet, *Le sens de la Terreure*, 35 COMMENTAIRE 436 (1986).

parency" of society. Social forms, as they exist, are and must remain irrelevant to politics. For the Jacobins, economic forms, however unequal, are immanent because they are determined by nature as well as reason. The domain of revolutionary politics is therefore to transcend but not to reshape the inevitable differences of material and social life. Jacobinism sidesteps social and economic problems. This escapist instinct explains those innumerable aspects of Jacobin rituals and *fêtes* that obsessively emphasized complementarity, whether of men and women, of the aged and the young, of choirs and soloists, of the past and the present.

Jacobinism, in the revisionist perspective, did indeed reject the hobbling limits that traditionalist corporatism had by its very nature placed on individual empowerment. But Jacobin doctrine accomplished this rejection only to insert individual becoming into a new and even more constraining ideological totalism, expressed intellectually in Rousseau's General Will, and politically in the rule of the Committee of Public Safety. The abbé Sieyes' prophetic *What is the Third Estate*, published in January 1789, justifies the rule of the bourgeoisie, but it also *excludes* the noble-born from civic rights through a joint reference to the inclusive principle of productivism and to the totalizing myth of national sovereignty. Jacobinism asserts the material status quo, decrees the death penalty for hypothetical agrarian communists, the partisans of the *loi agraire*, and simultaneously asserts the totalizing claims of republican fraternity.

In summary, 1789-91 can be perceived as a phase of individualist *dérapage* whose failure engenders in 1792-94 a second, antithetical but socially sterile communitarian sliding-out. In 1789-91, a possessing elite imposes its individuating will on the French nation. But unable to sustain that will ideologically, it perversely masks its determination to make private property the center of social life by elaborating in 1792-94 a deceptive rhetoric of falsely universal values.

C. Plasticity in the French Revolution

The point to consider now is the measure of plasticity present at any point of this Revolutionary drama if it is to be seen in the perspective that we have described. In the Marxist eschatology, plasticity is not basically at issue. It is at once fated and denied because history and the interaction of class move inexorably through the Le Chapelier law, to Jacobinism (with its successes and its failures), towards the eschatological emergence of an unpropertied class with its understood and promised goal.[24]

In the more recent views of Jacobinism, the verdict on plasticity is differently understood but no less severe. Jacobinism is presented here as

---

24 *See supra* Section II B 2 (1792-1794) (discussion of classical Marxist position).

a self-destructing snare. Its failure is pre-ordained: its simultaneous defense of property and universal myth cannot be sustained. It is of relevance as well that the full-blown appearance of Jacobinism as the cardinal principle of French politics is itself an effect of the earlier, liberal failure in 1789-91. Last but not least, as shall now be seen, our pessimistic argument also suggests that this initial liberal failure was itself largely pre-ordained. The French Revolution can thus be gloomily conceived as a series of interlocking catastrophes that play out in a concatenated way the earlier deformations of pre-revolutionary French life.

1. *Pre-revolutionary France.*—At stake here are recent studies on the curiously asymmetrical fate of organic traditionalism in pre-revolutionary, late monarchic France. On the face of things, that is to say, in terms of its *formal* institutions, Christian and corporatist organicism appeared to have been thoroughly discredited there. As Tocqueville pointed out a century and a half ago, its integrity had been sapped by the absolutist state, which used guilds and venal office as fiscal milch cows. Its social authority was mined as well by physiocratic, neo-capitalist, and Enlightened propaganda. So great was the dislike of corporatist practice that monetized relationships, which we see as central to relations of capitalist dominance, were perceived instead as liberating alternatives to the constraints of unequal feudal relationships. The rejection in the name of Enlightenment values of both formal corporatism and, after 1780, of bureaucratic centralism had deep roots.

As an *informal* system of values, however, the ethic of corporatism remained well-entrenched in French life. Individualism was negatively construed, not in entrepreneurial terms, but as aristocratic prowess, and as a mere brake against the ravages of despotic absolutism. Frenchmen might unite against the state, but they had little experience of positive political and social action. Corporate loyalty as a principle and conspicuous consumption remained instinctive to an aristocratic culture for which possessive individualism held only limited appeal. Even the French bourgeoisie did not see productive investment as the logical conclusion of thrift and prudence. For the peasantry, who kept their contact with the market to a minimum, property remained a means of social disengagement. The impact of Augustinian jansenism, with its fatalistic rejection of the world, ran very deep. Its Pascalian emphasis on inner intellectual coherence and on personal integrity certainly did turn the French legal bourgeoisie away from the traditionalist aristocratic state; but so did it preclude capitalistic venture and promethean self-empowerment. No longer feudal, seventeenth- and eighteenth-century France was nonetheless resolutely anti-modernist.

The Enlightenment complicated rather than resolved this cultural dilemma. Physiocracy, the first systemic presentation of a market economy, inflected but did not transform the particular conception of the self that had become instinctive for the French elite. True, physiocracy did legitimize capitalistic accumulation, albeit in a ruralist context, but for the physiocratic capitalist—as had been true for the jansenist and the aristocrat—society in a sense did not truly exist. The individual found his empowerment not in the world, but against it. For the friends and disciples of Dr. Quesnay, the inventor of physiocracy, the enrichment of those who already possessed presupposed the working out of Turgot's iron law of wages, which held that the poor could not rise above a level of subsistence barely exceeding starvation.[25] To Rousseau's vision of an individual whose true will could only be that of the community, the Physiocrats countered with a vision of *homo economicus* at war with the world. The physiocrat employer measured his prosperity by the distress of the masses. Here was a defense of individualism that might appeal before 1789 to those who despised the Ancien Régime, but it could not appeal in practice to the nation at large. It was the presence of the Ancien Régime that made physiocracy appealing, rather than the inherent strength of its world view.

The simultaneity of corporatist and anti-individualist presence and disappearance had a determining effect on France's cultural situation on the eve of the Revolution; older social institutions had, it seemed, collapsed. But the social principle they embodied remained deeply felt. New cultural constructs had emptied traditional society of its formal content, but without pointing the way to viable new social forms.

The economic trajectory of French society in the eighteenth century, it can be added, underwrote this mixed cultural ensemble. France, as the second commercial power in the world, did witness a considerable development of monetized relationships. But France, unlike England, did not witness any general movement of capitalistic rural enclosure. Capitalism, that is to say, economic individualism, did not transform French society, whose involvement in the international trade of the day resembled that of China's comprador economy during the nineteenth century. A more sustained capitalism might have given the principles of physiocractic individuals greater social resonance. That in turn would have stabilized the individualist *dérapage* of 1789-91. But capitalism in eighteenth-century France remained uncertainly grounded, an accretion rather than a transforming principle.

2. *1789: Plasticity and Failure.*—It was in this double context of a promising but illusory sense of social space that the French elite's dreams of empowerment and of political opening were set in 1787-91. The constraints of corporatism had been left behind, or so it then seemed, but contemporaries had no sense of the liabilities which physiocratic capitalism—soon to be deployed by industrialism—would visit upon them. The

---

25 *See* W. Reddy, The Rise of Market Culture (1984).

Revolution of 1789 was indeed the beginning of modern European history and the start of a "bourgeois" politics, but this was a beginning whose possibilities were far more limited than contemporaries envisaged.

The idea of foreordained revolutionary failure is not new. Tocqueville's fame, for example, rests on his interpretation of the revolutionary decade as a mere interlude within a single bureaucratic continuity. For this disillusioned aristocrat, French society in the 1780s was deeply divided against itself. The dissolving action of French absolutism, he explained, had reduced feudalism to a shadow of its former self, so that Frenchmen were now more alike than they had ever been. But the gap of memory and hope between them remained vast. To worsen matters even further, the destructive action of intellectuals exacerbated the many institutional differences that still separated nobles as a class from non-nobles as another class, differences encouraged by the fiscal policy of the state. For Tocqueville in 1856, the benevolent but weakened monarchy of 1789 could no longer impose its authority on a warring scene for which the state itself was largely to be blamed. The course of France under the Ancien Régime was set, it seemed to him, for both revolutionary upheaval and revolutionary failure. Politically inexperienced as they were, Frenchmen soon proved unable to resolve the chaotic problems that are typical of revolutionary times. 1789 was for Tocqueville not only the end of the monarchy, but the beginning of yet another historical cycle whose peak would be Napoleon's coup of 18th brumaire.

Our own analysis of pre-revolutionary France shifts the terms of the argument away from Tocqueville's emphasis on the state's fiscal policies and toward a judgment on the sterile content of individualism as defined by the forces at work in French history, be they economic, religious, or institutional. But the basic conclusion is unchanged, or made even more discouraging. Our view deploys Tocqueville's earlier and more institutional explanation of French political failure.

France in 1789 could not go on as a corporatist state, but its future either as a liberal society or as a civic Republic was uncertain. Looking backward, we can now apprehend that the aggressive, acquisitive individualism of the Feuillants in 1789-91 originated in an incomplete understanding of the importance of the corporatist ethos in French life. Looking forward to totalitarian regimes so foreign to Unger's inspiration, we can also see why the sequel of this rejected, over-individuated state should have so easily become the tyrannical reign of Republican virtue— a modernized and Rousseauist restatement of the fundamental reluctance of French culture to make of individualism the central value in either its politics or its social life.

III. CONCLUSION

In our observations on periods of plasticity in France and China, it is not our intent to minimize the place of popular struggles and movements in social change. Rather, we mean to question the role of polarization and clashing ideological conceptions in relation to the "directionality" of the social change to which they contribute. In social struggles, does the sharpening of ideological and practical conflict necessarily promote the goals the rival parties set out to accomplish? After so many painful historical examples of supposedly self-conscious movements achieving anything but the results they ostensibly intended, it seems we have to look again and seek the origin of this self-defeating tendency. In Unger's terms, this means finding out where the formative structures are "located" and what gives them the regenerative capacities they have so often shown over the course of the most severe upheavals.

Unger's overall *projet* engages our sympathy, and its optimism challenges us to strengthen our basic resolve to conciliate individual empowerment with the social good. If we are to find ways of making good the rationalism of our Enlightenment forefathers, we must indeed make new formative structures answerable to standards of Reason and Liberty and an adequate vision of Humanity.

Informed by a depolemicized study of history, willing to see something new, those in our own times with Unger's "transformative vocation" must then develop a keener understanding of the ruses of History and of society's awesome powers of resistance. They must find out what holds the formative structures in place, what reinforces them, what undermines them. Our brief survey of French and Chinese politics in periods of havoc reminds us that the sense of plasticity characteristic of "interesting times" can be painfully illusory. Intense, explicit polarization and the clash of rival currents in society has seldom produced unmixed results, whether definitive qualitative change, or the movement of society in the direction the contenders envision in advance. This of course comes as no surprise to a writer like Unger, who emphasizes the need for practical work for reform wherever it can be achieved, and who has himself undertaken that difficult assignment. Unger's opus has for us a powerful and durable message, but we add a caveat. Only with a sober look into the intricate interplay of warring conceptions can people nurture and properly cherish their "transformative vocation" and hone it to accuracy.

When given this historians' elaboration, the striking optimism of Unger's work is somewhat tempered. The first shoots of latent new possibilities may appear in conditions of plasticity, but how can they be brought to fruition intact? The moral of history may be that Unger is right to think that blows must be struck, but as Walter Benjamin remarked, they may have to be struck with the left hand.

SOCIAL THEORY AND POLITICAL PRACTICE: UNGER'S BRAZILIAN JOURNALISM

William H. Simon

Roberto Mangabeira Unger is a citizen of Brazil. While working on *Politics*, his large-scale treatise on social theory, he has been active in his country's politics. Among the fruits of these activities is a series of political and programmatic commentaries on Brazil published in the Brazilian press. The commentaries apply the style of political analysis and the general political program elaborated in *Politics* to the recent circumstances of Brazil. Thus, they give an extended illustration of Unger's general social theory.[1] At the same time, they exemplify a form of political writing that attempts to combine ambitious critical social theory with popular journalistic policy discussion.

Unger's major journalistic efforts, on which I will focus here, are two series of articles published in the largest Brazilian newspaper, *A Folha de Sao Paulo*. The first is *The Country in a Daze,* a seven-part essay published as part of a special supplement entitled *Brazil After Geisel* in January 1979.[2] The second is *The Transformative Alternative*, consisting of fourteen linked pieces published separately on the paper's "op-ed" page between December 1984 and April 1985.[3]

---

[1] Some of the themes of the Brazilian pieces are summarized in SOCIAL THEORY at 67-79.

[2] Unger, *O Brasil Depois de Geisel: O Pais As Tontas* [Brazil After Geisel: The Country in a Daze], Folha de Sao Paulo, Jan. 14, 1979, Caderno Especial. This and the Brazilian publications cited in notes 3, 6, and 11 are on file in the Harvard Law Library and at the *Northwestern University Law Review*.

[3] The series, entitled *A Alternativa Transformadora* [The Transformative Alternative], consists of the following pieces, each published on the "op-ed" page (page 3 of the "Opinao" section) of the *Folha de Sao Paulo* on the indicated date: (1) *O Problema e a Tarefa* [The Problem and the Task], Dec. 20, 1984; (2) *A Estrategia Politica da Transicao* [The Political Strategy of the Transition], Dec. 27, 1984; (3) *A Economia Politica da Transicao,* [The Political Economy of the Transition], Jan. 3, 1985; (4) *Uma Trajetoria Economica—Primeiro Estagio* [An Economic Trajectory—First Stage], Jan. 3, 1985; (5) *Uma Trajetoria Economica—Segundo Estagio* [An Economic Trajectory—Second Stage], Jan. 9, 1985; (6) *Uma Trajetoria Economica: A Politica de Conjuntura* [The Politics of the Short Term], Jan. 17, 1985; (7) *O Ideario Constitucional: Puntos de Partida* [The Constitutional Ideas: Starting Points], Jan 27, 1985; (8) *O Ideario Constitucional: O Presidencialismo Reformada* [The Constitutional Ideas: The Presidential Regime Reformed], Feb. 14, 1985; (9) *O Ideario Constitucional: A Burocracia Subordinado* [The Constitutional Ideas: The Bureaucracy Subordinated], Feb. 15, 1985; (10) *O Ideario Constitucional: A Decentralizacao Antioligarquica* [The Constitutional Ideas: Anti-oligarchical Decentralization], Feb. 19, 1985; (11) *O Ideario Constitucional: O Estado E As Organizacoes Populares* [The Constitutional Ideas: The State and the Mass Organization], Feb.

Unger's journalistic style in Portuguese differs little from the style of his theoretical writings in English. It eschews jargon, portrays abstract ideas with high drama, resorts constantly to dialectical (thesis-antithesis-synthesis) exposition, sweepingly and often ironically characterizes people and events, and is occasionally unabashedly hortatory. If one compares this work to the journalistic efforts of some of the classic social theorists, it resembles those of Marx and Keynes in its flair for dramatizing current events by infusing them with broad historical significance and in its ability to criticize contemporary figures through pithy characterization.[4] But Unger's journalism seems more integrated with his social theory than that of Marx or Keynes. Unger makes more of an effort to portray his general theoretical scheme in his journalism; much of the two *Folha* series summarizes major sections of the argument of *Politics*. In some respects, Unger's Brazilian writings seem more in the style of *The Federalist Papers* and the eighteenth century pamphlet literature from which it arose. Like *The Federalist Papers*, Unger's articles quite explicitly and systematically expound a general social theory in the course of addressing current political issues and events.

I propose to describe the analysis in Unger's Brazilian journalism, especially the two *Folha* series, that addresses most directly the circumstances of Brazil. What follows is partly interpretive summary, partly close paraphrase. I have supplied a few basic background facts about Brazil, but otherwise the account is drawn entirely from Unger's work.[5]

I. BRAZIL IN A DAZE

At the beginning of 1979, when *The Country in a Daze* appeared, Brazil seemed on the threshold of political liberalization. Increasingly divided internally, the military regime that had seized power in 1964 confronted economic stagflation and political challenge from a variety of newly invigorated forms of popular mobilization, including the industrial unions, rural workers, urban squatters, liberal professional organizations, and church-affiliated social action groups. The Geisel administration had moderated official violence, made concessions to civil liberties, and ac-

---

27, 1985; (12) *O Ideario Constitucional: O Direito de Desestalizar* [The Constitutional Ideas: The Destabilization Right], Mar. 7, 1985; (13) *O Problema Militar* [The Military Problem], Mar. 28, 1985; (14) *A Politica das Relacoes Pessoais* [The Politics of Personal Relations], Apr. 3, 1985. Related pieces published during this period are *A Crise Que O Brasil Ainda Nao Conhece* [A Crisis That Brazil Has Yet to Recognize], Jan. 3, 1985; *A Opcao Partidaria dos Socialistas Brasileiros* [The Party Option of the Brazilian Socialists], Mar. 19, 1985; *Diretas-ja* [Direct Elections Now], Nov. 23, 1985.

4 *See* J.M. KEYNES, ESSAYS IN PERSUASION (1931); K. MARX, *The Eighteenth Brumaire of Louis Napoleon*, in THE MARX-ENGELS READER 594 (R. Tucker 2d ed. 1978).

5 For relevant background on Brazil, see REDEMOCRATIZING BRAZIL (A. Stepan ed. forthcoming 1987); P. EVANS, DEPENDENT DEVELOPMENT: THE ALLIANCE OF MULTINATIONAL, STATE, AND LOCAL CAPITAL IN BRAZIL (1977); R. WESSON & D. FLEISCHER, BRAZIL IN TRANSITION (1983); Lothian, *The Political Consequences of Labor Law Regimes: The Contractualist and Corporatist Models Compared*, 7 CARDOZO L. REV. 1001 (1986).

ceded to a series of electoral reforms that seemed capable of leading to a relatively open political system. Geisel was scheduled to step down in March 1979, to be replaced by Joao Figuereido, a military candidate apparently committed to liberalization.

The dominant focus of *The Country in a Daze* is that of *Politics*—the way ideas create and limit possibilities of transformation. Unger portrays Brazil in one of those situations for which *Politics* evokes passionate interest: the established preconceptions about social organizations have been unsettled but not replaced. The limits of possible transformation have become blurred. Everyday struggles and ordinary ambitions now sometimes appear to implicate larger social projects. The distinction between fighting within the social system and fighting about the system, between the practical and the visionary, has become harder to draw.

Unger rejects the two most influential interpretations of the situation: the technocratic authoritarianism of the military regime's adherents and the Marxist or deep-logic social theory of the leftist intellectuals. According to the former, only by repressing or dampening social conflicts and permitting the further enrichment of the already wealthy can the nation achieve the savings and investment necessary to economic growth. Concessions to popular consumption are appropriate only as strategic maneuvers to stave off disruptive protest or as part of a gradual long-term plan for the incorporation of fragments of the populace into the regime. According to the latter interpretation, the military regime is the creature of its contradictory position in the class structure—a petty bourgeois group in the service of the high bourgeosie, crudely imitating its masters but at the same time deeply resenting them. Transformative politics must await the exacerbation of these contradictions and the undermining of the regime by economic crisis and consequent revolution.

In fact, the history of the military regime does not bear out either interpretation. Contrary to the first interpretation, there are possibilities in Brazil for combining economic growth with democracy. These possibilities result partly from an important development that the second interpretation ignores or denies: the course of economic development sponsored by the military regime subverted part of the power of the capitalist class in a way that went far beyond an expression of resentment, though it stopped far short of revolution. Moreover, the disintegration of the military regime has not occurred primarily through economic crisis, and it is neither necessary nor possible to await some profound economic crisis in order to fight effectively for democratization.

Unger pursues the theme of political possibility through examinations of Brazil's military, economy, class structure, and culture. Throughout, as in *Politics*, he portrays patterns and institutions that have structure but that preclude any deep or rigid logic; that are creatures of purposeful social activity but that often escape the purposes and even understanding of their creators in sometimes surprising and ironic ways; and that generate multiple possibilities for elaboration and development.

A. The Military

Unger sees in the conventional maneuvers and disputes of everyday political life a structure defined by interests and by preconceptions about social possibilities. In the case of the increasingly insecure military regime of 1979, this structure takes the form of five dilemmas.

The first revolves around the constitutional facade of military rule. On the one hand, the complete abandonment of constitutional pretensions would expose the regime to serious risks. It would alienate segments of the regime ideologically committed to "relative democracy." More fundamentally, it would further politicize the military to an extent that its own members might find alarming. In the absence of programmatic consensus within the regime, the military has depended on the restricted legislative and party system it has tolerated to resolve political disputes that arise within its leadership. Without this system, such disputes would have to be resolved entirely within the military. In this situation, the military would be highly vulnerable either to factionalism or to charismatic authoritarianism (*caudilhismo*). On the other hand, democratic concessions almost inevitably encumber the regime. The electoral process legitimates opposition, and the call for further democratization mobilizes and unifies the opposition. The opposition can occasionally thwart the regime in unanticipated ways through the electoral machinery, thus necessitating either unwilling substantive concessions or embarrassing and delegitimating retractions of previous electoral concessions. And the regime finds it difficult to cabin the political participation of the lower classes so as to prevent such participation from spreading conflict beyond the range acceptable to the electoral system.

The second dilemma concerns the means by which the military might extricate itself from its situation. To legitimate a formula for transition to a civilian regime, the military would have to negotiate with organizations representative of broad segments of the population. Yet the regime's political practice undermines the capacity of existing organizations to represent broad segments of the population. The regime refuses to strengthen or create representative organizations for fear of losing control of them. Existing organizations are strong enough to harass the regime, for example, in the congress and the press, but they are too weak to perform the representative function needed to legitimate a political transition.

The third dilemma concerns the attempt to maintain cohesion within the military regime. Basically, there are only two ways to accomplish this. One is constant deliberation among the officer class as a whole. However, this approach promises to turn the military corps into a forum of debate and intrigue. The other way is to concentrate power in a small circle of high officials, and ultimately, in the current president. Yet this approach would isolate the regime, already isolated from the rest of society, from the military itself.

The fourth dilemma arises from the divergence between the reigning fantasies of capitalist development and the realities of government control over the economy. If the regime limited itself to subsidizing capitalists without any control over the allocation of investments, it could not plausibly hope to achieve a satisfactory level of economic growth or a measure of independence from foreign capital. Thus, the regime is driven toward policies of economic control both by the need to protect its economic goals from private investors and from its desire not to be seen by the nation as the investors' lackeys. These controls earn it the ingratitude of big business without ingratiating the middle classes. To appeal to the latter, it would be necessary either to adopt policies of open-handed redistribution or to refocus the economy away from luxury consumption and expensive consumer durables, toward the more modest consumption goods of the urban and rural petty bourgeoisies. But such measures are unacceptable to the regime. Thus, the regime has committed itself to policies that isolate it even from the sectors of the society that it has most benefitted.

The fifth dilemma is the most fundamental. It arises from the military's aversion to strong leadership. If the officers could find among themselves a person of shrewd judgment, political talent, and popular appeal, they would fear him. Such a person would push the regime to take risks other than the ones of procrastination and obliviousness that the military is willing to run. This attitude has caused the elevation of official mediocrity from an unfortunate habit to a sacred principle. "For fear of political lions, Brazil is governed by political ostriches." Thus, the distance between the severity of the nation's problems and the capacity of the government to deal with them increases.

The common theme of the five dilemmas is a fatalistic sense of the inevitability of impasse. Failure of vision leaves the military regime incapable of taking the initiative and subjects it to the constant sense of being dragged along by events.

B. The Economy

Brazil's political economy presents a distinctive variation of the general problems common to the economies of the relatively wealthy capitalist nations. The general pattern (which is analyzed extensively in *Politics*) is this: The government commits itself to stimulating and maintaining economic growth by augmenting demand. In the early stages of the pattern, production and purchasing power can be increased together with relative ease because there is substantial idle capacity. New workers can be added to existing enterprises without difficulty. The government absorbs part of the newly created wealth and uses it to generate further demand through public expenditures and transfers. But the capitalists rarely respond to the increase in demand with the kind of ambitious investments needed rapidly to expand capital stock and increase productivity. They prefer a slower, more cautious rhythm of investment. Why? Because they distrust the willingness of the government to protect their profit margins and defend them from the demands of their workers. And they fear that the state will deprive them of their gains through taxation. The consequent slowness with which output and productivity expand in relation to demand contributes to inflation and aggravates the conflicts between employers and workers, as well as conflicts between different groups of workers. The government then feels compelled to fight inflation through fiscal austerity or monetary contraction. This policy is typically strong enough to provoke recession but not strong enough to control inflation. When the government again ventures to foster growth, it again resorts to fiscal and monetary demand-stimulation measures that entail the same problems. The large early gains in national wealth become a thing of the past.

The core of this pattern is a particular relation between government and the capitalists. On the one hand, no matter how redistributive the officials' ambitions, they cannot ignore the capitalists' interests. If a government of the left undertakes to redistribute too much or to curtail drastically control over capital, the capitalists withdraw their investments: economic growth stalls, inflation grows, the electorate becomes disillusioned, and the party in power finds itself abandoned by many of its former friends. On the other hand, no matter how pro-capitalist their loyalties, the officials have difficulty giving the capitalists the degree of support and security they require to make the level of investment needed for high productivity and employment. The required level of support and security would affront widely held notions of social justice. It would also subject government policy more and more to the discretion of big business and the wealthy. Moreover, the opposition and the unions can often frustrate such attempts, and the prospect of future elections is constantly threatening to disrupt economic policy.

There are two approaches to breaking the control that private capital and management exercise over the conditions of collective prosperity and to resolving the difficulties that arise from this control. First, the regime could consolidate a nationalized leadership sector of the economy. Second, it could try to influence the pattern of investment by placing general restrictions on capital. Both approaches are politically difficult to implement. Capital and labor interests often try to block them. More importantly, trying to implement such policies gradually creates difficulties of transition: before new centers of development can be consolidated, the old ones contract and disintegrate, creating both material losses and the threat of electoral defeat for the reforming government.

In Brazil during the authoritarian regime, both approaches have been carried further than they have in any of the advanced capitalist countries. The brutal imperative of accumulation, the dynamic of centralization of power, the confidence that domestic and foreign capitalists placed for many years in the government, and the manipulative flexibility created by the suppression of democracy converged to make possible a powerful public enterprise sector unprecedented in Brazilian history and unrivaled among the industrialized capitalist countries of the world. The nationalized sector developed into an economic engine capable of responding to the demands of public economic planning and of establishing an investment process substantially independent of private investors, and not—as in most Western countries—into a graveyard for declining industries or a mechanism of subsidizing unionized workers. At the same time, the government acquired preeminent influence over the profitability of private investment through its control over credit, prices, and currency exchange.

The fact that this subversion of the autonomy of capital has occurred simultaneously with the unprecedented enrichment of the capitalists and the repression of the workers shows that it does not represent a deliberate assault on the high bourgeoisie. Yet this development has an important consequence. While enriching the capitalists, the military regime has undermined the basis of their power. It has created a structure that could make the nation less vulnerable to the kind of blackmail in which capitalists threaten to disrupt the economy through disinvestment if their privileges are not respected or augmented.

This line of thought suggests that the primary concern of a democratic socialist movement in Brazil—or of any reform movement—should be to safeguard and strengthen this unintended legacy of the regime of 1964. This legacy is the structural precondition for an economic policy of institutional democratization and redistribution of wealth that is compatible with economic growth. The movement must subordinate—or ideally, coordinate—policies of redistribution and support for popular consumption to the goal of maintaining growth. Without growth, efforts at social transformation would flounder in economic chaos, and violence and dictatorship would be required for the reconstruction of the society.

The relative freedom of government action in planning economic policy makes it possible to continue the process of accumulation with less deference to the interests of private investors. It facilitates the mobilization of the savings of the middle and lower classes, since a state that possesses the instruments for guaranteeing the level of profitability of the investments of the wealthy already possesses the means for substituting the beneficiaries of such protection. It could give officials the ability to re-orient private and public investments toward popular consumption and the advantage of the work force. It could permit a redistribution of wealth through the tax system, allow the provision of social services, and permit the reform of administrative and pay hierarchies in enterprise. It could give the country the opportunity to achieve greater independence from the international capitalist system, while at the same time preserving its ability to enter into specific agreements with foreign investors.

C. Class Structure

Some aspects of the Brazilian social structure seem enigmatic, especially from the perspective of the wealthy Western countries. In order to come to terms with them, one must abandon the premise that in every historical situation, classes have well-defined boundaries and that they speak with a single voice.

The first fact that requires attention has been widely observed, though the reasons for it remain obscure. The urban middle classes—the great majority of merchants, professionals, and functionaries—have never gained in Brazil the relative independence of action that distinguishes comparable groups in Western Europe and North America. This is not merely a matter of dependence on the state for favors, since such dependence is common throughout the West. More fundamentally, it is a reflection of the fact that the economic and political power of this group has been so precarious, and the obstacles to the transmission of its achieved social status to its children have been so great that the group has remained in a social and ideological ghetto. This is so despite the fact that this group furnished a large number of the politicians who governed the pre-1964 parliamentary regimes, as well as most of the lawyers, journalists, and theorists who articulated the ideals of these regimes. Politically this group has often leaned either toward a contemptuous rejection of politics altogether or toward support for the dominant elites. Occasionally it has sublimated its resentment in grand reform campaigns that did not seriously challenge the status quo, but it has never developed a transformative political practice.

Another surprising fact of Brazilian history has been less noticed but in the long run is more important. This is the relative absence of hostility among the lower classes. Basic conflicts between the organized and relatively prosperous industrial workers on the one hand and the unorganized, under-employed, and generally disadvantaged urban masses on the other have not developed in Brazil. This is especially interesting because in Brazil the industrial working class continues to be a genuine labor aristocracy even as the military regime has suppressed much of its economic freedom. In the major industrial powers of the West, conflict between the relatively securely employed and well-paid organized working class and the under-employed, impoverished, and unorganized workers is one of the decisive facts of political life—one which forms a major obstacle to a working class movement committed to social transformation.

A second conflict conspicuously absent is the one that might have been expected between the middle and lower classes in the countryside and those in the city. Brazilian industrial development has occurred at the cost of the impoverishment of Brazilian agriculture, and thus urban wages are generally much higher than rural ones. The situation cannot be explained in terms of the deal between urban and rural interests that permits the latter to share in the fruits of industrialization. This deal has always been negotiated at the level of the elites; it does not explain the conduct of the masses. Nor is it sufficient to point to the ease of migration from the countryside to the cities. Large numbers of people remain in the countryside and have economic interests there, involving such matters as the prices of agricultural products, the rates of pay for rural labor, and export policy, all of which are directly opposed, at least in the short run, to those of the urban workers. Why have conventional politicians not taken advantage of this latent conflict, as they did in many European countries, such as nineteenth-century Germany?

Each of these paradoxes contains an important lesson for the conduct of a Brazilian working class party. Consider first the case of the urban middle classes. In the two recent periods in which the state achieved substantial autonomy from the elites, it failed to win the support of these middle groups and in fact ended up antagonizing them. In the Goulart era (1961-1964), they were alienated by an aggressive populistic rhetoric made all the more frightening by explosive inflation and consequent economic disorganization. The result was the aggravation of hostility between the middle classes and the politically active sectors of the masses and a close reconciliation between the middle class and the dominant elites. The subsequent military regime opened unprecedented opportunities of mobility for the middle classes, but it too failed to secure their support. They were disenchanted by the military's technocratic elitism with its open disdain for liberal rhetoric and by the modesty of the improvements in their economic position relative to that of the dominant elites. Thus substantial numbers of the middle class began to vote for the opposition party.

Although they have never gained the level of power they have sought, the middle classes have been one of the most important determinants of national politics. The attitudes of this group cannot be explained either in terms of a natural alliance of interests with the wealthy or in terms of a congenital tendency to be gulled by the ideas of the wealthy. One of the most delicate tasks of a Brazilian democratic socialist movement is to show to this group that its interests are not in conflict with such a movement. In programmatic terms, this means the protection of small property, both rural and urban; security against inflation for small investment, if necessary through the use of fiscal and monetary policy to subsidize it; the overhaul of the tax system to soak the rich and undermine inheritance; the design of public enterprises as models of efficiency and channels of mobility for the children of the middle classes; the scrupulous disdain for rhetoric calculated to incite indignation and fear among the middle classes; and the reinterpretation of the ideas of Brazilian liberalism as a more ample vision of democracy.

Now consider the second mystery: the absence of conflict between the organized industrial work force and the comparatively disadvantaged, under-employed urban masses. Various hypotheses might be advanced to explain the lack of such conflict, which is strikingly characteristic of the advanced capitalist countries. First, there is the rapidity and the unsettling effect of the rural-urban dislocation. A large part of the urban lower classes consists of people who arrived from the country too recently to have acquired fixed social identities and well-defined antagonisms. Second, even the best paid workers in the large industries live in a precarious state: they lack the organization necessary to defend their jobs and prerogatives against the mob beating at the doors. Third, Brazilian capitalism prefers to industrialize with advanced machinery oriented toward production of luxury goods. Since wages represent a relatively small fraction of the costs of this kind of production, industry has often been willing to pay wages well above what the market dictates in the hope of securing the loyalty of a docile and experienced workforce.

Fourth, the workers inside and outside the privileged sector have developed a complex network of family, patronage, and friendship relationships. The salary paid to the organized workers often goes to support less advantaged people. These ties have muted the impact of disparities between the two groups. Fifth, the weakness of the union movement and its repression under the authoritarian regime have blurred the lines separating the privileged and disadvantaged sectors. Large numbers of unionized workers become employed or unemployed in accordance with the fluctuations of the business cycle. In the wealthy capitalist countries, the unorganized sector of the masses is used to reconcile the guarantees won by the union movement with the freedom of the capitalists to expand or cut back production in accordance with fluctuations in demand. The unorganized sector, which can be employed or dismissed easily, suffers the brunt of economic instability. Because the boundary between the privileged and the disadvantaged fluctuates more in Brazil than in the advanced countries, a settled line of antagonism is less likely to develop.

Sixth, the subtlety of racial mixture in Brazil—the blurring of color and ethnic distinctions within the lower classes—accounts for a distinctive facet of popular unity. Color and ethnic distinctions accentuate the distance between the elites and the poor and gives them a sense of naturalness or necessity. It encourages the lighter-complexioned members of the lower classes to aspire for easier incorporation into the white middle classes. It aggravates distrust among the lower classes and furnishes an insidious racial vocabulary in which to articulate it. In Brazil, however, no clear racial and ethnic dichotomy exists to aggravate or solidify the economic distinctions between the privileged working class and the urban masses.

Even if all these hypotheses were confirmed by empirical research, there would remain an unexplicable element to the phenomenon. In spite of all the qualifications, the material interests of these two groups of workers are in conflict. The fact that this theoretical conflict has not become open antagonism must be credited in part to the styles of imagination and conduct that characterize the Brazilian working masses.

The absence of conflict between the privileged and underprivileged sectors of the lower classes is a valuable and unintended gift to the Brazilian popular movement. To safeguard this gift, the movement needs a specific social program. The starting point of this program would be the free, immediate, and total unionization of workers in every sector of the labor market. The more encompassing unionization becomes, the less the risk that union boundaries reflect or create hierarchical distinctions. This policy requires a principle of organization that avoids not only unionization along the lines of each separate enterprise (as in Japan), but also the limitation of each union to a single well-defined stage of the economy. To enhance both the political power of the unions and their capacity to exercise pressure on employers, they should be organized in terms of broad sectors that include all workers involved in a particular industrial or commercial area. For example, in the automobile industry, the union should include not only the employees in the large central production and assembly plants, but also the less organized and well-paid workers in the smaller satellite enterprises. The practical effect of this policy would be to weaken at the outset any conflict between aristocrats and plebes within the work force.

Other policies would also foster solidarity among the various elements of the working classes. In the short run, full employment policy would moderate tensions arising from competition for scarce jobs. In the long run, the reorientation of industry toward popular consumption and more labor-intensive technology would avoid the danger of an implicit alliance between industrial workers and rich consumers, an alliance likely to strengthen divisions within the working classes.

The other potential conflict conspicuously absent in Brazil is between the urban and rural masses. Modern regimes have favored industrial development at the expense of agricultural development, have squeezed rural producers to subsidize urban consumption, and have declined to confront the landed oligarchies that dominate the countryside through both open violence and control of political machines. This state of affairs has benefitted urban workers in some respects and swelled their ranks by encouraging mass migration from the country, but it has done little for small rural landowners and workers. The danger of this—as yet latent—conflict would increase as Brazil became more democratic and more socialist. As the rural masses became more politically active and self-conscious, they might come to see a divergence of interest with their urban counterparts over such matters as the relative pricing of agricultural and industrial products and the distribution of government assistance between agriculture and industry.

The danger would be less severe for development strategies that seek to strengthen small and medium-scale family operations through technical assistance, credit, and marketing facilities than it would be for the strategies of consolidating agricultural production in large-scale, capital-intensive enterprises favored by the state technocrats, the urban business elite, and the leftist intelligentsia. In embracing the latter strategies, some are influenced, not only by the preconceptions of both capitalist and Marxist theory about the necessary course of economic development, but also by a fear that the former strategy would necessarily foster a large reactionary petty bourgeoisie. In fact, from the point of view of the danger of rural-urban conflict, the strategy of capital intensive industrialization is the least risky, if only because it would empty the countryside. In other respects, outside of a few areas where large scale production is already established or required by technological considerations, the petty bourgeois strategy is more promising. It would most effectively engage the talents and ambitions of large numbers of small producers and workers who have strong commitments to agriculture. It would require less capital and cause less human dislocation. And most important, it would create the basis for a vigorous and autonomous electorate in the countryside.

Such an electorate would undermine the conservative rural party machines that, aided by the disproportionate representation of rural states in the legislature, have long provided powerful opposition to progressive reform. There is no reason to assume that this electorate would be conservative. A national progressive movement seriously committed to strengthening small and medium-scale agriculture and securing small rural property should be able to win its support. The petty bourgeois strategy would also avoid further swelling the cities and thus aggravating the accompanying social problems, and it would preserve valuable forms of social life in the countryside. Finally, the petty bourgeois strategy would limit the subordination of Brazilian agriculture to the international economy. The industrialization strategy makes the economy more vulnerable to domination by foreign capital and to the vicissitudes of international commodities markets.

Unger concludes this section with a warning of the dangers for a popular movement of rigid presuppositions about the identities of its possible allies and enemies, but he qualifies the point in a way that gives it a paradoxical quality. On the one hand, dogmatic presuppositions about the possible configurations of the political map restrict the left's strategic options and hamper its capacity to imagine social transformations. On the other hand, when a political movement treats all collective divisions as arbitrary and infinitely manipulable, it loses its grounding in a conception of goals and projects that transcends transitory party conflicts, and the fight for power becomes an end in itself. The only solution to this paradox is the attempt, always difficult and dangerous, to preserve a sense of distance between the movement's fundamental principles and its specific alliances and pronouncements. There is no rule as to when the principles require modification or abandonment of the alliances and pronouncements, and indeed experience with the latter will sometimes suggest modification of the former. Thus, the line between a movement's basic political identity and its immediate political circumstances can rarely be more than a precarious one.

D. Political Reform

In this section Unger sketches the vision that *Politics* calls "empowered democracy" which is more extensively elaborated in *The Transformative Alternative*, discussed below.

E. Cultural Style

This section is a portrait of the various strata of Brazilian society in terms of cultural style, that is "the kind of alliance worked out between the passions and institutions." Unger argues that the society's distinctive modes of sociability create and limit political possibilities and that a thoroughgoing political transformation would have to reach them.

He begins with an image of sociability that is often portrayed as the Brazilian national character but that is in fact characteristic principally of the elites. The image portrays a dialectic of cynicism and sentimentality. The sentimental dimension is expressed in the capacity to give a veneer of affection to relations of dependence and domination, in the tendency to devalue impersonal duties in favor of loyalty to family, friends, and clients; in the tendency to view the public world of work as a means of fulfilling private personal obligations; in the readiness to break established rules when they conflict with the demands of personal relationships; in the idea that amiability can excuse failures of reliability and integrity; and in the proclivity for extravagant demonstrations of affection. The cynical dimension appears in the indifference to solemn promises, obligations of work, and time schedules of every sort; in the shirking of collective tasks; in the skepticism toward ideals that would sacrifice immediate interests and personal ties to long term public goals; in the energetic quest for worldly pleasures; and in an intransigent agnosticism often masked in a confused religiosity. The sentimental and the cynical are two sides of the same coin: the cultivation of the immediate, the refusal to live for the transcendent.

This culture of the established elites has a shadow. The shadow culture is expressed in a set of institutions that convey an opposed vision of sociability. These institutions are the church, the armed forces, and the communist political parties. In Brazil these institutions have a distinctive affinity that arises from their opposition to the established elite culture. This affinity can be seen in various themes. First, there is the importance of ideals that generate rules of conduct. Second, there is the posture of asceticism, often genuine and noble. Third, there is the emphasis on ties of organization: the sanctity of promises, the sense of individual responsibility for collective goals, the sense of personal mission brought to public undertakings. Fourth, and overlapping the first three, there is the condemnation of the established elite culture, which is identified with the nation as a whole: a desire to wage war against society and reconstruct it in the image of the shadow culture (a desire moderated in the case of the church either by sympathy for the oligarchs or by genuine Christian charity).

The urban middle classes and professional groups have no coherent attitude toward the conflict between the established elite culture and the shadow culture. At times, they zealously mimic the elites; at times, they share the indignation of the shadow. Most often, they seem to do both at the same time, thus giving a paradoxical cast to Brazilian middle class culture.

Unger argues that this polarized cultural scene is a major obstacle to transformative politics. The type of sociability that characterizes the established elite culture is incapable of nurturing civic duty, collective solidarity, and devotion to ideals. On the other hand, the isolation of the shadow culture means that its institutions define themselves negatively. Viewing themselves at war with the society, they are unable to devise means of accommodation and dialogue between their own ideas and those they believe dominate the society as a whole. Saddest of all, the established elite culture and the shadow culture are both founded on the exclusion of the masses and an inability to understand them.

The Brazilian elites have always thought of the masses in terms of two wildly inaccurate images. On the one hand, they see the masses as exaggerated examples of the established elites—self-indulgent, hedonistic, irresponsible, sentimental, and cynical. On the other hand, they see them as an exaggerated version of the shadow culture—severe, implacable, and resentful. Both views rest on the elites' overwhelming ignorance about the Brazilian masses. In contrast to the sterile, simplistic, imitative, and monotonous culture of the elites, Brazilian popular culture embraces an exciting variety of forms of sociability and moral visions.

To give an idea of the panoply of forms of social life among the lower classes, Unger devotes much of the remainder of the discussion to a particular cultural system. This is the system characteristic of the northeastern and central regions of the country. It consists of four related elements: large-scale agriculture; small towns; areas of small and medium farms and villages; and metropolitan cities, which may be physically remote from the other three elements but have important ties to them. The important point is that all four elements are prominent in popular consciousness. The connection of the elements is particularly visible in the organization of work, for example, in the situation of seasonal agricultural workers who live in the small towns and large cities but depend on agricultural work.

In the areas of large-scale agriculture, hierarchical distinctions often take an especially naked and brutal form, and solidarity among the workers is often weak. The largely unchecked power of the landowners and their agents rests not only on their capacity for violence and the availability of state assistance, but on the inability of the workers to identify their fates with this kind of production. The harshness of their lives inspires, not resistance, but dreams of escape to family farms, small towns, or the metropolitan city. In these circumstances, collective fights and hopes never assume clear definition.

In turning away from the realm of large-scale agriculture, the worker looks in two directions: toward family farms and villages and toward the small towns. Despite their physical proximity and the ease with which people move between them, the two represent radically opposed modes of sociability. Life in the small farm sector is characterized by entrepreneurial pride, by norms of mutual assistance among neighbors, and by a sense of equality. It is a hard and even desperate life, but one with traces of nobility. In comparison, small town life is mercenary and competitive. Inequality is flaunted shamelessly and cruelly. Attitudes of conniving and demoralization overwhelm solidarity, and citizenship is degraded to parasitism. Even more than in the metropolitan cities, a vacuous, numbing popular culture consisting largely of television and soccer holds sway.

Unger suggests three social factors that underpin the contrast between the small farm and the town. First, in the realm of small agriculture, the relative physical separation of family farms, coupled with the dependence of neighbors, fosters autonomy and solidarity. In the small towns, on the other hand, where people lack space of their own and the necessities of cooperation are weaker, people tend to view each other as rivals and feel oppressively hemmed in by others. "In the countryside, distance unites people; in the small towns, proximity divides them." Second, the political circumstances of small agriculture are conducive to some measure of equality. The large landowners are unable to subjugate the small ones but generally are able to prevent them from growing into large ones themselves. Thus, there is a relatively stable equality in the relations of the small producers to each other. By contrast, the economic role of the small towns, as intermediaries between large-scale agriculture and the metropolitan cities, generates economic circumstances that facilitate hierarchy. Third, the small operator's experience of violent oscillation between the intimacy of the relatively isolated family farm and the economic sufferings imposed by the outside world (the large plantations, the towns) creates an atmosphere conducive to great hopes of collective redemption. The precariousness of the existence of the small operator and the elemental quality of his problems gives the small farmer a sense of participation in a collective historical drama. On the other hand, in the small towns, life is moderately more secure, and economic struggle is experienced as more petty, mundane, and competitive. Here it is easier to imagine salvation as the task of the individual soul, working against an unchangeable world and appealing to a remote, hidden God.

The final element of the system is the metropolitan city. Here lower class experience moves among three realities. There is the impersonal hierarchical order of large industry, a realm of relatively secure and privileged employment. Then there is a realm of less security and more personal dependence—the realm of employment in small business, domestic service, and odd job handiwork, and of patron-client relations with privileged aquaintances. The third reality is the disaster of unemployment and the disintegration of personal ties. The lower classes in the metropolitan cities are buffeted among these three experiences. Each type of existence is thus unstable: the fortunes of individuals and those to whom they are connected fluctuate constantly.

This sketch of the diversity of popular experience in this particular Brazilian social system is intended to illustrate three general points. First, lower class culture is not adequately portrayed in terms of stereotypes that preoccupy the elites. Popular experience cannot be reduced to a contrast between self-indulgence and truculence; rather it involves a deeper dialectic of suffering, resignation, and discovery. Second, the fluctuating quality of popular experience blurs the lines of group identity, interest, and commitment. Third, the lower classes are relatively open to messages of collective struggle and redemption. If they are capable of abandoning themselves to demogogic manipulation and charismatic authoritarianism (*caudilhismo*), they are also capable, with responsible leadership and collective organization, of transforming the uncertainties of the world into weapons of power and knowledge.

II. THE TRANSFORMATIVE ALTERNATIVE

The military regime ended in 1985 in a manner that reflected the confusion and internal division emphasized in Unger's 1979 analysis. The regime had established a procedure by which the new president would be elected in January 1985 by an electoral college constituted in a manner that gave its own party a majority. But divisions within the party intensified to the point that in the summer of 1984 the leader of the moderate faction of the regime party bolted and entered into an alliance with the Party of the Brazilian Democratic Movement (PMDB), the largest opposition party. The alliance pledged itself to vote for a slate consisting of the PMDB's Tancredo Neves for president, and Jose

Sarney, a member of the bolting wing of the party of the military regime, for vice-president. As the year went on the alliance solidified its position. By the time that the first articles of *The Transformative Alternative* appeared on December 20, it was clear that the Tancredo Neves-Sarney slate would be elected in January.

The PMDB was one of several parties that appeared in 1980 through the political opening sponsored by the military regime, which promised a gradual loosening of the electoral process and permitted relatively free organization of parties. It emerged through the reorganization of what had previously been the only opposition party recognized under the tightly controlled electoral rules. Unger was associated with the party at the time of its reorganization and drafted its "manifesto of foundation."[6] In accordance with Brazilian electoral law, the party submitted this document to the Superior Electoral Court as part of its official platform. (The law also requires that upon joining a party, members attest that they subsribe to the principles espoused in such documents.) The document is in both style and substance similar to the newspaper articles, though the dogmatic and hortatory qualities of the style are less restrained and seem far more familiar in the context of the manifesto form.

The manifesto emphasizes many of the central themes of *The Country in a Daze*: the importance but insufficiency of constitutional democracy; the need to carry democratization into the realm of private life; the importance of decentralized popular organization; the need for economic transformation that focuses on public support for small enterprise in the countryside and the cities; the importance of avoiding polarization of the organized working class and the petty bourgeoisie, and of rural and urban workers; and the possibility of a politics that attempts to transform mundane grievances into more far-reaching critique and opposition. Especially striking in the context of the manifesto is Unger's insistence that social change be viewed as provisional and not as a program designed to achieve its goals once and for all: "Through democratization and mobilization, all society would become, not the fulfillment of some ultimate destiny, but a field of experiment."[7] The manifesto outlines some of the institutional reforms elaborated in *The Transformative Alternative*.

The PMDB soon moved away from the relatively radical and unconventional tenets expressed in the manifesto. The manifesto had committed the party to reach out from its centrist base within the elite to the working class parties, labor unions, and local church-connected popular organizations. But in practice, the party sought to conciliate centrist and conservative groups. By the time of the electoral alliance with the mili-

---

[6] R. Unger, Programa: O Partido do Movimento Democratico Brasileiro E Sua Obra Futuro (unpublished manuscript) (available in Harvard Law School Library). The manifesto has been published and widely distributed in Brazil as part of a collection of the party's electoral documents.
[7] *Id.*

tary party, its program and rhetoric bore little resemblance to Unger's manifesto (despite the manifesto's continuing legal status as the party's official platform).

Shortly after his election as president in January 1985, Tancredo Neves died and was succeeded by Jose Sarney, the nominee of the moderate wing of the party affiliated with the military regime. It is not clear that this change had any significant effect on the programmatic direction of the PMDB. Certainly Unger felt that the programmatic shift away from the principles of the manifesto had occurred earlier.

Thus, while *The Transformative Alternative* elaborates on the program of the PMDB manifesto, it was written in opposition to the PMDB as it had evolved by the time of the 1985 elections. The program to which it is an "alternative" is explicitly that of the Tancredo Neves administration.

By this time Unger had become associated with the Democratic Workers' Party and its leader Leonel Brizola, a major figure in the Goulart regime who had recently returned from exile. A leftist populist-style leader, Brizola was one of the few Brazilian politicians with anything like a mass following and was probably the most popular. He was widely regarded among the elites as a demogogue and was the political figure most feared by members of the military regime.

The Transformative Alternative begins with a prediction that the imminent PMDB regime would frustrate the hopes of the middle and working classes and would fail to vindicate the ideals of political democracy. Unger describes the fundamental characteristics of this program as a desire to alleviate the grossly unequal distribution of income in Brazil without confronting entrenched economic privilege. This "redistributive but institutionally conservative"[8] program is committed to welfare measures and an income policy but does not propose to alter the productive structure of the economy. Unger argues that this program is bound to fail and that without fundamental institutional change, redistribution will impede growth and productivity.

Unger argues that the PMDB constitutional rhetoric has also taken a conservative direction. The party leaders have begun to balk at the notion of contested direct elections and to flirt with the idea of "democracy by acclamation."[9] They suggest that contested elections may be a luxury inappropriate to unstable times and that rallies, opinion polls, and plebiscites might adequately replace contested elections. Gradually becoming explicit in this rhetoric is a conservative constitutional project. One of its themes is an effort to combine presidential and parliamentary models in a way that restrains the aspects of presidentialism considered dangerous, which is to say, anti-elitist. These are the aspects that permit

---

8 *O Problema e a Tarefa, supra* note 3.
9 *Id.*

popular leaders to appeal directly to the masses over the heads of the party oligarchs and local interests. The other theme of the project is corporatism: social groups organized under the control of the state would be accorded representation in the decisional processes of the government. For example, labor and management representatives would have more or less official representatives in the economic planning process.

Unger argues that Brazil needs a constitutional regime exactly the opposite of this. Instead of a chastened *presidencialismo*, it needs a regime that retains the power of the president to appeal directly to the people, while adding measures that avoid the institutional stalemates that characterize presidential regimes. Instead of a conciliating, tutelary corporatism, it needs a system that fosters popular self-organization while emancipating it from the state.

The turning away of the PMDB from the concerns of the lower classes and from institutional innovation favors more contentious leaders capable of giving voice to popular discontents. But Unger acknowledges a danger here: that of repeating "the recurrent drama of contemporary Brazilian politics."[10] A tumultuous and confused populism could antagonize the middle classes and provoke the military to re-assume power. The risk seems particularly great because the process of redemocratization is occurring without any clear affirmation of the principle of civilian rule and without the institutional reforms necessary to it. Unger attributes this danger to the populist style associated in Brazil with Getulio Vargas, who ruled from 1930 to 1945 and from 1951 to 1954, first as a usurping dictator and then as a popularly elected president, and which many now attribute—not entirely without reason, Unger admits—to Leonel Brizola. This style, which emphasizes welfare spending and direct personal appeals to the masses by charismatic leaders, is ultimately ineffectual, first, because it neglects the tasks of mass organization and thus makes itself vulnerable to coups, and second, because it neglects the tasks of economic reform and thus makes itself vulnerable to inflation and disinvestment.

At the level of party politics, Unger sees three broad groups. The group of conservative development is committed to keeping things more or less as they are and responding to popular deprivation indirectly through general economic growth. The redistributive group (to which, Unger says, the leaders of the PMDB would belong if redistribution did not require taking away from some as well as giving to others) is committed to redistributing wealth and income within existing structures through fiscal, income, and welfare policy. Lastly, the group committed to institutional transformation includes the "independent leftists" of the PMDB, the Democratic Workers' Party, and the Workers' Party.

---

[10] *A Estrategia Politica do Transicao, supra* note 3.

None of the parties of the left has yet acquired a mass base. But the popular mobilization in the last years of the military regime, especially by labor unions and local church-affiliated groups, provides important opportunities. Unger insists that the Brazilian left is distinguished from the center at both the party and the popular levels, not by a commitment to statism over privatism, but rather by a preference for a more egalitarian, experimental, and participatory mode of decentralizing the economy than the dominant private rights model of Western political economy. A striking and paradoxical quality of the recent popular labor and ecclesiastical movements has been precisely that they express an aspiration to radically democratize the society in the language of socialism at the same time that they reject statism, the talisman of traditional socialist movements. So far, these aspirations remain vaguely formulated. Unger offers his program as a contribution to the effort to give concrete content to them.

Unger argues that the success of a more ambitious project of transformation depends on the willingness and ability of the Tancredo Neves-Sarney government to secure basic legal and economic rights, rights of organization, and welfare rights that alleviate the kind of severe misery that leaves people more prostrate than indignant. Thus, the independent leftists within the PMDB government have an important role to play in insuring that the government keeps its commitment to basic political liberties and economic rights. Unger doubts, however, that they can move their party very far to the left. He thinks that the electorate will so rapidly identify the party with the more conservative path it has charted that the party will compromise its ability to deepen its program.

The "independent" quarters of the PMDB, the Workers' Party, and Democratic Workers' Party are likely to contribute to the project of developing the organizational and programmatic bases for a more ambitious politics. But for the moment, those within the PMDB seem paralyzed by ambivalence about their relation to the party. And the Workers' Party has a social base—the radicalized sectors of the salaried middle classes and factory workers in the industrialized areas—and a doctrinal perspective—one that puts the conquest of the state before the transformation of society—that make it difficult for the party to perform the critical tasks of organizing the masses outside the industrial sector and of conciliating among the different political groups committed to transformative politics.

Leonel Brizola and the Democratic Workers' Party, which have a following among the unorganized workers and are less committed to the traditional preconceptions of socialist politics, seem better situated to undertake these tasks. To do so, however, they need to develop a concrete program of non-statist socialism, and they need to develop internal processes that are more impersonal, complex, and pluralist. At the same time, the independent leftists within other parties need to develop a fairer appreciation of labor history, of the phenomenon of popular leadership, and of Brizola himself.

In four articles of the series, Unger sketches the economic dimension of his program, and in the following six, he sketches the political dimension. Another article discusses the reform of the military, and the final one discusses "the politics of personal relations."

A. *Economic Change*

The sketch of Unger's economic program begins by rejecting two assumptions shared by the dominant currents on both the left and the right. The first assumption is that prosperity requires that development continue to focus on concentrated, large-scale industry. The second concerns the understanding of the meaning of decentralization adopted from liberal political economy—one which identifies centralization with government control of the economy and decentralization with private property rights. Unger's program proposes state interventions designed to foster decentralization and challenges some of the aspects of private property rights that in fact promote centralization, notably the control exercised by a small number of large-scale institutions in the name of property investment and capital.

Despite his emphasis on fundamental institutional change, Unger expresses some sympathy for those who say that the new government must attend to the most urgent economic problems in incremental fashion, and only turn to basic reform when immediate pressures abate. He does not deny this point, but rather argues that there are many possible incremental responses to immediate problems, and that some have more potential than others to contribute to further, more basic change.

The economic program has two stages. The first involves the creation of a partnership between the state and small enterprise. The idea is most readily illustrated in the agricultural sector, where programs in the United States and other advanced countries have attempted, albeit ambivalently and with mixed success, to support small enterprises through the provision of services and resources designed to compensate for the disadvantages of scale. Thus, through price regulation, favorable tax policies, and access to credit, the government makes small farmers less vulnerable to the market. It helps small producers take advantage of some scale economies without growing by providing technical assistance and by assisting in the organization and financing of cooperative marketing and development projects. Such a policy in Brazil would constitute a reversal of the longstanding practice of public subsidy and assistance to large-scale enterprise. Recently published data indicate that agricultural establishments of less than one hundred hectares account for twenty percent of the agricultural land in Brazil and receive thirty-four percent of agricultural finance but are responsible for fifty percent of agricultural production, while enterprises larger than one hundred hectares account for eighty percent of the land, receive sixty-six percent of finance, and contribute less than half of agricultural production. The most immediate victims of the established policies, and the potential beneficiaries of the proposed reform, are the underemployed and impoverished masses in the large cities, most of whom have emigrated from the countryside for lack of employment.

Though the model of state support for small enterprise is less familiar in the industrial sector, it could be extended there. For example, instead of nationalizing the banks or continuing to leave small entrepreneurs at the mercy of banks who invariably prefer large clients, the government would organize an alternative financial system designed to support small enterprise. It would organize industrial parks, even in areas already highly industrialized, that would provide technical and mechanical support to participants that would enable them to take advantage of technology with high minimum fixed costs while remaining small and would encourage experiments with cooperative and participatory work organization.

The point is not to abolish all forms of economic concentration in either agriculture or industry, but to divert the emphasis of economic policy from its traditional subservience to large-scale organization. Even a modest shift in emphasis, if shrewdly managed and complemented by popular political organization, could have revolutionary consequences for economic development and social equality.

One of the economic consequences would be to increase the productivity of the parts of the economy—rural and urban small enterprises—that employ the great majority of the Brazilian workforce. Instead of relying on the radiating effects from a nucleus of concentrated industry, which will never employ more than a small percentage of the work force, the policy would open to previously excluded masses of workers opportunities to participate in the central and dynamic mainstream of the economy. And it would enable Brazil to avoid playing the role being designed for the more advanced Third World countries by the dominant trends in the international division of labor—that of serving as a base for the kind of concentrated and bureaucratic industrial organization that the wealthy Western countries have already started to abandon.

The program would contribute to social equality by increasing employment and income. The increased purchasing power of the lower and middle strata would push industry to re-orient production toward popular consumption and away from its present focus on consumer durables, such as automobiles and appliances, that in Brazil are upper class luxuries.

However successful, this preliminary stage will be self-limiting. The limit will occur when the problem of radical inequality re-asserts itself among the newly developed businesses. The more successful will grow large; the less successful will try to hang on by pleading for increased state support. At this point a second stage of more fundamental reform becomes appropriate. The second stage involves the "revolving capital fund" program advanced in *Politics*. In this program, the government would establish broad parameters over such matters as the level of savings and investment and the permissible degrees of economic inequality. Below the government but substantially independent of it would be a series of investment funds. Each fund would specialize in a defined area of the economy and different kinds of investment, but the funds would overlap sufficiently to permit competition among them. The funds would make capital available strictly on a temporary and conditional basis. Some funds would be allocated through rationing; others through auction. Under rationing, funds would be lent subject to extensive conditions restricting the organization and activities of the recipients. The rationing criteria would give preference to the creation of new businesses rather than the expansion of established ones. Eligibility would be restricted to groups of workers committed to specified norms of democratic work organization. The recipients would pay interest to the fund, a portion of which would be remitted to the central government. Favoritism in allocating resources would be constrained in part by competition among the funds to achieve the highest possible returns within the rationing constraints.

The other funds would hold capital permanently at auction. Whenever new bidders demonstrate an ability to earn a higher return on resources than the current holders, the capital would pass to the new bidders. The prior holders would be compensated by a program of displacement benefits.

At the enterprise level, the program contemplates a broad range of autonomy in the organization and operation of businesses, especially in those funded by auctioned funds. Instead of having rights in a particular job in a particular industry—a kind of privilege that paralyzes social and personal innovation—workers would benefit from a permanent retraining system. And they will be secure against impoverishment through a welfare system financed by interest payments to the capital funds.

Unger argues that, while this program would diminish the sovereign character of property rights in capitalist economies, it would decentralize the economy. It would do so by divorcing the ability to take advantage of scale economies from the control of large concentrations of capital.

The economic discussion ends with an emphatic repudiation of many of the established practices of Brazilian public finance. It rejects the practices of redistributing through the manipulation of foreign currency exchange (as by overvaluing the national currency and then rationing foreign currency at the implicitly subsidized rates to favored users). The program would hold the state to strict standards of fiscal efficiency and responsibility. It would reject uncontrolled monetary expansion that feeds inflation and pushes up real tax rates. The program would also dispense with the practice of generalized salary adjustments unrelated to increased changes in productivity. It would address the salary question by refocusing investment so as to increase the relative productivity of the lower classes.

One of the aims of the program would be to combat financial speculation, which has assumed economically disastrous and humiliating proportions in the Brazilian economy. The program would sell public securities directly to individual savers rather than institutions, would prohibit their use as security for private borrowing, would require the banking system to internalize the financing of interbank transactions without state subsidy, would apply aggressive antitrust legislation to the banks, and would tax gains from speculative transactions at exceptionally high rates.

With respect to Brazil's high foreign debt, the program would seek creditor forbearance, but it would treat forbearance as space in which to pursue institutional reconstruction, not as a license to redistribute as much as possible before the ax falls.

Unger concludes by stating that, while he prefers redistribution through institutional reconstruction to redistribution through transfer payments, he recognizes the need for some transfers. On the other hand, his program would repudiate "at any cost" the type of redistribution favored by recent Brazilian governments that relies on hidden subsidies, currency manipulation, monetary magic, and featherbedding public employment.

B. *The Constitution*

The six pieces in the series sketching the constitutional aspects of the program were offered as proposals for the Constituent Assembly which was then planned and, subsequently in 1986, elected and convened to draft a new constitution for Brazil. Unger prefaces the constitutional discussion with two warnings. The first is that the temptation to view the new constitution as a means of establishing once and for all a permanent model of social organization imposing the policies and principles of the drafters on future generations should be resisted. The task, rather, should be seen as laying ground rules for a process of "permanent innovation." The critical precondition for such a process is preventing the possibility that any particular class or faction assumes dominant power. Unger asserts that this view does not mean that the constitution should be brief or dry. He rejects the suggestion that the American Constitution should be taken as a model. Neither the concision nor the long duration of the American Constitution, so widely admired in many quarters, are necessarily virtues from the point of view of the ideal of permanent social innovation.

The second caution stresses the importance of achieving a realistic understanding of the relation between constitutional thought and the claims of organized social movements. This requires taking account of some lessons of the Brazilian experience. When the institutions of the liberal democratic state are projected into circumstances of extreme inequality and unabashed elitism like those in Brazil, they suffer two perversions. In the poorer and more submissive areas of the country, they become mired in clientalism. In the more politicized areas of the country, these institutions confront a level of expectation and agitation, either from organized movements or more frequently from populist leaders speaking for disorganized masses, that they are unable to canalize or absorb.

It is said that these perversions would disappear with the achievement of greater equality. But the institutions Brazil has received from the Western liberal democratic tradition, instead of being part of the solution, are part of the problem. They make frequent far-reaching reform difficult by deploying an array of constitutional obstacles. At the same time, these institutions leave popular organizations without support or, as with the corporatist variations of liberalism, with the kind of support that crushes them.

This should not be surprising. The constitutionalism of the liberal democratic state, so readily identified as the natural essence of democracy, is in fact the contingent product of heterogeneous events and circumstances. One such circumstance is the type of political party—more than a mere alliance of professional politicians but less than a real mass organization—that took root in the early democracies in the nineteenth century. Another is the set of constitutional techniques, such as the classical scheme of the separation and balance of powers in the presidential regime, designed to restrict officials in a way that also rigidifies the social order, protecting it from agitations and agitators and conserving power in the hands of social elites.

Brazil needs new constitutional ideas and institutions in order to break the vicious cycle of its politics. It cannot attain or surpass the level of freedom and equality of the wealthy foreign democracies by imitating their political systems. To do so would perpetuate the pattern of clientalistic appropriation of the state, followed by extra-institutional mobilization, followed by impasse, and ultimately, by regime failure. Brazil needs a constitution that will foster a more flexible state, a more mobilized society, and a more contentious culture than those of the countries to which it looks for its models.

The constitutional program Unger proposes in response to these concerns emphasizes five features: first, a reformed presidential regime; second, the transformation of public administration; third, a set of norms and institutions that foster "self-organization" in workplaces and residential communities; fourth, a revised understanding of federalism; and fifth, a set of norms and institutions designed to impede and destabilize concentrations of power.

Unger embraces a strong, directly elected presidency in preference to the parliamentary models popular among the elites, not on the ground that it is intrinsically superior, but on the ground that presidential elections in Brazil traditionally have been privileged occasions of political mobilization that have anguished the elites and confounded their calculations. A strong presidential regime has the most promise of canalizing the energies for reform against the blocking efforts of the elites.

Unger rejects the complaints being advanced against *"presidencialismo."* The critics assert that presidential regimes produce omnipotent and repressive executives. Unger replies that some parliamentary regimes, such as England's, and to a lesser extent India's, have produced chief executives as strong as any in the world. Moreover, in Brazil, presidents have tended to be strong only in their capacity to give out favors; they have been weak in their capacity to execute the reform programs to which they have committed themselves. The former problem requires reforms that restrict particular kinds of presidential power, but the latter requires reforms that extend presidential power.

Another complaint is that the presidential regime provokes periodic political crises. But to an important extent, the "crises" are nothing more than reflections of the threat that presidential elections have represented to elite political control. The constitution should preserve this threat. It should protect the continuity of basic democratic commitments by strengthening the means for presidents to fulfill their electoral commitments and by safeguarding basic political rights, especially those of popular organization.

The critics also say that presidential regimes excessively personalize politics. But in a country where political leaders are accustomed to ideological posturing, a focus on personalities is not entirely a disadvantage. The emphasis on personalities often involves an effort to assess the real intentions of the candidates, so often hidden behind the misdirections and prevarications of campaign rhetoric.

Nevertheless, the classical presidential regime does suffer from a basic defect: a tendency toward impasse between a popularly elected president and a parliamentary opposition majority. This tendency is particularly severe in connection with efforts at fundamental reform. Brazil is a country in which the citizenry has been generally oppressed and has acheived freedom only when and to the extent that it has mobilized. And it is a country in which popular forces can gain the presidency more easily than they can achieve a legislative majority. In such circumstances, a tendency to impasse is fatal. It fuels the frustrating cycle of modern Brazilian politics: a centrist president . . . disillusionment of the working class electorate . . . a left-wing president . . . a congress opposed to presidential reforms . . . popular mobilization in support of the president . . . reaction, coup, and collapse of the democratic regime

. . . redemocratization . . . vacillations of chastened liberals . . . a centrist president . . . . It's time to put an end to this recurring history.

The solution is to reform the presidential regime to cure it of its tendency to impasse. This requires a means of quickly referring the basic disputes to the electorate in a way that facilitates both the resolution of basic issues and the replacement of the personnel identified with the rejected alternative so as to make possible governmental unity. The result might be viewed as a synthesis of parliamentary and presidential models, though it is radically opposed to the style of parliamentarism favored by conservative jurists in Brazil.

In this model, the congress would be empowered to dismiss the president within, say, a year of election for political or programmatic reasons. The dismissal of the president would trigger new elections for both the congress and the presidency. For his part, the president would be obliged to submit to the congress at the beginning of each session a reform plan setting out the general outlines of his program. Should the congress reject the program, the president could dissolve the congress and call new congressional elections. But the president could invoke this power a second time only by simultaneously triggering a presidential election for which he would be ineligible. The president would not be permitted to legislate by decree during the interval between the dissolution of the congress and the election of a new one.

This system of mutual dissolution and substitution of powers would also make liberal use of referenda, initiatives, and plebiscites. These techniques do not represent within the framework proposed here what they might elsewhere: an invitation to a popular leader to appeal to the people over the heads of constitutional institutions without modifying those institutions, and in effect to conduct a kind of permanent *coup d'état*.

A presidential regime reformed along these lines would have two basic virtues. It would contribute to a politics that repeatedly mobilizes the society to question its basic structure. And it would give the victorious party an opportunity to implement a program of basic reform.

The next feature of the constitutional reform confronts the features of the Brazilian state that make it a powerful instrument for handing out favors and punishments but a weak one for reforming society. At first glance, this situation might seem an irresolvable paradox; the state's power to affect society might seem to lie precisely in its capacity to dispense and withhold myriad forms of patronage. But this is a mistake. In fact, precisely the same factors that cause the state's hypertrophy as patron are responsible for its impotence as reformer.

The first of these causes is irresponsible functionalism. Elected officials control appointments to not only upper level government positions involving policy formulation, but also a vast and poorly defined array of middle level offices. The consequence is to place between policy level officials and the professional civil service an undisciplined and incompetent horde of friends of friends of the powerful. Meddlesome and politically unaccountable, this group, which is occupied largely with matters of patronage and profiteering, impedes the execution of any government program. The problem would be alleviated by ending the practice of patronage appointments below the policy level. More difficult but also necessary is the definition of ideas and the cultivation of attitudes that promote and distinguish the political responsibility of policy officials on the one hand and ministerial responsibility of civil servants on the other.

Another aspect of the dilemma is the corporatist practice that pervades Brazilian public administration. It is exemplified by the "mixed commissions"—official bodies with jurisdiction over some area of policy whose membership is composed in substantial part of representatives of interested private groups. The use of such practices to extend citizen representation within the state has striking defects. On the one hand, it facilitates the control by the state of the represented private groups; on the other hand, it permits the more powerful private groups to capture for their own benefit the public regulatory power they are supposed to be supervising. At the same time, this form of administration impedes the formulation and implementation of a coherent governmental program by the central government. It tends to dissolve government policy into a series of small private deals. The proper response to this situation is to purge public administration of all vestiges of corporatism. The state should try to strengthen popular organization in the ways discussed below, but it should stop doing so by according official executive status to the strongest private organized groups.

Still another dimension of the administrative problem is the proclivity for hidden and indirect redistribution through subsidies, unequal indexing for inflation, discriminatory price and foreign currency controls, and public job creation exempt from norms of productive efficiency and financial responsibility. Besides allowing perverse forms of redistribution that would be unacceptable if done explicitly and directly, this proclivity aggravates the dilemma of public administration. Indirect redistributive practices encourage an endless line of favor-seeking that distracts and encumbers the executive. It also permits the governing potential of the executive to be cannibalized by private interests and encourages particularistic solutions to broad social problems. The appropriate response is to ban hidden and indirect redistribution.

To create a state weak in its ability to hand out favors but strong in its ability to execute reforms, Brazil must dismantle the patronage state, which stagnates reform by the same means that it infantalizes and corrupts its citizens.

The third aspect of the constitutional program concerns the principles and instruments of citizen self-organization. The program contemplates the development of practices currently established in labor organizations and their extension to other areas of social life.

All discussions in Brazil of labor organization begin by rejecting the established system of corporatism; a system that, under the pretext of making unions part of the state, subordinates them to the state. But the rejection of corporatism should not lead to the embrace of pluralism, which permits rival unions to compete to represent the same groups of workers. On the one hand, pluralism dissipates the energies of the labor movement in internal fighting. On the other hand, it radically separates the union's confrontation with the employer from its confrontation with the state. In any case, pluralism favors a moderate level and an economistic style of labor militancy.

In the hands of an authoritarian government, a unitary union system serves as a means of repression, especially in combination with the weapons of political control that a corporatist system furnishes the government. But in the circumstances of developed democracy, unity has the opposite effect. It facilitates politicized union militancy, politicized in the sense of linking economistic claims to claims of institutional reform.

Unger proposes a union structure that combines unity with autonomy. As in the current system, the state would define a structure that would include a single representative organization for each group of workers. Different currents of opinion, whether or not linked to political parties, could compete for influence in these organizations, in much the same way that political parties compete for offices in the state. The two competing national labor organizations in Brazil today, which are not part of the official state-mandated structure, illustrate how competition can operate within a single-union structure. Without being part of the legal structure, they give organizational expression to the different currents of opinions among the workers and link the legally mandated union structure to the national political parties. Such organizations complement the official centralized organization that forms a part of the legally mandated structure.

Whether or not a system of state mandated unitary unions can be reconciled with genuine autonomy for these unions depends on the resolution of a series of concrete problems. For example, there is the issue of the classification of workers for the purpose of determining the scope of the bottom tier representative organizations. A unitary system requires a single set of classifications. But unitary classification does not necessarily mean classification by the state. An initial classification by the Ministry of Labor could be a provisional one subject to modification when a majority of the affected workers voted for a particular reclassification.

Another matter that raises the issue of the reconciliation of unity and autonomy is the labor tax, which under the established Brazilian corporatist regime the state collects from employers and returns to the unions to fund organizational expenses. It is not inevitable that the labor tax lead to oppression and corruption. But to avoid this, a series of reforms is essential. The majority of the receipts should remain in the hands of the base level union organizations. The system should be organized on the model of public political campaign finance systems, so that funds are available to finance competitors in contested union elections. The tax should be scaled to fall more heavily on capital-intensive enterprise so that it does not act as a disincentive to employment. Unions should be most generously funded in those sectors of the economy that can most easily isolate themselves from union pressures.

To the extent that the democratization of the economy proceeded along the lines proposed above, especially in terms of support for small enterprise, the unions might acquire new functions, not so much in terms of representing employees against employers, but in terms of representing the interests and aspirations of small entrepreneurs vis-à-vis the state.

Alongside the unions, a system of neighborhood organizations should be established. These organizations would act as a kind of counter-state, facilitating local political participation and competing with the municipal councils, not with respect to their legislative powers, but with respect to identifying problems and organizing pressures for change. These neighborhood organizations might in turn affiliate with any of a variety of national political organizations. No legal structure would be prescribed for the national organizations; they could adopt whatever structure seemed appropriate to their program.

The constitutional program also addresses the issue of decentralization. Legislative and administrative decentralization is widely favored in Brazilian political debate. Unger emphasizes that, from the left's point of view, decentralization as conventionally conceived would be dangerous. It could strengthen local oligarchies by immunizing them from political struggles that arise more readily at the national level. If centralized power has often taken the side of the wealthy and powerful, it has also been the only agency capable of threatening them and of opening space for transformative politics.

Unger proposes an approach to decentralization in which the national government permits and even encourages state and local legislative initiative but retains responsibility to guarantee that such initiative is not used to create or strengthen inequality and dependence. State and local initiative would be facilitated through a general doctrine of concurrent legislation that would permit governments to opt out of federal legislation in certain areas and through specific federal delegations of legislative power in other areas. Safeguards against the abuse of decentralized power would be enforced through federal judicial review of state and local concurrent legislation or legislation under specific delegations, through legislative revocations of improperly used delegations, and through citizen exercise of "destabilization rights."

The proposal for "destabilization rights" begins with a criticism of the dominant tendency of thought among Brazilian social democrats about constitutional rights. This tendency is to focus on guarantees of material welfare and to give little attention to guarantees of distribution of power. Unger argues that it is unlikely that constitutional welfare rights could ever be formulated so as to be effectively enforceable. On the one hand, if the rights were vaguely defined, almost any government program would survive review under them; on the other hand, if they were specifically defined, they would deprive the government of needed flexiblity to respond to economic contingency.

Rather than focus on guarantees of material welfare, Unger would focus on guarantees of opportunities to mount political resistance to perceived violations of substantive political values, including welfare rights. These guarantees include rights of free expression and of political organization. Most distinctively, they include destabilization rights: rights to provoke, through appeal to a fourth branch of government, the destabilization and reconstruction of organizations and practices whose structure of authority or membership conflicts with the minimal exigencies of the democratic order and which have become immune to the normal forms of electoral challenge. The practice or organization might be a way of organizing work or of assigning students to schools or providing treatment in hospitals or asylums. It might be a usurpation of decisional power. It might be an exclusion that victimizes women or minorities.

The constitutional program could provide, not only to the individuals and groups directly affected, but to any citizen, a right of action. If sustained, the claim would warrant intervention by the state to provide minimal conditions of dignity and autonomy to those oppressed by the challenged organization or practice. The enforcement of destabilization rights is a distinct activity separate from legislative and judicial functions and it should be confined to a distinct branch of government. This could take the form of a council composed of some members elected directly, the President of the Republic, and perhaps members appointed by the other branches.

Although these new rights and their distinctive enforcement mechanism may appear radically innovative, they merely generalize solutions already accepted under different names and in more truncated forms, in several contemporary democracies.

C.   The Military

All discussions of progressive reform in Brazil are haunted by a vague but pervasive fear of military veto. This is a condition intolerable to any democratic program, and thus Unger's program includes proposals for reforming the military.

Unger begins by observing that there is no plausible strategic role for the Brazilian military as it is presently organized. On the one hand, it is not and could never become strong enough to engage in war with a nuclear power, and it is not organized to conduct the kind of guerilla warfare that would be needed against an occupying great power. On the other hand, it is vastly larger than necessary to counter any plausible threat of invasion from a neighboring country.

Moreover, the military regime actually weakened the fighting capacities of the military. It left Brazil and its army divided internally between an arrogant semihereditary officer caste and a miserable, untrained, and immature rank-and-file. Far from being capable of the operational and technological flexibility modern warfare requires, the army's commanders seem to have been preparing to refight the Battle of Verdun in southern Brazil. The troops have been demoralized by their subordination to the domestic security unit during the military regime and corrupted by the use of the military career as a springboard to privileged state and private employment. Unger sketches a plan designed to make the military less prepared for domestic political intervention but more prepared for military combat.

The plan distinguishes between a "social-military service" and a "military center." The social military service would conscript young men and women for obligatory national service at the time they finished their studies. Part of their service would involve social projects, such as constructing schools, hospitals, irrigation and land reclamation projects, as well as providing educational, medical, and legal services. At the same time, they would undergo basic military training, and would go on after their period of full-time service to become reservists. The emphasis would be on general skills adaptable to a variety of circumstances and a changing military technology.

Inductees would be conscripted in the opposite order from that of the present system: the most educated people would come first; then the relatively less educated but only to the extent the system was prepared to provide them with significant education within the social-military service. The more educated recruits would share the more humble work with the less educated. Thus the armed forces would come closer to the image of a Brazil without social classes that those forces, in their best moments, have wanted to realize. The children of the elites would be required to serve and would thus be exposed to the darker side of Brazil.

The military center would be a separate organization. It would be a vanguard of highly trained officers, responsible for the development of a repertory of technological and organizational capacities and strategic conceptions. It would serve two purposes, which would have a variety of peaceful applications, taking advantage of the links between military and civilian technology. In this way, the system would continue the polytechnic tradition of the Brazilian officer corps. At the same time, the military center would supervise the military training and availability for combat of the recruits and reservists of the social-military service.

The military center would not have effective control over the troops of the social-military service. The latter would be organized in decentralized fashion and would have its own administrative officer corps which would not be a self-perpetuating elite. The goal of organization would be to enhance national security while at the same time to eliminate the possibility of a domestic military veto of political initiatives.

D. The Politics of Personal Relations

The last piece in the series argues that political transformation should involve, not only institutional change, but the self-conscious remaking of the tones and patterns of personal relations.

Unger suggests that the most distinctive characteristic of the Brazilian ideal of human relations lies in the obscure link between two tendencies that, at first glance, appear contradictory. One of these tendencies is the commitment to delicacy and softness in personal encounters and the conviction that immediate personal solidarity is more important than abstract differences of principle. The other tendency is the exaltation of an ideal of grandeur in personal style, a devotion to the grandiose, the excessive, and the impulsive qualities that enliven conventions and routines and that mirror on the plane of human encounters the unconstrained, superabundant qualities of nature. Thus, many of the major figures of Brazilian high literary culture juxtapose a fascination for spontaneous and disorderly vitality with the sober irony of decline, limitations, and frustration.

The most original mark of Brazilian culture is this conviction that there is a mode of self-affirmation that strengthens sensitivity and solidarity, rather than subverting them—that there is a way of being at once sweet and great. This ambition is distinctive within Western culture, where Christian paths of charity have often seemed incompatible with pagan ideals of grandeur.

But this distinctive vision is degraded by a variety of forces in Brazilian life. In contrast to the ideal that they undermine, these forces are not specifically Brazilian; they oppress the cultures of many subjugated peoples.

There is, first of all, the sentimentalization of power. The relations of exchange and work in Brazil are also relations of domination and dependence. These ties, at once contractual and hierarchical, become tolerable by sentiments of mutual loyalty that temper the force of fear and interest. In this situation, every show of tenderness risks turning into servility. And every rebellion appears to be a betrayal of venerable loyalties. Women, who are the major carriers of the distinctive aspects of Brazilian culture, are also the major victims of this confusion between sentiment and power. Thus, in Brazil the feminist movement is necessarily implicated in the attempt to desentimentalize power.

Then there is the dialectic of bureaucracy and paternalism. The omnipresence of paternalism leads to the imposition of rigid rules and centralized administration to protect people from extreme personal subjugation. But bureaucratization multiplies inefficiency and generates distrust. To make things work, it is necessary to reintroduce discretion, which reintroduces favoritism and paternalism. If the Czarist regime could be characterized as despotism tempered by assassination, the practice of personal relations in Brazil could be called bureaucracy tempered by patronage. For those who do not have patrons, or who do not want them, the solution is to fight for a style of relationship that is both more informal and more impersonal. But without paternalism, informality requires trust. And trust requires a minimum of autonomy and equality.

People who do not know each other, or even who are not connected by previously defined relations, tend to be indifferent and even brutal toward each other. Anyone who has driven an automobile in any of the large cities in Brazil knows this. This lack of civility among strangers arises from a difficulty in imagining other people as real and deserving of respect, which is in turn a function of a social structure of hierarchy and exclusion.

Institutional change is necessary to change these traits. But it is also necessary to practice an extra-institutional politics of personal relations in the places where people live and work: in schools, factories, and neighborhoods. It is necessary to develop more informal styles of sociability and conditions of trust through small-scale confrontation and experimentation. Everyday realities have to be changed through everyday practices. Only through such experimentation can Brazilian culture approach its ideal of becoming at once both sweet and great.

* * * * *

By 1987 the emphasis of *The Transformative Alternative* on the dangers and limits of institutionally conservative redistribution seemed prescient. As expected, the Sarney government committed itself to modest redistributive efforts and rejected ambitious institutional reform. It soon faced triple-digit inflation and declining investment, both aggravated by the pressures of a huge international debt burden. In early 1986 it responded with the Cruzado plan, a series of economic reforms including a new currency, temporary wage and price controls, various steps toward the de-indexation of the economy, and promises of responsible fiscal and monetary policies.

The plan was portrayed as a means of preserving the purchasing power of the wage earners, though Unger argued in the *Folha* that the wage controls were structured so that workers lost ground.[11] The plan had an initial success in spurring growth and arresting inflation and generated a wave of popularity for the administration. Riding this wave and looking toward the November 1986 elections, the administration main-

---

11 Unger, *O Plano de Estabilizacao—Um Golpe Branco Contra Os Trabahladores* [The Stabilization Plan—A Conservative Coup Against the Workers], Folha de Sao Paulo, Mar. 18, 1986 (Opinao), at 3.

tained price controls long after its economists thought appropriate, and it broke its promise of responsible monetary policy.

In consequence, the price controls discouraged production, buyers went on a purchasing binge that depleted inventories and then turned to imports until the country's foreign exchange reserves gave out. The administration's policy held until just after the November 15 elections, in which Sarney and his electoral alliance enjoyed a sweeping triumph. But almost immediately afterwards, shortages and investment declines became striking, and triple-digit inflation re-ignited. The administration was forced to relax price controls and fall back on indexing. Antigovernment street demonstration and strikes became frequent.

Thus, more than two years after its publication, the account in *The Transformative Alterative* of the dilemmas of centrist reform seemed as timely as ever.

III. CONCLUSION

Politics and Unger's journalism share a concern about the relation of the modernist critique of established and conventional thought with prescriptive and programmatic thought. In legal and moral discourse, Unger's style of modernist critique tries to show that the conclusions of conventional discourse do not follow from their premises or that the premises yield several, sometimes contradictory conclusions. In social theory, the critique attacks claims that events are necessarily linked in rigid sequences or that social circumstances combine in only a small number of patterns.

This style of critique seems to pose difficulties for programmatic argument, since any programmatic argument is vulnerable to the critical methods modernists apply to conventional thought. The modernists themselves have shown that there is no such thing as a discourse without premises and presuppositions; yet critique can always show that prescriptive conclusions are not rigorously or uncontroversially grounded in their premises or that the premises themselves are controversial. At the most extreme, this recognition has led modernists to deny or abandon prescriptive thought entirely or to adopt a nihilist or avant-gardist style that attempts to escape criticism by making a principle of arbitrariness.[12]

Unger rejects these more extreme moral claims of modernism. Unlike his first work, *Knowledge and Politics*, his more recent work does not aspire to a "total criticism"[13] that would encompass and transcend the most basic premises of the dominant modes of thought. It insists on the impossibility of entirely transcending the influence of the established conventions of thought and culture, while denying the necessity of surrender

---

[12] *See, e.g.*, Sontag, *The Aesthetics of Silence*, in STYLES OF RADICAL WILL 1-34 (1969); Luban, *Legal Modernism*, 84 MICH. L. REV. 1656 (1987).

[13] KNOWLEDGE AND POLITICS at 1-3.

to them. The style of argument in the journalism is one Unger has called "internal development" and "deviationist doctrine"[14] elsewhere, and one he defends at length in *Politics* as a combination of "internal" and "visionary" argument.[15]

Unger acknowledges that this style of programmatic discourse involves an irreducible element of will, but he argues that it also involves a style of meaningful argument and analysis involving the "mutual correction of abstract ideals and their institutional realizations."[16] The society's institutions are criticized in the light of its ideals, and its ideals are revised in the light of its experience with institutions. The practice is internal in the sense that it makes use of the established conventions of normative argument; it is visionary in the sense that it appeals to the more abstract and Utopian ideals of the culture to criticize and revise these conventions.

Several aspects of this style of argument seem well suited to the forms of journalism. One of these is the emphasis on the provisionality of political prescription. Provisionality seems both a virtue, since it reflects Unger's ideal of the continuously self-revising society, and a necessity, since from the perspective of modernist critique, any particular commitment seems an unstable compromise of conflicting concerns. A closely related aspect is the insistence on the contextual nature of social and political thought. In showing that the abstract propositions of social and moral theory do not yield the conclusions conventionally drawn from them, critique forces programmatic thought to focus more concretely on particular social circumstances.

Another relevant aspect of Unger's prescriptive style is its attenuation of the distinction between working within the system and fighting to change the system, or between reform and revolution. The conventional distinctions presuppose that the social system has a determinancy that deconstructive critique refutes. Unlike many theorists of the left, Unger both envisions dramatic social transformation and insists on the political meaningfulness of small-scale, incremental change. He suggests that transformative ideals can inform political projects of widely varying degrees of ambitiousness. Thus, he is able to point to short-term incremental reforms with the potential to contribute to broader transformative possibility, as well as more radical forms of reconstruction.

All these traits of Unger's theoretical approach would seem to make his style of argument compatible with some of the conventions of contemporary journalism. Indeed, one complaint that might be made about *The Country in a Daze* is that it is not journalistic enough, that it is too

---

14 THE CRITICAL LEGAL STUDIES MOVEMENT at 15-22.
15 FALSE NECESSITY at 355-95.
16 *Id.* at 580.

sweeping and abstract and does not entirely satisfy the appetite it awakens for concrete description.

Other characteristics of Unger's approach—his concern with explicating his theoretical presuppositions and the visionary aspects of his thought—square less readily with journalistic conventions, especially those of American journalism, which favor a pseudo-pragmatic style of discourse that is reluctant to acknowledge or examine its premises and which takes place within a narrow ideological range. And although American newspapers devote an increasingly large amount of space to policy debate, they do not present political discourse oriented around an explicit, comprehensive program of reform. It is hard to imagine a major American newspaper giving an individual or group the space that Brazil's largest newspaper gave Unger to develop a political analysis or program.

The portions of the newspaper pieces that summarize some of the critical theoretical arguments in *Politics* (most of which are omitted in the summary given here) strike me as considerably less successful in their journalistic form. It is hard to make clear the relevance of the critique of the premises of conventional discourse without a fairly elaborate analysis showing that the propositions discussed are in fact presupposed in conventional discourse. On the other hand, the more specifically programmatic portions of the argument do not suffer comparably from their more compressed exposition. They do acquire a more dogmatic and hortatory tone than they have in the treatise, but this seems appropriate to partisan political discourse, even one that aims to unsettle traditional boundaries of partisanship. Given space constraints and the prohibition on technical discussions, the articles cannot offer more than a superficial defense of the controversial positions of the platform. But for the purposes of refocusing discussion and interest, or more ambitiously, of defining a political movement, the brevity, accessibility, and liveliness of exposition seem advantageous.

Unger's Brazilian journalism offers a model of a style of argument that combines critical and programmatic discourse that overlaps but is partially distinct from that of *Politics*. The form of his jouralistic manifesto has great promise, as well as venerable antecedents, though it would take a considerable liberalization of the editorial practices of American journalism to accommodate its revival here.